USŪL AL-TAFSĪR

USŪL AL-TAFSĪR

The Sciences and Methodology of the Qur'ān

RECEP DOĞAN

TUGHRA
BOOKS
New Jersey

23 22 21 19   2 3 4 5

Published by Tughra Books
345 Clifton Avenue,
Clifton, New Jersey, 07011,
USA

www.tughrabooks.com

Library of Congress Cataloging-in-Publication Data Available

ISBN: 978-1-59784-321-8

Printed by
NBN-National Book Network

Contents

Chapter Five

Transliteration Table

ا = a	ح = ḥ	ص = ṣ	ك = k
ء = ‘	خ = kh	ض = ḍ	ل = l
ب = b	د = d	ط = t	م = m
ت = t	ذ = dh	ظ = z̲	ن = n
ث = th	ر = r	ع = ‘	ه,ة = h
ج = j	ز = z	غ = gh	و = w
	س = s	ف = f	ي = y
	ش = sh	ق = q	

Transliterations of Arabic expressions in this book are arranged according to the table below. In addition, (ū ī ā) are used for long vowels.

Foreword

The Holy Qur'ān has been a source of knowledge and wisdom for Muslims for centuries. It is the most fundamental principle of Islam, providing guidance on all aspects of life and the afterlife for those who follow it. The most important feature of the Qur'ān, which sets it apart from other religious scriptures, is that it is self-aware and has managed to preserve intact all the verses revealed over a 23-year period which were practised by the Prophet Muhammad, peace and blessings be upon him, himself. Since the early period of Islam up until the present day, Islamic civilizations have tirelessly exerted effort to understand the Divine message contained in the text of the Qur'ān contributing innumerable works of exegetical literature. Despite the protection of the classical exegesis' in the modern period, there are many new attempts at interpreting and understanding the Qur'ān today. In particular, the broad richness of modern Muslim geography, language, culture and ethnicity has brought about a wealth of different approaches and styles of modern readings of the Qur'ān. The participation of non-Muslims in discussions regarding Qur'anic exegesis has also in recent periods broadened the field.

Of course, the backbone of the search for a sophisticated and versatile technique is the question 'which kind of exegetical method' to apply. Today, the methodology of exegesis in the Islamic world is determined particularly by the works produced in the Arab world during the 19*th* and 20*th* centuries. It is impossible to ignore the strong influence of these works on later exegetical studies which have been written in almost every language spoken by Muslims. Zurqani, Subhi Salih, Dhahabi, and Manna' Qattan are just a few of such scholars. Sadly, it should be noted that the best examples of the classic works on the methodology of exegesis such as Zarkahshi's *Burhan* and Suyuti's *Itqan* no longer attract the attention of modern researchers. A large amount of methodological information set forth in the introductions of the classical commentators has unfortunately almost been completely forgotten. More importantly today, Muslims who work on the methodology of exegesis in different parts of the Islamic world, do so exclusively in Arabic or in the language spoken in their country of residence. Though much effort has been exerted in understanding the Divine word, which is the reason of existence for Muslims, there still exist shortcomings in these efforts.

Muslims now reside in almost every country of our globalized world with a growing population in the Western world. These Muslims, who are often second or third generation and fluent in the language of their resident country, study Islam through university departments of Middle Eastern Studies, Near Eastern Studies or Islamic Studies, where they can also be found working in small numbers. As the world's global language, English has had an unparalleled impact on education materials and has undeniably dominated the language of materials produced in Islamic Studies in the modern period. However, the later adaptation of Muslim communities to the academic field, as well as the prior existence of inadequate and imitative works, necessitates the need for new works to give new breath to the discipline. This is especially true when it comes to a multi-faceted scripture such as the Qur'ān, the need for works which provide a more in-depth and comprehensive method of understanding is unavoidable. As I see it, the existing works of Muslim scholars which fill an important gap in the topic of exegetical methods are limited in content and few in number. The works of some non-Muslims, however, give the feeling of manipulation due to certain deductions in their approaches to the Qur'ān. As a result, their works are far from satisfying for Muslims.

For this reason, a study that is conscious of Islamic sensitivity, rich and comprehensive in terms of content and understandable in terms of methodology is urgently needed. This valuable work on the methodology of exegesis by Dr. Recep Doğan, meets and exceeds these criteria and will serve as an important measure for future works in this area. With his expertise in the history and exegesis of the Qur'ān, as well as his familiarity and comprehensive understanding of Islamic disciplines, Dr. Doğan has managed to combine both classical and modern acquis. Those who benefit from this study will witness a centuries-old tradition at the same time learning modern developments and formations. Dr. Doğan displays a clear procedure for his readers with his method of explanation on the continuity of Qur'anic exegesis. He at all times maintains a serious balance and builds a meaningful bridge between the past and the present through the many examples he gives. This work contains detailed information on the history of the Qur'ān, its structure and linguistic qualities and important dynamics of the methodology of exegesis such as *Makkī* and *Madanī*, *asbab al-nuzul* (occasion of revelation), *muhkam mutashabih* (clear and ambigious verses) and *nasikh mansukh* (abrogating and abrogated verses), etc. Dr. Doğan comprehensively explains the topics of *ijaz* and *i'jaz* which are often only briefly mentioned in other modern works on methodology. Presenting a variety of different approaches, Dr. Doğan also offers a broad range of Western approaches in reading the Qur'ān.

Western institutes that offer and those who receive education in the 'introduction to the Qur'ān' or 'approaches to the Qur'ān' will especially appreciate this work. It will also serve as reference to those who have an interest in the field or any Muslim who wants to deepen their understanding of their Muslim identity in the light of the Qur'ān. For this reason, I thank and congratulate the architect of this work, Dr. Recep Doğan, whose work fills an important gap in its area and wish him success in future studies.

Prof. Dr. İsmail Albayrak

Preface

The Qur'ān is the eternal speech of God; it came from the eternal One and it will continue forever.

God sent Messengers as a conduit between Him and humankind to relay His guidance to attain eternal life in Paradise. The Prophet Muhammad (pbuh) was the last of these Messengers and received the final revelation, the Qur'ān, on behalf of humanity. The message he conveyed is the direct word of God, unchanged and unadulterated. As he recited the revelation he ordered scribes to record it in writing and checked the accuracy by listening to it. This copy of the Qur'ān was distributed among the Companions. Over centuries, Muslims have made great efforts to preserve the Qur'ān in its original language without any alterations. It is the foundation of the religion of Islam and without it, the religion cannot be practised.

The Qur'ān addresses the whole of humankind regardless of race or religion. It aims to guide all people to the truth without ignoring or causing injustice to anyone. The content of the Qur'ān has four main purposes and themes: demonstrating God's existence and unity; establishing Prophethood; proving and elucidating all aspects and dimensions of the afterlife; and promulgating the worship of God and the essentials of justice. The general topics of the Qur'ān are: the principles of creed; rules to govern human life; detailed information on the resurrection and the afterlife; prescript for the worship of God; moral standards; direct and indirect scientific information; principles for the formation and decay of civilizations; the history of previous civilizations, etc.

Amongst its many miracles, the most distinguished miracle of the Qur'ān is in its letters, words and verses. The Qur'ān uses the Arabic alphabet to create incomparable words, verses and *surah* (chapters). On the surface it would appear easy to produce words and verses similar to those of the Qur'ān, but throughout history even the most accomplished and eloquent Arab poets such as Walid, Labīd, Ā'shā and Ka'b bin Zuhayr were unable to produce even similar words, let alone similar chapters. This is because the Qur'ān is a miracle and inimitable.

To properly interpret the Qur'ān, the interpreter must realistically have a detailed knowledge of all of the Qur'anic sciences such as: the occasions of revelation (*Asbāb An-Nuzūl*); which verses were revealed in Mecca and which in Medina; the various forms of reading the Qur'ān (*Ahruf*); the abrogating and abrogated rulings and verses (*Nāsikh-Mansūkh*); the various classifications of the verses (*Muhkam, Mutashābih, Mutlaq, Muqayyad*, etc.); the inimitable style of the Qur'ān (*I'jāz*); the interpretation (*Tafsīr*); the grammatical analysis of the verses and the knowledge of the words which are no longer in common usage (*Gharīb al-Qur'ān*). In this book, all the related topics are covered to enable the reader to more fully understand the Qur'ān.

The nature of the communication between God and humankind has been a mystery since the beginning of human life on earth. God selected some of His servants (Prophets) to receive His message about His existence and unity and convey it to all humans. He endowed them with special abilities to receive this message. It is not possible to understand the method of this communication but we can understand and act on the revelation. We can use the analogy of a satellite and satellite dish to help us to understand the revelation experience. Communication is enabled via a transmitter and a receiver. The satellite dish on earth receives signals from the satellite and transforms them into meaningful images and sounds. Similarly, Prophets have the unique God-given ability to receive His revelation and convey it in a meaningful way to the rest of humankind. The method of communication however, is only known and understood by God and His Messengers. The important mission for humankind is to understand the revelation (the Qur'ān) as it was sent as a guide for every aspect of life. This book aims to cover the Qur'anic sciences to provide sufficient background for anyone who is not familiar with the Islamic sciences.

I praise and thank Allah, the One who gave this opportunity to me and let me serve in His way. The real success comes from Him and belongs to Him. Any defect is in this book belongs to me and for that I ask forgiveness from Allah. I pray for the Prophet (pbuh), who guided us to the straight path, explained the religion in the most exemplary way and did not leave us astray in the middle of the desert of ignorance. Finally, I would like to thank everyone who helped in the preparation of this book.

Dr Recep Doğan
Lecturer Centre for Islamic Sciences & Civilization (CISAC)
Faculty of Arts, Charles Sturt University

Chapter One

Introduction to the Methodology of Qur'anic Exegesis

Introduction to the Methodology of Qur'anic Exegesis

1.1 Definition of Qur'anic Sciences (*'Ulūm al-Qur'ān*)

The Qur'ān is the basis for all Islamic sciences and disciplines; without it they would not exist. In the early days of Islam, religious commandments were memorised and transmitted by oral tradition rather than transcribed. Religious rules and regulations in relation to creed, worship, and daily life were stored within the memories of the early Muslims. Since religious commandments were vital issues in a Muslim's personal and social life, scholars gave these issues priority and compiled books on religious commandments using the Qur'ān as guidance. Using the Qur'ān as their main source, Islamic jurists collected and codified books on Islamic law and its rules and principles pertaining to all fields of life, *Hadith* scholars (*muhaddithun)* established the Prophetic traditions and preserved them in collections, theologians dealt with issues concerning Muslim belief, exegetes of the Qur'ān dedicated themselves to studying its meaning and interpretation including issues that would later be called 'Qur'anic sciences', linguists used the Qur'ān as a base for their philological arguments, and *qurrā* (professionals in Qur'ān recitation)[1] used it for their studies.

In the third century of Islam, most Islamic disciplines established their methodology (*usūl*). *Usūl al-Tafsīr* or *'Ulūm al-Qur'ān* was one such discipline established in this period. Previously, the science of the Qur'ān came under the Hadith science and was recognised as the 'book of exegesis' (*kitāb al-tafsīr*). The two were later separated and each science established its own methodology. The sciences of the Qur'ān focused on the knowledge of those sciences that had a direct relationship with the recitation, history, understanding and implementation of the Qur'ān. In order to interpret the Qur'ān, it is essential to have knowledge of many subjects including, and not limited to, a thorough knowledge of Arabic grammar,

[1] (singular *Qārī*) – A professional class of Qur'ān reciters/interpreters. There are seven orthodox variants of interpretation.

Arabic rhetoric, and principles of jurisprudence (*fiqh)*, the various readings of the Qur'ān, the sciences of the exegesis, the Prophetic traditions and many more.

'Ulūm al-Qur'ān is understood by early scholars as the sciences and disciplines contained within the Qur'ān.[2] The Qur'ān is an inexhaustible source of all kinds of knowledge as well as being the subject of study for exegetical works. The sciences, which are derived from the Qur'ān or applied to it, were divided by scholars into many disciplines and collectively they created the Qur'anic sciences.

> We reveal the scripture unto you as an exposition of all things[3]
>
> And with Him are the keys of the unseen; none knows them except Him. And He knows what is on the land and in the sea. Not a leaf falls but that He knows it. And no grain is there within the darkness's of the earth and no moist or dry thing but that it is in a clear record.[4]

The Qur'anic sciences primarily cover; the occasions of revelation (*asbāb an-nuzūl*), the verses which were revealed in Mecca or Medina, the various forms of Qur'ān reading (*ahruf*), the abrogating and abrogated rulings and verses (*nāsikh-mansūkh*), the various classifications of verses (*muhkam, mutashābih, mutlaq, muqayyad,* etc.), the inimitable style of the Qur'ān (*i'jāz*), the interpretation (*tafsīr*), the grammatical analysis of the verses and the knowledge of words that have fallen out of usage in modern times (*gharīb al-Qur'ān*). A detailed knowledge of all Qur'anic sciences is essential in order to properly interpret the Qur'ān. Therefore, to name this subject the 'Methodology of Interpretation' (*Usūl al-Tafsīr*) instead of 'the Qur'anic sciences' would be more befitting.

Although the terms *'Usūl al-Tafsīr'* (the interpretation of the Qur'ān) and *'Ulūm al-Qur'ān* (the sciences and disciplines of the Qur'ān) are often used interchangeably, in the case of the methodology of interpretation there are some topics which are omitted or scarcely touched upon, such as the history and development of the oral and written Qur'anic scripture. As such, it is more correct to regard *'Usūl al-Tafsīr* as a subset of *'Ulūm al-Qur'ān*. Not all of the sciences related to the Qur'ān play a role in explaining its meanings, for example, the counting of the verses. The different classical authorities of Qur'anic recitation have different methods of counting the verses of each *surah*. The differences in these methods have no impact on the *tafsīr* of the Qur'ān even though they fall under *'Ulūm al-Qur'ān*.

---

2 Zarkashī , *al-Burhān Fi 'Ulūm al-Qur'ān*, 1/17.

3 Qur'ān, 16: 89.

4 Qur'ān, 6: 59.

According to Abū Bakr b. 'Arābī (468 – 543 A.H. / 1076 – 1148 C.E.), Qur'anic sciences encompass three areas; 1) *Tawḥīd* (unity and knowledge of God, His names, attributes, essential qualities, etc. within the scope of *Kalām*), 2) *Tadhkīr* (knowledge of *ẓāhir* (outer) and *bātin* (inner) meanings together with the after-life (*wā'd* 'giving good tidings' and *wa'īd* 'warnings'), paradise and hell, etc. these are the topics of *Tasawwuf*, 3) *Aḥkām* (knowledge of *ḥalal* (lawful) and *ḥaram* (unlawful) which is the topic of *fiqh*).[5] Tabarī (224 – 310 A.H. / 838–923 C.E.), categorizes these sciences differently as *tawḥīd*, *akhbār* (reports, history) and *diyānah* (religiosity).[6] Early scholars understood that the importance of the science is related with the importance of its content, therefore, understanding the Qur'ān is the most important study among all other Islamic sciences as the Qur'ān is prevailing and preeminent.

SUMMARY: DEFINITION OF QUR'ANIC SCIENCES (***'ULŪM AL-QUR'ĀN***)

1. The Qur'ān is the basis for all Islamic sciences.
2. In the early days of Islam Qur'anic knowledge was preserved and transmitted orally.
3. In the third century, the methodology of the Islamic disciplines was established. The Qur'anic sciences and Hadith were separated.
4. *'Usūl al-Tafsīr* is a subset of *'Ulūm al-Qur'ān*.
5. Qur'anic sciences encompass three areas; *tawḥīd*, *tadhkīr* and *aḥkām*.

1.2 The History of *'Ulūm Al-Qur'ān*

There are many different words that have been used to express the Qur'anic sciences such as *'fahm al-Qur'ān'* (comprehending the Qur'ān), *"ilm al-Qur'ān'* (knowledge of the Qur'ān) and *'fiqh al-Qur'ān'* (understanding the Qur'ān). *'Ilm al-Qur'ān* (the science of the Qur'ān) was used for the first time in history by 'Umar al-Wāqidī (130-207 A.H. / 748-822 C.E.) in his book *'al-Rāghib Fi 'Ilm al-Qur'ān wa Ghalat ar-Rijāl'*. Unfortunately, we don't have this book today so it is impossible to know how he discussed the notion of the Qur'anic sciences. From the early period to the present day, the works on the understanding of the Qur'ān (*Usūl al-Tafsīr*) are considered as one subset of the sciences of the Qur'ān (*'Ulūm al-Qur'ān*). The emergence of the technical expression 'sciences of the Qur'ān' has been credited to the twelfth, thirteenth, and even to the beginning of the eleventh centuries.

5 Zarkashī, *Burhān*, I.38
6 Zarkashī, *ibid.* I.40-1.

'Ilm al-Tafsīr provides the infrastructure for the *mufassir* (interpreter/exegete) in preparation for interpreting the Qur'ān. *Usūl al-Tafsīr* primarily affords the *mufassir* with a prescriptive step-by-step guide to interpreting the Qur'ān. *'Ulūm al-Qur'ān* is more comprehensive and contains both the *'ilm* and *usūl* of *tafsīr*. Therefore many exegeses are also called *'Ulūm al-Qur'ān*. Over time, *'Usūl al-Tafsīr* (the methodology of interpretation) gained prominence and *'Ulūm al-Qur'ān* lost its primacy. This is an example of one such shift in Qur'anic studies.

Some scholars consider disciplines which serve purpose in the interpretation of the Qur'ān, such as Hadith, *'Usūl al-Fiqh* (the methodology of jurisprudence) and others, as part of *'Ulūm al-Qur'ān*. Other scholars expand the content covered by *'Ulūm al-Qur'ān* by including myriad disciplines within its scope. According to these scholars, disciplines such as the notion of revelation, the collection of the Qur'ān, the occasions of revelation and clear and ambiguous verses are directly related to the *'Ulūm al-Qur'ān,* but other disciplines such as jurisprudence and theology are indirectly within its scope. Additionally, social and scientific disciplines such as psychology, sociology, politics, biology, physics and medicine that are dealt with and illuminated in the Qur'ān are also to be considered as one dimension of the Qur'anic sciences.

The historic development of *'Ulūm al Qur'ān* conjures the question of why was it developed so late. The reason for this can be extrapolated by examining Prophetic history. Prophet Muhammad (pbuh) warned his community against using their own opinion when interpreting the Qur'ān. Therefore, there were only a few Companions who were deemed qualified to undertake its interpretation. The other reason is that those early works were not under the title of *'Ulūm al-Qur'ān*. Nevertheless it is true to say that the sciences of the Qur'ān were, in fact, birthed during the time of the Prophet (pbuh) who explained the meaning of the verses and gave synonyms or explained metaphors in the verses. An example of this is when the following verse was revealed:

> They who believe and do not mix their belief with injustice, those will have security, and they are rightly guided.[7]

The Companions asked: 'O Messenger of God! Who amongst us does not do injustice?' Their understanding was that the verse referred to those believers who did not commit any injustice, or sin. The Prophet (pbuh) replied: 'The injustice referred to in this verse is associating partners with God'.[8]

---

7 Qur'ān, 6: 82.

8 Bukhari, *Saḥīḥ, Kitāb at-Tafsīr*, 153.

The Companions were so enthusiastic in seeking this knowledge that they were able not only to explain the meaning of any verse in the Qur'ān, but also give its history and the cause of its revelation. Ibn Mas'ud reports:

> I swear by Allah, besides whom there is no other god, there is no chapter in the Qur'ān that I don't know where it was revealed. And there is not a single verse in the Qur'ān that I don't know the reason behind its revelation. If there were any person who knew more about the Qur'ān than I know, and it was possible for me to reach him, I would ride on my camel to him to gain this knowledge.[9]

The other reason pertaining to the late development of the Qur'anic sciences is that, for a long time, *ta'wil* and *tafsīr* were used interchangeably to explain the Qur'ān. There are many books of different names, attributable to early generations, that dealt with the sciences of the Qur'ān such as, *I'rāb al-Qur'ān* (linguistic interpretation), *Ma'āni al-Qur'ān* (the meanings of the words used in the verses), *Wujūh wa al-Nazāir* (the different meanings of one word and the different words which have the same meaning), *Gharīb al-Qur'ān* (strange or unusual words), *Majāz al-Qur'ān* (metaphoric expressions), *al-Nāsikh wa al-Mansūkh* (abrogating and abrogated verses), *Rasm al-Muṣḥāf* (the writing of the Qur'ān), etc. There are early books pertaining to the sciences of Qur'ān such as, *Qatāda* (118 A.H. / 726 C.E.), *Mansūkh*, Zuhrî (124 A.H. / 742 C.E.), *an-Nāsikh wal-Mansūkh*, Muslim b. Maysara al-Khurasanī (135 A.H. / 757 C.E.), *al-Nāsikh wal-Mansūkh*, Ata b. Abī Rabah (114 A.H. / 732 C.E.), *Qarīb al-Qur'ān*, Muqātil b. Sulayman (150 A.H. / 763 C.E.), *al-Ashbah wal-Nazāir and Mutashābih al-Qur'ān*, Musa al-Azdî al-A'war (170 A.H. / 786 C.E.) and *Wujūh wal-Nazāir*. It must also be mentioned that, in addition to these books, many Hadith collections, such as the Saḫīḫ Bukhari and Muslim collections, included sections on various topics of the sciences of the Qur'ān.

Contrary to this approach, some scholars were of the opinion that the sciences of the Qur'ān developed very late, even after the development of the methodology of *fiqh* and Hadith. One example is Abū al-Faraj Ibn al-Jawzī who held that the early scholars neglected to produce a work on the *'Ulūm al-Qur'ān* similar to the methodology of Hadith. To address this Abū al-Faraj Ibn al-Jawzī (508 – 597 A.H.) wrote *Funūn al-Afnān Fi Uyūn 'Ulūm al-Qur'ān*, a comprehensive work on the sciences of the Qur'ān.[10] Zarkashī (1344/45 – 1392 C.E.) was also of the same opinion. He believed that Hadith, *fiqh* and other disciplines had established at least

9 Buhkari, *Saḫīḫ, Book of the Virtues of the Qur'ān*, 4716.

10 Abu al-Faraj Abd al-Rahman Ibn al-Jawzī, *Funūn al-Afnān fi Uyūn 'Ulūm al-Qur'an*, (ed.) Hasan Ziya al-Din Itr, Beirut: Dar al-Basair al-Islamiyya 1987, 141

the technical terms of their methodology whilst this was lacking in the case of the sciences of the Qur'ān. His book *al-Burhān Fi 'Ulūm al-Qur'ān* was an attempt to fill this gap. According to Zarqānī (1367 A.H.), no work was published on *'Ulūm al-Qur'ān* before the fifth century of Islam.[11] His explanation for this was that there was no need to publish books on this subject as the sciences of the Qur'ān were known to scholars. The first book in this field *al-'Aql wa Fahm al-Qur'ān* (the intellect and understanding the Qur'an), belongs to al-Hārith al-Muhāsibī (d.243 A.H. / 857 C.E.). In his book, al-Muhāsibī explains the sciences of the Qur'ān through the topics of; *naskh* (the abrogation of the verses), *muhkam* (clear verses), *mutashābih* (ambiguous verses), *fadāil al-Qur'ān* (the virtue of the Qur'ān), *khalq al-Qur'ān* (the created or uncreated nature of the Qur'ān), *uslūb al-Qur'ān* (the style of the Qur'ān), etc. Major chapters in his work include the reason and the understanding of the Qur'ān, the rejection of innovators and heretics and the subjects related to the sciences of the Qur'ān.[12] The other works of this period are Abū al- Ḫasan al-Ash'arī's (d. 324 A.H.) *al-Mukhtazan fî 'Ulūm al-Qur'ān* (apparently a voluminous work, which does not exist today and is infrequently referenced), Abū al-Mutarrif b. Isa Ashbagh (d. 402 A.H.) and Wāḫidī's (d. 468 A.H.) *Asbāb an-Nuzūl*, Hibat Allah b. Salama (d. 410 A.H.) and Abū Tālib al-Makkī's (d. 386 A.H.) *Nāsikh wal-Mansūkh*, Hasan b. Furak (d. 410 A.H.) and Qādi Abd al-Jabbār al-Hamadânî's (d. 415 A.H.) *Muhkam and Mutashābih*, Ali b. Ibrahim b. Sa'id al-Hūfī or Hawfi's (d. 430 A.H.) *al-Burhān fi 'Ulūm al-Qur'ān.* Ibn al-Anbari's (d. 328 A.H.) *Ajāib 'Ulūm al-Qur'ān* and Muhammad b. Halaf al-Marzaban's (d. 309 A.H.) *'al-Hāwi fi 'Ulūm al-Qur'ān'.*

The seventh century of Islam witnessed major contributions to the sciences of the Qur'ān. Many books containing comprehensive analysis of every branch of *'Ulūm al-Qur'ān* were published in this period. For example, Rāghib al-Isfahānī (d. 503 A.H.) wrote *Muqaddimāt al-Tafsīr,* (also known as *Muqaddimāt Jami al-Tafāsir*) of which there are various publications. Ibn al-Jawzī (d. 597 A.H.) wrote several books on the subject including, *Ajāib 'Ulūm al-Qur'ān* and *al-Mujtaba fi 'Ulūm al-Qur'ān.* Other contributing authors include, Najm al-Din Sulayman b. Abd al-Qawi al-Tufi's (716 A.H. / 1216 C.E.) book *al-Ikthīr fi Ilm al-Tafsīr* and Ibn Taymiyya's (728 A.H. / 1327 C.E.) book titled *Muqaddima fi Usūl al-Tafsīr.*

It can be said that al-Zarkashī's *Burhān* and al-Suyūtī's *Itqān* represent the culmination of centuries of Islamic studies on the Qur'ān. Even today, they (espe-

[11] Zarqānī/Zurgani, *Manāhil al-Irfan fi Ulūm al-Quran*, I.27-8.

[12] See for detailed explanation Adil Öksüz, *Tefsir Usûlü Açısından Hâris el-Muhâsibî'nin Fehmu'l-Kur'an'ı*, SAÜ Sosyal Bilimler Enstütüsü (unpublished masters theses) 1996.

cially the *Itqān*) remain the main sources for those writing 'new' handbooks on the sciences of the Qur'ān.

The sciences of the Qur'ān has some more modern works including; Tahir al-Jazâirî's (1388 A.H. / 1919 C.E.) *al-Tibyân li Ba'd al-Mabâhith al-Mutaallaqati bil-Qur'ān*, Muhammad Abd al-Azîm al-Zarqānī's (1367 A.H. / 1948 C.E.) *Manahil al-Irfan fi 'ulūm al-Qur'ān*, Subh al-Salih's *Mabahith fi 'ulūm al-Qur'ān*, Muhammad b. Muhammad Abū Shahba's *al-Madkhal ila dirasa al-Qur'ān al-Karim*, Manna' Khalil al-Qattan's *Mabâhith fi 'ulūm al-Qur'ān*, Abd Allah Mahmud Shahhâta's *Ulūm al-Qur'ān*, Muhammad Adnan Zarzur's *Ulūm al-Qur'ān*, Muhammad Ali al-Sabūnî's *al-Tibyan fi 'ulūm al-Qur'ān* and Ismail Cerrahoglu's *Tefsir Usūlu*.

SUMMARY: THE HISTORY OF *'ULŪM AL-QUR'ĀN*

1. In the early days of Islam there were many different expressions for the Qur'anic sciences with a general term emerging in the 4th/5th century.
2. *'Ilm al-Tafsīr* provides the infrastructure for the exegete in preparation for interpreting the Qur'ān. *Usūl al-Tafsīr* gives a prescriptive step-by-step guide to interpreting the Qur'ān.
3. Scholars differed in opinion as to what is covered by *'Ulūm al-Qur'ān* with some saying it was whatever aided in interpreting the Qur'ān and others including a myriad of disciplines within its scope.
4. Islamic sciences were birthed during the time of the Prophet (pbuh) but developed slowly. Some early works were produced.
5. Some scholars believed that the sciences were addressed much later than *fiqh* and Hadith disciplines and to fill the gap many notable works were produced in the 4th – 6th centuries.
6. The 7th century saw books produced covering every area of the Qur'anic sciences some of which are still used as main sources for today's scholars.

1.3 General Topics of *'Ulūm al-Qur'ān*

The richness of the content of the Qur'ān makes it difficult to categorise, however, Zarkashī categorises *'Ulūm al-Qur'ān* as:

1) The text of the Qur'ān (pauses, the beginning, ending and division of the chapters, the beginning of chapters, etc.)
2) The history of the text of the Qur'ān (the revelation, the collection of the Qur'ān, the occasions of revelation, knowledge of *Makkī* and *Madanī*, etc.)

3) The language of the Qur'ān (the notion of *i'jāz, muhkam-mutashābih*, seven letters, *balāghah*, etc.)
4) Qur'anic narratives (parables, unidentified figures in the Qur'ān, etc.)
5) The exegesis of the Qur'ān (*tafsīr, ta'wil, mushkil al-Qur'ān*, etc.)
6) Teaching the Qur'ān (etiquette, the recitation of the Qur'ān, *tajwīd*, etc.).

These categories also include the following subcategories:

1) The text of the Qur'ān (*ayah, surah, tartib al-ayah wal-suwar, tawfiqi, fawasil*, etc.).
2) The history of the Qur'anic text (the notion of revelation, the collection of the Qur'ān, etc.), *asbāb al-nuzūl, Makkī* and *Madanī, naskh*, etc.
3) Arabic language (*i'jāz, wujūh wan-nazāir, muhkam and mutashābih*, foreign words in the Qur'ān, seven letters, etc.).
4) The eloquence of the Qur'ān (*khabar and insha* (narrative and commandments), *ma'āni, bayān and badi', haqiqah and majāz*, etc.).
5) Narrative features of the Qur'ān (*qasas al-Qur'ān, amthal, jadal al-Qur'ān*, etc.).
6) Understanding the Qur'ān (*tafsīr, ta'wil, mushkil al-Qur'ān*, etc.).
7) Qur'anic education (*adab al-Qur'ān, qiraat al-Qur'ān, tajwīd al-Qur'ān, al-waqf wa al-ibtida al-Qur'ān*).

1.4 Benefits of Studying the Sciences of the Qur'ān

The study of the Qur'anic sciences is associated with innumerable benefits including an appreciation of its richness and wealth of knowledge, and the enabling of a more comprehensive understanding of the book itself. Through the study of various fields within the *'Ulūm al-Qur'ān* such as the history of revelation and collection, one is able to understand the terms used in the interpretation of the Qur'ān and benefit from this knowledge. This, for the believer, results in an increased and strengthened faith that can withstand any deception and false claims made by biased people. The affirmations of the Qur'ān's authenticity render the believer's heart tranquil. The Qur'anic challenge to both the human race and *jinn* to produce just one chapter similar to one of its chapters (a challenge made by God in response to claims that the book was written by man) has, throughout history, failed to produce any text similar to even the shortest chapter within the Qur'ān, thus establishing its authenticity. History testifies to this reality and the Qur'ān both predicts and affirms that no one will ever be able to present such a chapter.

The Qur'anic sciences enable its students to defend the Qur'ān against its extreme critics and their false claims. Students achieve a profound knowledge of the Qur'ān by studying these sciences and by interpreting its verses in a way meaningful to their time and conditions. This knowledge is the key to unlocking the meanings contained within the Qur'ān and without it, satisfactory interpretation is impossible.

1.5 Origin of the Term 'Qur'ān'

The majority of Islamic scholars agree that the word 'Qur'ān' is an infinitive form of the verb *'qa-ra-a'* meaning 'reading' or 'reciting'. Therefore, it literally means 'a thing recited by adding letters and words to one another'. This verb has another infinitive form, *qar'u*, which means 'to collect'. Based on this form, some scholars are of the opinion that 'Qur'ān' means 'the thing which collects'. There are other scholars who affirm that the word 'Qur'ān' was not derived from any existing word. They hold that it is the proper name given to the book which God sent to His final Messenger, Prophet Muhammad (pbuh).[13] The Qur'ān has other titles, each of which describes one of its aspects and therefore can be regarded as one of its attributes. Some of them are, the Book, the Criterion, the Remembrance, the Advice, the Light, the Guidance, the Healer, the Noble, the Mother of the Book, the Truth, the Admonishment, the Good Tiding, the Book Gradually Revealed, the Knowledge, and the Clear.

1.6 What Kind of Book Is the Qur'ān?

Since the Qur'ān is the direct word of God it can be described by Him best. So The Qur'ān describes itself as;

> Alif. Lam. Mim. This is the (most honoured, matchless) Book: there is no doubt about it (its divine authorship and it being a collection of pure truths). It is guidance for the God-revering, pious who keep their duty to God.[14]

The Qur'ān is a collection of revelations, compiled as a book, which were conveyed to Prophet Muhammad (pbuh) by the angel Gabriel over a period of twenty-three years. Whenever the Prophet (pbuh) received a verse, he instructed scribes to write it down and they collectively wrote every single verse of the

---

13 Rāghib al-Isfahānī, *Mufradaat*, p. 402.

14 Qur'ān, 2: 1-2.

Qur'ān. After the Prophet (pbuh) passed away, the Qur'ān was transmitted by the most authentic narrations (*mutawātir)* and has been preserved without a single change up until the present day. It is the verbatim Word of God (Allah) which has multiple aspects and its recitation is considered as worship in Islam. The Qur'ān is the holy book for Muslims but it also represents the best example of Arab literature. In fact, the Qur'ān is the oldest written form of Arabic literature.

The Qur'ān is beyond comparison with regards to its style, parables, method of explaining realities, its sciences, its description of God by His names, attributes and essential qualities, its guidance methodology, the information about the unseen world and many other areas. Bediuzzaman Said Nursi (1878 – 1960 C.E.) depicted this reality in his statement:

> The Qur'ān is an eternal translation of the great Book of the Universe and everlasting translator of it multifarious tongues reciting the Divine laws of the universe's creation and operation; the interpreter of the books of the visible, material world and the World of the Unseen; the discloser of the immaterial treasuries of the Divine Names hidden on the earth and in the heavens; the key to the truths lying behind events; the World of the Unseen's tongue in the visible, material one; the treasury of the All-Merciful One's favours and the All-Glorified One's eternal addresses coming from the World of the Unseen beyond the veil of this visible world; the sun of Islam's spiritual and intellectual world, as well as its foundation and plan; the sacred map of the worlds of the Hereafter; the expounder, lucid interpreter, articulate proof, and clear translator of the Divine Essence, Attributes, Names and essential Qualities; the educator and trainer of the world of humanity and the water and light of Islam, which is the true and greatest humanity; and the true guide of humanity leading them to happiness. For humanity, it is both a book of law, and a book of prayer, and a book of wisdom, and a book of worship and servanthood to God, and a book of command and call to God, and a book of invocation, and a book of thought and reflection. It is a comprehensive, holy book containing books for all spiritual needs of humanity; a heavenly book that, like a sacred library, offers numerous booklets from which all saints, eminently truthful people, all discerning and verifying scholars, and those well-versed in knowledge of God have derived their own specific ways, and which illuminate each way and answer their followers' needs.[15]

The Qur'ān differs from all other divinely revealed books in regard to its time of revelation, its effect on people, satisfying their worldly and spiritual needs in

[15] Said Nursi, *Words, The Twenty-fifth Word*, p. 388.

every aspect, its style, language and transmission. God endowed Moses and Jesus with miracles that were most suitable for their time and people; He gave the miracles of the *staff* and the *bright hand* to Moses, and gave the miracles of raising the dead and healing certain illnesses to Jesus. The Qur'ān is the chief miracle of Prophet Muhammad (pbuh) and its eloquence is its most notable attribute. At the time of the Prophet (pbuh) most people of the Arabian Peninsula were illiterate and they preserved their tribal pride, history, and proverbs in oral poetry. Eloquence was esteemed and highly prized so new or meaningful, unique expressions were memorized for their poetic form and eloquence and then handed down to posterity. Eloquence was so important that wars between tribes were started and ended on the words of prominent literary figures. The wall of the Ka'ba was adorned with gold inscriptions of the odes of seven poets, called the 'Seven Suspended Poems'. The Qur'anic revelation challenged the literary figures of the Arabian Peninsula: 'If you doubt what We have sent down on Our servant, produce a *surah* like it'.[16] As previously mentioned, this challenge has not been met by anyone up until now.

The Qur'ān speaks to the layman and the profound sage simultaneously, making the Qur'ān both universal and timeless. It is extremely difficult, if not impossible, to address different people with different intellectual capacities at the same time adequately, yet the Qur'ān (being guidance for all people and the Word of God) comprehensively addresses all people without ignoring or causing injustice to anyone. The Qur'ān aims to guide all people to the truth and has four main purposes and themes: demonstrating God's existence and unity, establishing Prophethood, proving and elucidating the afterlife with all its aspects and dimensions and promulgating the worship of God and the essentials of justice.[17] The Qur'ān is also a source of healing; its application in life provides a cure for almost all psychological and social illnesses. Additionally it is a book of cosmology, epistemology, ontology, sociology, psychology, and law. It was revealed to regulate human life in this world and it is not bound or limited to any time, place or people. It is for all times and for all peoples, universal and timeless.

The most distinguished miracle of the Qur'ān is in its letters, words and verses. The Qur'ān uses the Arabic alphabet and brings letters together to create words, verses and *surah*. It would seem rather easy to merge letters together and produce similar words to that of the Qur'ān. However, as history has attested, even the most eloquent Arab poets such as Walid, Labīd, Ā'shā and Ka'b bin

---

16 Qur'ān, 2:23.

17 Ali Unal, *The Qur'ān with Annotated Interpretation, foreword.*

Zuhayr could not produce similar words, let alone similar chapters, because the Qur'ān is a miracle and inimitable. The Prophet (pbuh) was unlettered as attested in the Qur'ān:

> You did not recite before it any scripture, nor did you inscribe one with your right hand. Otherwise the falsifiers would have had cause for doubt.[18]

Despite their lack of belief in the Qur'ān, polytheist leaders in Mecca could not resist listening to its recitation, due to its appealing nature and their appreciation of poetry. They would secretly go to the Ka'ba to listen to the Prophet (pbuh) reciting during prayer. 'Umar b. al-Khattāb was prepared to kill the Prophet (pbuh) yet upon hearing the recitation from *Surah Ta-ha* his heart was illuminated with the words of the Qur'ān and he consequentially converted to Islam.[19] Utba ibn Rabia set out to the Prophet's (pbuh) house with the sole purpose of defeating the Prophet (pbuh) in a debate. The Prophet (pbuh) listened silently to all Utbas' arguments. When he had finished, the Prophet (pbuh) recited the first thirteen verses of *Surah Fussilat*. Utba listened in shock and was greatly affected. When he returned to his friends, who were awaiting news of the outcome of the debate, Utba responded: 'I have listened to such words from him that I have never heard before. This is neither poetry, nor magic nor the words of soothsayers. It is not like of any of these. O Quraysh, pay attention and listen to me, leave him alone. If he cannot be successful the Arabs will destroy him, but if he is successful, his success is your success'.[20] Once Tufayl ibn Amir came to Mecca and was told by the polytheist leaders: 'O Tufayl, you came to our land; people who listen to Muhammad (pbuh) have separated from us, and our unity is being dissolved because of him. His words are very effective, like magic which separates a man from his father, his brother and even his wife. We are worried about you and your tribe, be careful and never listen to him'. Tufayl was scared by their warnings and whenever he went to Ka'ba, he refrained from listening to Muhammad (pbuh). He would even close his ears so as to not hear the words of the Prophet (pbuh). One day he said to himself, 'I am in a false belief, what is the harm in listening to his words, if the words are true; I have the capacity to understand it'. After that he listened to the Qur'ān and consequently converted to Islam. He was the first Muslim guide in his tribe.[21]

---

18 Qur'ān, 29: 48.

19 Ibn Hishām, *Sīrah*, vol.2 p. 187.

20 Ibn Hishām, *Sīrah*, 1/294.

21 Ibn Hishām, *Sīrah*, 1/382.

Sometimes listening to just one verse was enough for people to understand the Qur'ān and appreciate its value. When Sa'sa the uncle of Farazdaq heard the following verse: 'So whoever does an atom's weight of good will see it, and whoever does an atom's weight of evil will see it' he said, 'it is enough for me' and he became Muslim.[22] Arabs achieved deepened levels of understanding through the Qur'ān. An example was when Asma'i heard a pleasant poem from a village girl, he commented 'What a beautiful poem, how eloquent it is'. Thereupon the girl replied, 'What a bad man you are, my words are not more eloquent than this verse; 'We inspired to the mother of Moses, 'Suckle him; but when you fear for him, cast him into the river and do not fear and do not grieve. Indeed, We will return him to you and will make him one of the Messengers''.[23] She added; this verse contains two commands, two prohibitions and two good tidings.[24]

At the beginning of Islam, the Meccan leaders tried to refute the Qur'ān saying that Muhammad (pbuh) was insane or a poet or a soothsayer, but the majority of them eventually accepted Islam. In a short period of time, they understood that the Qur'ān was a divine revelation, a miracle and impossible to challenge.

The Arabs were differentiating between real and false Prophethood. For example, Talha an-Namari came to Yamama to speak with Musaylama[25]. After speaking with him, Talha said, 'I testify that you are a liar, you are not a real Prophet, and I testify that Muhammad (pbuh) is the real and true Prophet (pbuh). But the liar of the tribe Rabia is more beloved for me than the true Prophet of the Mudar tribe'.[26] Indeed, the impossibility of challenging or producing something similar to the Qur'ān was obvious to the Arabs, and despite some of their efforts to do so, they stood defeated confessing their inability to do this.[27]

One day, a great philosopher Kindi was asked by his friends to write something similar to the Qur'ān. He responded 'I can do it for some part of the Qur'ān'. After secluding himself and dedicating his time to the study of the Qur'ān in efforts to fulfil his friends' challenge, he attested to his friend 'I swear by God, I am incapable of doing this and I don't think anybody can do this either. When I opened the Qur'ān I encountered *Surah Maida,* the first verse is 'O you who have believed, fulfil all contracts. Lawful for you are the animals of grazing livestock

---

22 Qurtubī, *al-Jami' al-Aẖkām al-Qur'ān*, 20/153.

23 Qur'ān, 28: 7.

24 Qurtubī, *al-Jami' al-Aẖkām al-Qur'ān*, 13/252.

25 Musaylama – a false prophet from the Bani Hanifa tribe during the same time as Muhammad (pbuh).

26 Mustafa Sadiq ar-Rafi, *I'jaz'ul Qur'ān*, 195.

27 Mustafa Sadiq ar-Rafi, *I'jaz'ul Qur'ān*, 187-212.

except for that which is recited to you in this Qur'ān, hunting not being permitted while you are in the state of iḥrām. Indeed, God ordains what He intends'.[28] This verse starts with the fulfilment of contracts, then it prohibits breaking them, it regulates a general law about the meat of animals and then makes an exception from this general rule. After that God declares his power and wisdom. All these things cannot be phrased in two lines; no one can fit these things in small sentence, it is necessary to write volumes of books to explain these things'.[29]

Finally, it is imperative to note the definition of the Qur'ān given by the Prophet (pbuh):

> The superiority of the Qur'ān over all other words and speeches is like God's superiority over His creatures. The Qur'ān is a definite decree distinguishing between truth and falsehood. It is not for pastime. Whoever rejects it because of his or her despotism, God breaks his or her neck. It contains the history of previous peoples, the tidings of those to come after you, and the judgment on the disagreements between you. Whoever searches for guidance in something other than it, God leads him or her astray. It is God's strong rope. It is the wise instruction. It is the Straight Path. It is a book which desires cannot deviate and tongues cannot confuse, and which scholars are not fed up with, never worn-out by repetition, and has uncountable admirable aspects. It is such a book that they could not help but say: 'We have indeed heard a wonderful Qur'ān, guiding to what is right in belief and action and so we have believed in it.' Whoever speaks based on it speaks the truth; whoever judges by it, judges justly and whoever calls to it, calls to the truth.[30]

Summary: What Kind of Book is the Qur'ān?

1. A collection of revelations conveyed to Prophet Muhammad (pbuh) by angel Gabriel over 23 years.
2. First revelation was received in Ramadan, 610 C.E..
3. Taught the polytheist community belief in the oneness of God.
4. A holy book and also highest form of literature.
5. A book beyond comparison with regard to its content.
6. It is the chief miracle of Prophet Muhammad (pbuh) and cannot be matched by humans.

---

28 Qur'ān, 5: 1.

29 Qurtubī, *al-Jami' al-Aḥkām al-Qur'ān*, 8/31-32.

30 Tirmidhi, *Sunan, Thawab al-Qur'ān*, 14.

7. Speaks to all levels of people at the same time with the aim of guiding them to the truth.
8. Has four purposes: demonstrating God's existence and oneness, establishing Prophethood, proving and explaining the afterlife, transmitting the worship of God and the essentials of justice.
9. Contains information on worship, standards for living, science, history, psychology, law, sociology and many more.
10. Its letters, words and verses speak for themselves and turn hearts to the truth just by listening to it.

1.7 Concepts of the Exegesis, Interpretation and Translation (*Tafsīr and Ta'wil*)

In studying the Qur'ān, it is important to appreciate the origins, meanings and usage of the words *tafsīr* and *ta'wil* in the early days of Islam. The word '*tafsīr*' is in the infinitive form and comes from either '*fa-sa-ra*' or '*sa-fa-ra*'.[31] The root word '*fasara*' means to explain, to discover, to expose and to uncover.[32] The other root '*safara*' means to uncover something covered, to enlighten and open.[33] Evidently, both root words are close in meaning and it is possible that the word '*tafsīr*' may be derived from one of them. Amin al-Khuli alludes to some differences between these two root words. He states that, '*safara*' is to discover something material or the outer dimension of things, but '*fasara*' is to discover something immaterial or spiritual.[34]

Tafsīr in the Qur'anic sciences is related to discovering the meanings of the verses.[35] The real explanation is possible by the author of the words, so the real *tafsīr* of the Qur'ān is the one which God and His Messenger (pbuh) explained.

Ta'wil is the infinitive form of the root word '*a-wa-la*' which means to return,[36] to explain, to discover, to interpret, to translate and the result.[37] In terminology,

---

[31] Ibn Manzūr, *Lisan'ul 'Arab*, 55, Jawhari, *Sihah*, 2/781.
[32] Rāghib al-Isfahāni, *al-Mufradaat*, 380.
[33] Ibn Manzūr, *Lisan'ul 'Arab*, 6/369, Sihah, 2/686.
[34] al-Huli, *at-Tafsīr Maalimu Hayatihi ve Manhaj al-Yawm*, 5.
[35] Ibn Manzūr, *Lisānu'l 'Arab*, 55.
[36] Ibn Manzūr, *ibid.*, 11/32.
[37] *Lisānu'l 'Arab*, 11/33.

it is giving one of the possible meanings of the verses[38] or giving the meaning of the verses according to their context.[39]

The words *tafsīr* and *ta'wil* are both used in the Qur'ān. *Tafsīr* is used once in the following verse:

> And those who disbelieve say, 'Why was the Qur'ān not revealed to him all at once?' Thus [it is] that We may strengthen thereby your heart. And We have spaced it distinctly. And they do not come to you with an argument except that We bring you the truth and the best *explanation*.[40]

In this verse the word *tafsīr* is used to mean explanation.[41] The unbelievers disputed the revelation's coming in parts, thereupon Qur'ān answered their questions. However, the word '*ta'wil*' is used fifteen times within the Qur'ān. This word has multiple meanings, including; the interpretation of words,[42] dreams[43] and actions.[44] As such, its use is related to explaining the meanings of words, informing about the real facts of events, predicting results and interpreting dreams. Every use of *ta'wil* in the Qur'ān is related to people apart from one, which is related to God (*Surah Ali Imran, verse 7*).

The Companions were hesitant to talk about *tafsīr*, because they understood that, it is directly related to God and His Messenger (pbuh). In their time, *tafsīr* was understood as the explanations of God and the Prophet (pbuh). This *tafsīr* was the exact truth with no possibility of mistake. The Companions witnessed the revelation and its occasions; they knew at first hand the relationship between the rules and the verses. For this reason Ḫākim said:

> The explanations of the Companions can be used as evidence as they heard them from the Prophet (pbuh). Whatever they say about any verse in the Qur'ān, we agree with them because their words are comprised of the words of the Prophet (pbuh).[45]

In *tafsīr*, there is a sufficient and exact explanation of the verse, because it relies on evidence. If it does not rely on evidence, *tafsīr* is named *tafsīr bir-ra'y*

38 Zarkashī, al-Burhān, 2/148.
39 Tabarī, *Jami' al-Bayan*, 19/8.
40 Qur'ān, 25: 32-33.
41 Tabarī, *Jami' al-Bayan*, 19/8.
42 Qur'ān, 3: 7.
43 Qur'ān, 12: 36.
44 Qur'ān, 17: 35.
45 Ibn Qayyim al-Jawzī, *I'lami'l Muwaqqiin*, 2/231.

(*tafsīr* based on opinion). *Ta'wil,* on the other hand, implies multiple possible meanings and was therefore used more often by the Companions as a precaution. In *ta'wil,* there is no exact and certain explanation, but there is preference among the possible meanings for the verses. Imam Māturidī explains the difference between *tafsīr* and *ta'wil* as follows:

> *Tafsīr* refers to the Companions but *ta'wil* refers to Muslim jurists. The Companions witnessed the occasions, the history. of the verses and they knew the reasons behind the verses very well. For this reason, the explanation of the verses was clear for them and it was the real *tafsīr* of the verses. This type of explanation is like learning something directly from a scholar or witnessing it in person. When a person says 'this is the *tafsīr* of this verse' he means by this statement 'God is my witness and the certain meaning of this verse is as I say'. This is very dangerous and the Prophet (pbuh) warned people about this. He said, 'if any of you makes *tafsīr* on Qur'ān based on his opinion (without having necessary conditions for it) he better prepare his place in hell'.[46] In ta'wil, the scholar chooses one of the possible meanings for the verse, but it is very difficult to apply same thing in *tafsīr*. In *ta'wil,* a scholar doesn't show God as witness for his interpretation, he doesn't say, this is the real meaning of this verse, he does not claim that God's purpose is my interpretation in this verse, but he says that, these words are usually used in the language of people for these meanings and God knows the best.[47]

There were two classes of Companions when it came to Qur'anic interpretation. The people in the first group were extremely cautious in their approach and did not produce any *tafsīr* whilst the second group made *tafsīr* and explained certain Qur'anic verses more widely. However, this group was also cautious as the Prophet (pbuh) had warned his people about making *tafsīr* of the Qur'ān without relying on evidence. This reticence and the fear of making a mistake in interpretation passed on to further generations. Some Companions of the Prophet (pbuh) such as Abū Bakr, 'Umar and Ibn 'Umar avoided the issue altogether. In one incident, Abū Bakr was asked about the words 'fruit and grass'[48] in the verse, thereupon he replied, 'If I make interpretation of God's book without having knowledge about it I am afraid that earth does not let me live on it and sky does not let me shade beneath it.[49] 'Umar was also very strict in this matter. A

---

46 Tirmidhi, *Sunan, Kitāb at-Tafsīr,* 2951.

47 Māturidī, *Sharh-u Ta'wilat al-Qur'ān,* 2.

48 Qur'ān, 80: 31.

49 Tabarī, *Jami' al-Bayan,* 1/78.

man named Sābiq came to Medina and asked about *mutashābihāt* verses in the Qur'ān. When 'Umar learned of this, he summoned him and punished him severely, then sent him back to his hometown.[50] 'Umar is also reported to have said, 'I don't fear about people who hide their faith or who commit sins publicly. I fear about people who read the Qur'ān well but interpret it improperly'.[51] Amr b. Hafs is also reported to have said about that Sālim b. Abd Allah and Qâsım b. Muhammad 'were not interpreting the Qur'ān'.[52] Once Muhammad b. Sīrin asked Ubayda as-Salmani the meaning of one verse, Ubayda told him, 'fear from God, the people who knew the reasons behind the revelation of the verses died. Do not interpret the Qur'ān; this is the proper way for you'.[53] As a result of these documented approaches, Asma'i refrained from discussing the Qur'ān or Hadith; he didn't interpret even one verse and he declined answering any questions about them.[54]

The other class of Companions including Abd Allah b. Mas'ud and Abd Allah b. 'Abbās interpreted the Qur'ān and explained its verses.[55] These Companions were very careful about discussing the verses of the Qur'ān, for example; Ibn 'Abbās was asked about the day in the following verse, 'He arranges each matter from the heaven to the earth; then it will ascend to Him in a day, the extent of which is a thousand years of those which you count.'[56] He replied to this question with the following verse: 'The angels and the Spirit will ascend to Him during a day the extent of which is fifty thousand years'.[57] After this response the questioner said, 'I am asking about the day in the verse, you are answering me with another day in a different verse'. Thereupon Ibn 'Abbās said, 'these are the days which God mentioned in His book, I don't like to talk about the verses other than this'.[58] When Abd Allah b. Mas'ud was sitting with his friends, one man came and informed them about a man who interprets *Surah Dukhan*, verse 10 according to his own opinion. Upon hearing this Ibn Mas'ud become very angry and said, 'O People, fear God, if any of you knows anything, say it, if he doesn't know it well, he must say, God knows best'.[59] These examples demonstrate that when the Com-

---

50 Suyūtī, *al-Itqān Fi 'Ulūm al-Qur'ān*, 2/4.
51 Shātibī, *al-Muwafaqaat Fi Uṣūl as-Sharia*, 3/422.
52 Ibn Sa'd, *Tabaqaat*, 4/184.
53 Ibn Kathīr, *Tafsir* 1/6.
54 Ibn Qutayba, *al-Maarif*, 236.
55 Tabarī, *Tafsir*, 1/81.
56 Qur'ān, 32: 5.
57 Qur'ān, 70: 4.
58 Ibn Kathīr, *Tafsir*, 1/5-6.
59 Bukhari, *Saḫīḫ, Kitāb at-Tafsīr*, 297.

panions had knowledge regarding certain verses they shared that information with people. They did not speak according to their own opinion and they warned other people against doing so.

The sharing of such information by the Companions comes from the teachings of the Prophet (pbuh) who in many reports encouraged people to teach their knowledge to others. The Prophet (pbuh) said, 'The best among you is the one who learns the Qur'ān and teaches it to others'.[60] In order to teach something to others it is necessary to have a well-grounded knowledge of the subject to be taught. The Companions at the time of the Prophet (pbuh) would thoroughly learn ten verses from both a theoretical and practical perspective and, after applying those verses in their everyday lives, they would continue learning a further ten. Ibn 'Abbās says: 'there are different possible meanings in the Qur'ān, you should learn the best one among them'.[61] Said b. Jubayr has also been reported to have said: 'the person who reads the Qur'ān without interpreting it, is like a blind person'.[62] Mujahid is reported to have said: 'the most beloved of God's servants are the ones who know the Qur'ān best'.[63]

In conclusion, it is evident that the Qur'ān should be interpreted properly and this need can be met by the profound scholars in the Qur'anic interpretation. The early scholars such as Ibn Qutayba, Tabarī and Māturidī were very careful in this issue and thus they used the word *ta'wil* rather than *tafsīr* in the titles of their books as *tafsīr* implies the original explanations directly from the Prophet (pbuh) and his Companions.

Summary: Concepts of the Exegesis, Interpretation and Translation (*Tafsīr* and *Ta'wil*)

1. *Tafsir* is related to the discovery of meaning in the verses.
2. The real *tafsīr* is the explanation by God and His Messenger (pbuh).
3. *Ta'wil* is giving one of the possible meanings of the verses or giving the meaning according to the context.
4. Both words are using in the Qur'ān: *tafsīr* is used once to mean explanation; *ta'wil* is used fifteen times, relating to people (apart from one relating to God) and its use is related to explaining the meanings of words,

60 Bukhari, *Saḫīḫ, Book; the Superiority of the Qur'ān*, 4639.
61 Qasimi, *Tafsir*, 1/10.
62 Tabarī, *Tafsir*, 1/81.
63 Qurtubī, *al-Jami Li Ahkam al-Qur'ān*, 1/26.

informing about the real facts of events, predicting results and interpreting dreams.

5. The Companions were reticent to make *tafsīr* as during their time the *tafsīr* was the exact truth (the explanation of God and the Prophet (pbuh) and they were afraid of making mistakes.
6. *Ta'wil* was used more often by the Companions as this implies multiple meanings of which one is preferred whereas *tafsīr* implies an exact explanation based on evidence.
7. The Companions formed two groups with regard to Qur'anic interpretation: those who were extremely cautious and produced no *tafsīr*; those who made *tafsīr* and explained some verses more widely.
8. All Companions were cautious in explaining their knowledge and this reticence passed on to future generations.

1.8 The Differences between Interpretation (*Tafsīr*) and Translation (*Tarjama*)

The first step to understanding the Qur'ān is to understand its language. Language has the same meaning for a text as bodily features have for a human being. The essential existence of a text lies in its meaning, as that of a human being lies in his or her spirit. The bodily features are the externalized form which the spirit of a human being has taken on, and therefore serve as a mirror in which to see into his or her character.[64] In the same way, the language and styles of the Qur'ān are the form of its meaning and therefore cannot be separated from it.[65] It is due to its miraculous eloquence that the Qur'ān has such depth and richness of meaning. One of the elements on which the Qur'ān's eloquence is based is its creative style and richness in the arts. It frequently speaks in parables and adopts a figurative, symbolic rhetoric using metaphors and similes.[66] This is natural because it contains knowledge of all things and addresses all levels of understanding and knowledge.

In order to understand the differences between interpretation (*tafsīr*) and translation (*tarjama*) we should learn both the dictionary definition of the words and their use in Islamic terminology. *Tarjama* is translating something from one

---

[64] Ali Unal, *The Qur'ān with Annotated Interpretation, Foreword.*

[65] Ali Unal, ibid.

[66] Ali Unal, ibid.

language to another, giving a title for a topic, narrating one's life story, conveying a message to one who is not within reach, explaining one word in the same language, interpreting and explaining one word from one language to another and directly translating the words from one language to another.[67]

Tarjama in terminology means, transferring the meaning of a word, phrase, and piece of writing or speech from one language to another without either changing or diminishing the meaning from the original. In order to achieve an exact translation from one language to another, both languages must be equal in the following areas:

a. clear expression
b. proving
c. summarizing
d. explaining
e. general phrasing
f. specific phrasing
g. phrasing something without making any exceptions
h. phrasing something, making exceptions
i. power of phrasing
j. exactness of phrasing.
k. eloquence in phrasing
l. style of phrasing
m. knowledge, art, etc.

We should keep in mind that a language is not a set of moulds made up of letters and words. As the style of speech or writing gives a human being away, the language of a nation is a mirror to that nation's character, as moulded by its culture, history, religion, and even the land in which its people live.[68] It is almost impossible for any word used in a language to have an exact counterpart in another language.

The other difficulty in translation is that Arabic is a strictly grammatical language. The rules of its grammar are established and it is the richest language in the world with regards to its conjugation and derivation; there are three different types of infinitive in Arabic and a verb has 35 different infini-

---

67 Zabīdī, *Tāju'l Arūs*, 8/211, *as-Sihah*, 5/1928, *Manahilu'l Irfan*, 2/6.

68 Ali Unal, ibid

tive forms, each of which has different connotations and implications.[69] For example, the Qur'ān describes the events of Judgment Day in the past tense, although Judgment Day is yet to come in the future. Besides other reasons for this usage, the simple past tense in Arabic is also used to convey that a future event will undoubtedly take place.

Evidentially, it is impossible to achieve a complete and true translation of the Qur'ān from Arabic into another language. It is impossible to meet all the conditions in order to translate one piece of work exactly into another language without losing some of its essential meaning. Each language has different specifications, idioms, metaphoric expressions, grammar, phrasing styles, etc. and each language addresses the feelings, the logic, the reason, the heart and the inspirations behind those different styles. It is possible that a skilled translator may be somewhat successful in translating the obvious meaning of a text from one language to another but the subtle undertones, the feelings, implications, the logic and inspirations will be missed. In order to satisfactorily translate something from one language to another, it must be translated completely with all its meanings and intentions.

Summary: The Differences between Interpretation (*Tafsīr*) and Translation (*Tarjama*)

1. *Tarjama* is to directly translate the meaning of a word, phrase, piece of writing or similar from one language to another without losing or changing the meaning. For this to be achievable there are many areas in which both languages need to be equal.
2. Arabic is a strictly grammatical language and the world's richest in this sense making it very difficult to translate.
3. A complete and true translation of the Qur'ān into another language is impossible without losing some of its essential meaning.

1.8.1 Two Types of Translation (*Tarjama*)

There are two types of translation; literal (exact) translation and translation of the meaning through interpretation.

Literal translation: In this translation, an attempt is made to translate the text exactly into another language by finding equal expressions in the other language and replacing the original words with them. This type of translation is dif-

[69] Ali Unal, ibid.

ficult because generally the translator cannot find words of precisely equal meaning in another language to translate the exact meaning of the original text.

Translation in meaning: The priority of this type of translation is to express the meaning of the original text with words close to, or similar, in meaning. This type of translation is not exact as the translator finds ways to convey the meaning of the original text in another language, sacrificing structure where necessary. This type of translation is less deleterious than literal translations and requires fewer conditions than the former;[70] consequently, it is used more frequently.

With the obvious difficulties presented by the two different types of translation, it is natural that Muslim scholars differ in opinion on the question of whether it is possible to translate the Qur'ān into different languages. Some Muslim scholars hold that it is possible but they do not mean a literal translation; rather they mean that it is possible to translate the Qur'ān with additional necessary explanations, because any defects in the translation are ascribed to the translator not to the Qur'ān itself. For this reason, both the translation of the Qur'ān and the original text (the Qur'ān in Arabic) are presented side-by-side in Qur'anic translations. There is a general consensus among Muslim scholars that it is impossible to translate the Qur'ān exactly (literally) into another language. Any literal translation would necessitate changing the words exactly from one language to another. It is a requisite condition that the original text and the translation are identical; that is the translation must contain everything which is in the original text. This literal translation is impossible, as the Qur'ān is the speech of God. If it were deemed possible, the challenge of the Qur'ān would be met and the Qur'ān wouldn't be a miracle.

Many Western scholars have also confessed that it is impossible to translate the Qur'ān exactly into another language. As Edouard Montet states:

> Whatever we say or write about the *surah* of the Qur'ān, they don't contain the beauty of the original text, its perfect style and the high eloquence in it, all the western languages are deprived of the exact translation of the Qur'ān.[71]

Georges Sale holds that, 'I [Sale] struggled to translate the Qur'ān objectively, but the readers will find in my translation that, I couldn't continue to be loyal to this objective translation'.[72] Furthermore, Marmaduke Pickthall comments:

---

[70] Zarqānī, *Manahil-ul Irfan*, 2/ 9.

[71] Edouard Montet, *Le Coran (introduction)* Paris 1949, p. 53.

[72] The journel *Sebilurresâd*, year 1954, 7/310.

> Early scholars said that, it is impossible to translate the Qur'ān exactly to another language; I agree with them, I don't claim that I exactly translated the Qur'ān, but I just tried to transfer its meanings to another language. If I am somehow successful at this, that is my luck, however, this translation never takes the place of the original text and I never intended to do this.[73]

It is important here to highlight the differences between *tafsīr* (exegeses, interpretation) and *tarjama* (translation). As stipulated earlier, *tafsīr* is the explanation of the text or the words using different phrases to make it clear and more understandable. This activity can be produced in the same language as the original text or in different languages, therefore it is permissible to interpret or make exegeses on the Qur'ān in languages other than Arabic. *Tafsīr* can never take the place of the Qur'ān; indeed, it is just the scholar's understanding of the Qur'ān. Translation is absolutely different to *tafsīr* regardless of the category. Zarqānī mentions four differences between *tafsīr* and *tarjama;*[74]

1) *Tarjama* (translation) is the work which directly replaces the original text or words, but *tafsīr* is always related to the original text. Since *tafsīr* is an additional explanation of the original text for the purpose of making it clear, it must be connected to the original text all times; if disconnection occurs, the explanations are worthless.

2) Adding extra words is not permissible in *tarjama* but it is permissible, and sometimes even necessary, in *tafsīr* to enable an explanation of the original text. Only in the *tarjama* is it necessary for the translation and the original text to be similar to each other in words, structure and phrasing. The *mufassir* (the one who makes *tafsīr*) chooses a way or style for his *tafsīr* based on his need in order to clarify the original text. He gives explanations for the literal meanings of the words, the multi-layered meanings of words, the terminological meanings and which evidence he has used to support his *tafsīr.* For this reason, exegeses of the Qur'ān (*tafsīr*) contain many Qur'anic sciences such as literature, Arabic grammar, Islamic jurisprudence, the methodology of Islamic jurisprudence, theology, the occasions behind the revelations, abrogating and abrogated verses, social and natural sciences and many more. If a scholar makes mistakes by adding extra information which is not directly related to the original text in his expla-

---

[73] Ömer Rıza Doğrul, *Tanrı Buyruğu (God's Command), the preface for the first edition.*

[74] Zarqānī, *Manahil-ul Irfan*, 2/10-14.

nations, he warns people about this. This does not occur in translations, because the *tarjama* takes the place of the original. In *tarjama* the author cannot add anything to the translation which changes the meaning.

3) *Tarjama* in terminology contains the compromise between the original text and the translation in meaning and in aims, but it is not the case in *tafsīr* which focuses specifically on the explanation of the text. It may choose one aspect, all aspects, or the aims of the text; it may be a brief or a detailed explanation, but *tarjama* translates the exact meaning to another language without adding any additional information or diminishing the meaning in the original.

4) In Islamic terminology, *tarjama* is understood as the exact translation of the original text conveying exactly the same meaning and with the same purpose based on evidence. The translator must fully understand the meaning of the original text and its purpose based on evidence and must choose specific translations over other possibilities. *Tafsīr,* on the other hand, is not as exact. If a *mufassir* finds sufficient evidence for his explanations, he can be sure about his *tafsīr*; if he cannot find the necessary evidence he mentions all of the possible meanings (without preferring one over the others) and explains each of them. On occasion the *mufassir* notes the weakness in the explanation of one expression from the original by saying 'the author [God] knows best what is meant by this expression'. This type of confession is seen more frequently for the explanation of conjecture letters at the beginning of some *surah.* For example the letters *Alif Lam Mim* at the beginning of Surah Baqara.

With all this evidence we are able to conclude that a direct translation of the Qur'ān to another language is impossible. However, it is possible to explain it using parallel meanings to the original text, thought this can lead to the neglect or addition of some information. For this reason the translation of the Qur'ān to other languages is considered as '*meal*'.

Summary: Two Types of Translation (*Tarjama*)

1. Literal translation is the attempt to achieve a direct translation from one language to another by finding equal expressions in the other language.
2. Translation in meaning is to express the meaning of the original text through similar words and phrases sacrificing structure where necessary. This is used more frequently as it requires fewer conditions than literal translations.

1.8.2 *Meal*

The infinitive form of the Arabic word '*meal*' is '*a-wa-la*' with the Arabic letter '*mim*' (*mim masdar*).[75] Its literal meaning is 'the place of the thing or the purpose of the thing which it will reach'. *Meal* in Arabic also means 'liquid that intensifies and becomes solid'.[76] In *tafsīr* terminology it means closely, but not exactly, phrasing one word or statement in another language but losing some of the original meaning in translation. Since the exact translation of the Qur'ān is impossible, the word '*meal*' is the proper name for the translation of the Qur'ān into other languages. It is necessary to translate the Qur'ān for non-Arabs for them to understand God's speech and assist them in acquiring knowledge about Islam. The eligible Muslim scholars must meet this need otherwise non-eligible people may produce deficient translations of the Qur'ān.

It is important to emphasise that the exegeses, interpretations, translations or the *meal* will never take the place of the original text of the Qur'ān. In Islam they are never used in place of the Qur'ān for worship. When compared to the history of the Bible and Torah the significance of this statement can be better understood. The rigour and sensitivity surrounding the Qur'ān's unique original text has seen its absolute preservation throughout history.

SUMMARY: *MEAL*

In Islamic terminology '*meal*' means closely phrasing one word or statement in another language but losing some of the original meaning in translation. *Meal*' is the correct word for translations of the Qur'ān into different languages.

---

[75] Ibn Manzūr, *Lisānu'l 'Arab*, 11/ 32-40.

[76] Zabīdī, *Tāju'l Arūs*, 7/ 214-215.

Chapter Two

The Notion of Revelation (*Waḥy*)

The Notion of Revelation (*Waḥy*)

2.1 The Nature of Revelation

The meanings of revelation and inspiration include: telling someone about something, a suggestion or gesture, sending a Messenger, speaking to someone so privately that no one else can hear, conveying knowledge and information into someone's heart that he would otherwise be required to study, directing someone to act in a certain way without his willing it, and enabling him to succeed in some tasks or activities which would usually be beyond his control or capability.[77]

According to Islam, God (Allah) is the Absolute Creator and He is the One who not only brought about creation but also continues to sustain and direct it. He has two important laws to communicate with His creatures; the laws of nature or works of God (*shari'ah takwiniyyah*) and the revelation or the words of God (*shari'ah tanziliyya*). Interestingly, both are named in the Qur'ān as 'the sign' (*al-ayah*). God has been communicating with His most honourable creatures (human beings) since their first appearance on earth, by guiding them with His revelation. God sent Prophet Adam to earth but He did not leave him without guidance:

> We said: 'Go down, all of you, from there!' (And executed Our order). If, henceforth, a guidance (like a Book through a Messenger) comes to you from Me, and whoever follows My guidance (and turns to Me with faith and worship), they will have no fear (in this world and the next, for they will always find My help and support with them), nor will they grieve.[78]

God conveyed His guidance through Prophets whom he continually sent to mankind until the last Messenger, Muhammad (pbuh) received His final guidance. Exactly how God communicated with His Prophets is a divine secret; they were chosen individuals with special abilities to receive the divine revelations. Fethullah Gülen interprets the phenomenon of revelation as the transition from exis-

[77] Fethullah Gülen, *Emerald Hills of the Heart*, tr; Ali Unal, Tughra Books, 2000, vol.3, p.72.
[78] Qur'ān, 2: 38.

tence as knowledge to existence perceived. This interpretation can be viewed as the wilful, direct, or indirect effusion of divine knowledge in the form of an address to one endowed with the required intellectual and spiritual capacity.[79]

Receiving the divine revelation requires a special disposition as well as intellectual and spiritual endowments. The spiritual level of human beings increases in relation to their efforts in struggling against, or training their disposition against natural vices and desires. When they reach a certain level they can perceive certain metaphysical realities that stimulate the spirit toward moral and spiritual perfection.[80]

The Prophets conveyed the revelation to people without hiding any part of it. This was their primary duty:

> We have revealed to you (O Messenger) as We revealed to Noah and the Prophets after him; and We revealed to Abraham, Ishmael, Isaac, Jacob and the Prophets who were raised in the tribes, and Jesus, Job, Jonah, Aaron, and Solomon; and We gave David the Psalms. And Messengers We have already told you of (with respect to their mission) before, and Messengers We have not told you of; and God spoke to Moses in a particular way. Messengers (have been sent as) bearers of glad tidings and warners, so that people might have no argument against God after the Messengers (had come to them). And God is All Glorious with irresistible might, All-Wise.[81]

In Islam, revelation is an initiative of God. It is God who intends to reveal His will to the Prophets. According to the methodologists of the Islamic religious sciences, revelation is the conveyance of knowledge to the Prophets by God with or without a means.[82] The Prophet becomes a receptacle of the revelation and a relationship between God and the Prophet is established. The Prophet Muhammad (pbuh) however, was not reduced to the role of passive bystander. He was an active recipient in that he was conscious whilst receiving the revelation and witnessed in his heart the grandeur of the presence of the 'voice' of God. The importance of this experience lies in what was said, not in what was experienced, by the Prophet (pbuh) at the time.[83]

Gülen explains the notion of revelation in broad concept:

---

79 Gülen, *Emerald Hills of the Heart*, p. 77.

80 Gülen, *Emerald Hills of the Heart*, p. 78.

81 Qur'ān, 4: 163-165.

82 Gülen, *Emerald Hills of the Heart*, p. 72.

83 Abdullah Saeed, *Interpreting the Qur'ān*, p. 37.

> Revelation, which can be described as breathing into hearts, occurs within a wide area, ranging from various manifestations to the master of creation, upon him be peace and blessings, to the inspiration in the heart of the mother of Prophet Moses, as stated in the verse, 'We inspired into Moses' mother' (28:7), and thereafter to what we can define as God's direction or guiding, which is mentioned in the verse, 'Your Lord has inspired the honeybee' (16:68). Revelation sometimes occurs as a suggestion through a single sound, gesture or hint, without speech. So, when we mention Revelation, we may sometimes mean this, without meaning Revelation in the religious sense.[84]

At the time of Prophet Muhammad (pbuh) human kind had reached a certain level of understanding of universal values; therefore the Qur'ān revealed those values for the whole of human kind for the last time through the last Prophet (pbuh). The Quraysh leaders in Mecca were unable to understand and appreciate this favour of God upon His Messenger and upon all human kind:

> Does it seem strange to people that We reveal to a man from among them, saying: 'Warn all humankind (of the consequences of the way they follow), and give those who believe the glad tidings that they have a sure footing with their Lord (on account of their belief, faithfulness, and righteous deeds).' (Is it because of this that) the unbelievers say: 'This (man) is clearly a sorcerer?[85]

Muhyi'd-Din ibn ul-'Arabi regards revelation as a development from the rank of absorption toward the rank of elaboration, where the Divine Being manifests Himself with His speech. According to him, whatever there is in the name of existence consists of a development from a concentrated or compacted form toward elaboration or expansion.[86]

With the Prophet's (pbuh) death the revelation and the favours of God were completed. This was a great loss for the Companions who had lived at a time when God was constantly speaking to them and answering their questions through His Messenger (pbuh) and guiding them to the truth. After the Prophet's (pbuh) death, many of the Companions missed him and the revelation process, and wept as a result:

> Once Abū Bakr and 'Umar visited Ummu Ayman and found her crying. They said, 'do not be upset, for sure, the Prophet (pbuh) is now in a bet-

---

84 Gülen, *Emerald Hills of the Heart*, p. 73.
85 Qur'ān, 10: 2.
86 Gülen, *Emerald Hills of the Heart*, p. 77.

ter place than where he used to be'. Thereupon she said, 'I am not crying just because of the Prophet's (pbuh) death but I am also crying because God stopped the revelation to mankind'. When Abū Bakr and 'Umar heard this, they started to weep with her.[87]

Summary of the Nature of Revelation:

1. Revelation includes many different methods.
2. God has two important laws to communicate with his creatures: laws of nature and revelation.
3. God sent revelations through Prophets to mankind until the last Prophet, Muhammad (pbuh).
4. Receiving revelations requires a special character and spiritual endowments.
5. The primary duty of Prophets is to convey God's revelation to mankind without concealing any part of it.
6. In Islam, revelation is an initiative of God. Prophet Muhammad (pbuh) was an active recipient.
7. The Qur'ān revealed the values that God has bestowed upon mankind for the last time.
8. The final revelation was completed with the death of the Prophet Muhammad (pbuh).

2.2 The Meaning of Revelation (*Waḫy*)

Waḫy in its infinitive form means to inspire, to whisper, to command, to imply, to gesture, to rush, to call, to write a letter and to communicate secretly or in a swift manner.[88] *Waḫy* has been used linguistically in different places of the Qur'ān:

1) The laws of nature;

> ...so He fashioned them (the clouds of gaseous elements which then existed in the place of the heaven) seven heavens in two days and inspired in each heaven its tasks.[89]

2) Natural instincts;

> ...and your Lord inspired the (female) bee: 'Take for yourself dwelling place in the mountains, and in the trees, and in what they (human beings) may

87 Muslim, *Saḫīḫ, Kitāb al-Fadāil al-Saḫābah*, 6009.

88 Ibn Manzūr, *Lisānu'l 'Arab*, 15/379-382.

89 Qur'ān, 41: 12.

build and weave. Then eat of all the fruits, and returning with your loads follow the ways your Lord has made easy for you." There comes forth from their bellies a fluid of varying colour, wherein is health for human beings. Surely in this there is a sign for people who reflect.[90]

3) Inspiration;

...we inspired the mother of Moses, saying: 'Suckle him (for a time, without anxiety for his life), then when you have cause to fear for him, put him in the river, and do not fear or grieve. We will surely return him to you and make him one of our Messengers.[91]

4) Signals, or gestures, to communicate;

...so he (Zachariah) came out to his people from the sanctuary (where he had been praying in the Temple), and signified to them: 'glorify your Lord at daybreak and in the afternoon'.[92]

5) Evil whispers from Satan;

...the Satan do whisper and make suggestions to their confidants to contend with you".[93]

6) Divine inspiration to the angels;

...when (in the meantime) your Lord revealed to the angels: I am certainly with you, so make firm the feet of those who believe.[94]

7) Divine revelation to the Prophets;

...we have revealed to you (O Messenger) as we revealed to Noah and the Prophets after him; and We revealed to Abraham, Ishmael, Isaac, Jacob and the Prophets who were raised in the tribes, and Jesus, Job, Jonah, Aaron, and Solomon; and We gave David the Psalms. And Messengers We have already told you of (with respect to their mission) before, and Messengers We have not told you of; and God spoke to Moses in a particular way. Messengers (have been sent as) bearers of glad tidings and warners, so that people might have no argument against God after the

[90] Qur'ān, 16: 68-69.
[91] Qur'ān, 28: 7.
[92] Qur'ān, 19: 11.
[93] Qur'ān, 6: 121.
[94] Qur'ān, 8: 12.

> Messengers (had come to them). And God is All Glorious with irresistible might, All-Wise.[95]

Revelation which comes to the Prophets is an objective, binding phenomenon which takes place beyond the spheres of the human soul and physical sensations. Its certainty transcends the conviction which comes from mere knowledge.[96] The angel who brought the revelation of the Qur'ān taught the Prophet (pbuh) how to recite it.

2.2.1 The First Revelation

The Prophet (pbuh) received the first revelation during the month of Ramadan in 610 C.E. when he was forty years old. Scholars generally agree that the first day of revelation was a Monday. Prior to receiving the revelation the Prophet (pbuh) had been in the habit of retreating to the secluded cave of Hira for spiritual reflection. It was during one of these retreats that he experienced something extraordinary; Aisha reports:

> The commencement of the divine revelation to God's Apostle (pbuh) was in the form of good dreams which came like bright daylight (i.e. true) and then the love of seclusion was bestowed upon him. He used to go in seclusion to the cave of Hira, where he used to worship (God alone) continuously for many days before a desire to see his family arose. He used to take with him food for the stay and then return to (his wife) Khadija to replenish it until suddenly the truth descended upon him while he was in the cave of Hira. The angel (Gabriel) came to him and asked him to read. The Prophet (pbuh) reported: 'I replied; 'I do not know how to read'. Thereupon the angel caught me (forcibly) and pressed me so hard that I could not bear it any more. He then released me and again asked me to read and I replied, 'I do not know how to read'. Thereupon he caught me again and pressed me a second time till I could not bear it any more. He then released me and again asked me to read, but again I replied, 'I do not know how to read'. Thereupon he caught me for the third time and pressed me, and then released me and said: 'Read in and with the Name of your Lord, Who has created, created human from a clot clinging (to the wall of the womb). Read and your Lord is the All Munificent, Who has taught (human kind) by the pen, taught man what he did not know". Then God's Apostle (pbuh) returned with the revelation and with his heart beating severely. He went to Khadija bint. Khuwaylid and said, 'Cover

---

95 Qur'ān, 4: 163-165.

96 Gülen, *Emerald Hills of the Heart*, p. 76.

> me! Cover me!' They covered him till his fear was over and after that he told her everything that had happened and said, 'I fear that something may have happened to me.' Khadija replied, 'Never! By God, God will never disgrace you. You keep good relations with your kith and kin, help the poor and the destitute, serve your guests generously and assist the deserving calamity-afflicted ones'. Khadija then accompanied him to her cousin Waraqa b. Nawfal, who, during the pre-Islamic period became a Christian and used to write in Hebrew. He would write from the Gospel in Hebrew as much as God wished him to write. He was an old man and had lost his eyesight. Khadija said to Waraqa, 'Listen to the story of your nephew, O my cousin!' Waraqa asked, 'O my nephew! What have you seen?' God's Apostle (pbuh) described everything he had seen. Waraqa said, 'this is the same one who keeps the secrets (angel Gabriel) whom God had sent to Moses. I wish I was young and could live to the time when your people will turn you out'. God's Apostle (pbuh) asked, 'Will they drive me out?' Waraqa replied in the affirmative and said, 'anyone (man) who came with something similar to what you have brought was treated with hostility; and if I should remain alive till the day when you will be turned out then I would support you strongly'. But after a few days Waraqa died and the divine revelation was also paused for a while.[97]

Jabir ibn Abd Allah al-Ansari said that while speaking about the intermission of the revelation, the Prophet (pbuh) said:

> While I was out walking, I suddenly heard a voice from heaven. I raised my eyes and there was the same angel who had come to me at Hira. He was sitting on a chair between the sky and the earth. I was afraid of him and returned home and said, 'O you cloaked one (who has preferred solitude)! Arise and warn! And declare your Lord's (indescribable and incomparable) greatness. And keep your clothing clean! Keep away from all pollution'.[98] After these few verses, the revelation started coming strongly, frequently and regularly.[99]

2.2.2 Receiving the Revelation

Revelation is only experienced by the Prophet (pbuh) and it is therefore almost impossible to know what happened during the process. Many reports and anecdotes, however, have been preserved which describe different dimensions of the process. The Qur'ān describes *waḩy* (revelation) as a heavy speech: "We will sure-

[97] Bukhari, *Saḩīḩ, Revelation*, 3.
[98] Qur'ān, 74: 1-5.
[99] Bukhari, *Saḩīḩ, Tafsīr of the Prophet*, 448.

ly charge you with a weighty Word (and with applying it to your daily life and conveying it to others)".[100]

Revelation does not mean that God makes His Being known, it arises from His will; and His will, or testament, is revealed in a comprehensible human language. Despite being unable to give a scientific description of the experience, the Prophet (pbuh) firmly held that the context of revelation was objective, not subjective, and this objectivity was established by the fact that the message was relayed in his own language.[101]

During the revelation process the Prophet (pbuh) experienced intense feelings; he shook and trembled, his face was extremely pale, he sweated even in cold weather and he breathed heavily. If he was mounted on a camel when the revelation came, the camel would kneel down and the Prophet (pbuh) had to unmount it. Once the Prophet (pbuh) received the revelation when his knees were resting on top of the legs of Zayd b. Thabit; Zayd felt so much weight on his legs that they almost broke.[102]

Aisha reports:

> al-Harith ibn Hishām asked the Messenger of God (pbuh): 'Messenger of God! How does the revelation come to you?' The Messenger of God (pbuh) said, 'Sometimes it comes to me like the ringing of a bell, and this is the hardest on me, which then leaves me after I have fully understood and retained what was said. Sometimes the angel comes to me in the form of a man and speaks to me and I retain what he says'. Aisha said, 'I saw him when the revelation was descending upon him on a very cold day and when it left him his eyebrows was drenched in sweat.[103]

Ibn 'Abbās reports:

> The Prophet (pbuh) used to experience great difficulty while receiving the revelation and he used to move his lips in order not to forget the verses during the revelation process. God sent the verses 75: 16-18; 'Do not move your tongue trying to hasten it. Its collection and recitation are Our responsibility' Ibn 'Abbās said that 'collecting it' means 'in your heart and your reciting it as it was revealed'. 'So when We recite it, follow its recitation', means 'listen and be silent', 'Then its explanation is also Our

---

[100] Qur'ān, 73: 5.

[101] Abd Allah Saeed, *Interpreting the Qur'ān*, p. 37.

[102] Bukhari, *Saḫīḫ, Revelation*, 2-4, Muslim, *Saḫīḫ, the Book of Commentary*, 1817, Abu Dāwud, *Sunan*, 2/11.

[103] Bukhari, *Saḫīḫ, Revelation*, 2.

> responsibility' means that it is up to Us when you recite it. After that, the Messenger of God, (pbuh) would listen when Gabriel came to him. When Gabriel left, then the Prophet (pbuh) would recite it as Gabriel had recited it".[104]

The above verses clearly indicate that the Prophet (pbuh) was not permitted to use his intellect to memorise the revealed verses of the Qur'ān. Moreover, we can easily observe that the revelation came down any time that God willed it, not when the Prophet (pbuh) needed or desired it. The Qur'ān itself makes frequent reference to this fact:

> And this Qur'ān is not such that it could possibly be fabricated by one in attribution to God, but it is a (Divine Book) confirming (the Divine origin of and the truths that are still contained by) the Revelations prior to it, and an explanation of the Essence of all Divine Books, wherein there is no doubt, from the Lord of the worlds.[105]

The Companions were eager to witness the moment of revelation upon the Prophet (pbuh). Safwān ibn Ya'la ibn Umayyah reports:

> My father, Ya'la ibn Umayyah used to say (during the Prophet's lifetime), 'How I wish I could see the Prophet (pbuh) while the revelation comes down to him'. So, one day, the Prophet (pbuh) was at Ji'rānah, when a person came to him and said, 'O Messenger of God! What is the ruling for one who enters into the state of *iḫrām* while his clothes are soaked in perfume?' So the Prophet (pbuh) waited for a while, until the inspiration came to him. 'Umar ibn al-Khattab motioned to Ya'la, 'Come quickly!' so Ya'la came and stuck his head into the Prophet's (pbuh) tent to see him. He saw the Prophet (pbuh), his face was red (due to the revelation), and he stayed like that for some time, then it was lifted off him, and he called the questioner and said, for the perfume on your body, wash yourself three times, and as for your clothes, then replace them (with non-scented ones)"[106]

Gülen cautiously elucidates the process of revelation with the example of Morse code: Receptors transfer the signals of the alphabet of Morse code into everyday letters and words with every signal being equal to a specific letter. The operator of this receptor knows which sign is equal to which letter. This comparison can help us to understand the process of revelation: God enables Prophets to

---

104 Bukhari, *Saḫīḫ*, *Revelation*, 4.

105 Qur'ān, 10: 37.

106 Bukhari, *Saḫīḫ*, *Book of the Virtues of the Qur'ān*, 4700.

receive divine signals and know them as specific words by endowing them with thousands of spiritual receptors.

Summary of the Meaning of Revelation (*Waḫy*):

1. *Waḫy* means to inspire, to whisper, to command, to imply, to gesture, to rush, to call, to write a letter and to communicate secretly or in a swift manner.
2. It is used in various places in the Qur'ān to mention: laws of nature, natural instincts, inspiration, signals and gestures to communicate, evil whispers from Satan, divine inspiration to the angels and divine revelation to Prophets.
3. Revelation to Prophets takes place beyond the soul and physical sensations. It is objective and binding.

The First Revelation:

4. Prophet Muhammad (pbuh) received the first revelation in the year 610 C.E.. It was during Ramadan and is generally agreed to have been on a Monday.

Receiving the Revelation:

5. The revelation was only received by the Prophet (pbuh) so it is impossible to know what happened.
6. The revelation is not God revealing Himself. It is Him revealing His Will.
7. During the revelation process the Prophet (pbuh) experienced intense feelings and discomfort.
8. The Prophet (pbuh) was not permitted to use his intellect to memorise verses of the Qur'ān.

2.3 The Forms of Revelation

There are different forms of revelation; the Qur'ān mentions three of them:

> It is not for any mortal that God should speak to him unless it be by Revelation or from behind a veil, or by sending a Messenger (angel) to reveal, by His leave, whatever He wills (to reveal). Surely He is All Exalted, All-Wise.[107]

The Hadith also explain various forms of revelation and, taken together with those mentioned in the Qur'ān, there are seven channels which can be categor-

[107] Qur'ān, 42: 51.

ised in two ways: revelation with an intermediary and revelation without an intermediary.

2.3.1 Revelation without an Intermediary

The first of the two major categories of revelation: God directly sends revelations to his servants without the use of an intermediary. This type of revelation has the following subcategories:

a) Receiving the revelation in a dream. Aisha reports:

> ...the commencement of the divine inspiration upon the Prophet (pbuh) was in the form of good dreams; he never saw a dream about anything except that it came true like the rising of the sun.[108]

It is generally accepted that Prophet Muhammad (pbuh) did not receive any Qur'anic verses in this manner. His dreams were preparations for the revelations. During his Prophethood he saw many dreams and even though he interpreted some of them, he never told his scribes to write them as verses of the Qur'ān. God may inspire humankind through true dreams, but they are not objective and binding upon other people. The Prophet (pbuh) said: 'nothing is left from Prophethood but the glad tidings (*mubashshiraat*), when he was asked about the glad tidings, he said, 'a true dream'.[109] In another Hadith the Prophet (pbuh) said: 'a true dream is one out of forty-six parts of Prophethood".[110] The only type of inspiration left following the death of the Prophet (pbuh) is in the form of true dreams to humankind.

The best example for this form of revelation is when Prophet Abraham received guidance in a vision, while asleep, to sacrifice his son:

> ...then, when (his son) grew alongside him to the age of striving (for the necessities of life), he said: "O my dear son! I have seen in my dream that I should offer you in sacrifice. So think about this and tell me your view!' He said (unhesitatingly): 'O my dear father! Do as you are commanded. You will find me, by God's will, one of those who show steadfast patience (in obeying God's commands).[111]

b) Receiving the revelation through the direct speech of God. This is the way in which Moses received the revelation. God spoke with him directly but did not

---

[108] Bukhari, *Saḫīḫ*, *Revelation*, 3.
[109] Bukhari, *Saḫīḫ*, *Interpretation of Dreams*, 119.
[110] Dārimī, *Sunan*, 1/374.
[111] Qur'ān, 37: 102.

reveal Himself to Moses. The voice that Moses heard was created by God for the purpose of revelation but was not His actual voice, because God is beyond, time and space, nothing is similar to Him. The following verse is good example for this type of revelation:

> And when Moses came to Our appointed time, his Lord spoke to him. (Then, in the rapture of nearness to God arising from his being addressed by Him) he said: 'My Lord, show me Yourself, so that I may look upon You!' He (God) said: 'You cannot see Me (with your eyes in the world). But look at that mountain: if it remains firm in its place, then you will see Me.' And the moment his Lord manifested His glorious Majesty to the mountain, He made it crumble to dust, and Moses fell down in a faint (as if struck by lightning). When he awoke, he said: 'All Glorified are You (in that You are absolutely above having any defects and any resemblance with the created)! I turn to You in repentance (for my desire to see You), and I am the first of the (true) believers (who realize that You are beyond any resemblance to any creature and beyond the grasp of any creature's senses).[112]

Prophet Muhammad (pbuh) also received this type of revelation at least once in his Prophethood. It occurred during the time when he still lived in Mecca, on the night that he ascended to the heavens. Some scholars claim that the Prophet (pbuh) received the last two verses of *surah* Baqara in this manner; however, there is no authentic, explicit proof for this opinion.

2.3.2 Revelation with an Intermediary

The primary and most common method of revelation is with an intermediary: the angel Gabriel. God sent Gabriel to inspire His Messengers with His will. 'Ubāda ibn Sāmit reported:

> Whenever the revelation descended upon the Prophet (pbuh), the significance and importance that he gave (to the inspiration) could be seen, and his face became slightly pale. Also, the Prophet (pbuh) would lower his head during the revelation process, and the Companions, due to their love for the Prophet (pbuh), would also lower their heads, until the revelation had ended.[113]

The Prophet (pbuh) sometimes saw the angel and sometimes he didn't. The Qur'ān mentions Gabriel as the angel of revelation:

---

[112] Qur'ān, 7: 143.

[113] Muslim, *Saḫīḫ, the Book of Commentary*, 1817.

> This is not all. They feel enmity towards Gabriel because he brings the Qur'ān to you....[114]

This type of revelation has the following subcategories:

a) Gabriel was sent in human form to transmit the revelation: Most of the Qur'ān was transmitted to the Prophet (pbuh) in this way and it was the easiest way for him. The angel was appearing in the form of a Companion, Dihya al-Kalbī. Muslim scholars agree that this was the surest and clearest definitive process of revelation.

b) Gabriel revealed verses whilst the Prophet (pbuh) was awake but without being seen: During this process of revelation God created the awareness in the heart of the Prophet (pbuh) that this was not inspiration, it was revelation and thus a part of the Qur'ān.[115]

c) The revelation process started with the sound of a bell ringing: This form of revelation was used for verses about admonitions and forewarnings and was the hardest form of revelation for the Prophet (pbuh).[116] When he received this type of revelation the Prophet (pbuh) used to shake with fear.

d) Gabriel appeared to the Prophet (pbuh) in his true form and transmitted the revelation: This type of revelation occurred twice during his Prophethood. The first time was in the cave of Hira at the beginning of his Prophethood and the second time was when he ascended to the heavens.

2.3.3 The Stages of Revelation

The Qur'ān mentions two important words to describe the stages of revelations: *inzāl* (to descend) and *tanzīl* (to send down). Muslim scholars generally classify the descent of the Qur'anic revelation in three stages.

> Indeed it is a glorious Qur'ān (– a sublime Book revealed and recited), in a Preserved Tablet (guarded from every accursed devil, and secure from any falsehood).[117]

The above verse describes the first stage of revelation. God wrote everything in the 'preserved tablet', a divine project, a blueprint for all creation. The content of this written record never changes; all events, destinies and creations in

---

[114] Qur'ān, 2: 97.
[115] Suyūtī, *al-Itqān*, 1/46.
[116] Bukhari, *Saḫīḫ*, *Revelation*, 3.
[117] Qur'ān, 85: 21-22.

the heavens and earth happen according to it and will do until the end of time. The Prophet (pbuh) said:

> The first thing that God created was the pen. He said to it, write, it responded, 'O my Lord! And what shall I write? God said: write the destiny of all things, until the Day of Judgement.[118]

The second stage refers to the process where the preserved text on a heavenly tablet is sent down whole to the abode of glory or lower heaven (from *lawḫ al-maḫfūz* to *bayt al-'izzah*). The Qur'ān mentions that it was revealed in the month of Ramadan:

> We have surely sent it (the Qur'ān) down in the Night of Destiny and Power.[119]

This verse means the angel Gabriel heard the revelation and understood it, and revealed to him what he heard, and so the angel descended with the revelation from a higher place (the heavens) to a lower one (*bayt al-'izzah*).

The Prophet (pbuh) said:

> Whenever God desires to inspire a matter (to His servants), He speaks with the inspiration, and (because of this) the heavens themselves shake out of fear of God. When the inhabitants of the Heaven (i.e., the angels) hear of it, they fall down in a swoon and prostrate to Him. The first one to raise his head is Gabriel and God speaks to him with the inspiration that He wishes. Then Gabriel passes by the angels; whenever he goes by any heaven, the angels of that heaven ask him 'what did our Lord say, O Gabriel?' He answers, 'He has spoken the truth, and He is the Most High, the Most Great'.[120]

The final stage, referenced in many verses of the Qur'ān is that the revelation was sent down from the heavens to the earth throughout the twenty-three years of Muhammad's (pbuh) Prophethood. The verse in *surah* al-Shu'ara displays this process clearly:

> This (Qur'ān) is indeed the Book of the Lord of the Worlds being sent down by Him (in parts). The Trustworthy Spirit brings it down on your

---

118 Tirmidhi, *Sunan, the Destiny*, 94.

119 Qur'ān, 97: 1.

120 Bukhari, *Saḫīḫ, Kitāb at-Tawḫīd*, 14.

heart, so that you may be one of the warners (entrusted with the Divine Revelation), in clear Arabic tongue.[121]

Summary of the Forms of Revelation:

The Qur'ān mentions different forms of revelation:

1. Revelation without an intermediary; i.e. receiving the revelation in a dream (which didn't occur with Prophet Muhammad (pbuh)) or through the direct speech of God (which happened at least once to Prophet Muhammad (pbuh)).
2. Revelation with an intermediary; the angel Gabriel. This happened in different ways: Gabriel appeared in human form and transmitted the revelation; he transmitted it unseen; a bell sound announced the beginning of the revelation; Gabriel appeared in true form; Gabriel transmitted the revelation whilst the Prophet (pbuh) was asleep.

There are three stages of revelation classified by Islamic scholars: the preservation of Divine Will and creation on a heavenly tablet; the tablet being sent to lower heaven and the transmission of the content (revelation) to Prophet Muhammad (pbuh).

2.4 The Wisdom behind the Gradual Revelation of the Qur'ān

The Qur'ān was revealed in stages over a period of 23 years rather than as a complete book in one single act of revelation. There are a number of reasons for this and the most significant wisdom behind the gradual revelation of the Qur'ān is as follows:

1) The revelation being sent in parts during different times, served to strengthen the heart of the Prophet (pbuh) by addressing him continuously and whenever the need for guidance arose. The Prophet (pbuh) and early believers suffered constant persecution and faced many difficulties, therefore they needed constant support and God helped them continuously by answering their calls through revelation.

2) Revelation was a physically and psychologically difficult experience for the Prophet (pbuh). To support him in it God mentioned some past nations' stories and informed the Prophet (pbuh) that he was not alone on this path. He always helped the Messengers and He never left them alone. 'The prosperity belongs to

[121] Qur'ān, 26: 195-195.

the pious people, so you will be successful and people will accept Islam within a short time'.[122]

3) The revelation coming in parts enabled the new community to gradually implement the laws of God. It needed time for the people to discard their old customs, beliefs and habits and adapt to the new way of life. An example of this is the prohibition of the consumption of alcohol which occurred in four stages many years into the Prophethood of Muhammad (pbuh). Human nature cannot be changed immediately and this was the wisdom of revealing the Qur'ān in stages rather than in its entirety at once.

4) The gradual revelation of the Qur'ān enabled the people to understand and memorize them easily. The Companions learned by heart, understood and applied to their lives ten verses at a time before moving on the following ten verses. In this way they were able to be thorough and not make mistakes.

Summary of the Wisdom Behind the Gradual Revelation of the Qur'ān:

The Qur'ān being revealed over 23 years has the following benefits:

1. To strengthen the hearts and resolve of the Prophet (pbuh) and early believers who suffered constant persecution.
2. To support the Prophet (pbuh) by telling him of past Prophets' experiences.
3. To enable a gradual implementation of a new way of life and worship.
4. To enable the Companions to understand, memorise and implement the Qur'ān into their lives without making any mistakes.

2.5 The Scribes of the Qur'ān and the Materials for Writing the Qur'ān

As the Prophet (pbuh) was illiterate, he ordered many scribes to write down all the revealed verses from the beginning of his Prophethood until he died. In addition to this, each Ramadan, the Prophet (pbuh) recited the whole Qur'ān (whatever had been revealed up until that point) to the angel Gabriel to check his accuracy. This is called the '*arḏ*' in Islamic tradition. In his final year of life the Prophet (pbuh) recited it twice during Ramadan.[123] As a result, the Qur'ān was com-

[122] Qur'ān 12: 57.

[123] Bukhari, *Saḫīḫ*, 3/199.

pleted and accurately recorded in the memories of the Companions and in the writings of the scribes.

The scribes used the following materials to record the verses of the Qur'ān:

1) Palm tree branches and leaves
2) Thin white stones
3) Animal scapula
4) Animal skins
5) Pieces of wood, earthenware pots and some other materials.[124]

Some of the names of the scribes of the divine revelation are:

1) Abū Bakr
2) 'Umar
3) 'Uthman
4) 'Ali
5) Zubayr ibn Awwam
6) Āmir ibn Fuhayra
7) 'Amr ibn As
8) Abd Allah ibn Arkam
9) Thabit ibn Qays
10) Hanzala ibn al-Rabi'
11) Mughira ibn Shu'ba
12) Abd Allah ibn Rawaha
13) Khalid ibn Walid
14) Hudhayfa al-Yamān
15) Mu'awiya ibn Abī Sufyan
16) 'Ubayy ibn Ka'b
17) Zayd ibn Thabit.[125]

Summary of the Scribes and Materials used to Record the Qur'ān:

1. The illiterate Prophet (pbuh) ordered scribes to record the revealed verses of the Qur'ān over the whole 23 years of revelation.
2. Each year in Ramadan the Prophet (pbuh) recited the whole Qur'ān to the angel Gabriel (twice during his last Ramadan) to check the accuracy.

---

[124] Ahmad Amin, *Fajru'l Islam*, 166.

[125] Ahmad ibn Abī Ya'qub, *Tarīkhi Ya'qubī*, 2/64, Ibn Ḫajar, *Fatḫ al-Bari*, 9/18.

3. These practices ensured the Qur'ān has been preserved complete and unadulterated.
4. Different materials were used to record the verses (see list above) and many different Companions acted as scribes (see list above).

2.6 The Spoken and Written Word of God

God's attributes, names and essential qualities are unique and it is impossible for mankind to understand their exact nature although it is possible to comprehend the concept that any name or attribute refers to. The Qur'ān derives from God's attribute of *Kalām*, meaning the Qur'ān is the direct speech of God and, like God and His attributes, it is eternal. Belief in the Qur'anic revelation as the exact word of God is very clear in both classical and modern definitions of the Qur'ān provided by Muslim scholars. The Qur'ān is the communication of God to humankind in Arabic, which was revealed in both word and meaning to the Prophet Muhammad (pbuh), which has been preserved in the Book, which has been worshipped by reciting and which has reached us by the strongest transmissions. Furthermore, there exists within it a challenge to all humankind to produce something similar to it. On the nature of revelation, the theologian Nasafī (d. 508/1114) says:

> The Qur'ān is God's speech, which is one of His attributes. Now God in all of His attributes is one, and with all His attributes is eternal and not contingent, (so His speaking is) without letters and without sounds, not broken up into syllables or paragraphs. It is not He nor is it other than He. He caused Gabriel to hear it as sound and letters, for He created sound and letters and caused him to hear it by that sound and those letters. Gabriel memorized it, stored it (in his mind) and then transmitted to the Prophet (pbuh) by bringing down a revelation and a message, which is not the same as bringing down a corporeal object and a form. He recited it to the Prophet (pbuh), the Prophet memorized it, storing it up (in his mind), and then recited it to his Companions, who memorized it and recited to the Followers.[126]

The language of the Qur'ān, is extremely important and an essential part of revelation. No translation of the Qur'ān is considered by Muslims as equal to the Qur'ān in its original Arabic. The two, the Qur'ān and its language, are inseparable in the same way that the body is inseparable from its skin. Reciting the Qur'ān

[126] F. E. Peters, *A Reader on Classical Islam*, 173.

in its original language is believed to allow the reader to communicate directly with God where the reader can experience the revelation itself.

In many verses of the Qur'ān, God describes his attribute of speech:

> God spoke to Moses in a particular way[127]
>
> The word of your Lord (which He sent down in parts in different periods considering the conditions of each period) is perfected (with the Qur'ān) as the embodiment of truth and of justice: there is no altering of His words.[128]
>
> Say: 'If all the sea were ink to write my Lord's words, the sea would indeed be exhausted before my Lord's words are exhausted, even if We were to bring the like of it in addition to it.[129]
>
> God's word (His cause) is (always and inherently) supreme. God is All-Glorious with irresistible might, All-Wise[130]

The speech of God is not limited to the Arabic language. God revealed the Torah and the Bible in Hebrew, and this was also a part of His speech. Indeed He has knowledge of every human language. God sent the Prophets with the language of their nations to convey His message and to inform them about the outcome of disbelief.

During the reign of Caliph Mamun, (813-833 C.E.) when books from various languages were translated into Arabic, there was confluence of Arabic and non-Arabic doctrines. The Arabs, who enjoyed eminence in political and cultural fields, were the chief spokesmen of Islamic theology and thus faced many problems. These discussions led scholars to the problem of the Qur'ān as being eternal or created. If it was created then necessarily it would have to be accepted as not being co-existent with the Almighty.[131] The question of whether the Qur'ān was 'eternal' or 'created' was quite unnecessary and unworthy of discussion. Mamun strongly supported the Mu'tazalites[132] who considered the Qur'ān as *created*. He declared the belief as official and punished those who did not subscribe to this view. Even after Mamun's reign, the orthodox scholars suffered severe punish-

---

127 Qur'ān, 4: 164.

128 Qur'ān, 6: 115.

129 Qur'ān, 18: 109.

130 Qur'ān, 9: 40.

131 Hasanuddin Ahmed, *Introducing the Qur'ān*, p. 28.

132 School of Theology, this movement was founded in Basra in the first half of the second/eight ce - tury by Wasil b. Ata (d.131/748), subsequently became one of the important schools of Islam.

ments, including physical torture.[133] On the other hand the Ash'arī[134] and Salafī [135] scholars rejected the idea of the Qur'ān being created. Imam Ahmad b. Hanbal (164-241 A.H. / 780-855 C.E.) strongly opposed the Mutazalite view and declared that the words of the Qur'ān were from God and therefore, eternal. However, there was a consensus between both groups that God speaks and the Qur'ān is the speech of God.[136] In Islam 'revelation' means that God 'spoke', that He revealed Himself through language, and not in some mysterious non-human language but in a clear, humanly understandable language. This is the initial and most decisive fact. Without this act on the part of God, there would have been no true religion on earth according to the Islamic understanding of the word 'religion'.[137]

Izutsu analyses this issue as follows:

> In understanding the problem of God's speaking in Arabic, a human language, one option is to emphasize the difference between the revelations as it relates to the 'speech' of God (at the level of the unseen) and the revelation as it relates to a human language. Revelation at the unseen (*ghayb*) level is a theological mystery incapable of being grasped by human analytical thought. The phenomenon of revelation, in this respect, is something essentially mysterious, which does not allow for any analysis; it is something only to be believed in. Revelation in a human language, however, is capable of being analysed.[138]

It is difficult then, to resist the conclusion that although in so far as it is God's speech, revelation is something mysterious and has nothing in common with ordinary human linguistic behaviour, in so far as it is speech, it must have all the essential attributes of human speech. [139] In fact, the Qur'ān also uses other words in reference to revelation that are most commonly applied to ordinary, commonplace products of speech: for example, in *surah* al-Shūrā the word '*kalimah*' meaning 'word' is used. [140]

God's speech is beyond our experience unless it is somehow expressed in a human language form that we can understand. Ghazālī said:

---

133 *Introducing the Qur'ān*, 29.

134 School of Theology, it was founded by Abu al-Hasan al-Ash'ari (d. 324/935).

135 People who follow the path of the Prophet without making any changing in it are called *Salafi*.

136 Fakhr al-Rāzī, *al-Tafsīr al-Kabīr*, 27/187.

137 Toshihiko Izutsu, *God and Man in the Koran*, Tokyo, Institute of Cultural and Linguistic Studies, 1964, p.152.

138 Toshihiko Izutsu, *God and Man in the Koran*, p. 154.

139 Ibid.

140 Ibid.

> God expressed that attribute of speech in human images and words to mankind. If the glory and excellence of the words of God could not have been made understandable in the garb of words, heaven and earth could not stand to hear His words and all things between them would have been smashed to pieces.[141]

There are three levels of 'speech' in the Qur'ān: language and utterance (*lughah wa nutq*), letters and writing (*huruf and kitabah*) and spirit and meaning (*ruh wa ma'na*). It is only in the last sense that the Qur'ān, the speech of God, can be said to be uncreated; that is, coeternal with God.[142] Many verses refer to the revelation as a *qawl*, which may be translated as 'saying', 'word' or 'words' that are 'said', 'communicated' and then 'heard'. The root *'qa-wa-la'* and its derivatives, such as *'qāla'*, are also used many times in the Qur'ān to refer to God's 'speaking'.[143] These and similar verses indicate that the Qur'ān is primarily the spoken word coming from God. These terms fall within the broad category of 'speech'.[144] According to Izutsu:

> It is no wonder, then, that Islam should have been from the very beginning extremely language conscious. Islam arose when God spoke. The Islamic tradition and culture made its start with the historic datum that; God addressed man in a language, which he himself spoke. This was not a simple matter of God sending down a sacred Book. It meant primarily that God 'spoke'. And this is precisely what 'revelation' means. Revelation is essentially a linguistic concept.[145]

While there is much in the Qur'ān to suggest that it is primarily spoken words, it also contains many verses indicating that it is also a 'written' word. From the Qur'anic point of view, the spoken word and the written word appear to be two sides of the same coin. Even though terms associated with speech are used more frequently to refer to the Qur'ān, the use of writing-related terms is also common.[146] In fact, even the first verses of the revelation to the Prophet (pbuh) established the connection of revelation to the 'pen': "Read, and your Lord is the All-Munificent, Who has taught (humankind) by the pen".[147]

---

[141] Ghazali, *Ihya 'Ulūm ad-Din*, p. 268.
[142] Abdullah Saeed, *Interpreting the Qur'ān*, p. 31.
[143] Qur'ān, 2: 243.
[144] Abdullah Saeed, *Interpreting the Qur'ān*, p. 35.
[145] Toshihiko Izutsu, *God and Man in the Koran*, p. 152.
[146] Abdullah Saeed, *Interpreting the Qur'ān, p.* 35.
[147] Qur'ān, 96: 3-4.

The Qur'ān refers to the previous scriptures using several terms:

1) *Suḫuf* (scripture, pages): "this is surely contained in the former Scrolls (*Suḫuf*), The Scrolls of Abraham and Moses".[148]

2) *Asfār* (written scripture):

> The parable of those entrusted to carry the Torah, who subsequently do not carry it out in practice, is that of a donkey carrying a load of books (*asfār*).[149]

3) *Alwāḫ* (tablets):

> We recorded for him (Moses) on the *tablets* (*Alwāḫ*) whatever is necessary as instruction and guidance (to follow the way to God), and as explanation for all matters.[150]

4) *Kitāb Allah* (scripture of God or the book of God):

> And We granted them both (Moses and Aaron) *the clear Book*.[151]

> (The infant Jesus) said: 'surely I am a servant of God. He (has already decreed that He) will give me *the Book* (the Gospel) and make me a Prophet.[152]

> Those who reject faith (in the Qur'ān and God's Messenger (pbuh) from among the People of the Book and the polytheists would not abandon and deviate until there had come to them the clear evidence, a Messenger from God, reciting and conveying (to them teachings absolutely free from any falsehood) from *purified pages* in which are right, ever-true ordinances.[153]

In the last verse God describes the Qur'ān as *purified pages*, which only those cleansed of material and spiritual impurities (those who have performed ritual ablution) may touch. The Qur'ān is not just the speech of God, but it is also the scripture and the book which the following verses clearly indicate:

> Do not take God's revelations for a mockery and remember God's favour on you and what He has sent down on you of the Book and the wisdom wherewith He exhorts you (to guidance)[154]

148 Qur'ān, 87: 18-19.
149 Qur'ān, 62: 5.
150 Qur'ān, 7: 145.
151 Qur'ān, 37: 117.
152 Qur'ān, 19: 30.
153 Qur'ān, 98: 1-3.
154 Qur'ān, 2: 231.

> Recite (and teach) that which has been revealed to you from the Book of your Lord. There is none who can change His words (whatever the unbelievers may say or desire), and you will never find, apart from Him, any refuge[155]

Summary of the Spoken and Written Word of God:

1. The Qur'ān is derived from God's attribute of speech (*Kalām*) and it is the direct speech of God.
2. It is spoken in Arabic and no translation can equal it.
3. Recitation of the Qur'ān in Arabic allows Muslims to experience the revelation.
4. God has knowledge of all human languages. He revealed the Torah and Bible in Hebrew.
5. In Islamic history there has been much discussion on whether the Qur'ān is created or eternal which has resulted at times in conflict and persecution.
6. In Islam 'revelation' means that God spoke. Without this fundamental fact there would be no true religion on the earth.
7. God's true speech is beyond our experience unless it is expressed in a human language form that we can understand.
8. There are three levels of speech in the Qur'ān: language and utterance, letters and writing, spirit and meaning; only the last is uncreated.
9. The Qur'ān refers to itself as 'spoken' many times and also as 'written'. It contains many occurrences of writing-related terms with regard to both it and other scriptures.

In summary, the dominant Muslim view of revelation in Islam on the whole accommodates the following, notwithstanding differences among Muslims on specific elements: God revealed his Will (not his Being) to Prophet Muhammad (pbuh); revelation occurred through an intermediary, known as the Spirit or the angel Gabriel; this revelation to the Prophet (pbuh) was in Arabic, the language of the Prophet (pbuh), and came to be equated with the text of the Qur'ān; there is a clear distinction between God's 'word' and the Prophet's (pbuh) 'word'; while both are considered 'revelation', the former is 'recited' revelation (the Qur'ān) and the latter 'un-recited' revelation (the Hadith); revelation ceased to exist with the death of the Prophet Muhammad (pbuh) and therefore no further revelation is

[155] Qur'ān, 18: 27.

to be accepted; revelation is eternal and independent of specific socio-historical context.[156]

I'd like to finish this topic with the statement of Fethullah Gülen on the speech of God:

> The Qur'ān is the speech of God both in its words and by their meanings, yet the Qur'ān as written on paper is not considered eternal. The Qur'ān comes from God's attribute of *Kalām* (speech). Since the attribute of *Kalām* is eternal, the Qur'ān is also eternal. Thus, the Qur'ān existed before the creation of this universe, because God was speaking in Himself (*Kalām Nafsī*) and He was The Speaker (*Mutakallim*) even before creating the things into existence. God has two types of speech; one speaking with others and the other speaking in Himself. The Qur'ān is of the second type of God's speech; it neither has a beginning nor an end. This noble quality is only true for the Qur'ān and no other book has such a quality.[157]

[156] Abdullah Saeed, *Interpreting the Qur'ān,* 39.

[157] M Fethullah Gülen, *Kuranin Altin Ikliminde,* 29-30, Nil Yayinlari; Istanbul, 2011.

Chapter Three

Transmission of the Qur'anic Revelation

Transmission of the Qur'anic Revelation

3.1 Memorisation and Oral Transmission of the Qur'ān

Prophet Muhammad's (pbuh) main purpose was to convey God's revelation to people and ensure its preservation. On receiving the revelation, the Prophet (pbuh) was the first person to memorise the verses, but he did not do anything to memorise them, rather he found them imprinted in his heart; they were then memorised by his Companions. The Prophet (pbuh) encouraged them to read and memorise the Qur'ān.[158] The Prophet said: 'The most superior among you (Muslims) are those who learn the Qur'ān and teach it'.[159] Ibn Mas'ud reports:

> God's Apostle (pbuh) said to me, 'Recite (of the Qur'ān) for me'. I said: 'shall I recite it to you although it had been revealed to you?!' He said: 'I like to hear (the Qur'ān) from others'. So I recited *surah* Nisā till I reached: 'How (will it be) then when We bring from each nation a witness and We bring you (O Muhammad) as a witness against these people?'[160] Then he said: 'Stop!' Behold, his eyes were shedding tears then.[161]

During the Prophet's (pbuh) lifetime, many of the Companions memorised the whole Qur'ān. Suyūtī mentions more than twenty Companions who memorised the whole Qur'ān, among them Abū Bakr, 'Umar, 'Uthman, 'Ali, 'Abd Allah ibn Mas'ud, Āi'sha, Hafsa and Ummu Salama. Ibn Mas'ud reports: 'I shall ever love that man for I heard the Prophet (pbuh) saying: Take (learn) the Qur'ān from four: 'Abd Allah b. Mas'ud, Sālim, Mu'adh and 'Ubayy b. Ka'b'.[162] Qatāda reported:

> I asked Anas b. Malik: Who collected the Qur'ān at the time of the Prophet? He replied, four, all of whom were from the Ansār: 'Ubayy b. Ka'b, Mu'adh b. Jabal, Zayd b. Thabit and Abū Zayd.[163]

---

[158] Bukhari, *Saḫīḫ, Fadāil al-Qur'ān*, 20, Ahmed b. Hanbel, *Musnad*, 6/66.

[159] Bukhari, *Saḫīḫ, Fadāil al-Qur'ān*, 546.

[160] Qur'ān, 4: 41.

[161] Bukhari, *Saḫīḫ, Prophetic Commentary on the Quran*, 106.

[162] Bukhari, *Saḫīḫ, Fadāil al-Qur'ān*, 521.

[163] Bukhari, *Saḫīḫ, Fadāil al-Qur'ān*, 526.

The revelation contained in the Qur'ān has been transmitted to us by many people in both oral and written form. As new Muslims the Companions were very enthusiastic, the Qur'ān was very original for them and they were so eager to memorise the verses, they were reading them day and night. The first man to recite the Qur'ān aloud in Mecca after the Prophet (pbuh) was 'Abd Allah b. Mas'ud. The Prophet's (pbuh) Companions came together and mentioned that the Quraysh had never heard the Qur'ān directly. When Ibn Mas'ud arrived at the station of Abraham around the Ka'ba he read 'In the Name of God, the Compassionate, the Merciful', he raised his voice while reading this. 'Rahman (The Compassionate) who taught the Qur'ān ...'[164] they got up and began to hit him in the face but he continued to read in so far as God willed that he should read.[165] It is also reported that Abū Bakr used to recite the Qur'ān publicly in front of his house in Mecca. The leaders of Quraysh were extremely annoyed by his recitals which resulted in many people listening to him and some of them converting to Islam.[166]

As well as reading and teaching the Qur'ān in Mecca, the Prophet (pbuh) also sent Companions to other Arab tribes to inform them about Islam and teach them new verses of the Qur'ān. For example, a group of people from Medina came to Mecca and accepted Islam at 'Aqaba. They asked the Prophet to send someone to Medina to teach Islam and the Qur'ān. The Prophet sent with them his young Companion Mus'ab ibn 'Umayr. In a short time, many people accepted Islam in Medina and returned to 'Aqaba to pledge their allegiance to the Prophet (pbuh).[167] Another example is Mu'adh ibn Jabal who the Prophet sent to Yemen. Before he left the Prophet (pbuh) asked him 'How will you judge among the people?' Mu'adh said, 'I will judge with God's book and His Messenger's Sunnah'. The Prophet (pbuh) asked him again, 'What if you cannot find the answer in the Qur'ān and Sunnah?' Mu'adh replied, 'I will judge based on my opinion,' thereupon the Prophet (pbuh) praised God for He led his Companions to the straight path'.[168]

Summary of the Memorisation and Oral Transmission of the Qur'ān:

1. Prophet Muhammad (pbuh) memorised the revealed verses then taught them to his Companions.

---

164 Qur'ān, 55: 1.
165 Guillaume, E: *The Life of Muhammad*, London, 1955, 141-142; Ibn Hishām, *as-Sīrah*, 1/206.
166 Ibn Hishām, *as-Sīrah*, 1/206.
167 Ibn Hishām, *as-Sīrah*, 1/199.
168 Bukhari, *Saḥīḥ, the Book of Zakat*, 3585.

2. Many Companions memorised the whole of the Qur'ān.
3. The revelation has been transmitted to us by many people in oral and written form.
4. Prophet Muhammad, (pbuh), as well as teaching the Qur'ān to the people in Mecca, also sent Companions to other Arab tribes to teach them the Qur'ān and Islam.

3.2 The Written Text of the Qur'ān at the Time of the Prophet (pbuh)

The Prophet (pbuh), even more than his Companions, wanted to preserve the Qur'ān and ordered scribes to transcribe the revelation whenever he received it to record it accurately. The ability to write was not widespread at that time but there were some Companions who could write. For example, it is reported that Waraqa, Khadija's cousin, who had converted to Christianity in the pre-Islamic period, used to write Arabic and he wrote the Gospel in Arabic as much as God wished him to write.[169] The Prophet (pbuh) himself encouraged the Muslims to learn to write. It is related that after the battle of Badr, some of the Quraysh prisoners were granted freedom in exchange for teaching some of the Muslims to write.[170]

The Prophet (pbuh) encouraged his Companions to record the Qur'ān in writing as well as memorising it, to ensure its accurate preservation. There is no doubt that the Qur'ān was transmitted orally by many Muslims who had learned parts or all of the verses, but it was also written during the Prophet's (pbuh) lifetime which is shown by the following evidence:

1) Ibn Hishām (d.833) mentions:

> 'Umar had set out to kill the Prophet Muhammad (pbuh), when somebody informed him that Islam had already spread into his own family and pointed out to him that his brother-in-law, his nephew and his sister had all become Muslim. 'Umar went to the house of his sister and found her together with her husband and another Muslim. A dispute arose and 'Umar violently attacked both his brother-in-law and his own sister. They said to him 'Yes, we are Muslims and we believe in God and His Apostle (pbuh) and you can do what you like'. When 'Umar saw the blood on his sister, he felt pity for her and turned back and said, 'Give me this sheet which I heard you reading just now so that I may see just what it is which Muhammad has brought. When he said that, his sister replied that

169 Bukhari, *Saḥīḥ, revelation*, 3.

170 Ibn Sa'd, *Tabaqaat*, 2/19.

> she was afraid to trust him with it. 'Do not be afraid', he said and he swore by his gods that he would return it when he had read it. When he said that, she had hopes that he would become a Muslim and said to him, 'My brother, you are unclean in your polytheism and only the clean may touch it'. So 'Umar rose and washed himself and she gave him the page in which was written *surah* Taha and when he had read the beginning he said 'How fine and noble is this speech...[171]

This incident happened in the fifth year of the Prophethood and shows that the verses of the Qur'ān were written and memorised from the beginning of the revelation until its end.

2) Uthman ibn Affan said: 'Whenever a new revelation came down, the Prophet (pbuh) was calling one of his scribes and ordering him to write the verses and to put them in a specific *surah*'.[172] Uthman was one of the earliest Muslims and witnessed the whole period of revelation so his statement about the completion and transmission of the Qur'ān is strong evidence.

3) 'Abd Allah ibn Umar reported: 'The Messenger of God (pbuh) said: 'Do not take the Qur'ān on a journey with you, for I am afraid lest it should fall into the hands of the enemy'.[173]

4) The following verse was revealed to the Prophet (pbuh):

> Not equal are those of the believers who (when not all believers are required to mobilize for God's cause) sit still without justifiable excuse (and without doing any harm to God's cause) and those who strive (and fight) in God's cause with their wealth and their persons. God has exalted in rank those who strive with their wealth and their persons over those who sit still. To each God has promised the best reward (Paradise), and yet God has exalted those who strive over those who sit still by a tremendous reward[174]

The Prophet (pbuh) said, 'Call Zayd for me and let him bring the board, the ink pot and the scapula bone' (or the scapula bone and the ink pot). Then he said 'write the verse' (mentioned above).[175]

---

171 Ibn Hishām, *as-Sīrah*, I/368.

172 Ahmed b. Hanbel, *Musnad*, 1/57.

173 Ibn Majah, *Sunan, Jihad*, 45; Ahmed b. Hanbel, *Musnad*, 2/6,10,55,63,76.

174 Qur'ān, 4: 95.

175 Bukhari, *Saḥīḥ, Tafsīr, Surah* 4.

5) The Prophet (pbuh) said; 'Do not write anything from me except the Qur'ān'.[176]

6) Another report informs us that when people came to Medina to learn about Islam, they were provided with *the copies of the chapters of the Qur'ān*, to read and learn them by heart.[177]

7) 'Abd Allah b. Abī Bakr b. Ḫazm reported: The book written by the Apostle of God (pbuh) for 'Amr b. Ḫazm contained also that no man should touch the Qur'ān without ablution.[178] Malik said: And no one should carry the *Muṣḫāf* (written Qur'ān) by its strap, or on a pillow, unless he is clean. The book referred to as written by the Prophet (pbuh) (which means of course written upon his instruction) was sent with some Muslims for instruction in Islam of the people of Yemen.[179]

8) During his last pilgrimage, at the farewell sermon, which he gave to the large gathering of Muslims, the Prophet (pbuh) said: 'I have left with you something which if you hold fast to you will never fall into error, a plain indication, the book of God and the practice of his Prophet...[180] This advice from the Prophet (pbuh) to the Muslims implies that the revelation was available as book (writing) before his death, for otherwise he would have referred to it in some other term.[181]

9) Zayd ibn Thabit reported: 'We used to compile the Qur'ān from small scraps in the presence of the Apostle'.[182]

10) Uthman reported: 'When something was revealed to him, the Prophet (pbuh) used to call someone from among those who used to write for him, and said, 'place these verses in the *surah*, in which this and this is mentioned', and when (only) one verse was revealed to him, he said: 'place this verse in the *surah* in which this and this is mentioned'.[183] This proves that not only was the revelation written down during the lifetime of the Prophet (pbuh), but that he himself gave instructions for the placement of the verses.

11) The angel Gabriel used to recite the Qur'ān with the Prophet (pbuh) once a year, but he recited it with him twice in the year that he died. The Prophet (pbuh)

---

176 Muslim, *Saḫīḫ, Zuhd*, 16.

177 Muhammad Hamidullah, *Ṣaḫīfa Hammam ibn Munabbih*, Paris, 1979, p. 64.

178 Malik b. Anas, *Muwatta*, Hadith no: 462.

179 Imam Malik, *Muwatta*, 204.

180 Ibn Hishām, p. 651.

181 Von Denffer, *'Ulūm al-Qur'ān*, p. 41.

182 Suyūtī, *Itqān*, 1/99.

183 Ibn Abī Dāwud, *al-Masāḫif*, p. 31.

used to stay in *i'tikaf* (spiritual retreat in Ramadan) for ten days every year (in the month of Ramadan), but in the year of his death, he stayed in *i'tikaf* for twenty days.[184]

In addition to the above evidence, there is much more that shows the Qur'ān was recorded in writing by the command of the Prophet (pbuh), but these are sufficient.

Whenever the scribes finished writing the verses, they read them to the Prophet (pbuh) and he corrected any mistakes. Zayd ibn Thabit reported: 'The Prophet (pbuh) was ordering me to write the verses and when I finished writing, he was ordering me to read what I wrote, if I skipped any word or made a mistake, the Prophet (pbuh) corrected it. After this process I was informing the Muslims about the new verses.'[185] When the verse had been recorded accurately, the Prophet (pbuh) ordered the scribes to make copies and distribute them amongst the Muslims for them to learn. If they were able to write, the Muslims also made personal copies for themselves. At the end of this activity, the original script was given to the Prophet (pbuh) and he protected it in his home.[186]

According to one opinion, the Prophet (pbuh) was ordering his scribes to write the verses on temporary materials and they were later copied onto paper to preserve them permanently. The following statement of Zayd ibn Thabit supports this opinion: 'We used to collect the verses of the Qur'ān from some materials during the time of the Prophet (pbuh).'[187] The Prophet (pbuh) arranged the placement of the verses within the *surah* whenever he received the revelation and he then informed the scribes where to place them. The Prophet (pbuh) used the best available materials to write and to preserve the Qur'ān in his time. All the scripts were edited at least twice under the direct supervision of the Prophet (pbuh).

The transmission and completion of the Qur'ān took place in three stages; the Qur'ān was collected during the life of the Prophet (pbuh) for the first time, it was collected again for a second time during Abū Bakr's reign and it was collected for the third time during Uthman's caliphate.[188]

At this juncture, it is best to begin with the transmission and completion of the Qur'ān during the time of the Prophet (pbuh). The following verse was revealed in Mecca and refers to the Qur'ān as a written text:

---

[184] Bukhari, *Saḩīḩ*, 6/ 518,519,520.

[185] Haythamī, *Majma' az-Zawā'īd*, 8/257.

[186] Zarqānī , *Manāhil*, 1/247; Abu Shu'ba, *al-Madkhal*, p. 267.

[187] Zarkashī, *al-Burhān*, 1/237; Suyūtī, *al-Itqān*, 1/76.

[188] Zarkashī, *al-Burhān*, 1/237; Suyūtī, *al-Itqān*, 1/76.

> They also say: '(It consists of) only fables of the ancients who he has got written. They are being read to him in early mornings and evenings'[189]

This verse shows that the Qur'ān was written before *Hijra* (emigration to Medina) but doesn't indicate when the Qur'ān was written. As was previously mentioned, 'Umar read a written piece of the Qur'ān (*surah* Taha, the twentieth *surah* of the Qur'ān) that he took from his sister before he accepted Islam. 'Umar accepted Islam in the fifth year of Prophethood which indicates that the Qur'ān was being written during the early Meccan period of Islam. It is difficult to know the exact time that the scribes started to write the verses, however, when we check the reports about the completion of the Qur'ān we can conclude that only a short period of time passed between the beginning of the revelation and the transcription of the verses. An opposing view held by some Western scholars is that the Qur'ān was not written during the Meccan period. They deny all the reports which prove the recording of the Qur'ān in Mecca and instead claim that the Prophet (pbuh) and his Companions trusted their memories and recorded the verses later.[190] The report of 'Umar and also the verse from *surah* Furqan prove these claims to be groundless and that the Qur'ān was being written during the Meccan period, although the exact time is not clear. The sources of Islam state that the entire Qur'ān was written during the time of the Prophet (pbuh).[191] It is reported that Abū Bakr ordered Zayd ibn Thabit not to accept the papers which were not written during the life of the Prophet (pbuh) when he was collecting the Qur'ān.[192] This report shows that the Qur'ān was preserved in the earliest scripts written from the beginning of the Prophethood.

Summary of the Written Text of the Qur'ān at the Time of the Prophet (pbuh):

1. Prophet Muhammad (pbuh) wanted to preserve the text of the Qur'ān and ordered scribes to write the verses when they were revealed.
2. The Prophet (pbuh) actively encouraged Muslims to learn to write.
3. There is clear evidence that the Qur'ān was recorded in writing during the lifetime of the Prophet (pbuh).

---

189 Qur'ān, 25: 5.

190 Caetani, L., *the History of Islam*, 9/168.

191 Ibn Ḫajar, *Fatḫ al-Bari*, 9/12; Zarqānī, *Manāhil*, 1/248.

192 Ibn Ḫajar, *Fatḫ al-Bari*, 9/12.

4. The Prophet (pbuh) told scribes not to write anything from him except the Qur'ān.
5. When the scribes had written the verses, they read them back to the Prophet (pbuh) who ensured their accuracy.
6. When the writing was accurate they made copies and distributed them to the Muslims to learn. Some Muslims who could write also made personal copies.
7. The Prophet (pbuh) kept the original script and protected it in his house.
8. Evidence shows the Qur'ān was being written during the early Meccan period. Some Western scholars dispute this but Islamic sources prove the entire Qur'ān was written during the life of the Prophet (pbuh).

3.2.1 The Preservation of the Written Materials

There are two opinions about how the written text was preserved. Some scholars hold that the written Qur'ān was preserved in the home of the Prophet (pbuh) having been checked by him.[193] When Abū Bakr was collecting the Qur'ān he found many pages at the house of the Prophet (pbuh) and tied them together with rope.[194] These bound pages were not the entire Qur'ān; if they had been it wouldn't have been necessary for Abū Bakr to establish a committee under the leadership of Zayd ibn Thabit to collect the Qur'ān. It seems these papers belonged to the Prophet (pbuh) and were the most trustworthy written text. The Prophet (pbuh) ordered some of his Companions to write a copy of the whole Qur'ān for him but passed away before it was completed. It is likely that the Prophet (pbuh) had this idea just before he died otherwise the Qur'ān would have been compiled completely before his death. The second opinion held by scholars is that the scribes themselves preserved the text of the Qur'ān after editing and copying the verses. It was the practise of the Companions to copy the verses to easily and practically disseminate them.[195]As we know, the scribes were writing the verses immediately after their revelation by order of the Prophet (pbuh). Abū Bakr told Zayd, 'search for the copies of the Qur'ān and collect them carefully'.[196] Each scribe had preserved his copy and brought it to Zayd ibn Thabit for the compilation of the Qur'ān. This report shows that the Qur'anic text was preserved in the homes of the Companions in pieces.

193 Zarqānī , *Manāhil*, 1/247; Abu Shu'ba, *al-Madkhal*, p. 267.
194 Suyūtī, *al-Itqān*, 1/73.
195 Muhammad Hamidullah, *Islam Peygamberi*, 2/700-701.
196 Ahmed b. Hanbel, *Musnad*, 1/10.

SUMMARY OF THE PRESERVATION OF THE WRITTEN MATERIALS:

1) Two opinions about this: a) Some scholars hold the written Qur'ān was preserved in the home of the Prophet (pbuh). b) Some scholars hold that the scribes preserved the text of the Qur'ān after editing and copying the verses.
2) Evidence indicates that a large number of papers were found in the Prophet's (pbuh) house after his death but were not the entire Qur'ān.
3) In the reign of Abū Bakr each scribe brought his own copy of the Qur'ān to Zayd ibn Thabit to help compile a single copy.

3.2.2 The Collection of the Qur'ān (*Jam' al-Qur'ān*)

The Qur'ān was written in its entirety during the time of the Prophet (pbuh) but had not been compiled as a whole and, for this reason, the written records or documents had not been arranged in order.[197] But the Prophet (pbuh) informed the Companions orally about the places of the verses and their order in the *surah*.

The general meaning of '*jam' al-Qur'ān*' is 'to collect its pieces together'. *Jam' al-Qur'ān* refers to the process by which the Qur'anic revelations were brought together and preserved for posterity. As a part of this process, the revelation has been transmitted to us by numerous people, both orally and in written form. The expression *jam' al-Qur'ān* contains two aspects; memorising the whole Qur'ān in one's mind and writing all the verses of the Qur'ān in a book or on sheets. In classical literature, this term has various meanings: to learn the Qur'ān by heart, to write down every revelation, to bring together those materials upon which the Qur'ān has been written, to bring together the reports of people who have memorised the Qur'ān, and to bring together all such sources, both oral and written.[198]

There is unanimous agreement among scholars that the Prophet (pbuh) did not write down any of the revelation, because he was illiterate (*ummī*);

> You did not (O Messenger) read of any book before it (the revelation of this Qur'ān), nor did you write one with your right (or left) hand. For then those who have ever sought to disprove the truth might have a reason to doubt (it).[199]

The Prophet (pbuh) did not present the revelation to his Companions collected and arranged in a single written volume. He preserved every single verse

197 Suyūtī, *al-Itqān*, 1/41.
198 Ahmad Von Denffer, *'Ulūm al-Qur'ān*, p. 35.
199 Qur'ān, 29:48.

through memorization and written text (transcribed by the Companions) which was reviewed and corrected by him. There are a number of good reasons for this:

1) The Qur'ān was collected and compiled into one single book based on demand and need during the time of Abū Bakr and Uthman, but there was no such need at the time of the Prophet (pbuh) because, whilst he was alive, he was the insurance for the revelation and its protection. It was impossible to change the Qur'ān or alter it in any way while the Prophet (pbuh) was alive.

2) The last verse was revealed to the Prophet (pbuh) either nine or 81 days before he passed away. According to the majority of scholars the last verse came nine days before he died. It is obvious that, in this short time, it was impossible to collect the whole Qur'ān into a single book;[200] It took Zayd one year to be able to collect all of the verses of the Qur'ān.[201]

3) The Qur'ān was revealed in stages over 23 years at different times and according to different occasions and needs. As the revelation was continuous and didn't end until the Prophet's (pbuh) death, it was impossible to collect all the verses into one book.[202]

4) Whilst the revelation continued it was possible for some verses to be abrogated. Some scholars say that flexibility needed to be maintained for this otherwise it would cause too much confusion. In order to prevent this, the Qur'ān was only collected as a whole book after the revelation was completed.[203]

In conclusion, the nature of the revelation was continuous and it was only completed at the end of the Prophet's (pbuh) life. Due to the need for some verses to be abrogated and the fact that verses and *surah* were not always revealed in their final order, it was necessary for flexibility to be maintained. The Prophet (pbuh) lived only nine days after the final revelation and was severely ill, hence the Qur'ān could only be collected and compiled after his death.[204]

The Companions had all the necessary information to collate and compile the Qur'ān accurately. By the time of his death, the Prophet (pbuh) had ensured all verses had been preserved in writing as well as memorised by many Companions. The verses were written on loose materials enabling easy compilation

---

200 Abdurrrahman Cetin, *Kuran Ilimleri*, p. 92.
201 Cetin, *Kuran Ilimleri*, p. 100.
202 Zarqānī, *Manāhil*, 1.248.
203 Zarqānī, *Manāhil*, 1.248.
204 Ahmad Von Denffer, *'Ulūm al-Qur'ān*, p. 36.

in the correct order. The order of the verses was already fixed within the *surah* in the written form, as well as in the memory of the Companions.[205]

The Prophet (pbuh) was meticulous in his efforts to preserve the Qur'ān. From the beginning of the revelation, the Prophet (pbuh) taught the Muslims all the verses that were revealed for recital in the daily prayers. This necessitated that every Muslim memorize at least some portions of the Qur'ān. Whenever new verses were revealed, the Prophet (pbuh) ordered the scribes who were near him to record them in writing and then asked for them to be read back to him to check for mistakes. Additionally, under their own initiative, the Companions made personal copies of the verses. These methods of preservation ensured the Qur'ān was able to be collected and compiled accurately.[206]

It is most appropriate to conclude this topic with the statement of Harith al-Muḫāsibī;

> Writing of the Qur'ān was no novelty, for the Prophet (pbuh) used to order that it be written down, but it was in separate pieces, on scraps of leather, shoulder blades and palm rips, and when (Abū Bakr) ordered that it be copied from the (various) places to a common place, which was in the shape of sheets, these (materials) were found in the house of the Prophet (pbuh) in which the Qur'ān was spread out, and he gathered it all together and tied it with a string so that nothing of it was lost.[207]

Summary of the Collection of the Qur'ān (*Jam' al-Qur'ān*):

1) The Qur'ān was written during the lifetime of the Prophet Muhammad (pbuh) but was not collated into a single volume.
2) *Jam' al-Qur'ān* means 'to collect its pieces together' and applies to the process of compiling the revelation. It contains two aspects: a) memorising the whole Qur'ān and b) writing the whole Qur'ān.
3) There is unanimous agreement that the Prophet (pbuh) did not write any of the Qur'ān because he was illiterate.
4) Reasons why the Qur'ān was not presented as a finished work by the Prophet (pbuh) include: there was no need during his lifetime, the Qur'ān was compiled as a result of demand and need during the reigns of Abū Bakr and Uthman; there was no time to compile the Qur'ān during the time between the last revelation and the Prophet's (pbuh) death; as the

205 Denffer, *'Ulūm al-Qur'ān*, p. 43.
206 Hasanuddin Ahmad, *Introducing the Qur'ān*, pp. 68-69.
207 Suyūtī, *al-Itqān*, 1/41-73

revelation was continuous over 23 years it was impossible to collect into one work; whilst the revelation continued it was possible for verses to be abrogated so flexibility needed to be maintained to avoid confusion.

5) By the time of his death, the Prophet (pbuh) had ensured the whole Qur'ān had been both memorised by many Companions and written completely. Everything needed for the complete and accurate compilation was available.

3.2.3 The Collection of the Qur'ān during Abū Bakr's Time

As we mentioned earlier, during the Prophet's (pbuh) lifetime it was impossible to compile the Qur'ān as one single book because the revelation continued until his death. However, the Prophet (pbuh) memorised the Qur'ān completely and recited it to the angel Gabriel every year (twice in his last year). After memorising the revealed verses, he recited them to Companions who wrote and memorised them. This meant that the Qur'ān was preserved fully and accurately both on paper and in the minds of the Companions.[208]

Abū Bakr had various reasons for compiling the Qur'ān into a single book. Whilst the Prophet (pbuh) was alive, he was the insurance for Muslims for their everyday issues, including the preservation of the Qur'ān; however, Abū Bakr did not possess this quality so it was necessary to collect the scattered verses together into a book. Muslims hoped that the collection of the Qur'ān would be insurance for them and that it would unite them under its authority.[209]

Abū Bakr could have collected the Qur'ān from the scattered pieces preserved by the scribes as these were the texts which the Prophet (pbuh) himself had dictated to them. However, Abū Bakr didn't see this as sufficient. The dangers of this method included possible mistakes in the spellings or writing, the loss of some verses copied by only a limited number of scribes and the loss of abrogated verses which were no longer recited of which only some Muslims were aware. It was mandatory to compile an official Qur'ān (*Imam Muṣḥāf*) to avoid mistakes and prevent conflicts amongst Muslims. The official *Muṣḥāf* (Qur'ān) would gain authority after comparing it with the scribes' copies and the Companions' memories. Abū Bakr established a committee to actualize this.

---

[208] Osman Keskioglu, *Kur'an Tarihi*, p. 152.

[209] Suat Yildirim, *Kur'an Ilimlerine Giris*, p. 63.

Along with the above reasons, there was also another very important reason for producing an official *Muṣḫāf*. In the battle of Yamama many Qur'ān *hafiz* (someone who has memorised the whole Qur'ān) were martyred.

After the Prophet's (pbuh) death Abū Bakr was selected as the next caliph. Trying to benefit from the change in power, some tribes became disobedient and a number of false prophets declared themselves resulting in riots against Muslim rule. One of these false prophets was Musaylama. Abū Bakr sent an army to destroy him and in this battle (633 C.E.) up to 10,200 Muslims were martyred, including between 500-700 *qurra* (people with a good knowledge of the Qur'ān).[210] 'Umar commented that, 'the Companions of the Prophet (pbuh) died in the battle of Yamama as if butterflies fell down into fire'.[211] This result was dangerous for the Muslims losing such great numbers, but particularly dangerous for the collection of the Qur'ān which hadn't yet been compiled as a single book. The first Companion to perceive this danger was 'Umar who realised the difficulty in achieving the completeness of the Qur'ān if they lost anymore *qurra*. 'Umar went to Abū Bakr without losing any more time and related his fears to Abū Bakr and offered to collect the whole Qur'ān into one single book. At first Abū Bakr hesitated as he thought it could stop Muslims memorising the Qur'ān[212] and because this was not something that the Prophet (pbuh) had done. Within a short time, however, he accepted the offer and decided with 'Umar that the best candidate for the job was Zayd ibn Thabit.

Summary of the Collection of the Qur'ān during Abū Bakr's time:

1) Abū Bakr collected the Qur'ān into one single volume to be insurance for the Muslims and to unite them under its authority.
2) He established a committee to compile an official *Imam Muṣḫāf* which would be the definitive copy from which all others would be derived.
3) In the Battle of Yamama many *hafiz* were martyred which made the compilation of the Qur'ān an urgent need.
4) Zayd ibn Thabit was appointed as the head of the committee to compile the official Qur'ān.

---

210 George Zaydan, *Medeniyeti Islamiyye Tarihi (tr; Zeki Megamiz)*, Istanbul, 1329 AH, 3/1115.

211 Ar-Rafi', *I'jāz al-Qur'ān*, Egypt, 1926, p. 17.

212 Zāhid al-Kawtharī, *Maqālāt al- Kawtharī*, p. 9.

3.2.4 Zayd ibn Thabit and the Collection of the Qur'ān

As we mentioned earlier, in the Battle of Yamama, a large number of Muslims, who had memorised the Qur'ān were martyred. Hence it was feared that unless a written copy of the Qur'ān was prepared, a large part of the revelation might be lost. Zayd ibn Thabit reports this incidence as follows;

> Abū Bakr sent for me on the occasion of the deaths of those killed in the Yamama wars. I found 'Umar b. al Khattab with him. Abū Bakr said: 'Umar has just come to me and said, in the Yamama fighting death has dealt most severely with the *qurra* and I fear it will deal with equal severity with them in other theatres of war and as a result much of the Qur'ān will perish. I am therefore of the opinion that you should command that the Qur'ān be collected'. Abū Bakr added: 'I said to 'Umar, 'How can we do what the Prophet (pbuh) never did?' 'Umar replied that it was nonetheless a good act. He did not cease replying to my scruples until God reconciled me to the undertaking'. Abū Bakr continued, 'Zayd, you are young and intelligent and we know nothing to your discredit. You used to record the revelations for the Prophet (pbuh), so pursue the Qur'ān and collect it all together'. By God! Had they asked me to remove a mountain it could not have been weightier than what they would now have me do in ordering me to collect the Qur'ān. I therefore asked them how they could do what the Prophet (pbuh) had not done but Abū Bakr insisted that it was permissible. He did not cease replying to my scruples until God reconciled me to the undertaking as He had already reconciled Abū Bakr and 'Umar. Thereupon I pursued the Qur'ān collecting it all together from palm-branches, flat stones and the memories of men. I found the last verse of *surah* al Tawba in the possession of Abū Khuzayma al Ansari (Harith b. Huzayma), having found it with no one else, 'There has come to you (O people) a Messenger from among yourselves; extremely grievous to him is your suffering, full of concern for you is he, and for the believers full of pity and compassion'[213] to the end of the *surah*.[214]

Ibn Ḫajar draws special attention to Zayd's statement, 'I found the last two verses of *surah* Tawba with Abū Khuzayma', as demonstrating that Zayd's own writing and memorization were not deemed sufficient. Everything required verification. Abū Bakr had not authorized him to record anything unless it was available in writing. That is why Zayd refrained from including the final verse of *surah*

213 Qur'ān, 9: 128.

214 Bukhari, *Saḫīḫ, Fadāil al-Qur'ān*, 3.

Tawba until he came upon it in written form, even though he and his fellow Companions could recall it perfectly well from memory.[215]

It is possible to conclude two things from this report: firstly, that all the verses of the Qur'ān were written on paper or different materials during the lifetime of the Prophet (pbuh) but they were scattered and separated. It was during Abū Bakr's caliphate that these separated writings were collected into one single volume for the first time. Bayhaqī said:

> Even though there is a common understanding that Uthman collected the Qur'ān for the first time, it is not true. Indeed, Abū Bakr is the first one who collected the separated papers of Qur'ān into one single volume. However when Uthman became caliph he feared from conflicts because of different variants of readings of the Qur'ān and he ordered to copy the early collection of Qur'ān and distribute it to different cities.[216]

The second conclusion we can come to from the report of Zayd is that the collection of Qur'ān duty was given to him. It is relevant to ask why Zayd was chosen for this duty even though Abd Allah ibn Mas'ud, 'Ubay ibn Ka'b and many more Companions who had a personal copy of Qur'ān were present at that time?

SUMMARY OF ZAYD IBN THABIT AND THE COLLECTION OF THE QUR'ĀN:

1) Evidence indicates that Zayd ibn Thabit saw the project as a very weighty task.
2) Zayd's own significant writing and memorisation of the Qur'ān were not considered sufficient. Every verse had to be written and verified.
3) Evidence shows a) all verses were written in the lifetime of the Prophet (pbuh) but were scattered and b) Zayd ibn Thabit (not anyone else) was given the task of collecting them into a single volume.

3.2.5 The Reasons for Choosing Zayd ibn Thabit for the Collection of the Qur'ān

There are various reasons why Abū Bakr and 'Umar chose Zayd for this task:

1) Zayd was among the few Companions at the time of the Prophet (pbuh) who memorised the whole of the Qur'ān and was reciting it very well. For this

215 Ibn Ḥajar, *Fatḥ al-Bari*, 9.13.
216 Zarkashī, *al-Burhān*, 1.235.

reason, the Prophet (pbuh) gave him the flag of Banī Najjār in the battle of Tabuk and said, 'Zayd is the best who knows and memorises the Qur'ān'.[217]

2) Zayd was with the Prophet (pbuh) during the last joint recitation of the Qur'ān with the angel Gabriel (*al-arḏ al-ākhira*) during the Ramadan nights (in some reports, it is said that there were also other Companions present).

3) He was young and very intelligent. The Prophet (pbuh) admired these features and assigned him as the controller of his written communications. Zayd reported: 'The Prophet (pbuh) met me in Medina; he was told that, Zayd was from the tribe of Banī Najjār (the children of Najjār). The Prophet (pbuh) recited 17 *surah* from the Qur'ān and I repeated them immediately. The Prophet (pbuh) was amazed by this and said; 'Learn the writing of Jewish Hebrew'. After that I studied Hebrew and learned it in 15 days. I started to read the letters in Hebrew to the Prophet (pbuh) and I was translating the words of the Prophet (pbuh) into Hebrew to send to Jews'.[218] In another report Zayd said; 'The Prophet told me; 'I am ordering some tribes to write letters in Hebrew, but I am worried about whether they add extra words or exclude any of my words in the letters, you learn Hebrew'. After that I learned Hebrew in 17 days'.[219]

4) There was no accusation to discredit him and people trusted him.[220]

5) He was one of the main scribes of the Prophet (pbuh) and his writing was very accomplished.

6) He was a neighbour of the Prophet (pbuh) in Medina and, as such, had the opportunity to learn directly from him.

3.2.6 'Umar's Role in the Dissemination of the Qur'ān

When Abū Bakr was on his deathbed, he entrusted the Qur'ān to the next caliph 'Umar.[221] 'Umar made great efforts to spread the Qur'ān all over the Arab peninsula; the Qur'ān spread rapidly in his time. Besides many victories on the battle field, 'Umar's caliphate was distinguished by the rapid dissemination of the Qur'ān beyond the borders of the Arabian Peninsula. He sent at least ten Companions to Basra for the purpose of teaching the Qur'ān[222], likewise he sent Ibn Mas'ud

[217] Nawawī, *Tahthib*, 1.201.
[218] Ibn Ḫajar, *al-Isāba Fi Tamyīz as-Saḫābah*, 3.23.
[219] Ibn Ḫajar, *al-Isāba*, 3.23.
[220] Abū Shāma al-Makdisī, *al-Murshid al-Wajiz*, p. 69; Qurtubī, *al-Jāmi al-Bayan*, 1/53, Dhahabī, *Tathkiratu'l Huffaz*, p. 130.
[221] Abu 'Ubayd, *Fadāil*, p. 281.
[222] Dārimī, *Sunan*, hadith no: 135.

to Kūfa.[223] 'Umar was very cautious about the teaching of the Qur'ān; he wanted the teachers follow the official Qur'ān in their lessons. Once he was informed by a man that someone was teaching the Qur'ān from memory in Kūfa, 'Umar became very angry but when he learned that the teacher was 'Abd Allah ibn Mas'ud, his anger disappeared.[224]

The governor of Syria, Yazid b. Abī Sufyan, appealed to 'Umar for instructors to teach Muslims the Qur'ān and other Islamic matters. 'Umar selected three Companions for this mission; Mu'adh, 'Ubāda, and Abū ad-Dardā and instructed them to proceed to Hums in Syria. After achieving their objectives, one of them would go on to Damascus and another to Palestine. When they satisfied the need in Hums, Abū al-Dardā continued on to Damascus and Mu'adh to Palestine, 'Ubāda was left behind. Mu'adh died soon afterwards, but Abū al-Dardā lived in Damascus for a long time and established a highly reputable circle. The number of students under his tutelage exceeded 1600.[225] Abū ad-Dardā divided his pupils into groups of ten, he assigned a separate instructor for each and he checked on their progress. Those who passed this basic level then came under Abū ad-Dardā's direct instruction and enjoyed the dual privileges of studying with Abū ad-Dardā and acting as intermediary teachers for the beginners.[226] Abū Musa al-Ash'arī applied same method; he separated his students into groups in the Basra Masjid and supervised nearly 300 students.[227] 'Umar assigned Yazid b. Abd Allah for Qur'ān teaching to the Bedouins around Medina. Abū Sufyan was inspecting their educational progress on the instruction of 'Umar.[228] He also assigned three Companions for the education of children in Medina, each with a salary of fifteen dirhams.[229]

Summary of 'Umar's Role in the Dissemination of the Qur'ān:

1) On his deathbed Abū Bakr entrusted the Qur'ān to 'Umar.
2) 'Umar's reign was marked by the rapid dissemination of the Qur'ān throughout Arabia and beyond the Arabian peninsula.

---

223 Ibn Sa'd, *Tabaqaat*, 6.3.
224 Ibid.
225 Dhahabī, *Siyar al- Ālam an-Nubala*, 2.344-346.
226 Dhahabī, *Siyar al-Ālam an-Nubala*, 2.346.
227 Al-Faryabī, *Fadāil al-Qur'ān*, p. 129.
228 Ibn Ḫajar, *al-Isāba*, 1/83.
229 Bayḫaqī, *Sunan al-Kubra*, 6/124.

3) 'Umar sent at least 10 Companions to Basra to teach the Qur'ān and was very careful about the method of instruction.
4) He also sent instructors to Syria, Palestine, and to Bedouin around Medina achieving the instruction of thousands of students.

3.2.7 The Methodology in the Collection of Zayd

Zayd implemented a very tight and careful methodology for collecting the Qur'ān. He saw neither the written papers nor the memories of the Companions as sufficient in themselves. Instead, he accredited both the papers which were written in the presence of the Prophet (pbuh) and the memories of the Companions.[230] He applied a strict checking method; first he checked which materials were written in the presence of the Prophet (pbuh), which means the Prophet (pbuh) himself would have recited them and then checked and assured their accuracy. Then he compared those with the memories of the Companions to see whether they had memorised the same (without adding or omitting words). He required two witnesses to vouch that written materials had indeed been recorded in the presence of the Prophet (pbuh) because Abū Bakr and 'Umar told him, 'Sit at the entrance to the [Prophet's] mosque. If anyone brings you a verse from the Book of God along with two witnesses, then record it'.[231]

Some scholars maintain that the two witnesses are the written material and the memory of the Companions.[232] However, this does not fit with reality. If this were the case, Zayd would accept the contribution of anyone who memorised and wrote something of the Qur'ān. The reality was that Zayd only accepted contributions that were recited and dictated by the Prophet (pbuh) and testified for by two witnesses.[233] Without this criteria being met, Zayd didn't admit any verses to the Qur'ān. This methodology eliminated any doubt concerning the authenticity.of the Qur'ān. With these strict conditions the Qur'ān was collected into one single book with the help of Abū Bakr, 'Umar and Zayd b. Thabit within a year.

---

230 Ar-Rafi', *I'jāz al-Qur'ān*, p. 18.

231 Zarqānī, *Manāhil*, 1/252.

232 Ibn Ḫajar, *Fatḫ al-Bāri*, 19/16, Ibn Ḫajar says; As if what is meant by two witnesses are mem - ry [backed by] the written word. Or, two witnesses to testify that the verse was written verbatim in the Prophet's presence. Or, meaning they would testify that it was one of the forms in which the Qur'ān was revealed. Their intention was to accept only what had been written in the Prophet's presence, not [what had been penned] from their memory.

233 Suyūtī, *al-Itqān*, 1/77.

Summary of the Methodology in the Collection of Zayd:

1) To collate the entire Qur'ān in written form and authenticated by those who had memorised it.
2) To accept only those written portions of the Qur'ān which were found to be reliable.
3) To accept only that material of which at least two written copies were available.
4) To obtain testimony from at least two witnesses that whatever was submitted to the commission was written in front of the Prophet (pbuh), and whichever portions of the Qur'ān were recited before the commission were exactly the same as heard from the Prophet (pbuh) and were also recited before him.
5) To compare the written material with the last recitation of the Qur'ān by the Prophet (pbuh).

3.2.8 The Specifications of the Collection of Zayd

The result of Zayd's efforts and work was that the scattered pieces of the Qur'ān were collected and compiled into one single volume within one year. The Prophet's (pbuh) time in Medina had been a time of intense scribal activity: many Companions possessed verses which they had copied from the parchments of friends and neighbours. By limiting himself to the verses transcribed under the Prophet's (pbuh) supervision, Zayd ensured that all of the material he was examining was of equal status, thereby guaranteeing the highest attainable accuracy. Having memorized the Qur'ān and scribed much of it while seated before the Prophet (pbuh), his memory and writing could only be compared with material of the same standing, not with second or third-hand copies. Hence, the insistence of Abū Bakr, 'Umar and Zayd on receiving first-hand material only, with two witnesses to back this claim and assure 'equal status'.[234]

As, it has been related, the collection was written on different materials, Zayd ordered scribes to copy the writing onto skins and make a new edition of the Qur'ān. This made it accessible and easy to use.[235]

It appears that while initially the focus of the collection lay on the written word, once the primary written source was found - whether parchment, wooden planks, or palm leaves, the writings were verified, not only against each other,

---

[234] M.M. al-Azami, *The History of the Qur'anic Text*, p. 88.

[235] Manna Kattān, *Mabāhis*, 127-128.

but also against the memories of Companions who had learned them directly from the Prophet (pbuh). By placing the same stringent requirements for acceptance of both the written and memorised verses, equal status was preserved.[236]

The Muslims fully accepted this *Muṣḫāf* as the authority. Once complete the compiled Qur'ān was placed in the 'state archives' under the custodianship of Abū Bakr,[237] who, when he died passed it on to 'Umar's protection. When 'Umar died, Hafsa, his daughter and the Prophet's (pbuh) wife, protected this *Muṣḫāf*.[238] Hafsa didn't take this Qur'ān as her personal possession but looked after it as the new caliph had not yet been elected. This Qur'ān stayed with Hafsa until the Muslims needed to copy it during the time of Uthman; they borrowed this Qur'ān to copy it and then returned it to Hafsa.

When Hafsa died, the Qur'ān passed to the ruler Marwan b. Ḫakem (d. 749 C.E.) who burned it to remove conflicts between the Muslims when a man claimed that 'the Uthman's edition didn't contain everything which was in the edition of Abū Bakr'.[239] Marwan reported:

> I burned this Qur'ān because its content is written and protected by many copies. Also I am worried about that after long time has passed over the *Muṣḫāf* of Abū Bakr, one may claim that, there was something in Abū Bakr's *Muṣḫāf* but not in the copies.[240]

Marwan burned this copy of the Qur'ān because it contained seven dialects (seven letters) which had become a source of conflict amongst the Muslims. In Uthman's time the *Muṣḫāf* was copied based on the Quraysh dialect in order to prevent conflicts among Muslims because of the seven letters. Also the Prophet (pbuh) recited and compared the Qur'ān with Gabriel for the last time in the Quraysh dialect. It is not obligatory to contain all seven letters in the Qur'ān, rather it is permissible.[241] For this reason Abū Bakr collected the Qur'ān according to seven letters in the hope that it would not be a foundation for conflict among Muslims. But in the time of Uthman many conflicts arose due to this issue so, as a means of achieving peace, Uthman copied the Qur'ān based on the Quraysh dialect.[242]

---

236 M.M. al-Azami, *The History of the Qur'anic Text*, p. 89.

237 Bukhari, *Saḫīḫ, Fadāil al-Qur'ān*, 3.

238 Ibn Kathīr, *Tafsīr*, p. 10.

239 Ibn Abī Dāwud, *Kitāb al-Masāḫif*, p. 21; Zarqānī, *Manāhil*, 1.402.

240 Ibn Abī Dāwud, *Kitāb al-Masāḫif*, p. 25, Subhi Salih, *Mabāhis*, p. 83.

241 Tabarī, *Jāmi' al-Bayan*, 1.22.

242 Tabarī, *Jāmi' al-Bayan*, 1.20.

SUMMARY OF THE SPECIFICATIONS OF ZAYD'S COLLECTION:

1) The Qur'ān was collated according to the strongest methodology and scientific methods.
2) Abrogated verses were not written in this edition.
3) The verses of this collection were transmitted to us through the soundest channels '*mutawātir*'[243]; there is a general consensus on this.[244]
4) This *Muṣḫāf* (written Qur'ān) included the seven letters of the Qur'ān (seven *ahruf* of the Qur'ān).[245]
5) This Qur'ān was named '*Muṣḫāf*' by the recommendation of 'Abd Allah ibn Mas'ud.[246]

3.3 The Collection of the Qur'ān during the Time of Uthman

One of the most important activities for the preservation of the Qur'ān is its copying in numbers. When 'Umar passed away, Uthman became caliph for the Muslims and he served in this position for ten years.[247] His most important act of service was copying the Qur'ān and sending the copies to different cities to prevent conflicts among the Muslims. Of course there were some serious reasons which led Uthman to copy the Qur'ān again and to send it to different cities.

3.3.1 The Reasons behind the Copying of the Qur'ān

The first collection of the Qur'ān met the need of the Muslims and, until the time of 'Uthman's caliphate, there was no need to copy it. There arose a great need to multiply this Qur'ān and send copies to different cities of the Islamic world. When we look at the Islamic sources we see that disputes arose in Medina and other cities because of the seven readings of the Qur'ān. Abū Qilaba reported:

> The Qur'ān teachers were teaching the Qur'ān according to the different readings (seven letters); one's teaching was different from the other. The students were disputing and having disagreements among themselves because of reading issue. When they took this matter to their Qur'ān teachers, one was even denying the other one's reading style. When Uthman

[243] It refers to gathering information from multiple channels and comparing them, so that if the overwhelming majority agrees on one reading then that gives us assurance and the reading itself acquires authenticity.

[244] Zarqānī, *Manāhil*, 1.253.

[245] Manna Kattān, *Mabāhis*, p. 128.

[246] Zarkashī, *al-Burhān*, 1.282.

[247] Suyūtī, *Tarīkh al-Khulafa*, p. 153.

> was informed about this, he gave a sermon and said: 'If you dispute in our presence, the Muslims in far cities would dispute more. O Companions of the Prophet! Come together and write one *Imam Muṣḫāf* (one official and authority Qur'ān).[248]

The other report states:

> Hudhayfa b. al-Yamān came to Uthman direct from the Azerbaijan and Armenian frontier where, uniting the forces from Iraq and those from Syria, he had had an opportunity to observe regional differences over the Qur'ān. He advised that, 'Commander of the believers, take these Muslims in hand before they differ about the Book like Christians and Jews.' Uthman sent asking Hafsa to lend him the sheets [inherited by her father, 'Umar, from Abū Bakr, and now in her possession] so that we can copy them into other volumes and then return them. She sent her *Suḫuf* (the Qur'ān) to 'Uthman who summon Zayd b. Thabit, Sa'id b. al As, 'Abdurrahman b. al Harith b. Hishām and 'Abd Allah b. al Zubayr and commanded them to copy the sheets into several volumes. Addressing the group from Quraysh he added, 'Wherever you differ from Zayd, write the word in the dialect of Quraysh for it was revealed in that tongue'. When they had copied the sheets, Uthman sent a copy to each of the main centres of the Islamic state together with the expert reader with the command that all other Qur'ān materials, whether in single sheet form, or in whole volumes, were to be shredded or burned.[249]

These reports indicate that the disputes and disagreements among the Muslims had reached a dangerous level and, if not immediately solved, could cause serious conflict or even war in the Muslim communities.

There are two main reasons why the Muslims reached this point: the first is to do with the seven different dialects of the Qur'ān (it is permissible to read the Qur'ān according to any of the seven dialects which were collected in the time of Abū Bakr). The other reason is to do with personal copies of the Qur'ān owned by the Companions; some of these had explanations or interpretations written in the margin which were not the part of Qur'ān.

The Companions learned from the Prophet (pbuh) variant reading styles and went on to teach these (during 'Umar's caliphate) in different areas. Each Companion taught his own style in the place he went to.[250] The natural result of this was that Muslims learned different reading styles depending on which Com-

---

[248] Ibn Abī Dāwud, *al-Masāḫif*, p. 21.

[249] Bukhari, *Saḫīḫ, Fadāil al-Qur'ān*, 3; Ibn Abī Dāwud, *al-Masāḫif*, 18-19.

[250] Zarqānī , *Manāhil*, 1/255.

panion they learned from and this eventually caused disputes. Even though new Muslims were warned about the seven letters (different readings of Qur'ān) they couldn't prevent doubt about this issue taking root in their hearts[251] and for this reason, they had severe disputes among themselves even to the point of accusing each other of disbelief. The seven letters do not change the meaning of the Qur'ān but replace some words with their synonyms in that dialect. Another problem was caused by Companions adding words of explanation for their own personal usage to their copies of the Qur'ān. Later on, these explanations would be taken as part of the Qur'ān and became a source of dispute. Some people would say that the Companions' recitations differed from each other; some would understand the explanations to be part of the Qur'ān whilst others would understand them as just explanations. Due to these conflicts, and with the recommendation of Zayd ibn Thabit, Uthman started the collection and copying of the Qur'ān in the 25 year A.H..

Summary of the Reasons Behind Copying the Qur'ān:

1) Islamic sources show that disputes arose in Medina and other cities due to the seven variant readings of the Qur'ān.
2) Some Companions with personal copies of the Qur'ān had added notes of explanation in places. This ended up causing confusion and dispute about what was actually in the Qur'ān and what were added notes.
3) Companions, as taught by the Prophet (pbuh), were teaching different reading styles to their students. This also led to disputes.
4) Zayd ibn Thabit recommended to Uthman that a new copy of the Qur'ān should be made. This project started in 25 A.H..

3.3.2 The Methodology in the Collection of Uthman

According to Islamic sources Uthman ordered the committee assigned to collect and copy the Qur'ān to follow certain criteria:

1) To use the collection of Abū Bakr as an essential base for copying the Qur'ān.

2) To write the Qur'ān according to the last recitation of the Prophet (pbuh) to the angel Gabriel (*'arḏ ākhira*) in the Quraysh dialect only.[252]

---

[251] Ar-Rāfi', *I'jāz al-Qur'ān*, p. 19.

[252] Bukhari, *Saḫīḫ*, *Fadāil al-Qur'ān*, 3; Ibn Abī Dāwud, *al-Masāḫif*, p. 21.

3) To exclude abrogated verses in these copies. For example the verse about prohibition because of suckling 10 times (being milk mother and related rules regarding this) was reduced to five times and it was abrogated later on.[253]

4) If any dispute arose among the members of committee, the Quraysh dialect would be essential and the verses would be written according to it.[254]

5) To make multiple copies of the Qur'ān and send each to an Islamic centre and to burn any personal copies that differed from this copy.[255]

6) To arrange the order of the *surah* (chapters of Qur'ān) as we know it today. The order of the verses was the same in the collection of Abū Bakr and Uthman but the order of the *surah* was different in the Abū Bakr collection. Uthman ordered the members to arrange the *surah* order in the Qur'ān too.

7) To exclude any additional words of explanation from the copies.[256]

3.3.3 The Activities of the Committee for the Uthman Collection

Uthman assembled a committee of twelve (including 'Ubayy b. Ka'b and Zayd b. Thabit) from both the Quraysh and the Ansār (the residents of Medina), to manage the task by collecting and arranging all the Qur'ān parchments written in the Prophet's (pbuh) presence. The Companions who took part in the copying were: Zayd b. Thabit, Said b. As, Nāfi b. Zurayb, 'Ubayy b. Ka'b, Abd Allah b. Zubayr, 'Abdurrahman b. Hishām, Kathīr b. Aflah, Anas b. Malik, Abd Allah b. 'Abbās , Abd Allah b. Amr b. As, Malik b. Abī Amr, Abd Allah b. 'Umar. The historian Ibn Asakir reports in his *History of Damascus*:

> 'Uthman delivered a sermon and said, 'the people have diverged in their recitations, and I am determined that whoever holds any verses dictated by the Prophet himself must bring them to me'. So the people brought their verses, written on parchment and bones and leaves, and anyone contributing to this pile was first questioned by Uthman, 'did you learn these verses [i.e. take this dictation] directly from the Prophet himself?' All contributors answered under oath.[257] All the collected material was individually labelled and then handed to Zayd b. Thabit.

Malik b. Abī Amir related:

---

[253] For these verses see Muslim, *Saḫīḫ, ar-Radā*, 24; Imam Malik, *Muwatta*, ar-Radā, 18, Tirmidhi, *Sunan, ar-Radā*, 3.

[254] Bukhari, *Saḫīḫ, Fadāil al-Qur'ān*, 3.

[255] Manna Kattān, *Mabāhis*, p. 131.

[256] Zarqānī, *Manāhi*l, 1.257-260.

[257] Ibn Manzūr, Mukhtasar Tārikh Dimasq, 16.171-72.

> I was among those upon whom the *Muṣḫāf* was dictated [from the written sources], and if any controversies arose concerning a particular verse they would say, 'Where is the writer [of this parchment]? Precisely how did the Prophet teach him this verse?' And they would resume scribing, leaving that portion blank and sending for the man in question to clarify his writing.[258]

Hani al-Barbari, a client of Uthman, reported:

> I was with Uthman when the committee was comparing the *Muṣḫāf*. He sent me to 'Ubayy b. Ka'b with a sheep's shoulder bone containing [three different words from different *surah*: a word each from 2:259, 30:30, and 86:17. So 'Ubayy called for his writing utensils and [revised the spelling of these words].[259]

Harun ibn 'Umar reported:

> When Uthman wanted to make an official copy, he asked Āi'sha to send him those parchments which were dictated by the Prophet and which she kept in her house. He then ordered Zayd b. Thabit to correct accordingly, as he himself was not free since he wanted to devote his time to governing the people and judging among them.[260]

Gathering these narratives together gives us the following: Uthman prepared an independent copy relying entirely on primary sources, which included the Companions' parchments along with additional material held by Āi'sha.

The committee, under the ruling of Zayd ibn Thabit, completed their work within five years. During this five year period the committee had only one single disagreement which was about how to write the last letter of one word; the word '*al-tābūt*' in 2:248. Zayd said this letter should be written as circle 'ta' (ة) but when this matter was referred to Uthman he ordered them to write it as open 'ta' (ت).[261] The problem was resolved by intervention of Uthman. The committee of scribes wrote several copies of the Qur'ān during these years. There are different reports about the number of these copies; however, the majority accepts that there were seven.[262] One of these copies was left in Medina and the others

---

258 Ibn Abī Dāwud, *Masāḫif*, 21-22.

259 Abu Ubayd, *Fadāil*, pp. 286-287.

260 Ibn Shabba, *Tārikh al-Medina*, p. 997.

261 Ibn Abī Dāwud, *Masāḫif*, p. 20.

262 Abu Shāma, *al-Murshid al-Wajiz*, p. 73.

were sent to the following cities; Mecca, Kūfa, Basra, Damascus, Yemen, Bahrain.[263] The copy which was kept in Medina was named '*Imam Muṣḥāf*'.[264]

With the task complete there was no need for the numerous fragments of the Qur'ān in circulation to remain, so, after consulting the Companions, Uthman decided all such fragments should be burned.[265] The consultation and joint decision ensured no conflict arose. Ali b. Abī Tālib reported: 'By Allah, he only did what he did with these fragments in clear view of us all [i.e. and with our consent]'.[266]

The well-known personal copies of the Qur'ān belonged to 'Ali, 'Ubayy ibn Ka'b, 'Abd Allah b. Mas'ud and Abū Musa al-Ash'arī. There is no copy (*Muṣḥāf*) from these Companions transmitted to us. We merely have reports (mainly *khabar wāḥid*) about how they read some specific verse or word. Therefore, any comparison between Uthman's collection and so called *Muṣḥāf* Ibn Mas'ud, 'Ubayy, Ali, Ibn 'Abbās, (the last two collected in chronological order), or any other Companions are meaningless.

Uthman not only sent the copies to the centres of Islam but he also sent teachers (*qurra*) along with them to teach the recitation style. He sent Abd Allah ibn Sâib to Mecca, Mughira ibn Shihab to Damascus, Abū Abdurrahman as-Sulami to Kūfa and Āmir b. Qays to Basra.[267] Abū Fattah al-Qādi said:

> Each of these scholars recited to the people of his respective city in the manner he had learned through authenticated, multiple channels going back to the Prophet, insofar as these channels lay in complete agreement with each other and fit the *Muṣḥāf's* consonantal skeleton. Any mode of recitation arriving through a single channel (or containing verses that had been abrogated during the Prophet's lifetime) was discarded. Dispatching reciters with the *Muṣḥāf* meant limiting the possibilities that were compatible with the consonantal script to only those that enjoyed authenticated and multiple backing.... Sending a scholar with every *Muṣḥāf* was, therefore, elucidating that proper recitation was dependent on learning through direct contact with teachers whose transmission channels reached to the Prophet, not simply a product of script or spelling conventions.[268]

263 Ibn Abī Dāwud, *Masāḥif*, p. 34.
264 Manna Kattān, *Mabāhis*, p. 131.
265 Qurtubī, *al-Jāmi' al-Bayan*. 1.52.
266 Ibn Abī Dāwud, Masāḥif, p. 22.
267 Zarqānī, *Manāhil*, 1.396-397.
268 Azami, *The History of the Qur'anic Text*, p. 103.

It only took a short period of time for Muslims to completely trust these copies and as a result many copies were made in this one dialect.[269] Early copies of Uthman's *Muṣḥāf* were largely consonantal, frequently dropping vowels and containing no dots. These copies could be read erroneously in many ways. In undertaking this second compilation, Uthman's main purpose was to eliminate all occasion for disputes in recitation; sending a *Muṣḥāf* by itself, or with a reciter at liberty to devise any reading, was contrary to the unity Uthman sought to establish within the populace. The existence of total unity in the Qur'anic texts throughout the world for fourteen centuries, between all countries and all divergent Muslim sects, is proof enough of Uthman's unparalleled success in gathering all Muslims upon a single text.[270]

SUMMARY OF THE ACTIVITIES OF THE COMMITTEE FOR THE UTHMAN COLLECTION:

1. Uthman assigned a committee of 12 to collect and arrange all the Qur'ān parchments that were written in the presence of Prophet Muhammad (pbuh).
2. Uthman prepared an independent copy of the Qur'ān relying entirely on primary sources.
3. The committee completed their work within five years.
4. Seven copies were made. One was kept in Medina and the others were sent to Mecca, Kūfa, Basra, Damascus, Yemen and Bahrain.
5. The Medina copy was named *Imam Muṣḥāf.*
6. All previous fragments of the Qur'ān were burned on order of Uthman after consultation with the Muslim community.
7. Each copy of the Qur'ān was accompanied by a teacher to instruct in the recitation.
8. The Qur'ān was written in one dialect. This copy quickly gained authority and achieved the unity of recitation that was Uthman's main purpose.

3.3.4 What Happened to the Copies of Uthman?

There are three existing copies out of the seven Uthmanic Qur'ān's. Four were lost due to war, fire or similar incidents. The *Muṣḥāf* of Medina was lost in the time of Yazid b. Mu'awiya in 683 C.E., the *Muṣḥāf* of Mecca was lost in 689 C.E.,

[269] Ar-Rāfi', *I'jāz al-Qur'ān*, p. 41.
[270] Azami, *The History of the Qur'anic Text*, p. 104.

and the *Muṣḥāf* of Kūfa was lost in the year 748 C.E..[271] The *Muṣḥāf* of Bahrain was also probably lost.[272] Three *Muṣḥāf* have survived and one of them is now on exhibit at the Topkapi Museum in Istanbul, Turkey, the other two are in Tashkent and London.

The *Muṣḥāf* in Tashkent came to Samarkand (after the Umayyad had taken it from Medina to Morocco) in 890 A.H. (1485 C.E.), and remained there until, in 1869, the Russians took it to St. Petersburg. They returned it to Samarkand (close to Tashkent) in 1924, and it has remained there since.[273] The Russian authorities made copies of the *Muṣḥāf* which are available at a number of leading universities and private collections.

Muhammad Hamidullah says the following words about the three existing *Muṣḥāf*;

> The Turkish soldiers took some books from Medina when they left there after the first civil war. There was Uthman's *Muṣḥāf* among those books. For this reason, this *Muṣḥāf* was stipulated to return to Sharif Huseyin at the treaty of Sevres. But the Turkish Government'sresponse to this was that 'the book was in such place and it was lost because of flood'. There is blood of Uthman in this *Muṣḥāf* on the verse 'God suffices you against them'[274]

The third *Muṣḥāf* is in London in the library of the 'India Office'. The British took this *Muṣḥāf* from the palace of the King of Mogul and took it to England.[275] Hamidullah studied the pictures of these three *Muṣḥāf* and says they are exactly same in regard to their size, dictation specifications and calligraphy.[276]

It is of great historical importance to know exactly what happened to these copies. As for the *Muṣḥāf* of Abū Bakr, after he passed away it was given to 'Umar. On his deathbed, 'Umar did not nominate a successor, but rather a committee of six people. With no immediate caliph present the *Muṣḥāf* was naturally inherited by Hafsa, his daughter and a wife of the Prophet (pbuh). When Hafsa died, the Qur'ān passed on to the ruler Marwan b. Ḥakem (d. 749 C.E.) and was burned by him to remove the conflicts among the Muslims.[277]

---

271 Osman Keskioglu, *Tarihi Kuran*, p. 13.
272 Osman Keskioglu, *Tarihi Kuran*, p. 247.
273 Muhammad Hamidullah, *Kuran-I Kerim Tarihi Ders Notlari*, p. 31.
274 Qur'ān, 2: 137, Muhammad Hamidullah, *Kuran-I Kerim Tarihi Ders Notlari*, p. 31.
275 Hamidullah, *Kuran-I Kerim Tarihi Ders Notlari*, pp. 30-31.
276 ibid, p. 31.
277 Ibn Abī Dāwud, *Kitāb al-Masāḥif*, p. 25, Subhi Salih, *Mabāhis*, p. 83

Ibn Kathīr (d. 774 A.H.) wrote in his history book that he had seen one of Uthman *Muṣḥāf*. It had been sent from Palestine to Damascus, and it was very large, in beautiful clear, strong writing with strong ink, on parchment, probably made of camel skin.[278]

Ibn Battuta (d. 779 A.H.), the famous Muslim traveller, reports seeing many *Muṣḥāf* that were copied directly from the *Muṣḥāf* of Uthman. As for the Medina manuscript:

> Ibn Jubayr (d. 1217 C.E.) saw the manuscript in the mosque of Medina in the year 580 A.H. /1184 C.E. Some say it remained in Medina until the Turks took it from there in 1334 A.H. / 1915 C.E. It has been reported that this copy was removed by the Turkish authorities to Istanbul, from where it came to Berlin during World War I. The Treaty of Versailles, which concluded World War 1, contains the following clause: 'Article 246: Within six months from the coming into the force of the present treaty, Germany will restore to His Majesty, King of Hedjaz, the original Qur'ān (sic) of the Caliph Othman, which was removed from Medina by the Turkish authorities and is stated to have been presented to the ex-Emperor William II.' The manuscript then reached Istanbul, but not Medina.[279]

3.3.5 Differences between the Two Collections

The Uthman collection tradition was not opposed to that of Abū Bakr and 'Umar. It was to resolve conflicts arising from some personal "variant reading" and personal "variant *Muṣḥāf*" traditions. The reason behind the collections was different: in Abū Bakr's time the text was assembled for fear of losing parts of it as a result of the deaths of those who had memorised it. In Uthman's time, the reason was to unify the Muslims under one authoritative copy of the text. In the first collection there was no order of the *surah* (chapters) which is an important asset of the second collection. The two texts vary in their number of compilers and sheets. Abū Bakr's *Muṣḥāf* contains seven letters (*ahruf al-sab'a*). Seven letters are not *wujub* (necessary) but *mubah* (preferable).

3.4 Qur'anic Script

The Uthmanic *Muṣḥāf* was written in ancient Kūfī script which is almost incomprehensible to modern-day Arabic readers. The *Muṣḥāf* were written without any

[278] Kattān, p. 134.
[279] Von Denffer, p. 62.

hamzahs, dots (*nuqat*)[280] or vowel marks (*tashkeel*).[281] This was the traditional manner of writing at that time. Therefore, for example, a straight line could represent the letters *baa*, *taa*, *thaa* and *yaa*, and each letter could have any of the vowel marks assigned to it. It was only by context that the appropriate letters and vowels could be differentiated. The Arabs at that time were accustomed to such a script, and would substitute the appropriate letter and vowel depending on the context.[282] There were no indications signifying the ending of the verses in the *Muṣḥāf*, and the only sign that a *surah* had ended was the *basmala*. There were also no textual divisions (into thirtieths, sixtieths, etc.).[283]

When they immigrated to Medina the Muslims began to learn how to read and write. The Prophet (pbuh) encouraged them to learn the Arabic alphabet and many Arabs learned a primitive style of writing.[284] There were no vowel marks, dots or similar signs that are commonly used today to make the Arabic alphabet easy to read. For them it was not hard to read and understand it. However, many non-Arabs converted to Islam and could not read the Qur'ān correctly. Mistakes in reading were very common amongst non-Arab Muslims. It was necessary to protect the Qur'ān from recitation mistakes so the diacritical marks visible today, which make the Arabic alphabet easy for non-Arabs, were introduced.

The first change to be introduced was the addition of the diacritical marks the *tashkeel* by Abū al-Aswad ad-Dualī (d. 69 A.H.), who was the first to codify the science of Arabic grammar (*naḥw*). According to one report, 'Ali ibn Abī Tālib asked him to make the *Muṣḥāf* easier for people to read, but he initially declined to do so, since he did not believe it was necessary. However, he once heard a person recite a verse incorrectly:

أَنَّ اللهَ بَرِيءٌ مِنَ الْمُشْرِكِينَ وَرَسُولُهُ

> God disavows those who associate partners with Him (and break their treaty), and His Messenger likewise (disavows them).[285]

---

[280] The nuqat are the dots that are used to differentiate between different letters that have the same base structure.

[281] They are the diacritical marks of the *fatḥa*, *kasra*, and *damma* and other marks (such as the *shadda*) that are used to pronounce the particular letters correctly.

[282] Abu Ammaar Yasir Qadhi, *The Sciences of Qur'ān*, p. 141.

[283] Qadhi, *The Sciences of Qur'ān*, pp. 141-14.

[284] Caetani, L, *the History of Islam*, 9/156.

[285] Qur'ān: 9: 3.

When the person recited the verse inaccurately, the meaning was changed to: 'God disavows all ties with the pagans and His Apostle'. The mispronunciation of just one vowel led to this drastic change in meaning. Abū al-Aswad said, 'I did not think the state of the people had degenerated to this level!' He remembered the advice of 'Ali b. Abī Tālib and went to Ziyad ibn Abīhī, the governor of lraq and requested the supply of a scribe. Ziyad sent 30 scribes to Abū al-Aswad, but he chose just one of them and started his work. He told the scribe to use a different coloured ink for each mark: 'If I pronounce (the vowel) 'a', then write a dot above the letter. If I pronounce it as 'u', then write a dot in front of the letter. If I pronounce 'i', then write it below the letter'.[286] Abū al-Aswad controlled the writing and corrected any mistakes in them. He meticulously marked the whole Qur'ān from beginning to end.[287]

The benefit of this new system was the prevention of mistakes in the *i'rab* (the placement of words in the sentence, known by the sound of the last letter of each word). However, it was still difficult for non-Arabs to recognise the Arabic letters. For example, without dots, the following Arab letters look similar and it is very difficult to know which one is used in the word; *'baa'*, *'taa'*, *'tha'*, *'jim'*, *'haa'*, *'faa'* and *'qaf'*. There was a need to differentiate each of these letters to enable the proper reading of the text. The governor of Iraq, Ḫajjāj b. Yusuf, sensed this problem first and asked Nasr b. 'Asim and Yahya b. Ya'mar to do something to prevent these mistakes. Thereupon Nasr and Yahya invented the dots to separate each letter and marked these dots on the letters of the Qur'ān.[288] In the Qur'anic sciences, putting the dots on the letters is called *'I'jam'*. Zarqānī said:

> May Allah have mercy on these two scholars (Yahya ibn Ya'mar and Nasr ibn 'Asim), for they were successful in this endeavour (of adding dots to the Qur'ān), and completed the addition of the dots for the first time. They conditioned upon themselves not to increase the number of dots of any letter above three. This system spread and became popular amongst the people after them, and it had a great impact in removing confusion and doubts concerning (the proper recitation of) the *Muṣḫāf*.[289]

To prevent confusion of the vowels and dots, the scholars used different colours to write the Qur'ān letters and their marks. In the beginning, scribes used to write the dots in black and the *tashkeel* in red to distinguish them from the actu-

286 Ibn Abī, Dāwud, *Masāḫif*, p. 144.

287 Ibn Nadīm, *al-Fihrist*, p. 60, Zarqānī, *Manāhil*, p. 408.

288 Ibn Abī Dāwud, *Masāḫif*, p. 141.

289 Zarqānī, Manāhil, 1.407.

al text of the Qur'ān. There are hundreds of *Muṣḥāf* dating from the first two centuries of the *Hijrah* still present with this type of *tashkeel* system. We can see in these *Muṣḥāf* red, yellow, green and sometimes blue coloured inks.[290] The Qur'ān was read with this system for a hundred years, but later the profound scholar Ḫalil b. Ahmad (d. 791) invented the system which we still use today; he marked the Qur'ān with the modern system and ended this conflict forever.

There are some narrations from the early scholars showing their disapproval of these additions. It is narrated from Ibn Mas'ud, an-Nakhāī (d. 96 A.H.), Qatāda (d. 117 A.H.) and other scholars of the first two generations concerning the prohibition of adding these dots to the *Muṣḥāf*. Other scholars, however, such as Ḫasan al-Basrī (d. 110 A.H.) and Ibn Sīrin (d. 110 A.H.), did not see a problem with the addition of these dots.[291] Imam Malik (d. 179 A.H.) was asked concerning the addition of vowels and dots in the Qur'ān. He replied:

> The people continued to ask me concerning the addition of dots in the Qur'ān, so I say: As for the major *Muṣḥāf*, I don't think they should be dotted, nor should anything be added that is not in them. As for the minor *Muṣḥāf* - the ones that the children learn from - then I don't see any problem with it.[292]

Dānī reported:

> I happened to come across an old copy of the *Muṣḥāf*, written during the beginning of the Caliphate of Hishām ibn 'Abd al-Malik. Its date (of writing) was written on the last page: 'Written by Mughira ibn Mina, in Rajab, in the year 110 A.H. It had *tashkeel*, the *hamzahs* ... and the dots (*nuqat*) were in red.[293]

Both these quotes show that, eventually, the addition of *tashkeel* and *nuqat* was accepted as a part of the writing of the *Muṣḥāf*.

During the next few centuries, further developments occurred, such as the writing of the *surah* names at the beginning of the *surah*, and the separation of the verses by special symbols and numbers. Initially, the verses were distinguished by placing three dots at the end of a verse. For every five verses, the word '*khams*' (five) was written, and after every ten, '*ashr*' (ten), after which the numbering would start from the beginning, until the end of that particular *surah*. Soon after-

290 Ad-Dānī, *al-Muqnī Fi Rasmi Masāḥif al-Amsār*, p. 130.

291 Qadhi, *The Sciences of Qur'ān*, p. 143.

292 Ibn Abī Dāwud, *Masāḥif*, pp. 141-143.

293 Zarqānī, *Manāhil*, 1.410.

wards, the word *khams* was abbreviated to the letter *khaa*, and the word *ashr* to a the letter *ayn*, both of which were written in the margin of the *Muṣḥāf* Eventually, the verses were indicated by a circle at the end of each verse, and the sequential number of the verse was written in the circle, as is present in the *Muṣḥāf* of today.[294]

The early scholars were very careful not to make additions to the Qur'ān. It was only later as a good deed that the additions of marks, dots and vowels were added to enable more people to read the text.[295]

Summary of the Qur'anic Script:

1. The Qur'ān's modern script came to us in stages.
2. The Uthmanic text written in ancient Kūfī script contained no markings to differentiate the letters and sounds and no signs to indicate the end of the *surah.* The first Muslims had no problem reading this as they were used to it. However, non-Arab converts faced difficulties in reading this text and made many mistakes.
3. Abū Aswad al-Dualī, the student of Imam Ali b. Tālib, was the first person to introduce diacritical marks. There are also others names mentioned by the sources in this process such as 'Nasr b. Asım al-Laysi, Hasan al-Basrī, Yahya b. Ya'mer al-Adawani, all from Basra.
4. It is important to note that additions to the Qur'anic text they began with vowel marks (*tashkeel/haraka*) and then the diacritical marks (*nuqat* and *i'jam*).
5. The vowel demarcations helped people to read the Qur'ān but non-Arabs still faced difficulties in discerning the text, for example; 2:259 نسرها. Is it نشرها *nunshiruha* or ننشزها *nunshizuha*.
6. The governor of Iraq, Ḫajjāj al-Thaqafi, played a significant role by asking Abū Aswad's student to work on how to distinguish the letters' reading. He also played important role in determining the names of the *surah.*
7. Walid b. Abd al-Malik was the first Umayyad caliph to order the beautification of the *Muṣḥāf.* Khalil b. Ahmad first beautified and put today's *tashkeel* (*harakat*-vowel) in the Qur'ān. He also developed *sukun*, *shadda* and *hamza* which we use today.
8. Ibn Muqlah introduced the *naskh* script to the Qur'anic text.

---

294 Ad-Dānī, *al-Muqnī*, p. 130.

295 Zarqānī, *Manāhil*, 1.409.

9. In the sixth century, Muhammad b. Tayfur al-Sajâwandî (560 A.H. / 1165 C.E.) put stop (*wuquf*) marks at the end of the verses or where the meaning of the verse is completed. These signs are called ‘*sajawand*’.
10. Gustav Flugel (1841 C.E.) (using Hafiz Uthman’s script) introduced the verse numbers.
11. There were *Muṣḫāf* published in Kazan, Cairo, Tehran, and Istanbul. In 1925 King Fu’ad’s standard edition was published under the supervision of Shaykh Muhammad Ali Halaf al-Husayni.

Chapter Four

Form, Structure, Coherence and the *I'jāz* of the Qur'ān

Form, Structure, Coherence and the *I'jāz* of the Qur'ān

4.1 The Theory of *I'jāz*

The word *i'jāz* comes from 'a-j-z' which means 'to be incapable of, to be weak, to render powerless and to render dumb-founded'. The word '*mu'jizah*' which is derived from the same root means 'miracle'. A miracle is an extraordinary event that God Almighty brings about at the hands of a Prophet to prove his Prophethood, strengthen the believers' faith, and break the unbelievers' obstinacy. This word is not used in the Qur'ān but Muslim scholars used this term later. The Prophets performed miracles to challenge their people but the people were incapable of producing something similar. '*Mu'jizah*' is defined as an act of a miraculous nature, performed by Prophets, that humans are incapable of imitating. *I'jāz* is the concept; *mu'jizah* is the actual act.

Fethullah Gülen says the following about *mu'jizah*:

> The universe operates according to God's fixed laws. In the absence of His laws and the uniform character of natural events, everything would be in continual flux. In such an environment, we would be unable to discover the Divine laws of nature or make any scientific progress. Although recent discoveries in atomic physics have shown that whatever exists is a wave in continuous motion, on the surface everything occurs according to classical or Newtonian principles. This has forced scientists to admit that they cannot state that anything will exist in the same state as it did even one second ago. Normally, life has its own laws according to which we behave. We need food and water to satisfy our hunger and thirst, and go to a doctor when we are sick. We use animals for labour, but cannot talk to them. Trees are fixed in their places, and neither they nor stones and mountains greet us. We conform to the laws of gravitation and repulsion, and do not attempt to rise into the sky without first making the relevant calculations. All of these and other laws make human life possible. However, since God has determined them, He is not bound by them. Therefore, He may sometimes annul a law or change the ordinary flow

of events to allow a Prophet to perform what we call a miracle or to show that He can do whatever He wills at whatever time He desires.[296]

SUMMARY OF THE THEORY OF *I'JAZ*:

1. The word *i'jaz* comes from the root 'a-j-z' meaning 'to be incapable of, weak, render powerless and render dumbfounded'.
2. The word *mu'jizah* means miracle.
3. A miracle is an extraordinary act performed by a Prophet with the permission of God to prove his Prophethood.

4.1.1 Conditions of *Mu'jizah*

1) It is something that only happens by the command of God, and is created by Him. The Prophets cannot perform it without His permission.

2) It is something that is extraordinary and not part of daily things and events (*kharqu-l adah*). In order to draw attention to the message of God, the Prophets perform these extraordinary acts and prove that they are not liars; they are acting on God's command. These miracles prove their claim because as mere humans they are not able to change the laws of nature, but, as God created nature He is not bound by it so He can change the laws at any time to help His Prophets deliver their message.

3) The miracles cannot be repeated or imitated by others. The Prophets performed miracles and challenged the unbelievers to perform something similar. When we look at history, even though people witnessed the miracles and couldn't produce something similar, some of them still denied the existence of God.

4) The Prophets only performed miracles in the Name of God. First, they approached the people with their message of God, the afterlife and the path to salvation. If the people doubted them they offered to perform miracles in God's Name to prove their claim. The unbelievers would sometimes request a miracle, such as the Prophet Muhammad (pbuh) splitting the moon. The Prophet (pbuh) would generally perform the most appropriate miracle to curb the disbelief of the people.

5) *Mu'jizah* (miracle) must affirm the claim of the Prophet. If an extraordinary event contradicts their claim, it cannot be considered to be a miracle. For example, if a person claims Prophethood and says that a stone will confirm this

[296] Fethullah Gülen, Essentials of the Islamic Faith, pp. 194-195.

claim but when asked, the stone says the person is a liar, it cannot be considered as a miracle, even though it is an extraordinary incident. Anything that contradicts what a 'Prophet' claims does not confirm their Messengership.

6) *Mu'jizah* (miracle) happens in a way which confirms the claim, otherwise it is not considered a miracle. For example, if a person claims that a cow will give milk abundantly with the stroke of his hands, but in actual fact, the cow dies immediately after, it is not considered to be a miracle because it did not confirm his claim.

7) Miracles occur without any preparation and at a time when there is a demand for such an event. The Prophets never made preparations when performing miracles and never knew what would be demanded of them. They responded to the demands of the unbelievers at the time without any preparation or delay.

8) Miracles happen to support the Prophets and the believers. The God-given role of Prophethood is a difficult one and God supports it and strengthens the hearts of the believers as well as enduring the hardships with them. Miracles are one of the ways in which He supports them.

9) *Mu'jizah* is an aid to help people find and understand the truth. It does not force them to believe, they choose that using their free will. It opens the door for the intellect but doesn't take the free will away from human beings. The unbelievers witnessed many miracles in history, yet most of them didn't believe. A person who uses his intellect doesn't need to see a miracle to believe, because the message itself is sufficient for acceptance. A thinking person can grasp the idea and see the truth from the message itself.

Summary of the Conditions of *Mu'jizah*:

1. They are only performed with God's permission.
2. They are something extraordinary and not part of normal daily life.
3. They cannot be repeated by others.
4. Prophets only performed them in the Name of God.
5. They must affirm the claim of the Prophet that performs them.
6. They must happen in a way that confirms the claim.
7. They don't require preparation, they happen at the time of the demand.
8. They happen to support the Prophets and the believers.
9. They are an aid to help people find and understand the truth.

4.2 The Qur'ān is a Miracle (*Mu'jizah*)

The Qur'ān uses the terms '*ayah*' and '*bayyinah*' instead of miracle. *Ayah* actually means 'sign'. In technical language it is the shortest division of the Qur'anic text, i.e. a phrase or sentence. The revelation is guidance from God to mankind and it is therefore not at all surprising to find that its smallest divisions are called (guiding) 'signs'.[297] The Qur'ān states that the real miracle is the Qur'ān itself and this is enough to believe, but the unbelievers rejected it and produced many pretexts for it:

> And they say, 'We shall not believe in you until you cause a spring to gush forth from the earth for us; Or you have a garden of date palms and grapes, and cause rivers to gush forth in their midst abundantly; Or you cause the heavens to fall upon us in pieces, as you have pretended, or you bring Allah and the angels before (us) face-to-face; Or you have a house of adorable material (i.e., gold and silver), or you ascend up into the sky and even then we will put no faith in your ascension until you bring down for us a book that we would read!' Answer them (O Muhammad), 'Glorified be my Lord! I am just a man, sent as a Messenger![298]

4.2.1 The Challenge of the Qur'ān (*I'jāz al-Qur'ān*)

The unbelievers in Mecca claimed that the Prophet Muhammad (pbuh) was a liar who forged the Qur'ān, or a magician, or one possessed by *jinn*. They even claimed that they could imitate the Qur'ān:

> And when Our verses are recited to them, they say, 'We have heard this! If we wish, we can say something similar to it. These are nothing but stories of old'.[299]

Thereupon God challenged them to fulfil this claim of theirs in three stages:

1) First, God challenged the unbelievers to produce a book which is similar to the Qur'ān:

> Say: If all of mankind and jinn gathered together to produce the like of the Qur'ān, they could not produce it even if they help one another![300]

> Do they say, 'He has forged it!' Nay! (Rather) they do not believe! Let them, then, produce a book similar to it, if indeed they are truthful.[301]

---

297 Von Denffer, *'Ulūm al-Qur'ān*, p. 67.
298 Qur'ān, 17: 90-93.
299 Qur'ān, 8: 31
300 Qur'ān, 17: 88.
301 Qur'ān, 52: 33-34.

2) Next, the Qur'ān asked them to bring forward 10 chapters which are similar to itself:

> Do they say, 'He (Muhammad) has forged it? Say: Bring then ten forged chapters similar to it, and call upon whomsoever you can, besides Allah, if you are truthful.[302]

3) Finally, the Qur'ān challenged them to bring one chapter which is similar to any of its chapters:

> Do they say, 'He (Muhammad) has forged it!' Say: Bring then a one single chapter similar to it, and call upon whomsoever you can, besides Allah, if you are truthful.[303]

> If you are in doubt about what We have sent down to Our servant, then produce a chapter similar to it, if you are truthful. But if you do not do it and of a surety you cannot do it then fear the fire whose fuel are men and stones, prepared for the disbelievers.[304]

The Arabs at the time of the Prophet (pbuh) prided themselves on their poetic skill and eloquence, this is why God presented them with this particular challenge. However, the Qur'ān itself is a miracle until the Day of Judgement so the challenge remains open to the whole of mankind (and *jinn*) to produce something similar to the Qur'ān.[305] This challenge will continue to be operative until the Day of Judgement.

Said Nursi says the following words about this challenge:

> The people of 'Arabia were mostly unlettered at that time, and therefore preserved their tribal pride, history, and proverbs in oral poetry. They attached great importance to eloquence, and so any meaningful, unique expression was memorized for its poetical form and eloquence and then handed down to posterity. Eloquence and fluency were therefore in such great demand that a tribe treated its eloquent literary figures as national heroes. Those intelligent people, who would govern a considerable portion of the world after Islam's advent, were more eloquent than other nations. Eloquence was so esteemed that two tribes would sometimes go to war over a saying of a literary figure and then be reconciled by the words of another. They even inscribed in gold the odes of seven poets

302 Qur'ān, 11: 13.
303 Qur'ān, 10: 38
304 Qur'ān, 2: 23-24.
305 Abu Ammaar Yasir Qadhi, the Sciences of the Qur'ān, p. 263.

> and hung them on the wall of the Kaba. They were called the Seven Suspended Poems. At a time when eloquence was in such demand, the Qur'ān of miraculous exposition was revealed. Just as God Almighty had endowed Moses and Jesus with the miracles most suitable to their times—the miracles of Staff and Bright Hand to Moses, and those of raising the dead and healing certain illnesses to Jesus—He made eloquence the most notable aspect of the Qur'ān, the chief miracle of Prophet Muhammad, upon him be peace and blessings. When it was revealed, it challenged first the literary figures of the 'Arabian Peninsula: If you doubt what We have sent down on Our servant, produce a surah like it (2:23). It defeated their intellectual pretensions and humbled them by continuing: If you cannot, and you certainly cannot, fear the Fire, whose fuel is people and stones, prepared for unbelievers (2:24). Those self-conceited people could not dispute the Qur'ān. Although this was an easy and safe course to obstruct and falsify its message, they chose to fight it with swords, the perilous and most difficult course. If those intelligent people, skilled in diplomacy, could have disputed the Qur'ān, they would not have chosen the perilous, difficult course and risked losing their property and lives. Since they could not argue with it verbally, they had to fight it with swords. There were two powerful reasons for trying to produce something like the Qur'ān: its enemies strongly wished to dispute it to refute its claim of Revelation, and its friends had the desire to imitate it. The result was, and continues to be, innumerable books written in 'Arabic. All people, whether scholars or not, who read such books are forced to admit that they do not resemble the Qur'ān. So, either the Qur'ān is inferior—friend and foe admit that this is inconceivable —or superior to all of them. There are no other options.[306]

When the unbelievers asked for miracles from the Prophet (pbuh), God revealed that the Qur'ān itself is sufficient as a miracle:

> And they say, 'Why are not miracles sent down to him from his Lord?' Say: 'The signs are only with Allah, and I am only a plain warner.' Is it not a sufficient 'miracle' for them that We have sent down to you the Book which is recited to them? Verily, herein is a mercy and a reminder for a people who believe.[307]

The Prophet (pbuh) also indicated the Qur'ān's status as a miracle:

> There has not been a single Prophet except that Allah gave him miracles because of which people believed in him. I have been given (as my mira-

[306] Said Nursi, Words, The Twenty Fifth Word, 390-391.

[307] Qur'ān, 29: 50-51.

> cle) the Inspiration (i.e., the Qur'ān) which Allah revealed to me. I hope, therefore, that I will have the largest number of followers on the Day of Judgement.[308]

The miracles of Prophet Muhammad (pbuh) were not limited to the Qur'ān. The most authentic Hadith books record more than one thousand miracles performed by him, the most well-known of which are: the splitting of the moon, increasing a small amount of food to a large quantity, the speaking of stones, animals and trees, and an abundance of water gushing from his hands in a time of need. None of the miracles he performed were permanent; they were performed for specific groups of people at specific times and places. Detailed narrations exist about these events which Muslims are required to believe in. The fact remains, however, that later generations must believe in the narrations of those who were present at the time of the miracle, for they themselves were not present.[309]

Ibn Khaldun (d. 808 A.H.) says the following words in his book '*Muqaddima*':

> Know that the greatest of all miracles, and the most sacred and blessed, and the clearest in proof, is the Qur'ān that was revealed to the Prophet. This is because all other miracles, in general, were brought forth separate from the actual inspiration (that the Prophet received), as a means of proving the truthfulness of the inspiration. As for the Qur'ān, it is the inspiration and the miracle in one, and is therefore not in need of any external miracles (to prove itself), unlike all the previous inspirations. It is, therefore, the clearest and most powerful miracle, since it combines the claim and the proof in one. This is the meaning of the Prophet's statement, '...I hope, therefore, that I will have the largest number of followers on the Day of Judgement'. This shows that a miracle as clear and powerful as this one -for it is the inspiration in its essence - must have the greatest number of believers and followers.[310]

Summary of the Challenge of the Qur'ān:

1. The Meccan unbelievers claimed that Prophet Muhammad (pbuh) was a liar who forged the Qur'ān. They claimed they could imitate it.
2. God presented a three stage challenge to them to a) produce a book similar to the Qur'ān b) produce 10 chapters similar to the chapters in the Qur'ān c) produce one chapter similar to a chapter of the Qur'ān.
3. The challenge is for all mankind until the Day of Judgement.

---

[308] Bukhari, *Saḥīḥ, Holding fast to the Qur'ān and Sunnah*, hadith no: 379.

[309] Qadhi, *The Sciences of the Qur'ān*, 264.

[310] Ibn Khaldun, *Muqaddima*, p. 113.

4. The Qur'ān is a miracle of God and is inimitable.
5. The Prophet Muhammad (pbuh) performed more than 1000 miracles in his lifetime. The Qur'ān is the one miracle that all mankind can bear witness to.

4.2.2 The Works against the Challenge of the Qur'ān

In history some attempts have been made to meet the challenge of producing something similar or equal to the Qur'ān. The reason for these are varied and include false Prophets claiming they have received a divine text and the work of artists who conceived they could rival the text of the Qur'ān with their own work. The following are examples of texts written to meet the challenge of the Qur'ān but which were met with ridicule even from the authors' most intimate friends and followers.

1. Musaylima al-Kadhdhab (the liar) was a false prophet. He wanted to acquire a kingdom and offered his terms for peace to the Prophet (pbuh). Musaylima claimed that the angel Rahman brought him the revelation. One of his compositions is as follows:

> frog! croak! How much do you croak? Neither You can trouble the water nor you can repulse the water-seeker.

Musaylima tried to imitate the following two chapters (*surah*) of the Qur'ān:

> Have you considered how your Lord dealt with the people of the Elephant? Did He not bring their evil scheme to nothing? He sent down upon them flocks of birds (unknown in the land), shooting them with bullet-like stones of baked clay (an emblem of the punishment due to them), and so He rendered them like a field of grain devoured and trampled.[311]

> The sudden, mighty strike! What is the sudden, mighty strike? What enables you to perceive what the sudden, mighty strike is? The day (when it occurs) humans will be like moths scattered about; and the mountains will be like carded wool. And then, the one whose scales are heavy (with faith and good deeds), he will be in a life of contentment. Whereas the one whose scales are light (as devoid of faith and accepted good deeds), he will have his home in a bottomless pit, what enables you to perceive what it is? It is a fire burning fiercely.[312]

[311] Qur'ān, 105: 1-5.
[312] Qur'ān, 101: 1-11.

Musaylima fabricated the following words to try to meet the challenge of the Qur'ān:

> The elephant! What is the elephant? And what would explain to you what the elephant is? It has a hard tail and long trunk and a strong tail, and few among the creatures of our Lord.
>
> Haven't you not noticed your Lord how he did with the pregnant? He pulled out of her soul, quickly moving between the epigastrium and intestine.

2. Aswad al-Ansi was famous for his eloquence and poetry. He pretended that he received the revelation from God. He was defeated against the eloquence of Qur'ān and his claims disappeared.

3. Nadr b. al-Harith was a contemporary of the Prophet (pbuh). He did not pretend to be a Prophet. He is said to have written a history of the Persians and other stories in the style of the Qur'ān. On account of his foolish assertion and the nature of his compositions, his stories have not been taken as a serious rival to the Qur'ān.

4. Ibn al-Muqaffa (d. 142 A.H. / 759 C.E.) was an eminent scholar and a poet of his age. His contemporaries asserted that he was inclined to accept the challenge of the Qur'ān and to produce similar compositions. Upon hearing a young boy recite the following verse he exclaimed and said, 'verily this is not a human utterance and it is impossible to compose anything likewise'.

> It was said: 'O earth, swallow up your waters! And, O sky, cease (your rain)!' And the waters were made to subside, and (by God's will) the affair was accomplished. Then the Ark came to rest on al-Judi, and it was said: 'Away with the wrongdoing people!'[313]

5. Ahmad b. Yahya Abū al-Hasan al-Rawandi (d.293 A.H. / 906 C.E.) was an atheist and wrote many books against Islam, but he couldn't meet the challenge of the Qur'ān nor could he refute claims of the Qur'ān. Ibn Kathīr refuted all his arguments which he used against the Qur'ān.

6. The famous poet Ahmad b. Husayn Mutanabbi (d. 354 A.H. / 965 C.E.) claimed in his early life to be a Prophet and said a book was revealed to him. Later he gave up his pretention.

7. Abū 'Ala al-Ma'arri (d.449 A.H. / 1057 C.E.) produced a book to meet the challenge of the Qur'ān named: *al-Fusūl wa al-Ghayat fi Murajaat al-Suwar wa al-Ayat*. The style of the work is totally different from that of the Qur'ān and is

---

[313] Qur'ān 11: 44

not considered to be a serious work against the Qur'ān. He even expressed the excellence of the Qur'ān.

SUMMARY OF THE WORKS AGAINST THE CHALLENGE OF THE QUR'ĀN:

1. There have been various attempts to meet the challenge of producing something similar to the Qur'ān.
2. These attempts have been made by false Prophets and poets, the most notable of which are Musaylima, Aswad al-Ansi, Nadr b. al-Harith, Ibn al-Muqaffa, Ahmed b. Yahya Abū al-Hasan al-Rawandi, Ahmed b. Husain Mutanabbi and Abū 'Ala al-Ma'arri.
3. None of the attempts to produce something similar to the Qur'ān were successful and some of the challengers even admitted the superior excellence of the Qur'ān.

4.3 Arguments for the Divine Authorship of the Qur'ān[314]

The Qur'ān's words, style, and meanings are unique. The Qur'ān is not similar to any previous books, it did not imitate any book, nor can any book imitate it, because it is the Word of God and above all other books.

The Qur'ān was sent down to the unlettered Prophet Muhammad (pbuh) and presented an eternal challenge to humanity which no one has been able to successfully meet:

> If you are in doubt about what We have sent down to Our servant, then produce a chapter similar to it, if you are truthful.[315].

Revealed over a period of 23 years, the Qur'ān deals with the truths about God, metaphysics, religious beliefs and worship, prayer, law and morality, the afterlife, psychology, sociology, epistemology, history, scientific facts, and the principles of a happy life. It never contradicts itself, in fact, the Qur'ān clearly declares that it contains no contradictions and is therefore a word of God:

> Do they not contemplate the Qur'ān (so that they may be convinced that it is from God)? Had it been from any other than God, they would surely have found in it much (incoherence or) inconsistency.[316]

---

[314] The arguments are mostly taken from Fethullah Gülen, *Essentials of Islamic Faith*, 224-230, please see there for more details.

[315] Qur'ān, 2: 23.

[316] Qur'ān, 4: 82.

Eloquence, poetry, and oratory enjoyed great prestige in pre-Islamic Arabia. The unlettered Prophet (pbuh) had never been heard to say even a couple of lines of poetry. However, the Qur'ān he brought eventually forced all known poetry experts to surrender. The Qur'ān is a literary masterpiece that cannot be duplicated. Its styles and eloquence, even its actual sentences, words, and letters, form a miraculous harmony. With respect to its rhythm, music, and even geometric proportions, mathematical measures and repetition, each is in its exact place and perfectly interwoven and interrelated with each other.[317]

Despite the high level of poetry existent at the time, Arabic's vocabulary was too primitive to adequately express metaphysical ideas or scientific, religious, and philosophical concepts. Islam, using the words and expressions of a simple desert people, made Arabic so rich and complex that it became the language of the most magnificent civilization, one that made many entirely original contributions to scientific, religious, metaphysical, literary, economic, juridical, social, and political arenas.[318] How could an unlettered person achieve all these?

On a first reading, the Qur'ān appears to be a basic text that can be understood by anyone, however its meanings are deep and multi-layered. Many scientists in different fields have been illuminated by the Qur'ān and the Qur'ān fulfils everyone's needs both for their studies and for their daily lives.[319] Poets, musicians, orators, sociologists, psychologists, scientists, economists, jurists and many more have benefitted from the Qur'ān for their studies. In this sense the Qur'ān has no equal.

It is not common for a person to read a book more than three times, yet here the Qur'ān also differs from other texts. It has been read and re-read by Muslims with increasing interest and enthusiasm every day for more than fourteen centuries. No one became bored of it or left it, on the contrary, its readers acknowledge that the more they recite it, the more they benefit from it. Muslims never get tired of its recitation, meaning, and content, and it never loses any of its originality and freshness.[320] As time passes, it breathes new truths and meanings into minds and souls, thereby increasing their activity and liveliness.

The Qur'ān describes all our physical and spiritual aspects, and contains principles to solve all social, economic, juridical, political, and administrative prob-

---

317 Fethullah Gülen, *Essentials of Islamic Faith*, 224.

318 ibid.

319 Ibid.

320 Ibid.

lems regardless of time or place.[321] Furthermore, it satisfies the mind and spirit simultaneously and guarantees happiness in both worlds.

Over the years of revelation, the Prophet (pbuh) experienced and practised the Qur'ān, first by himself, and by teaching it to his Companions. The perfect life outlined in the Qur'ān was represented by the Prophet (pbuh) first. The Qur'ān designed the Prophet's (pbuh) character and similarly the Prophet (pbuh) guided his followers to the best human values. When Āi'sha, the wife of the Prophet (pbuh), was asked about his character she said, 'Don't you read the Qur'ān? His character was the Qur'ān'.[322]

The Qur'ān is as universal and objective when dealing with particular issues as it is exact and precise when dealing with universal matters.[323] Authors are usually limited by the time and the conditions in which they exist, it is impossible to escape this influence in their work. However, the Qur'ān uses precise expressions even while describing the beginning of creation and the end of time, and humanity's creation and life in the other world.[324] Just as it sometimes draws universal conclusions from particular events, it sometimes goes from universal principles to particular events. This typical Qur'anic style cannot be found in any human work.

The Qur'ān not only contains many different scientific fields but also phrases them accurately. There is no other such book which contains many different fields without making contradictions. The Qur'ān also contains the principles of all branches of knowledge, either in summary or in detail, and not even one piece of this knowledge has ever been contradicted.

Scientific conclusions change constantly. Some so called 'truths' from the past are no longer held as true today. No author can claim that their book will remain true forever, but the Qur'ān remains as true and fresh today as it was at the time it was revealed. It continues, even now, to conquer new hearts and reveal its hidden unlimited treasures, to bloom like a heavenly rose with countless petals.

The Prophet (pbuh) is admonished in the Qur'ān. If he were its author, would he give such a noticeable place to the grave slander against his wife? His uncle Abū Tālib, who raised him from the age of eight and protected him for 10 years after his declaration of Prophethood, never embraced Islam. The Prophet (pbuh)

---

321 Ibid.

322 Gülen, 225.

323 Fethullah Gülen, *Essentials of Islamic Faith*, 226.

324 Ibid.

loved his uncle deeply and desired his conversion, but was told in the revelation: "You guide not whom you love, but God guides whom He wills. He is best aware of those who are guided"[325]. If he were the Qur'ān's author, he could have claimed that Abū Tālib had embraced Islam.

Many verses begin with "They ask you" and continue with "Say (in answer)." These were revealed to answer questions asked by the Muslims and non-Muslims, especially the Jews of Medina, about permissible or prohibited matters, the distribution of war booty, (astrological) mansions of the moon, Judgment Day, Dhul-Qarnayn (an ancient believing king who made great conquests in Asia and Africa), the spirit, and so on. A person without an all-encompassing knowledge could not answer such questions but the answers of the Prophet (pbuh) satisfied everybody showing that he was instructed by God, the All-Knowing.[326]

The Jews and Christians were very strong opponents of the Prophet (pbuh) eventually resulting in several conflicts with, and finally the expulsion of, the Jews of Medina. Despite this, the Qur'ān mentions Prophet Moses about 50 times and Jesus many times; it mentions Muhammad's (pbuh) name only four times. Why should a person who falsely claims Prophethood mention the Prophets of his opponents?

The Qur'ān also refers to certain facts of creation only recently established by modern scientific methods. How, except by Divine authorship, could the Qur'ān be correct on matters of which the people listening to it had no idea?[327]

Summary of the Arguments for the Divine Authorship of the Qur'ān:

1. Its words, meanings and styles are unique.
2. It was sent down to an illiterate Prophet and issued a challenge to humanity which has not been successfully met.
3. Despite its numerous and detailed subject matter it contains no contradictions.
4. There is a miraculous harmony in its styles and eloquence; its rhythm, music, geometric proportions, mathematical measures and repetition are perfectly interwoven and interrelated.

---

[325] Qur'ān, 28: 56.

[326] Fethullah Gülen, *Essentials of Islamic Faith*, p. 227.

[327] Gülen, p. 228.

5. The Qur'ān made the Arabic language so rich it launched a philological revolution unparalleled in human history.
6. Its meanings are deep and multi-layered but it speaks to people of all levels without losing its balance.
7. It fulfils everyone's needs for their daily lives whether scholars, jurist, musicians, poets or ordinary laymen.
8. Muslims have read and re-read it every day for fourteen centuries without tiring of its content. The more they read it the more they benefit from it. As time passes it breaths new truths and meanings.
9. The Qur'ān describes all our spiritual and physical aspects and contains the principles for all aspects of life.
10. It is not limited by the time and condition in which it was revealed; it is universal.
11. It contains many scientific fields and is completely accurate. It contains the principles for all branches of knowledge, none of which has ever been contradicted.
12. If Prophet Muhammad (pbuh) was the author he would not have included events in the Qur'ān which caused him much suffering.
13. The Qur'ān answers all the questions of the Muslims and non-Muslims regardless of subject matter. A person without an all-encompassing knowledge would not have been able to answer these questions but for the help of God.
14. The Qur'ān mentions many times the Prophets of the people who were the enemies of Prophet Muhammad (pbuh) but only mentions him four times.
15. The Qur'ān refers to facts of creation only recently established by modern science.

4.4 The Types of *I'jāz* in the Qur'ān

Why is the Qur'ān *mu'jizah*? What aspects of the Qur'ān make it inimitable? There are many books which discuss these questions in detail and the results of these studies are so numerous it is impossible to relate all of them. The following two categories detail some of the main reasons why the Qur'ān is a miracle: the first details its language, forms and structure and the second deals with the meanings.

4.4.1 The Language of the Qur'ān

At the time of the Prophet (pbuh), as was mentioned earlier, most of the people of Arabia were unlettered and therefore preserved their tribal pride, history, and proverbs in oral poetry. They attached great importance to eloquence, so any meaningful, unique expression was memorized and then taught to the next generations. Eloquence and fluency were in such great demand that a tribe treated its eloquent literary figures as national heroes. Due to this pride that was prevalent among the Arabs, the miracle that was given to the Prophet (pbuh) was of a similar nature; God revealed the Qur'ān in an Arabic that was so eloquent the Arabs could clearly see it was a miracle.

The Qur'ān's styles and eloquence, even its actual sentences, words, and letters, form a miraculous harmony. The eloquence of the Qur'ān is mainly related to three aspects; the abundant meanings in its forms, the beauty in its expressions and the greatness in its style. Examples below elaborate each of these aspects.

4.4.2 The Abundant Meanings in Its Words and Forms (*Jazalat an-Nazm*)

The word *jazalat* is an Arabic word meaning; abundance, blessings, multiple ways, fertility, being strong and based on evidence, never been to exposed to infertility, etc. We can see all these meanings in the forms of the Qur'ān. When reading the Qur'ān, at first the meaning seems simple and singular but on a deeper reading, multiple-levels of meaning reveal themselves showing the true blessings of the Qur'ān.

The following examples will show this:

وَلَئِنْ مَسَّتْهُمْ نَفْحَةٌ مِنْ عَذَابِ رَبِّكَ لَيَقُولُنَّ يَاوَيْلَنَا إِنَّا كُنَّا ظَالِمِينَ

> If but a breath of your Lord's punishment touches them, they are sure to cry: 'Oh, woe to us! We were indeed wrongdoers!'[328]

To indicate the severity of God's punishment, the above clause points to the smallest measure or slightest element of it. As the entire clause expresses this slightness, all of its parts should reinforce that meaning. The words 'If but' (*la-in*) signify uncertainty and therefore imply slightness (of punishment). The Arabic verb '*massa*' means 'to touch slightly', also signifying slightness. The Arabic word '*nafhatun*' (a breath) is merely a puff of air. Grammatically, it is a derived form

---

[328] Qur'ān, 21: 46.

of the word used to express singleness, which again underlies the slightness. The double 'n' (*tanwin*) at the end of '*nafhatun*' indicates indefiniteness and suggests that it is slight and insignificant. The particle '*min*' implies a part or a piece, thus indicating paucity. In Arabic, the word '*adhab*' (torment or punishment) is light in meaning compared to '*nakal*' (exemplary chastisement) and '*iqab*' (heavy penalty), and denotes a light punishment or torment. The use of '*Rabb*' (Lord, Provider, Sustainer), suggesting affection, instead of, for example, All-Overwhelming, All-Compelling, or Ever-Able to Requite, also expresses slightness. Finally, the clause means that if so slight a breath of torment or punishment has such an effect, one should reflect how severe the Divine chastisement might be. We see in this short clause how its parts are related to each other and add to the meaning. This example concerns the words chosen and the purpose in choosing them.[329]

وَمِمَّا رَزَقْنَاهُمْ يُنْفِقُونَ

> Out of what We have provided for them (of wealth, knowledge, power, etc.,) they spend (to provide sustenance for the needy and in God's cause, purely for the good pleasure of God and without placing others under obligation)[330]

The parts of the above sentence point to five conditions that make alms-giving acceptable to God[331];

First condition: While giving alms, believers must not give so much that they are reduced to begging. 'Out of' expresses this. For this reason, the Prophet (pbuh) didn't allow some of his Companions such as Ka'b b. Malik and Sa'd b. Abī Waqqas to give the whole of their possessions as charity. The Prophet (pbuh) prevented his Companions from extreme inclinations; when Sa'd insisted on giving all of his wealth as charity, the Prophet (pbuh) told him to give just one-third. He explained, 'leaving your family rich and self-sufficient is better than leaving them to beg from others'.[332]

Second condition: They must give out of what they have, not out of what others have. We have provided for them points to this. The meaning is "give (to sustain life) out of what We have provided you with" expresses that the charity must be given from *ḫalal* provision. For example, if anyone gives his whole rev-

---

329 Said Nursi, *The Words, The Twenty fifth Word*, p. 392.

330 Qur'ān, 2: 3.

331 This example has been taken from Said Nursi, *The Words*, 392-393.

332 Bukhari, *Saḫīḫ*, *Wasaya* 16, *Jihad* 103.

enue as charity which he gained by unlawful means, or if he goes to *Hajj* with this money, it is never accepted.

Third condition: The charity-giver must not remind the recipient of their kindness. 'We' indicates this, for it means: "I have provided you with the thing out of which you give to the needy as sustenance. As you are giving some of that which belongs to Me, you cannot put the recipient under obligation." Another verse clearly explains this:

> O you who believe! Render not vain your almsgiving by putting (the receiver) under an obligation and taunting – like him who spends his wealth to show off to people and be praised by them, and believes not in God and the Last Day.[333]

Fourth condition: They must give to those who will spend it only for their livelihood, not in illicit ways, indicated by the phrase; 'They give as sustenance'.

Fifth condition: They must give it for God's sake which is indicated by; 'We have provided for them'. It means: 'You are giving out of My property, and so must give in My name.'

Together with those conditions, the word 'what' (*ma*') signifies that whatever God bestows is part of one's sustenance or livelihood and is a general expression (not restricted). Believers must give out of whatever they have been given by God. This is not limited to possessions; for example, a good word, some help, advice and teaching are all included in the meaning of '*rizq*' (sustenance or provision) and '*sadaqa*' (alms). This short sentence contains and suggests a broad range of meanings for the giving of alms and offers it for our understanding.[334]

4.4.3 The Beauty in Its Expressions

The expressions used in the Qur'ān are unusual but they are not strange. Instead when reciting they come across as very appealing, fresh and attractive. When comparing these with the expressions and styles of previous poets, authors and orators we find the Qur'ān is not similar to any of them, rather it is totally unique. There has not been any other book written since the revelation of the Qur'ān that can be compared to it. Instead of being put off by the unusual style and expression of the Qur'ān, the people who received it found it new and exciting and appealing. They could appreciate its quality and even when the unbelievers in Mecca

[333] Qur'ān, 2: 264.
[334] Nursi, *The Words*, 392-393.

listened to it they could appreciate its unique style and greatness even if they could not open their hearts to its message.

> Utba ibn Rabia was once sitting with other members of the Quraysh, and the subject of Muhammad (pbuh) came up. The elders of the Quraysh began complaining about all the problems that this new message had caused among their people, and started to discuss various ways that they could rid themselves of this irritating problem. Utba suggested that perhaps the Prophet (pbuh) could be convinced of giving up his message, if only it was explained to him in a gentle manner the problems that his message had been causing. Common sense, Utba argued, would prevail. As proof of his convictions, Utba himself volunteered to be the one to go and talk to the Prophet (pbuh). He therefore set out to meet the Prophet (pbuh), and started to try to convince him to abandon preaching this 'new' message, and let the Quraysh return to the paganism of their ancestors. After finishing his plea to the Prophet (pbuh), he asked, 'Have you finished, O Abū al-Waled? When he applied in the affirmative, the Prophet (pbuh) recited the following verses:
>
> Ha. Mim. (This is) the Book being sent down in parts from the All-Merciful (Who embraces all beings with His Mercy), the All-Compassionate (Who has special mercy for the believers). A Book whose communications have been spelled out distinctly and made clear, and whose verses are in ordered sequence, a Qur'ān (Recitation) in Arabic for a people who have knowledge (and so can appreciate excellence in the use of the language); (Being sent) as a bearer of glad tidings (of the recompense for faith and righteousness), and a warner (against the consequences of misguidance). Yet most of them (the Meccan people) turn away, and they do not give ear to it (being inwardly averse and deaf to its excellence).[335]
>
> The Prophet (pbuh) continued to recite, until he finished. Utba sat quietly, entranced by what he was hearing. Then the Prophet (pbuh) said, 'You have heard what you have heard, so do as you please'. When Utba returned to his people, they said to themselves, 'I swear by the Lord of the Ka'ba, this Utba is not the same as the Utba that left us'. When Utba came to them, he said, 'O people! I have heard a speech the like of which I have never heard before. I swear by God, it is not magic, nor is it poetry, nor is it sorcery. O gathering of Quraysh, listen to me. Leave this man alone, for I swear by God, the speech that I have heard from him (meaning the Qur'ān) will soon be news (among the other tribes) ..."[336]

---

335 Qur'ān, 41: 1-4.

336 Ibn Hishām, *Sīrah*, 1/142, Hakim, *Mustadrak*, 2/550.

The Qur'ān has unique, original styles that are both novel and convincing. Its styles, which have always preserved and still preserve their originality, freshness, and "bloom of youth" do not imitate and cannot be imitated. The uniqueness of the expressions and the style of Qur'ān can be explained in two categories; one is related its letters, especially conjecture letters (*huruf al-muqatta'*) at the beginning of the some *surah*, the other one is related to the encompassing meaning which is seen in the whole Qur'ān.

4.4.4 The Greatness in the Detached Letters

The letters of the Qur'ān, their placement in the structures and forms are unique and original, especially the conjecture letters. The letters of the Arabic alphabet have different categories according to their pronunciation; some of them are soft letters and some are heavy. The conjecture letters make up half of the Arabic letters and they appear at the beginning of 29 different *surah*.

The cipher-like *muqatta'at*, the separated, individual letters (e.g., *Alif-Lam-Mim, Alif-Lam-Ra, Ta-Ha, Ya-Sin, Ha-Mim,* and *'Ayn-Sin-Qaf,* with which some *surah* begin), contain many miracles. For example, they comprise half of each category of the well-known categories of letters—emphatic, whispered, stressed, and soft (*Ba, Jim, Dal, Ta, Qaf*). Taking more than half from the "light" letters and less than half from the "heavy" letters, neither of which are divisible, the Qur'ān has halved every category.[337]

The conjecture letters are the letters of the Arabic alphabet like *'alif-lam-mim'* and they are used for the first time in the Qur'ān at the beginning of some *surah*. This type of usage and encoding was never seen until the revelation of the Qur'ān. The secrets of the Qur'ān are encoded in its spirit and the keys for this encoding are the conjecture letters. We can think of this as similar to an encoding system: secret messages are encoded into numbers and sent to the receiver side encrypted. If the receiving side doesn't know the numbers' values and codes, the message cannot be understood, but with decoding information they are safely transmitted and understood. We can compare the secrets of the Qur'ān to this encoding system; the conjecture letters are the ciphers of the secrets of the Qur'ān. Muhyiddin ibn 'Arābī, Imam Rabbānī, Said Nursi and many more discovered a lot of the secrets of the Qur'ān from these letters. They wouldn't have been able to discover the secrets of the Qur'ān without these conjecture letters.

[337] Said Nursi, *the Words*, 395.

There is purposeful usage in the conjecture letters; the soft letters are used twice as many times as the heavy letters. This cannot be random usage, they must be chosen deliberately, and indeed the classification of the conjecture letters alone is sufficient evidence to prove the miracles of the Qur'ān. For example, the Arabic alphabet letter '*qaf*' is used in the Qur'ān twice as a conjecture letter; one is used in the *surah* 'Qaf' and the other one is used in the *surah* 'Shura'. For *ish'ari* (Sufi) interpreters the letter '*qaf*' represents a cipher. 57 '*qaf*' letters are used in each of these two *surah* and the total is 114. This is equal to the total number of *surah* in the Qur'ān. It seems that the letter '*qaf*' in each *surah* indicates the number of *surah* in the Qur'ān in an encrypted way.[338] Indeed the content of both *surah* is very much related with the Qur'ān; the *surah* Qaf starts with the verse:

> *Qaf.* By the Qur'ān most sublime. (We have indeed, in spite of what they say, sent it to you to warn people that they will be raised from the dead to account for their lives)' and it ends with the verse, 'remind and warn by the Qur'ān him who fears My threat'.[339]

The *surah* Shura starts with the verse:

> Ha. Mim. 'Ayn. Sin. *Qaf.* Just so: He reveals to you as (He did) to those (whom He chose as Messengers) before you, (being as He is) God, the All-Glorious with irresistible might, the All-Wise' and the surah end with the verse, 'And thus (in the ways mentioned) We have revealed to you a spirit of Our command (the life-giving Message, the Qur'ān). You would not (otherwise) have known what the Book was (with all the knowledge it contains and the way of life it establishes), and what faith was (as described by the Book and with all its principles, requirements, and implications). But We have made it a light by which We guide whom We will of Our servants. And certainly you, (by God's guidance) guide (people) to a straight path – The path of God, to Him belongs whatever is in the heavens and whatever is on the earth. Be aware: all affairs are ultimately referred to God.[340]

It is clear that the letter '*qaf*' is related with the Qur'ān; the beginning and the end of the *surah* indicate this. Also *surah* Qaf was not the last revelation, many *surah* were revealed after it indicating that God chose these letters and placed them at the beginning of some *surah* as ciphers. The Prophet (pbuh) could not have known that the total number of *surah* would be 114, because he received the

338 Fethullah Gülen, *Kur'anin Altin Ikliminde*, pp. 76-77.

339 Qur'ān, 50: 1, 50: 45.

340 Qur'ān, 42: 1-3, 42: 52-53.

final revelation just nine days before he died. He could not have used the letter '*qaf*' as cipher for the Qur'ān and the 114 *surah*.

4.4.5 The Encompassing Meaning of the Qur'ān

The Qur'ān has a matchless and unique style in regard to addressing all levels of people who lived in different times and places. The Qur'ān uses such a tongue that not only people who lived at the time of its revelation understood it but also, centuries later, people today can easily understand it. The Qur'ān is an eternal discourse speaking to and teaching humanity at all levels and times; it contains, intends, and alludes to all of those meanings. Humankind has many levels in terms of intellect, inclinations, abilities, etc., but the Qur'ān is able to address all these people and meets all of their needs at the same time, without losing the balance of its expressions. The angel Gabriel understands the Qur'ān according to his level and the Prophet (pbuh) comprehends it as well. The shepherd understands the Qur'ān for his level of intellect while the profound scholars delve into its deeper meanings. Similarly, the farmers, the labours, the housewives, the scholars, the scientists, etc. all understand the Qur'ān according to their intellect and capacities and are satisfied by it.

The imams of the major schools of thought such as Abū Hanifa, Malik, Shafi, Ahmad b. Hanbal were students of the Qur'ān and established their schools on this basis. Even ordinary people are able to receive many meanings and blessings when they apply to the Qur'ān, because the Qur'ān has a generosity for everyone. It is common knowledge that the level of an individual and their ability to utilise their capabilities is affected greatly by their family and social situation. A person who grew up on the streets is not the same as a person who grew up in a palace with the best private teachers. It is very difficult to address people with all different levels of education, intellect and ability at the same time without losing the balance among them. If you speak at the level of a person who grew up in a palace, a person who grew up in the streets would not be able to understand the speech. On the other hand, if you speak at the level of a person who grew up in the street, a person who grew up in a palace would be bored and lose interest quickly. However, the Qur'ān is different; it takes one who grew up in the street and one who grew up in the palace into its presence as students, addresses both with same expressions but each understands it according to his level. This is the meaning of the expression 'the encompassing meaning of the Qur'ān'. This characteristic of the Qur'ān is phrased by the following words of the Prophet (pbuh): 'Each verse has outer and inner meanings, limits and a point of comprehension, as well as boughs, branches, and twigs'.[341]

Each phrase, word, letter, and even an omission has many aspects. Each person who hears it receives his or her share through a different door. Muslim jurists, Qur'anic interpreters, and scholars of religious methodology agree and the differences in their understanding of verses and the conclusions they derive demonstrate that all aspects and meanings understood from the Qur'ān can be considered among its meanings if they accord with Arabic's grammatical rules, Islam's basic principles, and the sciences of rhetoric, semantics and eloquence. The Qur'ān has placed a sign, either literal or allusive, for each meaning according to its degree. If allusive, there is another sign from either the context (the preceding or the following verses) or from another verse to point to the meaning. Thousands of Qur'anic commentaries prove its wording's extraordinary comprehensiveness. I will give some examples to elaborate this aspect of the Qur'ān.

First example:

> And (we made) the mountains as masts?[342]

Said Nursi explains this verse as follows:

> God Almighty means: "I have made mountains like masts and stakes for your earth." Ordinary people see mountains as if driven into the ground and, thinking of the benefits and bounties thereof, thank the Creator. Poets imagine the earth as a ground on which the heavens' dome is pitched, in a sweeping arc, as a mighty blue tent adorned with electric lamps. Seeing mountains skirting the heavens' base as tent pegs, they worship the All-Majestic Creator in amazement.
>
> Desert-dwelling literary people imagine the earth as a vast desert, and its mountain chains as multifarious tents of nomads. They see them as if the soil were stretched over high posts and as if the posts' pointed tips had raised the "cloth" of the soil, which they see as the home for countless creatures. They prostrate in amazement before the All-Majestic Creator, Who placed and set up such imposing and mighty things so easily. Geographers with a literary bent view the earth as a ship sailing in the ocean of air or ether, and mountains as masts giving balance and stability to the ship. Before the All-Powerful One of Perfection, Who has made the earth like a well-built orderly ship on which He makes us travel through the universe, they declare: "All-Glorified are You. How sublime is Your Glory!

341 Abdurrazzaq, *Musannaf*, 3/358, Tabaranī, *Mu'jam al-Awsat*, 1/236.

342 Qur'ān, 78: 7.

Sociologists or anthropologists see the earth as a house, the pillar of whose life is animal life that, in turn, is supported by air, water, and soil (the conditions of life). Mountains are essential for these conditions, for they store water, purify the atmosphere by precipitating noxious gases, and preserve the ground from becoming a swamp and being overrun by the sea. Mountains also are treasuries for other necessities of human life. In perfect reverence, they praise the Maker of Majesty and Munificence, Who has made these great mountains as pillars for the earth, the house of our life, and appointed them as keepers of our livelihood's treasuries.

Naturalist scientists say: "The earth's quakes and tremors, which are due to certain underground formations and fusions, were stabilized with the emergence of mountains. This event also stabilized the earth's axis and orbit. Thus its annual rotation is not affected by earthquakes. Its wrath and anger is quietened by its coursing through mountain vents." They would come to believe and declare: 'There is wisdom in everything God does'.[343]

Another verse is explained by the same author as follows[344]:

The sun runs its course to a resting place destined[345]

The particle *li* (written as the single letter *lam*), translated here as "to," expresses the meanings of "toward," "in," and "for." Ordinary people read it as "toward" and understand that the sun, which is a moving lamp providing light and heat, one day will reach its place of rest and, ending its journey, assume a form that will no longer benefit them. Thinking of the great bounties that the Majestic Creator bestows through the sun, they declare: "All-Glorified is God. All praise and gratitude are for God."

Learned people also read *li* as "toward," but see the sun as both a lamp and a shuttle for the Lord's textiles woven in the loom of spring and summer, as an ink-pot whose ink is light for the letters of the Eternally Besought One inscribed on the pages of night and day. Reflecting on the world's order, of which the sun's apparent movement is a sign and to which it points, they declare before the All-Wise Maker's Art: "What wonders God has willed," before His Wisdom: "May God bless it," and prostrate.

For geographer–philosophers, *li* means "in" and suggests that the sun orders and propels its system through Divine command and with a spring like movement on its own axis. Before the All-Majestic Creator, Who cre-

[343] Said Nursi, *The Words*, 411.

[344] Said, Nursi, *The Words*, 412-413.

[345] Qur'ān, 36: 38.

ated and set in order a mighty clock like the solar system, they exclaim in perfect amazement and admiration: "All greatness and power is God's," abandon materialistic philosophy, and embrace the wisdom of the Qur'ān.

Precise and wise scholars consider *li* to be causal and adverbial. They understand that since the All-Wise Maker operates behind the veil of apparent causality, He has tied the planets to the sun by His law of gravity and causes them to revolve with distinct but regular motions according to His universal wisdom. To produce gravity, He has made the sun's movement on its axis an apparent cause. Thus a resting place means that "the sun moves in the place determined for it for the order and stability of its own (solar) system." For it must be a Divine law that motion produces heat, heat produces force, and force produces gravity. On understanding such an instance of wisdom from a single letter of the Qur'ān, wise scholars declare: "All praise and gratitude be to God! True wisdom is found in the Qur'ān. Human philosophy is worth almost nothing."

The following idea occurs to poets from this *li* and the stability mentioned: "The sun is a light-diffusing tree, and the planets are its moving fruits. But unlike trees, the sun is shaken so that the fruits do not fall. If it were not shaken, they would fall and be scattered." They also may imagine the sun to be a leader of a circle reciting God's Names, ecstatically reciting in the circle's centre and leading the others to recite.

Summary of *I'jaz* in the Qur'ān:

1. Some of the main reasons why the Qur'ān is a miracle are: due to its language, forms and structure and also its meanings.
2. God revealed the Qur'ān in a form of Arabic so eloquent the Arabs could clearly see it was a miracle.
3. The Qur'ān's styles and eloquence, even its actual sentences, words, and letters, form a miraculous harmony.
4. The eloquence of the Qur'ān is mainly related to three aspects; the abundant meanings in its forms, the beauty in its expressions and the greatness in its style.
5. The word *jazalat* is an Arabic word which can be related to the forms in the Qur'ān. It means; abundance, blessings, multiple ways, fertility, being strong and based on evidence, never been exposed to infertility, etc.
6. When reading the Qur'ān, at first the meaning seems simple and singular but on a deeper reading, multiple-levels of meaning reveal themselves.

7. The order of the words in the Qur'ān's sentences has many similar aspects, and the words have a wide range of relationships with one another.
8. The expressions used in the Qur'ān are very appealing, fresh and attractive and totally unique. No other comparable book has been written.
9. Even non-believers in Arabia consented to its superior quality.
10. The uniqueness of the expressions and the style of Qur'ān can be explained in two categories; one is related to its letters, especially conjecture letters (*huruf al-muqatta'*), at the beginning of the some *surah*, the other is related to the encompassing meaning which is seen in the whole Qur'ān.
11. The conjecture letters are the letters of the Arabic alphabet like *'alif-lam-mim'* and they are used for the first time in the Qur'ān at the beginning of some *surah*. This type of usage and encoding was never seen until the revelation of the Qur'ān. The secrets of the Qur'ān are encoded in its spirit and the keys to unlock this encoding are the conjecture letters.
12. The Qur'ān has a matchless and unique style in regard to addressing all levels of people who lived in different times and places. The Qur'ān uses such a tongue that not only people who lived at the time of its revelation understood it but also, centuries later, people today can easily understand it.

4.6 The Thematic Unity of the Qur'ān

The thematic unity within the whole Qur'ān is another of its miracles. The Qur'ān is like a masterpiece from the hand of an artist in which the colours are very coherent, and the materials are placed in their proper places. There is not a single thing in the Qur'ān which bothers the eyes or ruins the pleasure.

The Qur'ān is so wonderfully comprehensive in style that a single *surah* may contain the whole ocean of the Qur'ān, in which the universe is contained. One verse may comprehend that *surah*'s treasury. It is as if most verses are really small *surah* and most *surah* are little Qur'ān's. This miraculous conciseness is a great gift of ease from God, for although everyone always needs the Qur'ān, not all people read the whole of it. So that they are not deprived of its blessings, each *surah* may be read as the whole Qur'ān and each long verse for a short *surah*. Moreover, people of spiritual discovery and scholars all agree that the whole Qur'ān is contained in *surah* al-Fatiha, which is itself contained in the *basmala* (In the Name of God, the All-Merciful, the All-Compassionate).

As we mentioned earlier, the Qur'ān and its verses were revealed at different times, on different occasions and in different places, but there are very strong interrelations among the verses as if they were all revealed in one place, on one occasion and at one time. The whole Qur'ān is in '*basmala*' as a seed, this seed sprouts into *surah* Fatiha, grows and has branches in *surah* Baqara and it gives fruits in the whole Qur'ān. The relationship between a seed and a fruit is in between the verses of the Qur'ān. It is impossible to show every single relationship between the verses here, but the following example demonstrates the thematic unity in the Qur'ān.

There is strong interrelationship between '*basmala*' and *surah* Fatiha; it seems that '*basmala*' is like one of its verses. Many scholars accepted '*basmala*' as the first verse of Fatiha. '*Basmala*' starts with the Name of God who is eternal; there was nothing with Him while He is. He created everything based on His knowledge. In the beginning, God created the universe with his 'Rahman' (The Most Merciful) name from His own divine will. After that he gave us free will, reason, the five senses and many more abilities with his 'Rahim' (The Most Compassionate) name. With these God-given abilities we are able to understand the meaning of the universe.

Surah Fatiha is like a thank-you message to the mercy in '*basmala*', because nothing is excluded from this mercy and it attracts everything to itself. That is why we start to read the Qur'ān by reciting '*Basmala*'. In order to thank God for His Mercy, Fatiha begins with praising God. 'O God, thank You, You bestowed on us many favours, we cannot count them, You are so merciful, all praise is Your right and our duty'.

Having been given free will and the other abilities humankind became responsible on the earth but, not knowing the right path, in need of divine guidance. God guides the ones who use their free will to find Him. First, God bestows on us existence, second He creates us as human beings and then He guides us to Islam and honours us as being the follower of Muhammad (pbuh). The chapter Fatiha reminds us of all these facts with its beautiful expressions.

The Qur'ān contains three main ideas: belief, worship and life. Belief consists of all things which are mandatory to believe in, worship includes all the deeds and practises which are performed for God, and life pertains to applying the rules outlined in the Qur'ān regarding individuals, family, society and the government. The whole Qur'ān deals with these three essential principles and similarly every *surah* of the Qur'ān also mentions these principles.

Now we can study Fatiha from this perspective:

> All praise and gratitude (whoever gives them to whomever for whatever reason and in whatever way from the first day of creation until eternity) are for God, the Lord of the worlds, The All-Merciful, the All-Compassionate, The Master of the Day of Judgment

In these verses belief is explained; they introduce God as the one who deserves all the praise, this is the essence of oneness of God, He administers all the events in the universe, nothing happens without His permission, He creates, sustains and controls everything. The expression 'The Master of the Day of Judgment' includes resurrection after death, accounting in the Judgment field, the divine scale (Mizan), Paradise, Hell, rewards and punishments. God is the Owner and Master of this day. All of the principles of belief are explained by these three short verses.

> Only You, we worship

This explains the other essential principle which is 'worship'. All kinds of worship are included in this statement; physical or financial, daily prayers, *zakat*, fasting, *Hajj* and struggling in the way of God.

> Only from You, we ask for help

This emphasizes that the most important source for the servant is God and it takes the servant to the higher levels of worship. To worship God alone is our duty and His right, so we just worship God alone and never associate partners with him in any kind of worship.

> Guide us to the Straight Path, The Path of those whom You have favoured, not of those who have incurred (Your) wrath (punishment and condemnation), nor of those who are astray

This verse is related to the 'life' principle. Fatiha's orbit is the straight path and the whole *surah* turns around this. In this path there is no room for any kind of extremism, this path is the balanced way and the most proper way for human beings. On this path the desires and spirituality are well-balanced and the reason and heart are in the same line. The summary of Fatiha based on the three essential principles is as follows; 'O God, guide us to the straight path in belief, in worship and in our lives'.

The themes of the Qur'ān are all mentioned in *surah* Fatiha as a foundation for life. It is impossible to find the truth in thought, in worship, in belief and in daily life without these principles.

4.7 The Predictions of the Qur'ān

4.7.1 The Predictions about the Past

The Qur'ān gives news of the past. Although communicated by an unlettered one, the Qur'ān mentions in a solemn and powerful manner the important experiences of Prophets from the time of Adam to the Islamic period, as well as the main aspects of their mission. The information it provides usually coincides with the commonly agreed descriptions of the previous scriptures. It also corrects the points on which their corrupted forms disagree. Thus, the Qur'ān has an all-seeing vision that knows the past better than the previous scriptures.

The Qur'ān speaks of past events as if seeing them. It extracts the kernel of a long series of events and presents its argument through that kernel. The extracts, summaries, and indications found in the Qur'ān demonstrate the eternal vision of God.

The Qur'ān mentions the stories of many Prophets and previous nations. The Prophet (pbuh) had no recourse to such information. He had lived amongst the Quraysh for forty years, and during this time had never studied under any priest or monk, nor had he read any history. Yet, despite his illiteracy, all of a sudden, he started to inform his people about the histories of previous nations.

4.7.2 The Predictions about the Future

For scholars of the inner aspects and innermost meanings of the Qur'ān and creation, the Qur'ān is full of predictions. The following section concentrates on one of these and gives some examples.

The Qur'ān says to the Prophet (pbuh):

> So be patient: Surely God's promise is true. (30:60)
>
> You will enter the Sacred Mosque, if God wills, in full security, with your heads shaved, your hair cut short, and without fearing (48:27)
>
> It is He who has sent His Messenger with the guidance and the Religion of truth, that He may uplift it above every religion. (48: 28)

These and other similar verses predicted and promised that the Prophet (pbuh) and his Companions would be victorious in the near future, despite the pressure they were under from the Quraysh. A short while later, the Prophet (pbuh) conquered Mecca and defeated his enemies. This is one of the proofs of the divine authorship of the Qur'ān.

> The Byzantine Romans have been defeated in the nearer part of the land; and, after their defeat, they will be the victors in a few years. To God belongs the Command. (30:3-4)

Before the advent of Islam, the Persians had attacked the Romans and conquered a part of Syria which had been under Roman control. A few years before the *Hijra* of the Prophet (pbuh), the Romans retaliated and tried to regain their lost territory. The Muslims in Mecca were hoping that the Romans would win, as they were Christians (and thus closer in faith to them), while the disbelievers of Mecca were hoping that the Persians would win, since they were fire-worshippers. The Persians won this battle which was a cause of great celebration for the disbelievers of Mecca. Exactly seven years after the revelation of these verses, the Romans attacked the Persians again; this time they were victorious and managed to regain their territory. The battle occurred on the same day as the Battle of Badr when the Muslims were themselves rejoicing because of their victory over the Quraysh. Thus, this verse predicted two events: the victory of the Romans, and the victory of the Muslims.

> If you are in doubt about (the Divine authorship of) what We have been sending down on Our servant (Muhammad), then produce just a surah like it... If you fail to do that—and you will most certainly fail... (2:23-24)

> We will show them Our signs in the outer world and in themselves, until it is clear to them that it is the truth. (41:53)

> Say: 'If humanity and jinn banded together to produce the like of this Qur'ān, they would never produce its like, even though they backed one another'. (17:88)

> God will bring a people He loves and who love Him, humble toward believers, mighty and dignified against unbelievers, (people) who strive in God's cause, and fearing not the reproach of any reproacher. (5:54)

> God has promised those of you who believe and do righteous deeds that He will make them successors in the land, even as He made those (of the same qualities) who were before them successors, and that He will establish their religion for them, that He has approved of for them, and He will replace their present state of fear with security. (24:55)

All the predictions in the above verses came true. Despite being subjected to strong criticism and persecution, the Prophet (pbuh) confidently communicated these verses, showing that the information he was conveying was received from God, not his own fabrication.

4.7.3 The Predictions about the Unseen Truths

The Qur'ān's explanations of divine truths and the information it contains about the creation, which shed light on many aspects of the universe, are among the most important pieces of information about the unknown.

The Qur'ān gives information about the events, conditions and stages of the afterlife which would otherwise be unknown. No one is able to learn this information by themselves, but it can be understood through the Qur'ān.

Summary of the Predictions of the Qur'ān:

1. The Qur'ān gives detailed information of the experiences of Prophets and nations from the beginning of creation until the Islamic period.
2. The information it provides usually coincides with the commonly agreed descriptions of the previous scriptures. It also corrects the points on which their corrupted forms disagree.
3. The Qur'ān speaks of past events as if seeing them. The extracts, summaries, and indications found in the Qur'ān demonstrate the eternal vision of God.
4. The Prophet (pbuh) was illiterate and had received no formal education, yet all of a sudden he started to inform his people of the histories of the previous nations.
5. Scholars of the inner aspects and innermost meanings of the Qur'ān and creation have seen that the Qur'ān is full of predictions, many of which have already come true.
6. The Qur'ān gives information about the events, conditions and stages of the afterlife which would otherwise be unknown.

Chapter Five

History of the Interpretation and Interpreters of the Qur'ān

History of the Interpretation and Interpreters of the Qur'ān

5.1 The History and Development of Exegeses of the Qur'ān *(Tafsīr)*

5.1.1 The Need for *Tafsīr*

The Qur'ān is the primary source of Islam and it is essential to Muslims that they understand it to enable them to practise the religion in the correct way. To enable the Qur'ān to be understood and its teachings implemented in the best way, it must be explained and interpreted according to the conditions and the needs of the time. Many of the verses and expressions in the Qur'ān cannot be understood by the layman without an explanation by an expert.

The Qur'ān provides guidance for humankind to save them in this life and the afterlife. It is important for explanations to be provided so that all liable people can understand its contents which were revealed in a specific literary style and contain many scientific facts and general principles. The Qur'ān doesn't contain the solutions for every single problem that all Muslims will meet until end of time, but it does contain main rules, general principals and basic criteria which can be used as a base for the solutions of all kinds of problems. Based on these, expert interpreters can enlighten the way for Muslims.

The Qur'ān contains much more than scientific findings and principles. If it contained just these there would be no need for a divine religion, because humankind could learn these facts through scientific studies. The Qur'ān is much deeper and must be understood through expert interpretation as it gives guidance on all moral and spiritual issues, removing the bad habits of humans and leading them to a purposeful and moral life. The first addressees of the Qur'ān, the Arabs, had no other book to refer to. They were attracted by the rules, the stories and the unique style of the Qur'ān and, for them, the most important aim was to read and understand it. They worked tirelessly at understanding and incorporating its guidance into their individual, family, social and governmental life. They believed fully in its teachings and practised them properly. When confronted with problems, the early Muslims always turned to the Qur'ān first for the solution and it was this perspective that enabled them to comprehend it very well.

Some of the verses of the Qur'ān are *muhkam* (clear, understandable), but some are *mutashābih* (unclear, ambiguous). In the time of the Prophet (pbuh), the Muslims believed these verses literally and didn't struggle to comprehend their meanings. The Qur'ān mentions those people who try to comprehend them in improper ways as those who have sickness in their heart.[346] The Prophet (pbuh) also warned the Muslims about following these types of people.[347] The first four caliphs were also very strict in this matter, because the people who were struggling in their interpretation of these verses aimed to cause doubt in the minds of the Muslims through their works.

The verses about the rulings of things as *halal* (permissible) or *ḫaram* (forbidden), the *ṣalah, Hajj, zakat,* and fasting, etc. are *muhkam* verses. In other words, the verses are clear, have one meaning and don't need any other explanation. *Muhkam* verses are understood from the literal meanings of the words. On the other hand, *mutashābih* verses have many possible meanings and need extra evidence to choose one of the meanings over the others. The scholars of *tafsīr* categorized the *mutashābih* verses into two; the first group can be understood by comparing them to the *muhkam* verses, however, the second group cannot be fully understood.[348] Some verses are *mutashābih* only because of the meaning but some are *mutashābih* because of both the meaning and the wording. For example, the conjecture letters (*huruf al-muqatta'*) at the beginning of some *surah* signify the *mutashābih* verses.

The literal meaning of *mutashābih* verses is known but it is difficult to comprehend the deeper meaning of these verses. Therefore, the early scholars didn't interpret them and they referred their knowledge to God. Later scholars attempted to study and understand those verses because of their belief that the human intellect cannot be limited. Indeed, there was a great need to interpret those verses accurately to prevent inaccurate interpretations of them and to protect the Muslims from the consequences of those. The benefit of struggling to understand the meanings of the *mutashābih* verses is twofold; first it helps to train the human intellect which works hard to comprehend the real meaning of the

---

[346] Qur'ān, 3: 7.

[347] Bukhari, *Saḫīḫ*, 6/42, Tirmidhi, *Sunan*, 11/115-116.

[348] Ibn Manzūr, *Lisan al-'Arab*, 9/32-40.

verses, (Islam encourages the freedom of thought in this sense), and secondly, the works in this area helped to strengthen the foundations of Islam. These verses were not explained in the time of the Prophet (pbuh) because they have many possible meanings. Explaining the multiple meanings could have caused confusion and doubt in the minds of the early Muslims who were uneducated people. Later, as the intellectual capacity of the Muslims increased, this fear was removed and scholars tried to understand these verses. To enable this they needed to study and learn the different disciplines of the Qur'anic sciences.

When certain deviated groups used some Qur'anic verses as a base for their views, it forced early scholars to make a true *tafsīr* of these verses. The unbelievers, or deviated sects, created some confusing questions to corrupt the Muslim mind, but the scholars answered all their questions by interpreting these verses according to the fundamental beliefs of Islam and the authentic Sunnah. The Qur'ān warns people against making improper interpretations of these verses, but it doesn't prohibit the Muslims from making proper explanations. Indeed, the interpretations of those verses that are based on good intentions, the basic principles of Islam, the authentic Sunnah and logic, are necessary and accepted. Later generations of Muslims lacked the strong faith of the Companions which made the logical interpretation of those verses necessary to remove any doubts about the Qur'ān. Therefore, the Muslims needed the *tafsīr* of the Qur'ān.

The Qur'ān is the book of religion and it contains many words which are used in different concepts. The Arabs knew the literal meanings of the words but there was a need to explain their terminological meanings. For example, the Qur'ān uses the word '*ṣalah*' which literally means praying and supplication, but in Qur'anic terminology it refers to the prescribed daily prayers; '*zakat*' means blessings and cleansing but in terminology it means the obligatory charity upon rich people; *Hajj* means purpose or intention, but in terminology it is visiting the house of God, the Ka'ba, in Mecca.

There are some words in the Qur'ān which have multiple meanings and also multiple words that have the same meaning (*al-Wujūh wan-Nazāir*) and it was necessary to explain these to avoid them seeming contradictory and to save the Muslims from doubt. The Qur'ān declares that it contains no contradictions:

> Do they not contemplate the Qur'ān (so that they may be convinced that it is from God)? Had it been from any other than God, they would surely have found in it much (incoherence or) inconsistency.[349]

[349] Qur'ān, 4: 82.

Muslims scholars felt themselves obliged to explain those verses which seem to contradict to each other. For example, Ibn Qutayba (d. 889 C.E.) defended the Qur'ān against people who claimed that it contains contradictions.

Moreover, the metaphoric expressions, allegoric explanations, the unseen objects, the stories, the ambiguous verses, etc. all require expert interpretation. After the time of the Prophet (pbuh) the Islamic world saw rapid expansion of its borders and Muslims met with many new issues and problems which needed to be resolved. In order to solve those problems and make new laws to address them it was necessary to interpret the Qur'ān as this is the primary source for Islamic law. The Qur'ān doesn't contain the rulings for every case for all time, but it does contain the main principles and criteria which can form the basis of new legal opinions (*ijtihad*). So, an interpretation of the Qur'ān is necessary for Muslim jurists to be able to make *ijtihād.*

Due to the revelation taking place over a long period of time, the subject matters in the Qur'ān are spread out across the book rather than organised into neat categories. A person with insufficient knowledge of the whole Qur'ān may reach wrong conclusions if referring to just one section. A proper interpretation of the Qur'ān avoids this issue by explaining the subjects in an orderly way.

The Qur'ān was revealed to Prophet Muhammad (pbuh) and he was the best person to teach it to the Muslims. His explanations are the basis for all later interpretations of the Qur'ān. He was directly responsible for conveying God's message to humankind and explaining it to them. As a result, the first work of interpretation of the Qur'ān was started by the Prophet (pbuh). God says in the Qur'ān:

> O Messenger! Convey and make known in the clearest way all that has been sent down to you from your Lord. For, if you do not, you have not conveyed His Message and fulfilled the task of His Messengership. And God will certainly protect you from the people. God will surely not guide the disbelieving people (to attain their goal of harming or defeating you)[350]

This verse clearly indicates that conveying God's message to people and explaining it to them is the Prophet's (pbuh) essential mission and responsibility. As a Prophet of God it is obvious that Muhammad (pbuh) knew and understood the revelation better than anyone else; therefore, when we talk about the exegeses of the Qur'ān it is he who comes to mind first. For humankind, only the human Messenger must teach and explain the book of God. God says in the Qur'ān:

---

350 Qur'ān, 5: 67.

> (We sent them with) clear proofs of the truth and Scriptures. And on you We have sent down the Reminder (the Qur'ān) so that you may make clear to humankind whatever is sent down to them (through you of the truth concerning their present and next life), and that they may reflect.[351]

Ibn Taymiyya says based on this verse: 'it is obligatory upon the Prophet (pbuh) to inform his followers about the meanings of the Qur'ān and explain it to them'.[352] Tabarī says for this verse:

> It is understood from this verse that without the explanation of the Prophet (pbuh), it is impossible to know the interpretation of some verses like commanding verses which make law as *wajib*, *mandub* or guidance; the types of prohibitions; the rights; the penal law and the responsibilities of human kind towards each other. It is not true to speak about these matters without having explanations from the Prophet (pbuh) or the evidence which explains them.[353]

Summary of the Need for *Tafsīr*:

1. As the Qur'ān is the primary source of Islam it is essential that Muslims understand it to practise the religion correctly.
2. It must be explained and interpreted according to the conditions and the needs of the time.
3. The Qur'ān has to be explained by an expert.
4. Some of the verses of the Qur'ān are *muhkam* (clear, understandable), but some are *mutashābih* (unclear, ambiguous). The latter have many possible meanings and need extra evidence to choose one of the meanings over the others.
5. When certain deviated groups used some Qur'anic verses as a base for their views, it forced early scholars to make a true *tafsīr* of these verses.
6. Later generations of Muslims lacked the strong faith of the Companions which made the logical interpretation of the unclear verses necessary to remove any doubts about the Qur'ān. Therefore the Muslims needed the *tafsīr* of the Qur'ān.
7. Words and verses in the Qur'ān which have multiple meanings and also multiple words that have the same meaning (*al-Wujūh wan-Nazāir*) and

---

351 Qur'ān, 16: 44.
352 Suyūtī, *al-Itqān*, 2/208.
353 Tabarī, *Tafsīr*, the interpretation of the verse 16/44.

also verses that seem contradictory had to be explained to avoid confusion and doubt.

8. When the Muslim world expanded, it was necessary to explain the Qur'ān to new Muslims who faced different and new challenges.
9. The Qur'ān was revealed to Prophet Muhammad (pbuh) who was the first to teach it to the Muslims; his explanations are the basis for all later interpretations of the Qur'ān.

5.2 Conditions for the Interpretation of the Qur'ān

Before starting to interpret the Qur'ān, there are some conditions that need to be met by the interpreter (*mufassir*). Without these conditions being met, interpreting the Qur'ān was strongly prohibited by the Prophet (pbuh). The exegeses of the Qur'ān is a great responsibility, because when a man interprets the Qur'ān, his words and explanations are understood as the word of God; therefore people without the necessary qualifications cannot interpret the Qur'ān. The conditions for the interpretation of the Qur'ān can be studied under two categories; the first category is related to the religious aspect of the interpreter and his moral values; the second category is related to the interpreter's knowledge of the Qur'anic sciences.

5.2.1 Religious and Ethical Conditions for the Interpreter

The interpreter of the Qur'ān must have true Islamic belief and strong faith. He must adopt the morality of Qur'ān and follow the Sunnah of the Prophet (pbuh) strictly. If a person with false belief interprets the Qur'ān he explains his wrong belief by misinterpreting it. If a person who doesn't follow the Sunnah of the Prophet (pbuh) interprets the Qur'ān, his interpretation won't be trusted and will be deprived of blessings. If corrupt people interpret the Qur'ān it is not permissible for Muslims to read those books because they aim to destroy Islam by their false interpretation.

The person who wants to interpret the Qur'ān must be sincere in his intention and do it for the sake of God alone, not for any other purpose. In other words, he must interpret the Qur'ān in proper ways with the intention to achieve God's pleasure, to serve the Qur'ān and Muslims. It is not permissible to interpret the Qur'ān with the intention to achieve worldly gains. Many people of innovation and deviated sects have interpreted the Qur'ān to support their claims based on their false beliefs, personal whims and misguided purposes. Some of these interpreters posed as pious Muslim believers but aimed to cause harm to Islam by sowing the seeds of doubt in the minds of Muslims.

In conclusion, the interpreter must be pious (*taqwa*), be just (*adalah*) and have knowledge that is practised. He must abstain from major sins and devote himself to Islam and God in worship.

Summary of Religious and Ethical Conditions for the Interpreter:

1. He must have true Islamic belief and strong faith.
2. He must adopt the morality of the Qur'ān and follow the Sunnah of the Prophet (pbuh) strictly.
3. He must be sincere in his intention and do it for the sake of God alone.
4. The interpreter must be pious (*taqwa*), be just (*adalah*) and have knowledge that is practised. He must abstain from major sins and devote himself to Islam and God in worship.

5.2.2 The Required Sciences for the Interpretation of the Qur'ān

A person who wants to interpret the Qur'ān must have a detailed knowledge of the many areas listed below:

1. Arabic philology (grammar, lexicography, words and their meanings, rhetorical studies etc.).
2. Science of Eloquence (*Balāghah*) including *Mean*, *Bayan* and *Badi'*.
3. Science of Hadith and the methodology of Hadith.
4. *Fiqh* and *Usūl al-Fiqh*.
5. Sciences of the Qur'ān such as the occasions behind the revelation of the verses, the abrogating and abrogated verses, *muhkam* and *mutashābih* verses, etc.
6. Science of recitation of the Qur'ān (*Qiraat*).
7. Theology (*Kalām*).
8. For the modern interpretation of the Qur'ān, one also should have a good knowledge of sociology, physiology, astronomy, physics, chemistry, medicine, history, etc. These sciences are necessary for the trusted interpretation of Qur'ān. A person who does not have sufficient knowledge in these areas makes many mistakes in his interpretations.
9. They must have the ability for precise comprehension of the verses.

10. They must abstain from the use of mere whimsical opinion.
11. They must start this interpretation of the Qur'ān with the Qur'ān itself first.
12. They must seek guidance from the words and explanations of the Prophet (pbuh).
13. They should refer to the reports from the Companions.
14. They should consider the reports from the *tabi'un* (the generation following the Companions).
15. They should consult the opinions of other eminent scholars.

Besides having all these qualifications some scholars say that the exegeses of the Qur'ān cannot be carried by one interpreter alone. Said Nursi says, today the exegeses of the Qur'ān should be carried out by a group of scholars from different fields of sciences, because the Qur'ān contains all kinds of knowledge in different levels and one scholar cannot have sufficient knowledge of all these areas. Therefore, the exegeses of the Qur'ān must be written by a group of scholars together.

5.3 *Tafsīr* of the Qur'ān by the Qur'ān

The first and primary source for the interpretation of the Qur'ān is the Qur'ān itself. Some facts in the Qur'ān are briefly mentioned in some verses but explained in detail in other verses. There are some verses which are explained by other verses, completing the meaning. Many of the questions which may arise out of a certain passage of the Qur'ān have their explanation in other parts of the very same book, and often there is no need to turn to any sources other than the word of God which, in itself, contains *tafsīr*. Reading the Qur'an in the light of the Qur'an is the first and foremost duty of the *mufassir*. It is only if this does not suffice that he will refer to other sources of *tafsīr*.[354]

The examples for the *tafsīr* of the Qur'ān by the Qur'ān:

> We sent it down on a night full of blessings; surely We have ever been warning (humankind since their creation)[355]

It is unclear which night is this blessed night in which the Qur'ān was sent down but the following verse clarifies this:

---

[354] Suyūtī, *al-Itqān*, 2/181-182.

[355] Qur'ān, 44: 3.

> We have surely sent it (the Qur'ān) down in the Night of Destiny and Power.[356]

Another example:

> Adam received from his Lord words that he perceived to be inspired in him. In return, He accepted his repentance. He is the One Who accepts repentance and returns it with liberal forgiveness and additional reward, the All-Compassionate[357]

In this verse, it is not clear which words Adam received from his Lord, but the Qur'ān explains these words in different verse:

> They said (straightaway): 'Our Lord! We have wronged ourselves, and if You do not forgive us and do not have mercy on us, we will surely be among those who have lost!'[358]

5.4 The *Tafsīr* of the Prophet (pbuh)

God sent the Prophet Muhammad (pbuh) to deliver and explain the Qur'ān to all people. As he was the one who received the revelation, the Prophet (pbuh) was the best person to explain it. His explanations are the primary source in the science of Qur'anic exegeses. His methodology was teaching ten verses at a time to his Companions.[359]

The Sunnah of the Prophet (pbuh) employed two methods for explaining the content of the Qur'ān. The first was the Prophet (pbuh) giving explanations of the brief expressions in the Qur'ān, (*bayān mujmal*), for example; he explained the times of the obligatory prayers (*ṣalah*), the amount of *zakat*, the *Hajj* rituals, etc. The second method was through making new laws which were not mentioned in the Qur'ān. There are many verses proving the Prophet (pbuh) was permitted to make laws himself which are not included in the Qur'ān, some of which are detailed below:

> He who obeys the Messenger (thereby) obeys God, and he who turns away from him (and his way), (do not be grieved, O Messenger, for) We have not sent you as a keeper and watcher over them (to prevent their misdeeds and be accountable for them)[360]

---

356 Qur'ān, 97: 1.
357 Qur'ān, 2: 37.
358 Qur'ān, 7: 23.
359 Suat Yildirim, *Peygamberimizin Kur'ani Tefsiri*, 33-34.
360 Qur'ān, 4: 80.

> Whatever the Messenger gives you accept it willingly, and whatever he forbids you, refrain from it. Keep from disobedience to God in reverence for Him and piety. Surely God is severe in retribution[361]

> When God and His Messenger have decreed a matter, it is not for a believing man and a believing woman to have an option insofar as they themselves are concerned. Whoever disobeys God and His Messenger has evidently gone astray[362]

When the Prophet (pbuh) made a new law it was obligatory upon Muslims to observe it. The Prophet (pbuh) made some things obligatory for Muslims and other things forbidden for them. For example, in the Qur'ān God forbids men to marry with two sisters[363] at the same time; the Prophet (pbuh) extended this prohibition so that a man cannot marry a woman and her maternal aunt or paternal aunt together at the same time.[364] God mentions in the Qur'ān:

> Forbidden to you (O believing men) are your mothers (including stepmothers and grandmothers) and daughters (including granddaughters), your sisters (including full sisters and half-sisters), your aunts paternal and maternal, your brothers' daughters, your sisters' daughters, your mothers who have given suck to you, your milk-sisters...[365]

The Prophet's (pbuh) Sunnah extended the prohibition because of the linkage of breast milk between the people including paternal and maternal aunts, the daughter of one's brother (milk brother) and the daughter of one's sister (milk sister).[366]

The Qur'ān made general rules and the Sunnah made more detailed explanations for those general rules. Since the beginning of Islam the Prophet's (pbuh) Sunnah has always been the second source of information after the Qur'ān. The Hadith books contain a section called '*kitāb at-tafsīr*' (the book of exegeses) which is the *tafsīr* of the Prophet (pbuh). The Prophet (pbuh) made exegeses in response to the questions from his Companions. The Companions did not ask many questions so the amount of *tafsīr* from the Prophet (pbuh) is

---

361 Qur'ān, 59: 7.

362 Qur'ān, 33: 36.

363 Qur'ān, 4: 23.

364 Bukhari, *Saḫīḫ,Nikāḫ*, 27, Muslim, *Saḫīḫ,Nikāḫ*, 37.

365 Qur'ān, 4: 23.

366 Bukhari, *Saḫīḫ*, *Shahada*, 7, *Nikāḫ*, 20; Muslim, *Saḫīḫ*, *Rada*, 1,2,9.

quite small but there are some *tafsīr* examples from the Prophet (pbuh) in the most authentic Hadith books.[367]

Summary of The *Tafsīr* the Prophet (pbuh):

1. God sent Prophet Muhammad (pbuh) to deliver and explain the Qur'ān.
2. The Prophet (pbuh) was the best person to explain the revelation.
3. The Prophet (pbuh) used to teach ten verses at a time to his Companions.
4. He employed two methods for explaining the content of the Qur'ān: a) giving explanations of the brief expressions in the Qur'ān, (*bayān mujmal*); b) making new laws which were not mentioned in the Qur'ān.
5. The Qur'ān made general rules and the Sunnah made more detailed explanations for those general rules.
6. The Prophet (pbuh) made exegeses in response to the questions from his Companions.

5.5. The Types of *Tafsīr* of the Prophet (pbuh) and Examples

5.5.1 His *Tafsīr* by the Qur'ān

The best and the most reliable of *tafsīr* is the *tafsīr* of the Qur'ān by the Qur'ān itself. In some verses the Qur'ān mentions some rules in a general way and then restricts them in other verses; in other areas it mentions rules briefly and then explains them in more detail in later verses. There are many examples of this in the Qur'ān. The Prophet (pbuh) explained some verses of the Qur'ān by reciting other verses. For example:

> Those who have believed and not obscured their belief with any wrongdoing, they are the ones for whom there is true security, and they are rightly guided[368]

When this verse was revealed the Companions struggled to understand it and said to the Prophet (pbuh): 'is there any of us who did not wrong to himself'. Thereupon the Prophet (pbuh) explained the wrong doing (*zulm*) which is mentioned in the verse by explaining that this was a different type of wrong doing than what they understood; this is as Luqman preached to his son:

---

367 Ismail Cerrahoglu, *Tefsir Tarihi*, 1/41-47.
368 Qur'ān, 6: 82.

> When Luqman said to his son by way of advice and instruction: 'My dear son! Do not associate partners with God. Surely associating partners with God is indeed a tremendous wrong'.[369]

The Prophet (pbuh) used a different verse of the Qur'ān to explain the type of wrong doing alluded to in the verse which had caused misunderstanding, thus clarifying the meaning for the Companions.[370]

5.5.2 His *Tafsīr* by Explaining What Is Mentioned Briefly in the Qur'ān

In the following verse, God introduces a general rule:

> For the thief, male or female: cut off their hands as a recompense for what they have earned, and an exemplary deterrent punishment from God. God is All-Glorious with irresistible might, All-Wise[371]

The Prophet (pbuh) restricted this general rule by setting a limit on it. He explained: 'If one steals a quarter dinar or more, the punishment is applied for him (not for the one who steals less than a quarter dinar)'.[372]

There are many examples of the Prophet's (pbuh) *tafsīr* on the subject of *ibadat* (worship) which can be found in the *fiqh* books.

5.5.3 His *Tafsīr* by Strengthening the Meaning of the Verse

Some of the *tafsīr* of the Prophet (pbuh) was to strengthen and enforce the meaning of the revealed verses. The meaning was already stated in the verse and the Prophet's (pbuh) *tafsīr* supported it. For example:

> O you who believe! Intoxicants, games of chance, sacrifices to (anything serving the function of) idols (and at places consecrated for offerings to other than God), and (the pagan practice of) divination by arrows (and similar practices) are a loathsome evil of Satan's doing; so turn wholly away from it so that you may prosper (in both worlds)[373]

---

369 Qur'ān, 31: 13.
370 Bukhari, *Saḫīḫ, Tafsir*, 20.
371 Qur'ān, 5: 38.
372 Abu Dāwud, *Sunan, Hudud*, 11.
373 Qur'ān, 5: 90.

When this verse was revealed the Prophet (pbuh) supported the ruling of the verse by saying 'alcohol is prohibited'.[374]

5.5.4 His *Tafsīr* by Explaining the Contradicting Expressions (*tawdih al-mushkil*)

If two verses in the Qur'ān appear to contradict each other they are known as '*mushkil*'. However, there are some verses that when read superficially, appear to contradict each other. To avoid confusion about these verses, they were explained by the Prophet (pbuh), the Companions and later scholars. For example, the Muslims felt a great burden upon them when the following verse was revealed to the Prophet (pbuh):

> Those who hoard up gold and silver and do not spend it in God's cause (to exalt His cause and help the poor and needy): give them (O Messenger) the glad tidings of a painful punishment[375]

The Muslims understood this verse to prohibit inheritance:

> 'Umar came to the Prophet (pbuh) and asked him to explain this verse. The Prophet (pbuh) explained the verse by his following statement; 'God made *zakat* obligatory upon you on your extra wealth to clean it, but He prescribed to you the inheritance on your wealth when you die'.[376]

He explained that, making money through *ḫalal* (lawful) means and saving it is not *ḫaram* (unlawful). The threat in the verse is for those who store their wealth but do not give its due *zakat*.

5.5.5 His *Tafsīr* by Explaining the Ambiguous Expressions

Some expressions in the Qur'ān are ambiguous. Based on wisdom these are left as they can only be explained through revelation either by the Qur'ān itself or by the Sunnah. For example:

> Be ever mindful and protective of the prescribed Prayers, and the middle Prayer, and stand in the presence of God in utmost devotion and obedience[377]

---

[374] Suyūtī, *al-Durr al-Mansur*, 11/314.
[375] Qur'ān, 9/34.
[376] Hakim, *Mustadrak*, 11/333.
[377] Qur'ān, 2: 238.

In this verse 'the middle prayer' is unclear and ambiguous. The Prophet (pbuh) explained it as the *'Asr* prayer.[378]

5.5.6 His *Tafsīr* by Explaining the Abrogated Verses (*Bayān al-naskh*)

Naskh means the abrogation of one verse's ruling by another verse. There are no Hadith which inform us about the abrogation of a verse's rule. The rulings in the Qur'ān can only be abrogated by the Qur'ān itself and the Sunnah explains this abrogation. For example, in the following verse God forbids fighting during the holy months:

> They ask you about the Sacred Month and fighting in it. Say: 'Fighting in it is a grave sin...'[379]

This verse is later abrogated by the following verse:

> Nevertheless, fight all together against those who associate partners with God just as they fight against you all together; and know well that God is with the God-revering, pious who keep their duties to Him.[380]

It is only possible to understand that this verse abrogated the ruling of the previous verse by looking at the practise of the Prophet (pbuh). In the sacred months of Shawwal and Dhul Qa'da he fought against the Hawāzin in Hunayn and against the tribe of Thaqīf in Taif. If the verse had not abrogated the original ruling, the Prophet (pbuh) would not have fought during these months, nor would he have allowed his Companions to fight.[381] It is the Sunnah that indicates that the ruling in the first verse was abrogated by the second verse.

5.5.7 His *Tafsīr* by His Practises

The Prophet's (pbuh) behaviour was an explanation of the rules commanded in the verses. He practised the rules himself first and indicated their purpose through his actions. Salman reported:

> Once a man came to the Prophet (pbuh) and greeted him by saying 'al-salam alayk' (peace be upon you). The Prophet (pbuh) returned his greeting by saying 'wa alayk wa rahmat Allah' (peace and God's mercy upon

---

[378] Tirmidhi, *Sunan,Tafsir al-Qur'ān*, 3.
[379] Qur'ān, 2: 217.
[380] Qur'ān, 9: 36.
[381] Tabarī, *Jami' al-Bayan*, the interpretation of 2: 217.

> you). Than another man came and greeted the Prophet (pbuh) by saying 'as-salam alayk wa rahmatullah' (peace and God's mercy upon you), the Prophet (pbuh) returned his greetings by saying *wa alayk wa barakat Allah* (peace, God's mercy and His blessings upon you). After that, a third man came and greeted the Prophet (pbuh) by saying 'as-salam alayk wa rahmatullah wa barakatuhu' (peace, God's mercy and His blessings upon you), the Prophet (pbuh) replied him with same expressions. The third man asked, 'O Messenger of God, may my mother and father be ransom to you, you replied to the two persons before me with extra words from their greetings, but you replied my greeting with same words?' thereupon the Prophet (pbuh) answered; 'you didn't leave us any extra word (you said all the good words for the greeting and I returned with same words), God says in the Qur'ān; 'When (whether traveling or at home, or in war or at peace) you are greeted with a greeting (of peace and goodwill), answer with one better, or (at least) with the same. Surely God keeps account of all things'[382] I returned your greeting with same expressions.'[383]

The Prophet (pbuh) explained the ruling of the previous verse through his practise.

5.5.8 His *Tafsīr* by Philological Explanations

When the Prophet (pbuh) was questioned about the meaning of some words in the verses he tried to answer in the shortest way without giving too much detail for the benefit of the questioner. For this reason, sometimes he just told the synonyms of the word or just explained the purpose of the word. Only if it was necessary would he explain in detail. For example:

> Those who return in repentance to God, and those who worship God, and those who praise God, and those who are '*saihun*' ....

When asked the meaning of the word '*saihun*' by his Companions the Prophet (pbuh) explained it as 'people who fast'.[384]

5.5.9 His *Tafsīr* by His Descriptions

One of the types of *tafsīr* of the Prophet (pbuh) was to give detailed explanations of the subjects in the verses. This helped to strengthen the faith of the Muslims by deepening their understanding. The intention of his explanations included: encour-

---

[382] Qur'ān, 4: 86.

[383] Tabarī, *Jami' al-Bayan*, the interpretation of 4: 86.

[384] Hakim, *Mustadrak*, 11/335.

agement, warning (*targhib-tarhib*), explaining a religious concept and giving information about past people or places as good or bad examples. For example:

> Thus, whomever God wills to guide, He expands his breast to Islam[385]

The Prophet (pbuh) described this verse as: 'When the light of faith enters to the heart of a person, his breast expands and opens'. The Companions asked him, 'What is the sign of this expansion; is there apparent sign for this?' The Prophet (pbuh) replied, 'Facing towards the eternal life whole heartedly and denouncing and escaping from the deceiving world and preparing for death before it comes'.[386]

5.5.10 His *Tafsīr* by Parables

Parables occur frequently in the Qur'ān. They are used to explain situations in a way that is easy to understand. They are used to remind, encourage, deter, teach, strengthen, to explain obscure meanings, and so on. In the Qur'ān, God used many parables to convey His message and the Prophet (pbuh) also made use of them. Jabir reported:

> One day the Prophet (pbuh) came and told us, 'I saw the angel Gabriel in my dream. He was at the side of my head and the angel Michael was at the side of my feet. One was telling the other, 'Give a parable about this man (the Prophet)', thereupon the other angel said, 'May your ears hear better and your heart comprehend well, the case of you and the case of your *umma* (the followers of the Prophet) is like this parable: A king possessed a property and constructed a house there. Afterwards, he organised a feast there. He sent a Messenger to invite people to his feast. Some of the people accepted the invitation and came to the feast; others rejected it. The king is God, the property is Islam, the house is Paradise and O Muhammad is the Messenger. Whoever gives ear to him enters Islam; whoever enters Islam, enters Paradise and benefits from the favours there'.[387]

This parable explains the following verse:

> God invites to the Abode of Peace (where they will enjoy perfect bliss, peace, and safety,) and He guides whomever He wills to a Straight Path. For those who do good, aware that God is seeing them is the best (of the rewards that God has promised for good deeds), and still more. Neither

[385] Qur'ān, 6: 125.

[386] Ibn Kathīr, *Tafsir*, the interpretation of 6: 125.

[387] Tirmidhi, *Sunan, Amthal*, 1

stain nor ignominy will cover their faces. They are the companions of Paradise; they will abide therein.[388]

5.6 *Tafsīr* by the Companions

Whilst the Prophet (pbuh) was alive the Companions used him as a source of information and explanation for the parts of the Qur'ān they did not understand. After his death in 632 the Companions naturally became the authority on the Qur'ān. They had observed the events during the life of the Prophet (pbuh) and knew the occasions that had prompted the revelations; this, coupled with their firm faith, enabled them to understand the Qur'ān better than anyone else. They had learned the Qur'ān from the Prophet (pbuh) piece by piece, memorised the verses and implemented its commands into their daily life.

The Companions were made up of different people with different levels of education and knowledge; they were not all at the same level in their ability to understand the Qur'ān. The education, cultural background and time spent with the Prophet (pbuh) are all important criteria for their knowledge of Islam. The most knowledgeable of the Companions delved into *tafsīr* and gave explanations of the verses of the Qur'ān. The first four caliphs are usually esteemed in their *tafsīr* authority. This work requires the extensive knowledge of the Arabic language and of old Arab poetry whose unusual words may help us better understand some of the words used in the Qur'ān. Additionally, knowledge of the customs and life of the old Arabs is beneficial as is knowledge of the conditions of the 'people of the book' at that time. There were not many Companions who had all of these qualifications.

When the Companions wanted to interpret verses from the Qur'ān they were first checking the Qur'ān and then the Sunnah to see whether they had observed anything from the Prophet (pbuh) about those verses. If the Qur'ān explained the matter itself, they did not say anything about it. If neither the Qur'ān nor the Sunnah had any explanation, they were using their personal opinion to interpret the verses. They also looked to some other scriptures to interpret some of the verses (*israiliyyat*), but they compared this information with the Qur'ān and the Sunnah before using it in their interpretation. If the information from other scriptures didn't contradict the Qur'ān and Sunnah, the Companions used it in their *tafsīr*, if it did, they omitted this information. The majority of the *tafsīr* of the Companions was explaining the occasions behind the revelation of the verses. If

[388] Qur'ān, 10: 25-26.

they interpreted the verses based on their opinions, it was mostly from the linguistic and religious perspective. They used different methods to explain ambiguous or seemingly contradicting verses. When forming their opinion they utilised their knowledge of Arabic grammar and Arab poetry.

The following is a good illustration of the *tafsīr* of the Companions:

> Spend in God's cause (out of whatever you have) and do not ruin yourselves by your own hands.[389]

Abū Ayyub al-Ansari explained the meaning of this verse as: 'if you do not spend your wealth in the way of God, you will contribute to your own destruction with your own hands.'

The Companions did not produce a comprehensive *tafsīr* of the whole Qur'ān; this was not necessary for them as they had lived together with the Prophet (pbuh) and already had a good knowledge of most of it. They only needed to interpret areas that were difficult for them. The work of *tafsīr* was expanded by later generations long after the time of the Prophet (pbuh) when the expressions in the Qur'ān became difficult to understand without explanations for the ordinary Muslims.

The *tafsīr* of the Companions is accepted as the first step in the development of *tafsīr* science. The Companions at the time of the Prophet (pbuh) had a very strong and sincere belief and they accepted matters without questioning them. Therefore, in their *tafsīr* there are no theological debates or conflict of ideas as they were very close to each other in thought and faith. There is also no interpretation of *fiqh* in their *tafsīr* as they learned the application of those verses directly from the Prophet (pbuh).[390]

The *tafsīr* of the Companions are important in understanding the Qur'ān, no one can ignore this fact. After the Prophet (pbuh) they are the ones who knew the Qur'ān the best and their interpretation counts above any personal opinion. If there is an authentic narration from the Companions about the *tafsīr* of one verse, it is not right to ignore that narration and choose personal opinion for the interpretation of the verse. Even if the Companions are talking about the occasions behind the revelation of the verses without stating that they learned the information from the Prophet (pbuh), their words are accepted as the word of the Prophet (pbuh), because in these types of subjects they didn't make *ijtihad* (using

[389] Qur'ān, 2: 195.
[390] Dhahabi, *Tafsir*, 1/97-98.

personal opinion). As a result, on matters that are not open to interpretation, such as the occasions of revelation, the *tafsīr* and narrations of the Companions are binding.[391]

There have been different views as to how binding the *tafsīr* of the Companions are but the majority of scholars (including Abū Hanifa) agree that the *tafsīr* and narrations of the Companions are binding on matters that are not open to interpretation. Their *tafsīr* on the parts of the Qur'ān that are open to different interpretations is preferable but not binding.[392]

Companions who are famous for exegesis are: 'Ali ibn Abū Tālib (d. 661 C.E.), 'Abd Allah ibn 'Abbās (d. 687 C.E.), 'Abd Allah ibn Mas'ud (d. 654 C.E.), 'Ubayy b. Ka'b (d. 650 C.E.), Zayd b. Thabit (d. 665 C.E.), 'Abd Allah ibn Zubayr (d. 692 C.E.), Abū Musa al-Ash'arī (d. 664 C.E.).

SUMMARY OF *TAFSĪR* BY THE COMPANIONS:

1. Having been taught first hand by the Prophet (pbuh) the Companions became the authority on the Qur'ān after his death.
2. The most knowledgeable of the Companions delved into *tafsīr* and gave explanations of the verses of the Qur'ān.
3. When interpreting verses the Companions checked the Qur'ān and the Sunnah for explanations before using their personal opinion.
4. The majority of the *tafsīr* of the Companions was explaining the occasions behind the revelation of the verses.
5. When forming their opinion they utilised their knowledge of Arabic grammar and Arab poetry.
6. The *tafsīr* of the Companions is accepted as the first step in the development of *tafsīr* science.

5.7 *Tafsīr* by the *Tabi'in* (the Successors)

Islam expanded greatly during the time of the first four caliphs and with new territorial conquests Islam spread outside of the Arabian Peninsula. The rulers and the teachers among the Companions were sent to new lands to teach Islam. For example, Mu'adh b. Jabal was sent to Yemen during the time of the Prophet (pbuh); 'Abd Allah ibn Mas'ud was sent to Iraq in the time of 'Umar. The Companions initiated Islamic education in every land they went to. They established

[391] Dhahabi, ibid, 1/95.
[392] ibid, 1/128.

circles of education in all Islamic cities and taught the *tabi'in* whatever they had learned from the Prophet (pbuh) with regard to Islam and the Qur'ān.

With the rapid spread of Islam, the Islamic world faced new problems including corruption, turmoil and conflict. Different groups and sects emerged and each group tried to support their views using verses from the Qur'ān, sometimes misinterpreting the Qur'ān to justify their thoughts. In order to prevent conflicts and unite the Muslims, there was a great need to interpret the Qur'ān correctly. This attracted many people to the education circles of the Companions; people wanted to learn the truth of Islam and the accurate interpretation of the Qur'ān. Many non-Arabs ('*mawali*') attended and learned the knowledge of the Companions and they in particular became outstanding in the field of *tafsīr*. Nāfi', Ikrimah, Ata ibn Rabah, Said ibn Jubayr and Hasan Basrī are well-known *tabi'in* in the fields of jurisprudence and exegesis. As non-Arabs, these scholars brought a new perspective to the Islamic sciences and initiated the movements in Islamic Thought. As a result, some schools were established in the field of *tafsīr*. These schools were based in Mecca, Medina and Kūfa (Iraq).

5.7.1 The School of Mecca

The Meccan school was established by the profound scholar 'Abd Allah ibn 'Abbās (d. 687 C.E.) with large contributions by Āi'sha and other Companions in Mecca. 'Abd Allah ibn 'Abbās was named as the 'ocean of knowledge' and 'the translator of the Qur'ān'. Indeed ibn 'Abbās is the founder of *Tafsīr* as a science. Ibn Taymiyya said: 'The most famous scholars in the field of *Tafsīr* from amongst the *tabi'in* are the students who were educated in the school of Mecca, because 'Abd Allah ibn 'Abbās educated them'.[393] The most outstanding students of this school were Said ibn Jubayr (d. 714 C.E.), Mujahid ibn Jabr (d. 721 C.E.), Ikrimah (d. 723 C.E.), Ata ibn Abī Rabah (d. 732 C.E.) and Tāwus b. Kaysan (d. 724 C.E.).

5.7.2 The School of Medina

The school of Medina was particularly important as the city was still inhabited by Companions for a very long time after the death of the Prophet (pbuh). The Companions who stayed in Medina taught the Qur'ān and the Sunnah for the new Muslims there. This school was established by the profound scholar and Companion 'Ubayy ibn Ka'b (d. 650 C.E.). His famous students were Abū al-Aliya (d. 708 C.E.), Muhammad b. al-Qurazi (d. 736 C.E.) and Zayd b. Aslam (d. 753 C.E.).

---

[393] Ibn Taymiyya, *Muqaddima Fi Uṣūl at-Tafsir*, 78-79.

5.7.3 The School of Kūfa

One of the leading scholars in the fields of *Fiqh* and *Tafsīr* was the Companion 'Abd Allah ibn Mas'ud (d. 654 C.E.). He was one of the scribes of the Prophet (pbuh) and early Muslims. Having been with the Prophet (pbuh) for a very long time he had often witnessed the explanations of the verses directly from him. 'Umar knew his qualifications and profound knowledge and sent him to Kūfa to teach Islam. Ibn Mas'ud established his school on the rational principles in Kūfa. 'Abd Allah ibn Mas'ud is considered as the first seed for the development of the *ijtihad* movements and his school was named the 'Iraq Rational School'. Famous students emanating from this school were; Masruq b. al-Ajda' (d. 683 C.E.), Aswad b. Yazid (d. 694 C.E.), Murra b. al-Hamadani (d. 708 C.E.), Amir as-Sha'bi (d. 721 C.E.), Hasan Basrī (d. 728 C.E.), Qatāda b. Diama (d. 735 C.E.) and Ibrahim an-Nakhāī (d. 726 C.E.).[394]

These schools brought a new movement to the field of Islamic thought.[395] Since these schools were established by different Companions in different cities, there were differences between them, but also some similarities. For example, the schools of Mecca and Medina did not incorporate analogy and personal opinion in their instruction, but in the school of Kūfa they were very important and often applied for the solution of problems.

Characteristics of the *Tafsīr* of the *Tabi'in*:

1. Their exegesis was applied to the whole Qur'ān and in many cases words and expressions were explained in detail.
2. Legal rulings that emerged from the analysis of verses were also included together with historical information.
3. Arabic poetry was utilized to explain the meaning of words used in the Qur'ān. Poetry acted as a dictionary.
4. Jewish and Christian sources were used to explain and give detail of stories in the Qur'ān.
5. *Tafsīr* knowledge was passed on from master to student in the class setting. No *tafsīr* publication was produced.

With the previous information it is true to say that the history of *tafsīr* and the *mufassir* can be studied chronologically in five periods;

The first period is the Companions' *Tafsīr*. The most important *mufassir* among them are the four caliphs; most of the reports about the *tafsīr* of the Qur'ān

394 ibid.
395 Suyūtī, *al-Itqān*, 11, 242.

are coming from 'Ali ibn Tālib. Since Abū Bakr died soon after the Prophet (pbuh) there are not many reports from him regarding *tafsīr*. Suyūtī said there are not more than ten reports from Abū Bakr. Besides the four caliphs the following Companions are also well-known in the field of *Tafsīr*; 'Abd Allah ibn Mas'ud, 'Abd Allah ibn 'Abbās , 'Ubayy ibn Ka'b, Zayd b. Thabit, Abū Musa al-Ash'arī and Abd Allah ibn Zubayr.

The second period is the *tabi'in' Tafsīr*. According to Ibn Taymiyya, the most important *mufassir* among the *tabi'in* are from the school of Mecca, because they learned from 'Abd Allah ibn 'Abbās. Some of the *tabi'in mufassir* are Ata ibn Rabah, Mujahid, Ikrimah, Said ibn Jubayr and Tāwus b. Kaysan. Mujahid narrates fewer reports about *tafsīr*, but he is the most trusted one among them. All the scholars trusted and accepted his *tafsīr*.

The third period is the time when later scholars began to write *tafsīr* books. They report all the information regarding *tafsīr* from the Companions and *tabi'in* including the chain of transmission. The most well-known among them are; Sufyan ibn 'Uyayna, Waqi' ibn al-Jarrah, Shu'ba ibn al-Hajjaj, Yazid ibn Harun, Abd al-Razzaq, Isḫāq ibn Rahuwayh and Abū Bakr ibn Abī Shayba.

The period of time covering the first three centuries of Islam (632 – 900 C.E.) is also known as the 'formative' period (pre-Tabarī). There are some important names during this period including: Ali b. Abī Talha (d. 143 A.H. / 760 C.E.), Muqātil b. Sulayman (d. 150 A.H. / 767 C.E.), Sufyan al-Thawrī (d. 161 A.H. / 778 C.E.), Yahya b. Sallam (d. 200 A.H. / 816 C.E.), Abd al-Razzaq b. Hammam (d. 211 A.H. / 826 C.E.). There were also linguistics who wrote *tafsīr* works such as: Al-Farra (d. 207 A.H. / 822 C.E.) and his work "*Ma'āni al-Qur'ān*"; Abū Ubayda (d. 210 A.H. / 825 C.E.) and his work "*Majāz al-Qur'ān*".

The fourth period starts with Ibn Jarir at-Tabarī. Following the fourth period the field of *Tafsīr* was separated from Hadith and become a stand-alone science. From this time the *mufassir* interpreted the verses in chronological order. The first *mufassir* who wrote a *tafsīr* book covering all the verses of the Qur'ān was Tabarī and it was due to him that the science of *Tafsīr* became an individual science. Before Tabarī, *tafsīr* was the explanation of some words and the narration of some reports. Few *mufassir* were using their personal opinion to interpret the verses. Tabarī and his *tafsīr* book will be covered in more detail later.

The fifth period started after the first five centuries of Islam and continues until the present day.

Summary of ***Tafsīr*** by the ***Tabi'in*** (the Successors):

1. With the expansion of Islam under the first four caliphs, teachers from the Companions were sent to new cities to teach Islam and Islamic law and circles of education were established in all Islamic cities giving education to the *tabi'in*.
2. Many non-Arabs (*'mawali'*) who wanted to learn the truth about Islam became outstanding in the field of *tafsīr*.
3. Schools were established in the field of *tafsīr* based in Mecca, Medina and Kūfa (Iraq). The Companions were teaching and the *tabi'in* were learning in these schools.
4. Characteristics of the *Tafsīr* of the *Tabi'in*: exegesis is applied to the whole Qur'ān with detailed explanations; they included legal rulings and historical information; they utilised Arabic poetry as a dictionary to explain meanings of words; they used Jewish and Christian scriptures to explain stories; *tafsīr* knowledge was passed on from master to student in the class setting. No *Tafsīr* publication was produced.

5.8 Tradition or Reason-Based *Tafsīr*

In general, classical *tafsīr* falls into two broad categories: tradition/narration (*riwāyah*) and reason-based/intellectual (*dirāyah*) *tafsīr*.

5.8.1 Narration (*Riwāyah*) *Tafsīr*

Tradition-based *tafsīr* means the interpretation of the Qur'ān should be guided by the Qur'ān, the Prophet (pbuh) and the earliest Muslims. In other words, the interpretation should reflect, as far as possible, the original sources of Islam. Moreover, when the source is a reported saying of the Prophet (pbuh), or a Companion or successor (*tabi'in*), the narration (*riwāyah*) should have a sound basis; that is, a sound and complete chain of narrators (*isnad*) whose narrations are truthful and reliable.[396] Naturally, the explanation of the Qur'ān by the Qur'ān and the explanation of the Qur'ān by the Prophet (pbuh) are the two highest sources for *tafsīr*, which cannot be matched nor superseded by any other source. Next in rank are the explanations of the Companions, since they were witnesses to the revelation, were educated and trained by the Prophet (pbuh) himself and were closest to the period of the first Muslims.[397] Typically, the authors of this type of *tafsīr* included the *isnad* of the narrations, or at least referenced the work

396 Abdullah Saeed, *Interpreting the Qur'ān*, 42.
397 Von Denffer, *'Ulūm al-Qur'ān*, 124.

where the *isnad* was found. A number of scholars (both classical and modern) have argued that tradition-based *tafsīr* is the most reliable and preferred method of interpretation. Manna' al-Qattan said:

> What we have to follow and hold onto is the *tafsīr* based on text/tradition. This is because it is the path of true knowledge. It is also the safest way of guarding [oneself] against [attributing] error and deviation to the Book of God.[398]

Because these types of *tafsīr* primarily relied on narrations they also included stories from Jewish and Christian sources. The word *'Isra'iliyat'* meaning 'of Jewish origin' refers to explanations derived from non-Muslim sources, especially from the Jewish tradition, but also including other *'ahl al-kitab'* (people of the book) in general. Such material was used very little by the Companions, but more by the *tabi'in* and even more by later generations. There are many aspects of the Qur'ān which can be explained by referring to such sources, when there is common ground between the Qur'ān and the other traditions. However, the information taken from such sources must be used with great caution and cannot be considered sound according to the standards of science of Hadith, unless traced back to the Prophet (pbuh) himself and his Companions.[399]

5.8.2 Intellectual (*Dirāyah*) *Tafsīr*

The second kind of *tafsīr* is the so-called *tafsīr dirāyah* or *tafsīr bi'l ra'y* (*tafsīr* based on personal opinion). This is not based directly on the transmission of knowledge by the predecessors, but on the use of reason and *ijtihad*. Reason-based (*dirāyah*) exegesis emerged as a necessity in the developing Muslim world which was confronted with new issues and challenges. In addition to narration, this type of exegesis also relies on the Arabic language, poetry and other sciences to better understand the verses of the Qur'ān. Scholars would first look to the Prophet (pbuh) and Companions' traditions for explanations of the verses and if these didn't exist they would examine the verses and give their interpretation. They would examine the nuances of the phrasing in a verse, the various linguistic connotations carried by a word and other factors. Of course, this does not imply that the narrations of the Prophet (pbuh) and Companions are absolutely ignored in

---

398 Abdullah Saeed, *Interpreting the Qur'ān*, 42.

399 Von Denffer, *'Ulūm al-Qur'ān*, 133.

these works, but rather they also used their personal opinions together with all these sources.

It was largely in the wake of the first and second century disputes in early Islam that the debate over the two types of *tafsīr* (reason-based and tradition-based) emerged. The debate was, however, more closely related to *fiqh* than to the interpretation of the Qur'ān. Abū Ḫanifa sometimes preferred *ra'y* (personal opinion) over the text in a number of his juristic views. This was in cases where the tradition brought hardship and it would be for the benefit of the public (*istiḫsan*). *Tafsīr* methodology became involved in what was primarily a *fiqh* debate, the latter having emerged as s discipline a lot earlier.

The Prophet (pbuh) warned the Muslims not to interpret the Qur'ān based on their mere opinion without having the necessary qualifications to make *tafsīr*. Only when one has the necessary qualifications are they permitted to interpret the Qur'ān. This is necessary for the Muslim world as the Qur'ān is the source for all kind of solutions and must be interpreted constantly. The scholars classified this area of *tafsīr* into two categories: *tafsīr* based upon praiseworthy *ra'y*, and *tafsīr* based upon blameworthy *ra'y*. The first includes that which is in agreement with the sources of *tafsīr*, the rules of religion and the Arabic language. The second is that which is done without proper knowledge of the sources of *tafsīr*, the religion and the Arabic language; it is therefore based on mere opinion and must be rejected.

Summary of Tradition or Reason-Based *Tafsīr*:

1. Classical *tafsīr* falls into two broad categories: tradition-based/narration (*riwāyah*) and reason-based/intellectual (*dirāyah*) *tafsīr*.

Tradition-based *tafsīr*: the interpretation of the Qur'ān should be guided by the Qur'ān, the Prophet (pbuh) and the earliest Muslims.

2. The explanation of the Qur'ān by the Qur'ān and the explanation of the Qur'ān by the Prophet (pbuh) are the two highest sources for *tafsīr*. Next in rank are the explanations of the Companions.
3. Authors of this type of *tafsīr* included the *isnad* of the narrations, or at least referenced the work where the *isnad* was found.
4. Because these types of *tafsīr* primarily relied on narrations they also included stories from Jewish and Christian sources.

Reason-based *tafsīr* (*tafsīr dirāyah* or *tafsīr bi'l ra'y*):

5. This is not based directly on the transmission of knowledge by the predecessors, but on the use of reason and *ijtihad.*
6. This type of exegesis emerged as a necessity in the developing Muslim world which was confronted with new issues and challenges.
7. It relies on the Arabic language, poetry and other sciences to better understand the verses of the Qur'ān.
8. Scholars would first look to the Prophet (pbuh) and Companions' traditions for explanations of the verses and if these didn't exist they would examine the verses and give their interpretation.
9. Only when one has the necessary qualifications are they permitted to interpret the Qur'ān.

5.9 The Well-Known *Tafsīr* Scholars

This section mentions examples of some of the famous *tafsīr* scholars and their works in chronological order. There are many *tafsīr* works in different categories; the most important ones are outlined below.

5.9.1 Abd Allah Ibn 'Abbās

'Abd Allah b. 'Abbās (d. 687 C.E.) is considered to be the most knowledgeable of the Companions in *tafsīr*. He has been called *'tarjuman al-Qur'ān'*, the interpreter of the Qur'ān, and *'hibr al-umma'* the scholar of the Muslim nation. He was a cousin of the Prophet (pbuh) and his maternal aunt, Maymuna, was one of the Prophet's (pbuh) wives; therefore he was very close to the Prophet (pbuh) and learned much about the revelation. It is said that he saw the angel Gabriel twice.[400] As well as having a detailed knowledge of all aspects of *tafsīr*, he is also credited with having emphasised one of the basic principles of the science of *tafsīr* which has remained important to this day; that the meaning of the words, especially unusual words, in the Qur'ān ought to be traced back to their usage in the language of pre-Islamic poetry.

5.9.2 Muqātil b. Sulayman

Muqātil b. Sulayman (d. 767 C.E.) was born in Balkh, studied in Baghdad and Marw and settled in Basra until he passed away. His *tafsīr* is considered the first proper, independent *tafsīr* work. However, many scholars criticised his work due to his tendencies towards some deviated sects in Islam. In his exegesis he did not

[400] Von Denffer, 126.

use *isnad* (chain of narrators) and it is said he frequently asked non-Muslims for information. After his death, his *tafsīr* was mostly ignored by scholars for one and half centuries. Tabarī did not narrate any report from him when compiling his *tafsīr*. However, there are also many other scholars such as Ahmad b. Hanbal and Shāfi'i who consider him as an authority in exegesis. Remarkably, the earliest references to his *tafsīr* are found in the commentary of Abū Mansur al-Māturidī (d. 945 C.E.). Abū as-Suud (d. 1544 C.E.) shows his profound respect for Muqātil by adding the expression *radiya Allah anhu* (May God be well pleased with him) after mentioning his name in his *tafsīr*.

Muqātil wrote many works on *tafsīr*, the most famous of which was '*Kitāb at-Tafsīr al-Kabīr*'. Major features of this book include: extensive usage of reports on the occasion of revelation, regular practice in etymological (derivation of words), analysis of the unseen (*ghayb*), all ambiguous (*mubham*) words and interpretations of similar passages in the Qur'ān.

5.9.3 Yahya b. Sallam

Yahya b. Sallam (d. 816 C.E.) was born in Kūfa (Iraq) in 741 C.E. and went to Qayrawan (in North Africa) in 798 C.E.. Very little is known about his life. His *tafsīr* is known as '*Tafsīr Yahya*'. Yahya's *tafsīr* is quite different from Muqātil's. Yahya paved the way for Tabarī. He was not only a narrator but was critical in his selection of some reports. He used Prophetic traditions, reports from Companions and the *tabi'in* in his *tafsīr*. He paid attention to the variant readings of the Qur'anic text in his analysis and gave his own opinion. He was also heavily involved in the linguistic analysis of Qur'anic words but he did not use Arabic poetry to explain their meaning. His *tafsīr* is a good example of the formative period of *tafsīr* science.

5.9.4 Muhammad b. Jarir at-Tabarī

Muhammad b. Jarir at-Tabarī (d. 922 C.E.) was born in 839 C.E. in Amul/Tabaristan (on the southern coast of the Caspian Sea, in present day Iran). During his life he travelled to Ray, Basra, Medina, Baghdad, Syria and Egypt. He memorised the Qur'ān when he was 7 years old. He was an expert on almost every single Islamic discipline: exegesis, history, jurisprudence, variant readings of the Qur'ān, tradition, theology, ethics, and other areas. He even initiated his own legal school which became extinct.

The full title of Tabarī's *tafsīr* is '*Jami' al-Bayan an Ta'wil al-Qur'ān*'. Some of the sources for his *tafsīr* are Ibn 'Abbās, Ibn Mas'ud, Mujahid, Said b. Jubayr,

Ikrimah, Qatāda, Farra and Abd al-Razzaq b. Hammam. His *tafsīr* is valuable and has no equal for its thorough usage and referencing of *tafsīr* works written in previous centuries which, mostly lost over time, are preserved through Tabarī's work. It is one of the most famous *tafsīr* books and is perhaps the most voluminous work we have on the subject. It belongs to the class of *tafsīr bi al-riwāyah* and is based on the reports from the Prophet (pbuh), the Companions and the *tabi'in*, noting the various chains of transmission and evaluating them. However, it also contains reports that are not sound, without clearly indicating this, including so-called *israiliyyat*.

Some of the features of *Jami' al-Bayan* are: interpretation of the Qur'ān in the light of the Qur'ān first; the use of many narrations from the Prophet (pbuh), the Companions and the *tabi'in*; the use of many poems to explain words in the Qur'ān; the use of Arab philological analysis, especially when there are no available narrations about a verse; the occasional use of *israiliyyat* reports (some of which are intellectually problematic) and the non-acceptance of the existence of foreign vocabulary in the Qur'ān. In his *tafsīr* Tabarī discusses some theological matters and mainly takes the Sunni position against the Mutazalite doctrines. He discusses matters of Islamic law, narrates different opinions, makes critical analysis and takes preference. He also takes into account different readings of words in the Qur'ān sometimes narrating some improper readings (*shadhdh*), but making it clear that they are improper.

5.9.5 Ibn Abī Hatim

Ibn Abī Hatim (d. 939 C.E.) was born in Ray in 854 C.E. near present day Tehran in Iran. He learned Hadith from an early age from his father, the famous Hadith scholar Abū Hatim al-Rāzī (d. 890 C.E.). He travelled to and studied in Damascus, Egypt and Isfahan. His area of expertise was *Rijal* (criticism of the Hadith transmitters). He is said to be one of the greatest Hadith scholars after the famous compilers of the six Hadith collections.

His *tafsīr* is titled '*Tafsīr al-Qur'ān al-Aẕīm Musnadan an Rasul was-Sahaba wat-Tabi'in*'. Similar to Tabarī, he also narrated from the Prophet (pbuh), the Companions and the other scholars for the interpretation of the verses. In his *tafsīr* he minimised his own comments and compiled thousands of narrations from the Prophet (pbuh) and the early scholars. His *tafsīr* was only printed recently and is one of the classic works in the field of *tafsīr bi'l riwāyah*. He was a major source for such well-known scholars as Ibn Kathīr and Suyūtī. Ibn Kathīr said Hatim's *tafsīr* contains the entire body of transmitted knowledge and surpasses any previously written *tafsīr* including Tabarī's.

Some of the features of his *tafsīr* are: the use of revelation reports and reference to the notion of abrogation and the frequent use of Hadith terminology; there are16,283 reports in the book of which the ratio Prophetic Hadith is only 4%. It is also observed that in this commentary 22% of the reports reach back to the Companions. Interestingly, 80% of the reports which reach back to the Companions also come from Ibn 'Abbās and 74% reports are attributed to the *tabi'in.*[401]Ibn Abī Hatim does not give any of his opinions in relation to the interpretation of the verses; he mainly just reports narrations related to *tafsīr*. He disagreed with Tabarī that there are no non-Arabic words in the Qur'ān; he held that a few words were used that were part of the Arabic language at the time of revelation but no longer existed in Arabic, for example, he said the word *'jibt'* in the Qur'ān was the Abyssinian name for Satan.

5.9.6 Zamakhshari

Abū al-Qâsım Mahmud Ibn 'Umar al Zamakhshari (d. 1144C.E.) was born in the town of Zamakhshar/Khwarizm (Central Asia). He was a Mutazalite[402] scholar and tried to spread these views in his *tafsīr*, for example, his *tafsīr* begins with 'all praise is due to Allah, who created the Qur'ān'. He placed great emphasis on Arabic grammar, lexicography and the notion of *i'jāz* (the eloquence of the Qur'ān). Rather than focus on reports from the early generations, he gave priority to the use of reason over narration.

Examples from his *tafsīr*:

> Some faces on that Day will be radiant (with contentment), looking up toward their Lord[403]

He views that 'looking' in this verse means 'expecting mercy' because the Mutazalite School holds that God cannot be seen in this life or the afterlife. Some scholars warned against Zamakhshari's *tafsīr*, but many benefited from it in various ways.

---

401 See the detailed information in Mehmet Akif Koç, *İsnad Verileri Çerçevesinde Erken Dönem Tefsir Faaliyetleri: İbn Ebî Hâtim (ö.327/939) Tefsiri Örneğinde Bir Literatür İncelemesi*, Ankara: Kitâbiyât 2003.

402 Muʿtazilah is an Islamic school of theology based on reason and rational thought that flourished in the cities of Basra and Baghdad during the 8th–10th centuries

403 Qur'ān, 75: 22-23.

5.9.7 Fakhr ad-Din al-Rāzī

Muhammad b. 'Amr al-Husain al-Rāzī, (d 1209 C.E.) was born in Ray in 1149. He was a profound scholar and a very famous theologian, philosopher, grammarian, commentator and scientist. His book '*Tafsīr al-Kabīr*' is one of the most comprehensive in the field of reason-based (*dirāyah*) *tafsīr* covering many areas, sometimes beyond the actual field of *tafsīr*. Some scholars were critical of this and remarked that his *tafsīr* included everything with the exception of interpretation. He was very influential for the generations that followed him. Tabarī's *tafsīr* was the peak of the *riwāyah* (narration-based) *tafsīr* and Rāzī's *tafsīr* was the best of the *dirāyah* (reason-based) *tafsīr*. Despite being reason-based, his *tafsīr* is also full of narrations.

Some of the features of his *tafsīr* are: common use of the interpretation of the Qur'ān in the light of the Qur'ān; the importance of the thematic unity between the verses and passages of the Qur'ān (the first scholar to focus on this); the frequent use of linguistic analysis; frequent and detailed use of scientific interpretation; use of rational explanation, for example, he explained many miracles in the Qur'ān in rational way. There are many divisions and subdivisions in his interpretations. He is critical of using *israiliyyat* sources and held that they cannot be relied on due to their weakness in authenticity. He was critical of Mutazalite and other non-Sunni school of thoughts in Islam but he based his criticism on reasoned arguments.

5.9.8 Ibn Kathīr

'Imad ad-Din Abū al-Fida Ibn Kathīr (d. 1373 C.E.) was born in Damascus and was a pupil of Ibn Taymiyya and Hafiz Mizzi. He has been named as the second Tabarī. He wrote many books on various Islamic disciplines and was careful to use both Christian and Jewish scriptures for the interpretation of some verses of the Qur'ān. His book '*Tafsīr al-Qur'ān al-Aẕīm*' is one of the better-known books on *tafsīr*, perhaps second only to Tabarī. It emphasises the soundness of reports, in particular rejecting all foreign influences such as *Isra'iliyyat*, and it discusses the *sanad* of various reports often in detail, which makes it one of the more valuable books of *tafsīr*.

Some of the features of his *tafsīr* are: the inclusion of many Prophetic traditions and quotations from the Companions; *isnads* (the chain of narrators) are mentioned when he reports from the Prophet (pbuh) or the Companions; the interpretation of the Qur'ān in the light of the Qur'ān first; selectiveness when considering different opinions and giving priority to the strongest opinion; rejection of the idea that there are foreign influences on the interpretation of the Qur'ān (*israiliyyat*). Ibn Kathīr gives variant recitations of the Qur'ān and selectively and discerningly narrates from Tabarī, Ibn Abī Hatim and Ibn Atiyya.

Other well-known books of *tafsīr* are:

-*Tafsīr al Samarqandi*, by Abū al-Layth al-Samarqandi (d. 983 C.E.), under the title *Bahr al-'ulūm* with many reports from the Companions and the *tabi'in*, but without *sanad*.

-*Tafsīr al Tha'labi*, by Ahmad b. Ibrahim Tha'labi an-Nisabūri (d. 993 C.E.), under the title *'al-Kashf wal-Bayan an Tafsīr al-Qur'ān'* with some *sanad* and some unsound tales and stories.

-*Tafsīr al-Baghawi*, by Hasan b. Mas'ud al-Baghawi (d. 1116 C.E.), under the title *'Ma'alim at-Tanzil'* being an abridgement of Tha'labi with its weaknesses but with more emphasis on soundness of Hadith.

- *Tafsīr as-Suyūtī*, by Jalal ad-Din as-Suyūtī (d. 1505 C.E.), under the title *'ad-Durr al-Manthur fi't Tafsīr bi'l Ma'thur'*.

- *Anwar at-Tanzil*, by 'Abd Allah b. 'Umar al-Baydawi (d. 1286 C.E.), a summary of Zamakhshari with additional material to counterbalance the *mu'tazila* stance of the *kashshaf*.

- *Ruh al-Maani*, by Shihab ad-Din Muhammad al-Alusi al-Baghdadi (d. 1854 C.E.), criticises unsound reports and is considered to be among the best of *tafsīr bi'l ra'y*.

Summary of the Well-Known *Tafsīr* Scholars:

1. **'Abd Allah b. 'Abbās** (d. 687 C.E.) is considered to be the most knowledgeable of the Companions in *tafsīr*. As well as having a detailed knowledge of all aspects of *tafsīr*, he is also credited with having emphasised that the meaning of the words in the Qur'ān ought to be traced back to their usage in the language of pre-Islamic poetry.
2. **Muqātil b. Sulayman** (d. 767 C.E.). His *tafsīr* is considered the first proper, independent *tafsīr* work. In his exegesis he did not use *isnad* (chain of narrators) and it is said he frequently asked non-Muslims for information.
3. **Yahya b. Sallam** (d. 816 C.E.). He used Prophetic traditions, reports from Companions and the *tabi'in* (the followers of the Companions); he paid attention to the variant readings of the Qur'anic text in his analysis and gave his own opinion.

4. **Muhammad b. Jarir at-Tabarī** (d. 922 C.E.) His *tafsīr* is valuable and has no equal for its thorough usage and referencing of *tafsīr* works written in previous centuries which, mostly lost over time, are preserved through Tabarī's work.
5. **Ibn Abī Hatim** (d. 939 C.E.). He does not give any of his opinions in relation to the interpretation of the verses; he mainly just reports narrations related to *tafsīr*. He held that a few words were used that were part of the Arabic language at the time of revelation but no longer existed in Arabic.
6. **Abū al-Qâsım Mahmud Ibn 'Umar al Zamakhshari** (d. 1144 C.E.). He placed great emphasis on Arabic grammar, lexicography and the notion of *i'jāz* (the eloquence of the Qur'ān). He gave priority to using reason over narration.
7. **Muhammad b. 'Amr al-Husain al-Rāzī**, (d 1209 C.E.). His book is one of the most comprehensive in the field of reason-based (*dirāyah*) *tafsīr* covering many areas, sometimes beyond the actual field of *tafsīr*. Despite being reason-based, his *tafsīr* is also full of narrations.
8. **'Imad ad-Din Abū al-Fida Ibn Kathīr** (d. 1373 C.E.). His book discusses the *sanad* of various reports often in detail, which makes it one of the more valuable books of *tafsīr*.

5.10 New Interpretation of Islam: Main Feature of Modernist Qur'anic Scholarship

There are some important modern figures in exegeses of the Qur'ān; before giving their names it is good to know the general characteristics of this term. Although each scholar has a different style for interpreting the Qur'ān they all share some common qualifications[404]:

1) They return to the Qur'ān only, disregarding the traditions, sometimes they criticise Prophetic traditions;

a) They believe that everyone has a right to think on the Qur'ān, religious scholars have no special authority; all learned Muslims can interpret Islam.
b) They place emphasis on the translation of the Qur'ān.
c) They hold that the meaning of the Qur'ān is very clear (there is no ambiguity or real *mutashābih* in the Qur'ān).

[404] See detailed explanation in Ismail Albayrak, *Klasik Modernizmde Kur'an'a Yaklaşımlar/Approaches to the Qur'an in Classic Modernism*, İstanbul: Ensâr Publication 2004.

d) They reject Hadith that are based on later compilations of Hadith and *isnad* and hold that considering them implies that the Qur'ān is not enough.

2) They reject the legal schools and the notion of *ijma* (consensus of Muslim scholars). Charagh Ali rejects all literature of Islamic law and suggests creating a new legal school of thought which is uniquely based on the Qur'ān. The natural extension of this approach is to open the door of *ijtihad* as wide as possible.

3) They deny the classical Islamic sciences and institutions saying that they are not enough to understand Islam today.

4) The removal of the *bid'a* (un-Islamic belief or innovation).

5) The rationalisation of religious concepts. They hold that reason does not contradict revelation. They rationalise many Qur'anic narratives and miracles.

6) They deal with many current issues and relate them with the Qur'ān such as social, political, and economic issues. For example; democracy, polygamy, interest, family planning, women, education, right of divorce, equality, justice, etc.

7) *Tanasub* or *munasabat* (the interrelationships between the verses and the chapters) is a very important device during the modern period.

8) Modern scholarship puts human beings in the centre of its approach. Human beings are free creatures with reason and responsible for their actions.

9) They emphasize the aim of the Qur'ān (*maqasid al-Qur'ān*).

10) They criticize the partial approaches to the Qur'ān.

11) They separate legal rules from the ethical ones; legal rules are temporary and the ethical values are eternal.

12) They differentiate between interpretation and understanding.

The following scholars are important figures in modern exegeses;

Shah Wali Allah al-Dahlawi (d. 1762 C.E.), Sir Sayyid Ahmed Khan (d. 1898 C.E.), Rashid Rida (d. 1935 C.E.), Muhammad Iqbal (d. 1938 C.E.), Nasr Hamid Abū Zayd (d. 2010 C.E.), Muhammad Arkoun (d. 2010 C.E.).

Summary of New Interpretation of Islam: Main Feature of Modernist Qur'anic Scholarship:

Many modern Qur'anic scholars follow a reason-based method of interpretation which involves rejecting many of the more mystical and spiritual interpretation methods and practises in Islam. This method rejects classical interpretation and the wealth of knowledge that has been built up by scholars over the centuries and instead relies on the Qur'ān alone (even to the point of rejecting narrations) for interpretation. These scholars' interpretations tend to be more worldly and literal than classical interpretations, prioritising worldly affairs and reducing miracles and Qur'anic stories to rational or scientific explanation. See above for the detailed list of characteristics.

5.10.1 M. Fethullah Gülen and His *Tafsīr*

His life[405]**:** One unique modern scholar who has combined classical and modern interpretation in his books is M. Fethullah Gülen. He was born in Erzurum, in eastern Turkey, in 1941; He is an Islamic scholar and thinker, and a prolific writer and poet. He was trained in the religious sciences by several celebrated Muslim scholars and spiritual masters. Additionally Gülen studied the principles and theories of modern social and physical sciences. Displaying exceptional skills in learning and focused self-study, Gülen soon surpassed his peers and in 1959 he was awarded a state preacher's license (in Edirne). In 1966 he was promoted to a post in Izmir, Turkey's third largest province. In Edirne, Gülen used his sermons to emphasise the pressing social issues of the times encouraging the younger generation into a social activism based on core Islamic values. Through his travels and lectures in Anatolia, Gülen grew in popularity among the population and gained the attention of the academic community, particularly the student body. In addition to religious matters Gülen also talked about education, science, Darwinism, the economy and social justice gaining respect amongst a wide audience.

Gülen retired from formal teaching duties in 1981, having inspired a whole generation of young students. His efforts, dating from the 1960s, especially in educational reform, have made him one of the best-known and most well-respected figures in Turkey. From 1988 to 1991, he gave a series of sermons as preacher emeritus in some of the most famous mosques in major population centres, while continuing to deliver his message in the form of popular conferences, not only in Turkey, but also in Western Europe.

Gülen's vision is of a twenty-first century which will witness the birth of a spiritual dynamic that will revitalize long-dormant moral values; an age of tolerance, understanding, and international cooperation that will ultimately lead, through intercultural dialogue and a sharing of values, to a single, inclusive civilization. In the field of education, he has spearheaded the establishment of many charitable organizations to work for the welfare of the community, both within Turkey and internationally. He has inspired the use of mass media, notably tele-

[405] This introduction is cited from the book 'Essentials of the Islamic Faith', M. Fethullah Gülen, tr; Ali Unal, 'about the author', The Light, New Jersey, 2005.

vision, to inform the public of matters of pressing concern to them, individually and collectively. Gülen believes that good quality, universal education is the key to ensuring sufficient understanding and tolerance to secure respect for the rights of others and justice for all. To this end he has encouraged all areas of society to support quality education through financial donations. With these donations, educational trusts have established many schools, both in Turkey and abroad. Gülen believes in a peaceful activism to persuade people to commit to this vision. He holds that democracy, in spite of its many shortcomings, is now the only viable political system and people should strive to modernize and consolidate democratic institutions in order to build a society where individual rights and freedoms are respected and protected and where opportunities for all are equal.

His *Tafsīr*: The following examples of Gülen's *tafsīr* are from his book 'Reflections on the Qur'ān'. This book is exegeses on selective verses of the Qur'ān. It presents subtle points and details revealed in these Qur'anic verses while expounding on them in the sequential order in which they appear in the Qur'ān. The exegeses displays Gülen's knowledge of classical commentary as well as further contemporary insight and views within the boundaries of the science of Qur'anic exegesis.[406]

Examples[407]:

1) First example:

> In the very center of their hearts is a sickness, and God has increased them in sickness. For them is a painful punishment because they habitually lie.[408]

Some interpreters of the Qur'ān interpret the expression, 'God has increased them in sickness,' in relation to the ruling: 'the punishment is in keeping with the crime.' However, it would be more fitting to understand this expression as follows: "God has increased them in sickness," not only because their intentions are filled with evil but also because they put these intentions into action whenever they have the opportunity. The results are that the more evils they commit, the greater their sickness becomes, ending in a vicious cycle. Evil intentions that cannot be uprooted from the heart, or worse, if the person does not even intend to get rid of such evil intentions, they generate other evil thoughts and deeds; this is how the hypocrite is ruined. Thus, it is more reasonable to interpret the

406 M. Fethullah Gülen, Reflections on the Qur'ān, Foreword by Suat Yildirim.

407 This information is directly cited from his book, Reflections on the Qur'ān, 5-6.

408 Qur'ān, 2: 10.

second half of this verse—"God has increased them in sickness"—as the natural consequence of such a vicious cycle. Just as good health is our essential nature and illnesses are accidental, we are born with a sound disposition (to good); spiritual illnesses are also accidental. Those who neglect to take care of the health of their hearts or to impose quarantine conditions will find that this divine faculty has been infected by viruses. There are diverse paths that open from one error to another, from one wrongdoing to a more grievous sin, which may even lead to unbelief, the greatest sin of all. A small diversion at the centre may end up at an unimaginably wide angle on the periphery. If the illness in the heart is a corruption or suspicion in faith, this is potential unbelief or denial; if the chains that extend from sin to unbelief are not broken through Divine help then such a sin is likely to end up in denial and unbelief. Sometimes, such hypocrites, who are doubtful about everything that extends from God to their souls, feel as if everyone is suffering in the claws of the same illness, aggravating their inner anguish. This, in turn, burdens them with more layers of doubt and denial, and they writhe in the pain of the tides of their souls; they are choked by the numerous afflictions they have conceived in their imagination, one heaped upon another, for they consider everyone to be as faithless, inconsiderate, and unreliable as themselves.

Another example:

> God taught Adam the names, all of them.[409]

The teaching of the names is not exclusive to Adam, peace be upon him, rather it includes all human beings. What was taught to Adam were seeds of the whole of knowledge or sciences, which would be taught to humanity in its worldly life, just as every race and blood group was included in Adam's loins. Later generations have developed these seeds and produced sciences and disciplines. The teaching of the names to Adam might have happened in the way that God Almighty implanted or sown the seeds of fundamental knowledge of all things in his spirit in the same way the Prophets and God's Messengers were informed of many unknown things through Revelation. It could also be that He enabled Adam to be aware of both the names and the things to be called by the names through the feelings of neediness intrinsic to humanity and the desire and capacity of learning that He ingrained in its very being. Indeed, much has been said concerning the names taught to Adam. Do they refer to the capacity of speaking or language with which humanity has been made distinct from other species? Is there a ref-

[409] Qur'ān, 2: 31.

erence here to the human ability or distinction to think about or reflect on things and their names in the way to reach the Owner of everything? Do they refer to the physical and metaphysical dimensions of existence or to the names of the angels and the names of all the human beings who would descend from Adam until the Last Day? All of these are particulars of the issue beyond our discussion.[410]

Summary of M. Fethullah Gülen and His *Tafsīr*:

1. His vision is of a twenty-first century which will witness the birth of a spiritual dynamic that will revitalize long-dormant moral values that will ultimately lead to a single, inclusive civilization.
2. He has spearheaded the establishment of many charitable educational organizations to work for the welfare of the community, both within Turkey and internationally.
3. He has inspired the use of mass media to inform the public of matters of pressing concern to them.
4. He holds that good quality, universal education is the key to ensuring sufficient understanding and tolerance to secure respect for the rights of others and justice for all.
5. He holds that democracy is the only viable political system and people should strive to modernize and consolidate democratic institutions in order to build a society where individual rights and freedoms are respected and protected and where opportunities for all are equal.
6. His *tafsīr* displays his knowledge of classical commentary as well as further contemporary insight and views within the boundaries of the science of Qur'anic exegesis.

[410] Gülen, 17.

Chapter Six

Occasions of Revelation (*Asbāb al-Nuzūl*) and *Isra'iliyyat*

Occasions of Revelation (*Asbāb al-Nuzūl*) and *Isra'iliyyat*

6.1 The Occasions of Revelations (*Asbāb an-Nuzūl*)

God created everything based on wisdom and nothing was created without a purpose. It is possible for us to know some of the wisdom behind created things but we cannot know all of it. The revelation of the verses of the Qur'ān at specific times and in specific places has much wisdom behind it. There are two categories of verses regarding knowing the reason behind the time of their revelation. The first category, which covers the majority of verses in the Qur'ān, contains verses that were revealed without relating to any particular occasion or reason. For example, the verses following the one below were revealed to inform Muslims about the hypocrites but were not related to any occasion or reason:

> Among them are some who vowed to God: 'Surely, if God grants us out of His grace and bounty, we will most certainly (pay the Prescribed Alms and) spend in alms for His sake, and we will most certainly be among the righteous'.[411]

Tabaranī reported that these verses were revealed in relation to Tha'laba b. Khatib and many *tafsīr* scholars have used this report in their explanations. However, the narration is not authentic as one of the transmitters in the *sanad*, Ali Yazid al-Hani, is not trustworthy so Hadith scholars abandoned his reports.

The second category covers verses that were revealed to specifically address certain reasons and occasions or as an answer to questions put to the Prophet (pbuh). Verses or *surah* revealed to answer a question put to the Prophet (pbuh) are called '*asbāb an-nuzūl*' (occasions of the revelation) in the sciences of the Qur'ān (*'ulūm al-Qur'ān*). *Sabab* means reason (*illa*), cause or purpose. *Asbāb an-nuzūl* is the knowledge about the reasons behind the revelations and know-

[411] Qur'ān, 9: 75.

ing the relationship between revelation and the events that occurred during the twenty-three year period of revelation.

There are three types of reason connected with the revelation of particular Qur'anic passages:

1) Revelation in response to an event or a general situation. For example:

> May both hands of Abū Lahab be ruined, and are ruined are they, his wealth has not availed him, nor his gains. He will enter a flaming Fire to roast; and (with him) his wife, carrier of firewood (and of evil tales and slander), around her neck will be a halter of strongly twisted rope.[412]

Abū Lahab was an uncle of the Prophet Muhammad (pbuh). Abū Lahab, meaning 'the father of flame', is a nickname that was given to him while he was a child because of the rosy glow on his cheeks. He was one of the fiercest enemies of the Prophet (pbuh) and Islam. Since he was an uncle of the Prophet (pbuh) he knew him very well and, therefore, was expected to believe in him. But he stubbornly rejected him and actively opposed him. He cursed him, saying: 'May your hands ruin', meaning 'May you be left with no good at all and perish!' Due to his limitless enmity the Qur'ān designated him as the 'Father of the Flame', signifying that he was destined to be among those who would suffer the greatest torment in hell. The Qur'ān foretold that he would perish without accepting the faith and this came true; he died in great sorrow when he learned that the Meccan army had been badly defeated at the Battle of Badr. He was suffering from a contagious illness which made people afraid to approach his body even in death. After a few days, the people dug a pit, pushed his body into it using long cudgels and threw stones from a distance to bury it.

Abū Lahab's wife, Arwa Umm Jamil, equalled her husband in her opposition to the Prophet (pbuh). She scattered thorns in his path and in front of his house. She slandered both him and his message trying to stir up enmity towards him and his followers. The Qur'ān announced the type of punishment that she would suffer in hell; she would burn in the fire and carry wood for the fire around her neck like the precious necklaces that she wore.[413]

2) Revelation in response to a particular question that has been asked by someone (a person, a group or even by the Prophet (pbuh) himself). Below is one of many examples of this type of revelation:

---

[412] Qur'ān, 111: 1-5.

[413] Ali Unal, The Qur'ān with Annotated Interpretation, surah 111; 1-5.

> God has indeed heard (and accepted) the words of the woman who pleads with you concerning her husband and refers her complaint to God. God hears the dialogue between you. Surely God is All-Hearing, All-Seeing.[414]

This verse references a pre-Islamic custom (*ẕihar*) among the pagan Arabs. If a husband was angry with his wife he would tell her, 'You are henceforth as my mother's back to me,' thus forbidding himself from conjugal relations with her. This meant an irrevocable divorce, but a woman thus divorced was not allowed to remarry. The Qur'ān took the first step towards abolishing this custom in verse 4 of Surat al-Ahzāb (revealed before the above *surah*) by declaring that a woman whose husband had pronounced her to be as his mother's back was in no way his mother in reality. Aws ibn Sāmit, from the Aws tribe, among the Muslims of Medina, was angry with his wife and declared that she was as unlawful to him as his mother's back. Afterwards, he regretted having done so, but according to custom, he was not able to return to his wife. So his wife, Hawlah bt. Tha'labah, appealed to the Prophet (pbuh); she told him that her children had grown up and she lived alone with her husband and would be left unprotected if he left her. She added that her husband would agree to re-accept her as his wife. God revealed the above verse and it's following verses on the same subject during her conversation with the Prophet (pbuh), thereby decisively and permanently abolishing the pagan custom.[415]

The following is an example of the revelation coming in answer to a question of the Prophet (pbuh). Ibn 'Abbās reported:

> The Prophet (pbuh) said to the angel Gabriel, 'What prevents you from visiting us more often than you visit us now?' So there was revealed[416]; '(In response to an interval in the coming of Revelation, Gabriel explained:) We do not descend but by your Lord's command only. To Him belongs whatever is before us and whatever is behind us and whatever is between (all time and space and whatever we do at all times in all places). And your Lord is never forgetful (so do not fear that He forgets you)'[417]

3) Some verses were revealed as warnings or to explain a particular event. For example, the following was revealed about a hypocrite:

---

414 Qur'ān, 58: 1.

415 Ali Unal, The Qur'ān with Annotated Interpretation, surah 58: 1.

416 Bukhari, Tafsir, 255.

417 Qur'ān, 19: 64.

> If you ask them (about what they were saying), they will say: "We were merely jesting and being playful." Say: "Was it God and His Revelations and His Messenger that you were mocking?[418]

This hypocrite said the following words while sitting in the Battle of Tabuk: 'We have not seen anybody like the Qur'ān readers who are fat, lying a lot and very cowardly when they meet the enemy'. He meant the Prophet (pbuh) and his Companions by his statement, the Prophet (pbuh) was informed about his statement and then God revealed the verses about hypocrites. After that, the man came to the Prophet (pbuh) and excused himself but God answered him with the above mentioned verse.[419]

Summary of the Occasions of Revelations (*Asbāb an-Nuzūl*):

1) There are two categories of verses regarding knowing the reason behind the time of their revelation.
   a. The first category: verses that were revealed without relating to any particular occasion or reason.
   b. The second category: verses that were revealed to specifically address certain reasons and occasions.
2) *Asbāb an-nuzūl* is the knowledge about the reasons behind the revelations and knowing the relationship between the revelation and the events that occurred during the twenty-three year period of the revelation.
3) There are three types of reason connected with the revelation of particular Qur'anic passages:
   a. Revelation in response to an event or a general situation.
   b. Revelation in response to a particular question that has been asked by someone (a person, a group or even by the Prophet (pbuh) himself).
   c. Some verses were revealed as warnings or to explain a particular event.

6.1.1 The Benefits of Knowing the *Asbāb an-Nuzūl*

In the sciences of the Qur'ān, it is very important to know the reasons behind the revelation. This knowledge brings many benefits, some of which are outlined below:

1) On some occasions, when the Prophet (pbuh) was asked questions he was waiting for the revelation to come. This showed that the Qur'ān was revealed by

[418] Qur'ān, 9: 65.

[419] Tabarī, *Jami' al-Bayan*, 10/172, Ibn Kathīr, *Tafsir*, 2/368.

God. There were times when the Prophet (pbuh) was asked about subjects he did not have good knowledge of, for example:

> They ask you about the spirit. Say: 'The spirit is of my Lord's Command, and of knowledge, you have been granted only a little'[420]

'Abd Allah ibn Mas'ud reported:

> While I was in the company of the Prophet (pbuh) on a farm, and he was reclining on a palm leaf stalk, some Jews passed by. Some of them said to the others: 'Ask him about the Spirit.' Some of them said: 'What urges you to ask him about it.' Others said: '(Don't) lest he should give you a reply which you dislike', but they said, 'Ask him.' So they asked him about the Spirit. The Prophet (pbuh) kept quiet and did not give them any answer. I knew that he was being divinely inspired so I stayed in my place. When the divine inspiration had been revealed, the Prophet (pbuh) recited the verse (which is mentioned above).[421]

Another example:

> They say: 'For certain, if we return to Medina, those with more status and power will drive out from it the weaker and lowlier ones'. But all glory and might belong to God, and (by His leave) to His Messenger (pbuh) and the believers. But (being incapable of knowledge of the truth) the hypocrites do not know this.[422]

When the Prophet (pbuh) immigrated to Medina, the Arab tribes, al-Aws and al-Khazraj of Medina, were preparing to crown 'Abd Allah ibn Ubayy ibn Salul as their king, but this plan was never carried out, because of the Prophet's (pbuh) arrival. Ibn Ubayy never forgave the Prophet (pbuh) and, though he accepted Islam outwardly, he was always a fierce enemy of the Prophet (pbuh) and Islam. He collaborated with the Meccan polytheists and Medinan Jews and tried to instigate dissension among the Muslims. The events described in the above verses occurred in the fifth year of *Hijra* during the return from the military expedition against the Banī Mustaliq. Availing himself of a quarrel that had broken out between two Muslims, one from Medina and the other from Mecca (an emigrant), when the army had halted halfway for a rest, Ibn 'Ubayy tried to incite the *Ansār* (helpers) against the *Muhajirin* (emigrants). Zayd ibn Arqam heard him saying 'For cer-

---

[420] Qur'ān, 17: 85.

[421] Bukhari, *Saḫīḫ, Kitāb al-Ilm*, 125.

[422] Qur'ān, 63: 8.

tain, if we return to Medina, those with more status and power will drive out from it the weaker and lowlier ones', meaning they were the ones with status and power and the Prophet (pbuh) and his Companions were the weaker and lowlier ones. Zayd informed his uncle of this insult who in turn informed the Prophet (pbuh). The Prophet (pbuh) called Ibn 'Ubayy and his friends to his side. When challenged, they swore vehemently that they didn't say those words. The Prophet (pbuh) accepted their denial but then God revealed the verse and informed the Prophet (pbuh) about the true essence of the matter.[423]

2) We learn through *asbāb an-nuzūl* that God always supported the Prophet (pbuh) and defended him against the unbelievers. For example:

> Those who disbelieve say (by way of yet another false argument for unbelief): "Why has the Qur'ān not been sent down on him all at once?" (We send it down in parts) so that We may (impress it on your mind and) establish your heart with it, and We are conveying it distinctly and gradually, (one part supporting the other, and providing guidance and instruction for emerging occasions)[424]

Another example is the incident of slander against 'A'isha:

In the sixth year of the *Hijra* when returning from an expedition to the Banī Mustaliq, 'A'isha was inadvertently left behind when the Muslim army left the camp. After several hours she was found by Safwān ibn al-Mu'attal, one of the emigrants who had participated in the Battle of Badr, whose duty it was to make sure that nothing and no one got left behind. 'A'isha got on his camel and they re-joined the army at the next encampment. Ibn 'Ubayy and his followers raised a malicious scandal about 'A'isha, but God defended her and the Prophet (pbuh) against this slander in the following revelation:

> Surely those who invented and spread the slander (against 'A'isha, the Messenger's (pbuh) wife) are a band from among you. However, do not deem this incident an evil for you; rather, it is good for you. (As for the slanderers,) every one of them has accumulated sin in proportion to his share in this guilt, and he who has the greater part of it will suffer a tremendous punishment...[425]

3) We understand through *asbāb an-nuzūl* that God removes the difficulties of the believers and relieves them. For example:

---

[423] Bukhari, *Sahīh*, *Tafsir*, 334.

[424] Qur'ān, 25: 32.

[425] Qur'ān, 24: 11-20

> But if you are ill or on a journey, or if any of you has just satisfied a call of nature, or you have had contact with women, and can find no water, then betake yourselves to pure earth, passing with it lightly over your face and hands (and forearms up to and including the elbows). Surely God is One Who grants remission, All-Forgiving[426]

'A'isha (the wife of the Prophet (pbuh)) reported:

> We set out with God's Apostle (pbuh) on one of his journeys till we reached Al-Bayda' or Dhāt al-Jaysh, where a necklace of mine was broken (and lost). God's Apostle (pbuh) stayed there to search for it, and so did the people along with him. There was no water at that place, so the people went to Abū-Bakr and said, 'Don't you see what 'A'isha has done? She has made God's Apostle (pbuh) and the people stay where there is no water and they have no water with them'. Abū Bakr came while God's Apostle (pbuh) was sleeping with his head on my thigh, He said to me: 'You have detained God's Apostle (pbuh) and the people where there is no water and they have no water with them. So he admonished me and said what God wished him to say and hit me on my flank with his hand. Nothing prevented me from moving (because of pain) but the position of God's Apostle (pbuh) on my thigh. God's Apostle (pbuh) got up when dawn broke and there was no water. So God revealed the verses of *tayammum* (ablution with sand). So they all performed *tayammum*. Usayd b. Khudayr said, 'O the family of Abū Bakr! This is not the first blessing of yours'. Then the camel on which I was riding was caused to move from its place and the necklace was found beneath it.[427]

Another example:

> To God belong the East and the West (and therefore the whole earth with its east and west: wherever you are, you can turn to Him in the Prayer). Then, in whatever direction you turn, there is the "Face" of God. God is All-Embracing (with His mercy), All-Knowing[428]

Without knowing the *sabab* (reason) for this revelation, one might easily conclude that this revelation permits Muslims to face any direction when performing prayer, while it is well known that to face *qibla* is one of the conditions without which prayer becomes invalid. The following report helps us understand this verse better:

---

426 Qur'ān, 4: 43.

427 Bukhari, *Saḫīḫ, Tayammum*, 330.

428 Qur'ān, 2: 115.

> A group of Muslims travelled on a dark night and they did not know where the *qibla* was, so they later realised that they had prayed in the wrong direction. They asked the Prophet (pbuh) about it (if their prayers were accepted) and he kept silent until the above verse was revealed.[429]

When the reason for the revelation is considered, it is impossible to come to the wrong conclusion that the direction of prayer is unimportant.

4) It is very important to know *asbāb an-nuzūl* to understand the original intent of the verses. For example:

> (The hills of) as-Safa and Marwa are among the emblems God has appointed (to represent Islam and the Muslim community). Hence, whoever does the *Hajj* (the Major Pilgrimage) to the House (of God, the Ka'ba) or the *'Umrah* (the Minor Pilgrimage), there is no blame on him to run between them (and let them run after they go round the Ka'ba as an obligatory rite).[430]

Without knowing the reason behind this revelation one could mistakenly conclude that running between the two hills Safa and Marwa is voluntary and not an obligatory ritual of *Hajj.* However the following report makes it clear and helps us understand it better;

'Urwa reported:

> I asked 'A'isha, 'how do you interpret the statement of God: 'Verily! as-Safa and al-Marwa are among the symbols of God, and whoever performs the *Hajj* to the Ka'ba or performs *'Umrah*, it is not harmful for him to perform *tawaf* between them (Safa and Marwa).' (2.158). By God! (it is evident from this revelation) there is no harm if one does not perform *tawaf* between Safa and Marwa'. 'A'isha said, 'O, my nephew! Your interpretation is not true. Had this interpretation of yours been correct, the statement of God should have been, 'It is not harmful for him if he does not perform *tawaf* between them'. But in fact, this divine inspiration was revealed concerning the *Ansār* who used to adopt *iḫrām* (special attire for *Hajj* and *'Umrah*) for worshipping an idol called 'Manāt' which they used to worship at a place called al-Mushallal before they embraced Islam. Whoever adopted *iḫrām* (for the idol), would consider it not right to perform *tawaf* between Safa and Marwa. When they embraced Islam, they asked God's Apostle (pbuh) regarding it, saying, 'O God's Apostle! We used to refrain from *tawaf* between Safa and Marwa'. So God revealed: 'Verily; Safa and Marwa are among the symbols of God'. 'A'isha added,

[429] Wāḫidī, *Asbāb an-Nuzūl*, 21.

[430] Qur'ān, 2: 158.

> 'Surely, God's Apostle (pbuh) set the tradition of *tawaf* between Safa and Marwa, so nobody is allowed to omit the *tawaf* between them'. Later on I ('Urwa) told Abū Bakr b. 'Abdurrahman (of 'Aisha's narration) and he said, 'I have not heard of such information, but I heard learned men saying that all the people, except those whom 'A'isha mentioned and who used to assume *iḫrām* for the sake of Manāt, used to perform *tawaf* between Safa and Marwa. When God referred to the *tawaf* of the Ka'ba and did not mention Safa and Marwa in the Qur'ān, the people asked, 'O God's Apostle! We used to perform *tawaf* between Safa and Marwa and God has revealed (the verses concerning) *tawaf* of the Ka'ba and has not mentioned Safa and Marwa. Is there any harm if we perform *tawaf* between Safa and Marwa?' So God revealed: 'Verily as-Safa and al-Marwa are among the symbols of God'. Abū Bakr said, 'It seems that this verse was revealed concerning the two groups; those who used to refrain from *tawaf* between Safa and Marwa in the pre-Islamic period of ignorance and those who used to perform the *tawaf* but after embracing Islam refrained from performing it as God had enjoined *tawaf* of the Ka'ba and did not mention *tawaf* (of Safa and Marwa) till later.[431]

This report shows that the verse was revealed to show the old belief was incorrect; it is not a sin to run between the two hills even if it is part of the *Hajj* rituals.

5) We know through *asbāb an-nuzūl* whether the meaning of a verse is specific or general. Sometimes verses can be wrongly understood as specific and knowing the occasions behind the revelation helps to avoid these misunderstandings. For example:

> Say (O Messenger): I do not find in what has been revealed to me anything made unlawful to one who would eat except it be carrion or blood outpoured (not that which is left in the veins of such organs as the liver and spleen), or the flesh of swine, which is loathsome and unclean, or that which is profane, having been slaughtered in the name of other than God (or without pronouncing God's Name over it). Yet whoever is constrained by dire necessity (to eat thereof), provided he does not covet nor exceed (the bounds of the necessity): (no sin shall be on him). Your Lord is indeed All-Forgiving, All-Compassionate.[432]

Without knowing the reason behind this revelation one can mistakenly believe that there are only four unlawful things and the rest are lawful. However, this verse

---

[431] Muslim, *Saḫīḫ*, *Hajj*, 1278.

[432] Qur'ān, 6: 145.

was revealed about the unbelievers who make lawful things unlawful or make unlawful things lawful. This verse rejects their claim but it does not limit the unlawful things to four; there are other verses which explain different unlawful things and all the verses must be considered together for the correct understanding.

Another example; Ibn 'Abbās reported:

> Hilal b. Umayya accused his wife before the Prophet (pbuh) of committing illegal sexual intercourse with Sharik b. Sahma. The Prophet (pbuh) said, 'Produce a proof, or else you would get the legal punishment (by being lashed) on your back'. Hilal said, 'O God's Apostle! If anyone of us saw another man over his wife, would he go to search for a proof'? The Prophet (pbuh) went on saying, 'Produce a proof or else you would get the legal punishment (by being lashed) on your back'.[433] Thereupon God revealed the following verse to the Prophet (pbuh):

> As for those who accuse their own wives of adultery but have no witnesses except themselves, such a person must testify four times swearing by God in each oath that he is indeed speaking the truth, and the fifth time, that God's curse be upon him if he is lying. But the punishment will be averted from the wife if she testifies four times by swearing by God in each oath that the man is surely telling a lie, and the fifth time, that the wrath of God be upon her if the man is speaking the truth[434]

This procedure is called *li'an* (oath of condemnation and mutual cursing). When a man accuses his wife of adultery, he must testify four times and swear by God. The fifth time he must invoke God's curse upon himself if he is lying. This verse was revealed about Hilal b. Umayya when he accused his wife of adultery, but the ruling is not limited or specific to him, rather it is a general ruling covering all Muslims. The evidence for this is the following report:

> 'Umaymir al-'Ajlani came to 'Asim ibn 'Adi al-Ansari and said to him, "Asim, what do you say about a man who finds another man with his wife? Should he kill him? What else should he do? 'Asim, ask the Prophet (pbuh) about that for me.' 'Asim asked the Prophet (pbuh). The Prophet (pbuh), disliked such questions and considered them to be blameworthy. What 'Asim heard the Prophet (pbuh) say was hard on him. When 'Asim returned to his family, 'Umaymir came and said, "Asim, what did the Prophet (pbuh) say to you?' 'Asim said, 'You have not brought me any good! The Prophet (pbuh) disliked the question which I asked him.' 'Uwaymir said, 'By Allah, I will not stop until I ask the Prophet (pbuh)

---

433 Bukhari, *Sahīh, Shahādah*, 2571.

434 Qur'ān, 24: 6-9.

> about it!' So 'Uwaymir went to the Prophet (pbuh) who was in the middle of the people and said, 'Messenger of Allah, if a man finds another man with his wife, should he kill him and then you kill him in turn (as retribution for murder)? What else should he do?' The Prophet (pbuh) said, 'Allah has sent down revelation about you and your wife. Go and bring her.' So they carried out the process of *li'an* while I was present among the people with the Prophet (pbuh). When they finished, 'Umaymir said, 'I would be lying about her if I were to keep her, Messenger of Allah.' So he divorced her three times before the Prophet (pbuh) commanded him to do so."Ibn Shihab said: So divorce was the tradition for all those who were involved in a case of *li'an*.[435]

This report shows that the Prophet (pbuh) applied the ruling of the verse for Hilal and for other people as well.

The other benefits in knowing the *asbāb an-nuzūl* are:

6) The knowledge of *asbāb an-nuzūl* means that the immediate meaning of a verse can be understood within its original context helping to avoid any misinterpretation.

7) We understand the wisdoms and reasons behind legal rulings, this understanding strengthens the faith of the believers and helps the unbelievers to see the truth and come to the right path.

8) *Asbāb an-nuzūl* helps Muslims to understand the chronology of the revelation.

9) The reports show us the historical situation at the time of the Prophet (pbuh).

10) We learn from *asbāb an-nuzūl* the person who caused the revelation.

11) *Asbāb an-nuzūl* provides narrative context.

12) With this knowledge the verses can be applied in the proper manner.

13) Knowing the occasions of the revelations enables us to connect the life with the meanings.

14) These reports help Muslims to memorise the Qur'ān more easily.

Summary of the Benefits of Knowing the *Asbāb an-Nuzūl*:

The knowledge of the reasons behind the revelation brings many benefits.

1) On being questioned, the Prophet (pbuh) waited for God to send the revelation proving it wasn't coming from him.

---

[435] Bukhari, *Sahīh, Tafsir*, 423, Muslim, *Sahīh, Li'an*, 1492.

2) *Asbāb an-nuzūl* show that God always supported the Prophet (pbuh) and defended him against the unbelievers.
3) *Asbāb an-nuzūl* show that God removes the difficulties of the believers and relieves them.
4) To understand the original intent of the verses it is important to know *asbāb an-nuzūl.*
5) We know through *asbāb an-nuzūl* whether the meaning of a verse is specific or general.
6) The immediate meaning of a verse can be understood within its original context helping to avoid misinterpretation.

6.1.2 Status of the *Asbāb al-Nuzūl* Reports from Companions

Due to the reasons listed below, the Companions are considered as the sources of the *asbāb al-nuzūl* reports:

1) The Companions did not try to understand the Qur'ān on the basis of textual analysis, but followed Qur'anic teachings and immediately put into practice what they had learnt.

2) The Companions had witnessed the actual revelations.

3) Their *asbāb* reports are not *ijtihad* (personal reasoning) because they received their knowledge from the Prophet (pbuh), whether directly or indirectly (*ḫukman marfu*).

4) The differences among the reports coming from them are not contradictory differences but various interpretations of the same issue.

5) Ghazālī said, if the reports from the Companions do not come from the Prophet (pbuh), it means they are giving their own opinions like us.

6) The interpretation of the Companions cannot be considered as mere *ijtihād.*

7) The consensus of the Companions on the reports should be considered as *hujjah* (clear evidence).

8) Abū al-Dardā said, 'if a scholar cannot widen the scope of a verse or interpret it in various ways; he should not be considered a real *fāqih* (not in the sense of jurist, but meaning a person who has a deep understanding of Islam).

9) There are two types of reports from the Companions: a) narrations from the time of the Prophet (pbuh) (*sabab al-nuzūl*), b) narrations from their own experience (*ta'wil*).

Scholars are divided into three groups of opinion about about *asbāb* reports from the *tābi'in.* The first group says the successors reports must be accepted because they must have come from the Companions, even if they do not mention the Companion's name or quote directly from the Prophet (pbuh). These *mursal* reports can be used in *tafsīr* but not in theology or Hadith works. The second groups says that if their reports do not come from the Prophet (pbuh) or the Companions, they are not accepted. The third group says that reports concerning the *asbāb* will only be accepted from those successors who were well known for their association with the Companions such as Mujahid (d. 103 A.H.), Ikrimah (d. 104 A.H.), Said b. Jubayr (d. 95 A.H.) and Qatāda (d. 110 A.H.).

SUMMARY OF STATUS OF THE *ASBĀB* REPORTS FROM COMPANIONS:

1) The Companions are the source of *asbāb* reports.
2) The Companions followed Qur'anic teachings and immediately put into practice what they had learnt.
3) They witnessed the revelations so we have to accept whatever they narrate from the Prophet (pbuh).
4) They received their knowledge directly from the Prophet (pbuh) so their reports are not *ijtihād*.
5) Any difference between their reports are not contradictory just various interpretations of the same issue.
6) The consensus of the Companions on the reports should be considered as clear evidence.
7) There are two types of reports from the Companions: narrations from the time of the Prophet (pbuh); narrations from their own experience.
8) There are three different opinions about *asbāb* reports from the *tābi'in*: 1) some scholars say their reports must be accepted even if they do not mention the Companion's name or quote directly from the Prophet (pbuh); 2) some scholars say if their reports do not come from the Prophet (pbuh) or the Companions, they are not accepted; 3) other scholars say that reports concerning the *asbāb* will be accepted from only those successors who were well known for their association with the Companions.

6.1.3 The Wording of *Asbāb al-Nuzūl* Reports

It is essential to discuss the different phrases that the Companions used when narrating the *sabab an-nuzūl* of particular verses, and how these are to be interpreted. This is because, occasionally, the Companions intended to imply that a particular act came under the ruling of a verse, and not necessarily that it was the *sabab an-nuzūl* of that verse. At other times, they conveyed their own uncertainty about the *sabab an-nuzūl*.[436]

Not only *asbāb* reports but also some Qur'anic verses indicate the background dialogue, for example:

- *Yastaftunaka* - (they ask you a *fatwa* (a question on a specific matter))
- *Yas'alunaka* - (they ask you.....)
- *Qul* - (Say or Tell to them....)

There are two primary forms that the Companions used in narrating such incidents. The first manner of phrasing is clear and unequivocal concerning the *sabab an-nuzūl* of the verse, the second type of phrasing, however, is not explicit in nature.

The following are examples of the phrases used which inform about the occasion of revelations:

1) *Sabab nuzūl al-ayah* - (the reason this verse was revealed is...)

2) *Fa-anzal Allahu hadhih al-ayah* - (for this reason, God sent this verse...)

3) *Sabab nuzūl al-ayah kadha* - (the reason for the revelation of this verse is like this...)

4) There are also narratives beginning with the letter 'f/ "ف" (called in Arabic '*fa al-sababiyyah*') which indicates reason:

- *Haddatha kadha fa-nazalat* - (The Prophet (pbuh) talked about this issue or said something about this 'then/*fa*' this verse was revealed').
- *Waqa'a kadha fa-nazala* - (this event happened then the word of Glorious God was revealed).
- *Su'ila an kadha fa-nazalat* - (The Prophet (pbuh) was asked, then it was revealed).

5) There are other phrases where the clear evidence is not mentioned. Scholars have differed in their opinion with regards to the acceptance of this type of report as *sabab an-nuzūl*. This is because this type of statement does not necessarily imply that the particular act mentioned was the *sabab an-nuzūl* of the verse. It could imply that the ruling of the verse applies to that case, or it could also imply that the act was the *sabab an-nuzūl*. In other words, due to the ambiguity in the wording of the statement, it does not give certain knowledge, and can be interpreted either way.[437] The expressions for this type are:

---

[436] Qadhi, *The Sciences of the Qur'ān*, 110.

[437] Qadhi, 110.

- *Su'ila Rasul Allah (pbuh)an kadha* - (the Messenger of God (pbuh) was asked about this issue...).
- *al-sababiyya tufhamu min al-maqam* - (Despite the absence of *'fa'* here many Muslim scholars state that it can be understood from the context that this is a *sabab* report).
- *al-ayah nazalat fi kadha* - (this verse is revealed about ...).

Summary of The Wording of *Asbāb al-Nuzūl* Reports:

1) The wording of the reports is significant in that it tells us the Companions' certainty about the verse and also how it is to be interpreted.
2) Not only *asbāb* reports but also some Qur'anic verses indicate the background dialogue.
3) There are two primary forms that the Companions used in narrating such incidents. The first manner of phrasing is clear and unequivocal concerning the *sabab an-nuzūl* of the verse, e.g. *Sabab nuzūl al-ayah* - (the reason this verse was revealed is...).
4) The second type of phrasing, however, is not explicit and unequivocal in nature, e.g. *Su'ila Rasul Allah an kadha* - (the Messenger of God (pbuh) was asked about this issue...).

6.1.4 Specific and General

When one has knowledge about the *sabab al-nuzūl* of the verses it is still necessary to decide whether the revelation has a specific implication only for the particular occasion it was connected with, or whether it is of general implication and needs to be applied by all Muslims at all times.

Those verses that came as a direct response to specific questions should not be considered only as answers to those specific queries. In the famous technical formula: 'the specific nature of the *sabab* (occasion) does not hinder the generality of the rule. Thus there is no need to limit the meaning of the verses with these reports'. The notion of *nadrat al-nusus ma'a kathrat al-waqa'i* (we have a limited number of verses but the events and incidents are limitless). These *sabab* reports cannot restrict the meaning of the verses.

For example:

> Who is greater in doing wrong than he who bars God's places of worship, so that His Name be not mentioned and invoked in them, and strives to

> ruin them? Such people might never enter them, save in fear. For them is disgrace in the world and in the Hereafter a tremendous punishment[438]

When considering the occasion for the revelation of this verse it can be seen that it targets those who prevented the Jewish people from praying in the temple in Jerusalem; however, viewing it only in this context narrows the scope of the verse. Once Meccan pagans tortured and prohibited Prophet Muhammad (pbuh) from praying at the Ka'ba, consequently, this verse can be applied to every tyrant who hinders or impedes believers from praying in their places of worship.

6.1.5 Types of Reports

The reports about the occasion of revelation can generally be classified into two types:

1) **Definite/*dalālah*:** These reports clearly indicate that the event which is narrated is *sabab an-nuzūl.*

For example:

> O you who believe! Obey God and obey the Messenger (pbuh), and those from among you who are invested with authority; and if you are to dispute among yourselves about anything, refer it to God and the Messenger (pbuh), if indeed you believe in God and the Last Day. This is the best (for you) and fairest in the end[439]

Ibn 'Abbās reported that this verse was revealed in connection with 'Abd Allah b. Huzafa b. Qays b. 'Adiy when the Prophet (pbuh) appointed him as the commander of an army detachment.[440]

2) **Probable/*ishārah*:** these reports seem like an interpretation and sometimes do not fit the textual context of the verse. The narrator does not indicate clearly that the event narrated is the *sabab an-nuzūl*, but suggests this probability.

For example; 'Urwa reported:

> Zubayr quarrelled with a man from the *Ansār* (the residents of Medina) because of a natural mountainous stream at al-Harra. The Prophet (pbuh) said: 'O Zubayr, irrigate (your land) and then let the water flow to your neighbour. The *Ansari* said: 'O God's Apostle (this is because) he is your cousin?' At that moment, the Prophet (pbuh)'s face became red (with anger) and he said: 'O Zubayr. Irrigate (your land) and then withhold the

---

[438] Qur'ān, 2: 114.

[439] Qur'ān, 4: 59.

[440] Bukhari, *Saḫīḫ. Tafsir*, 108.

water till it fills the land up to the walls and then let it flow to your neighbour. So the Prophet (pbuh) enabled Zubayr to take his full right after the *Ansari* showed some kind of disobedience to the Prophet.

The Prophet (pbuh) had previously given an order that was in favour of both of them. Zubayr said: 'I don't think but this verse was revealed in this connection[441]; "But no! By your Lord, they do not (truly) believe unless they make you the judge regarding any dispute between them, and then find not the least vexation within themselves over what you have decided, and surrender in full submission".[442]

Summary of Types of Reports:

1) There are two types of report about the reason for revelation:
2) Definite/*dalālah*: These reports clearly indicate that the event which is narrated is *sabab an-nuzūl.*
3) Probable/*ishārah*: these reports seem like an interpretation and sometimes do not fit the textual context of the verse. The narrator does not indicate clearly that the event narrated is the *sabab an-nuzūl*, but suggests this probability.

6.1.6 Multiple *Asbāb* for One Verse

It appears from the reports of the Companions that particular passages of the Qur'ān were revealed in response to more than one event, situation or question, or that the application of a particular passage of the Qur'ān was for more than one particular occasion. There is no obstacle for the multiple *asbāb* if dealt with by scholars in the light of the criteria of Hadith studies. When there are multiple narrations concerning *asbāb an-nuzūl* for a single verse, the following guidelines are used:

1) If one of the *sabab* reports is weak and the other is strong and authentic, the authentic one is accepted and, therefore, there are no multiple occasions. For example, Bukhari and Muslim report:

> Once the Prophet (pbuh) did not receive inspiration for a few days, so one of the women of the Quraysh ridiculed him, saying, 'O Muhammad, I think your Satan has left you'. God then revealed these verses (the *surah* Duha) in response to her.

---

441 Bukhari, *Saḫīḫ, Tafsir*, 109.

442 Qur'ān, 4: 65.

On the other hand, there is another narration from Tabaranī, stating:

> The Prophet (pbuh) did not receive inspiration for a few days, so he started worrying about this. This caused the servant of the Prophet (pbuh) to clean the house, and she discovered a dead puppy under the bed. When she removed it, this *surah* Duha was revealed.

Since the second narration is weak, it is rejected as *sabab an-nuzūl.*

2) If both narrations are authentic then it is investigated to see if there are any grounds for preferring one narration over the other. For example, if one of them is narrated in a clear manner as being the *sabab an-nuzūl* (i.e., the first type of phrasing mentioned in the previous section), whereas the other is not, then the former narration is accepted. If one of the narrations is reported by a Companion who witnessed the *sabab an-nuzūl* and who was present at the time of revelation, his narration is preferred over another. For example, there are two authentic narrations as the occasions of the following verse:

> They ask you about the spirit. Say: "The spirit is of my Lord's Command, and of knowledge, you have been granted only a little"[443]

The first report is from 'Abd Allah ibn Mas'ud:

> While I was in the company of the Prophet (pbuh) on a farm, and he was reclining on a palm leaf stalk, some Jews passed by. Some of them said to the others: 'Ask him about the Spirit.' Some of them said: 'What urges you to ask him about it?' Others said: '(Don't) lest he should give you a reply which you dislike', but they said, 'Ask him'. So they asked him about the Spirit. The Prophet (pbuh) kept quiet and did not give them any answer. I knew that he was being divinely inspired so I stayed at my place. When the divine inspiration had been revealed, the Prophet (pbuh) recited the verse (which is mentioned above).[444]

The second report is from Ibn 'Abbās:

> The polytheists of Mecca asked the Jews to give them a question that they could ask the Prophet (pbuh) in order to baffle him. The Jews told them to ask about the Spirit, and when they did, God revealed these verses.[445]

---

[443] Qur'ān, 17: 85.

[444] Buhkari, *Saḫīḫ, Kitāb al-Ilm*, 125.

[445] Wāḫidī, *Asbāb al-Nuzūl*, 148.

In this report, it is the Quraysh who are asking the Prophet (pbuh) not the Jews. Faced with these two reports, precedence is given to the first since Ibn Mas'ud was present at the time of revelation, whereas Ibn 'Abbās was not.[446]

3) If both reports are equivalent in authenticity and there is not any means of giving preference to either one of them, this implies the verse was revealed in response to both of the incidents (*jam' bayn al-asbāb*). For example, there are two equivalent reports in authenticity for the following verse:

> As for those who accuse their own wives of adultery but have no witnesses except themselves, such a person must testify four times swearing by God in each oath that he is indeed speaking the truth, and the fifth time, that God's curse be upon him if he is lying.[447]

The first report is from Ibn 'Abbās:

> Hilal b. Umayya accused his wife before the Prophet (pbuh) of committing illegal sexual intercourse with Sharik b. Sahma. The Prophet (pbuh) said, 'Produce a proof, or else you would get the legal punishment (by being lashed) on your back'. Hilal said, 'O God's Apostle! If anyone of us saw another man over his wife, would he go to search for a proof'? The Prophet (pbuh) went on saying, 'Produce a proof or else you would get the legal punishment (by being lashed) on your back'. Upon this the verses which are mentioned above were revealed.[448]

The second report:

> 'Uwaymir walked to God's Apostle (pbuh) in the midst of people, and said, 'O God's Apostle! If a man sees another man with his wife, would he kill him, whereupon you would kill him, or what should he do?' God's Apostle (pbuh) said, 'God has revealed some decree as regards you and your wife's case.[449]

Faced with these two authentic reports, it is concluded that both of these incidents occurred in a similar time frame and the verses of *li'an* were revealed in response to both of these cases.

4) If both reports are equally authentic but the time frames are known to be far apart, then this implies that the verse was revealed more than once. In other words, if there is more than one report of *asbāb an-nuzūl*, all of which are authen-

---

446 Qadhi, *The Sciences of the Qur'ān*, 113.
447 Qur'ān, 24: 6-9.
448 Bukhari, *Saḫīḫ, Shahādah*, 2571.
449 Bukhari, *Saḫīḫ, Tafsir*, 423, Muslim, *Saḫīḫ, Li'an*, 1492.

tic, and none of which can be given preference over the others, and it is inconceivable that all of these incidents occurred simultaneously, and then this implies that the verse was revealed on all of these occasions.[450] Zarkashī stated:

> It is possible that a verse is revealed twice, to signify its importance, and to remind people of it ... And the wisdom behind all of this (meaning the multiple revelation of a single verse), is that it is possible that a certain incident or question should be the cause of the revelation of a verse, but a verse has already been revealed before it that gives the ruling concerning that incident. Therefore, the same verse is re-revealed to the Prophet (pbuh), so that the people can be reminded of it, and to show them that the verse also contains the ruling of that incident.[451]

The example for this type is the following verse:

> It is not for the Prophet (pbuh) and those who believe to ask God for the forgiveness of those who associate partners with God even though they be near of kin, after it has become clear to them that they (died polytheists and therefore) are condemned to the Blazing Flame[452]

There are three reports concerning the revelation of this verse, all of which are equally authentic. In addition, it is not possible for all of these incidents to have occurred simultaneously. Faced with these three authentic narrations, it is concluded that this verse was revealed three separate times, on each of these occasions.

Summary of Multiple *Asbāb* for One Verse:

1. Some passages of the Qur'ān were revealed in response to more than one event, situation or question, or that the application of a particular passage of the Qur'ān was for more than one particular occasion.
2. There is no obstacle for the multiple *asbāb* if dealt with by scholars in the light of the criteria of Hadith studies. When there are multiple narrations concerning *asbāb an-nuzūl* for a single verse, the following guidelines are used:
3. If one of the *sabab* reports is weak and the other is strong and authentic, the authentic one is accepted and therefore there are no multiple occasions.

---

[450] Qadhi, 113-114.
[451] Zarkashī , *al-Burhān*, 1/29-31.
[452] Qur'ān, 9: 113.

4. If both narrations are authentic then it is investigated to see if there are any grounds for preferring one narration over the other.
5. If both reports are equivalent in authenticity, and there is not any means of giving preference to either one of them, then this implies the verse was revealed in response to both of the incidents (*jam' bayn al-asbāb*).
6. If both reports are equally authentic but the time frames are known to be far apart, then this implies that the verse was revealed more than once.

6.1.7 Multiple Revelations for One Occasion (*Sabab*)

It is also possible that one *sabab*, or reason, can be the cause for the revelation of several verses. A well-known example for several revelations which are connected with one particular circumstance are three verses which, according to reliable reports, came down in response to the question of Umm Salama about whether or why only the men had been referred to in the Qur'ān as being rewarded. According to Ḫākim and Tirmidhi the verses 3: 195, 4:32 and 33: 35 were revealed in response to this question.

SUMMARY OF MULTIPLE REVELATIONS FOR ONE OCCASION (*SABAB*):

1. It is also possible that one *sabab* or reason can be the cause for the revelation of several verses.
2. A well-known example for this is three verses which came down in response to the question of Umm Salama about whether or why only the men had been referred to in the Qur'ān as being rewarded.

6.1.8 Some Issues Related to the Occasion of Revelation

Before reporting *asbāb an-nuzūl* narrations it is very important to know the following issues:

1) There are some contradictions between the reports and the historical facts. Unfortunately, some scholars of *tafsīr* included those reports in their books before checking their authenticity.

> Who is greater in doing wrong than he who bars God's places of worship, so that His Name be not mentioned and invoked in them, and strives to ruin them?[453]

[453] Qur'ān, 2: 114.

In relation to the verse it is mentioned as *sabab nuzūl* in *tafsīr* books that Bukhtunasr (Nebuchadnezzar) from Babylon together with the Christians attacked the Jews. Bukhtunasr lived in the 7*th* century BC and therefore it is impossible for him to have collaborated with the Christians, so this report is not authentic

2) There are some contradictions in the reports themselves, they are ambiguous and very difficult to understand. This confusion and ambiguity might be caused because some people tried to connect the reports to events which happened later.

> Prosperous indeed is he who purifies himself (of sins and of his wealth by spending from it in God's cause and for the needy)[454]

Some scholars inferred the charity of *fitr* (charity which is given in Ramadan) from this verse but this verse was revealed in Mecca and charity of *fitr* was commanded in Medina.

3) The occasions of the revelation are one of the reasons for the appearance of sects in Islam. The sects misused these reports by changing them to provide justification and evidence for their views.[455]

4) Due to the variant readings of the Qur'ān there can be varying *asbāb* reports related to the same verse. For example:

> Assuredly We have sent you as a Messenger with the truth as a bearer of glad tidings and as a warner. You will not be questioned concerning the Companions of the Blazing Flame.[456]

One word is recited in this verse in two different recitations: *tus'al* (passive form: being questioned) and *tas'al* (active form: to question). According to first reading 'If God wills the Jews become Muslims' whereas according to second readings 'the Prophet (pbuh) wanted to know what would happen to his relatives'.

5) There is flexibility in the identification of pagan and Jewish opponents such as Abū Jahl, Uqba b. Muayt, Walid b. Mughira and so on in the reports regarding the occasions of the revelation.

6) The Companions used to note certain verses that were revealed concerning them, as this was a source of honour and distinction for them. 'Umar b. Khattab and Sa'd b. Abī Waqqas are two important examples.

Sa'd reported:

---

454 Qur'ān, 87: 14

455 Qasimi, *Mahasin at-Ta'wil*, 1/29-38.

456 Qur'ān, 2: 119.

Four verses of the Qur'ān were revealed concerning me. The first one was due to the fact that my mother promised not to eat or drink until I leave the Prophet Muhammad. Therefore, God revealed the following verse:

But if they (parents) strive with you to make you associate with Me something of which you certainly have no knowledge (and which is absolutely contrary to the Knowledge), do not obey them. Even then, treat them with kindness and due consideration in respect of (the life of) this world.[457]

The second verse was revealed concerning the booty we had captured in war. There was a sword that I really liked, so I asked the Messenger of God to give it to me. Upon this God revealed this verse:

They ask you concerning the spoils of war...[458]

The third verse was revealed when the Prophet visited me when I was sick. I asked him, 'O Prophet! I wish to distribute my wealth, should I give away half of it?' He answered, 'No!' I then asked, 'A third?' He did not respond to this, so from then onwards (a bequest) of a third was allowed. And the fourth one occurred when I was drinking wine with a group of the *Ansār*. One of them hit me on my nose (because he was drunk), so I went to the Prophet (to complain), and then God revealed the verse prohibiting of wine.[459]

Summary of Some Issues Related to the Occasion of Revelation:

1. Before reporting *asbāb an-nuzūl* narrations it is very important to know the following issues:
2. There are some contradictions between the reports and the historical facts.
3. There are some contradictions in the reports themselves, they are ambiguous and very difficult to understand. This might be caused because some people tried to connect the reports to events which happened later.
4. The occasions of the revelation are one of the reasons for the appearance of sects in Islam.
5. Different *asbāb* reports in accordance with the variant readings of the same verse can be occur.
6. There is flexibility in the identification of pagan and Jewish opponents such as Abū Jahl, Uqba b. Muayt, Walid b. Mughira and so on in the reports regarding the occasions of the revelation.

---

457 Qur'ān, 31: 15.

458 Qur'ān, 8: 1.

459 Zarkashī , 1/33.

7. The Companions used to note certain verses that were revealed concerning them, as this was a source of honour and distinction for them.

6.1.9 Summary of *Asbāb an-Nuzūl*

It is good to summarize this topic in order to give the reader a better view on this and help them to understand the true notion of *asbāb al-nuzūl.*

1) The occasion of revelation is an auxiliary means to help understand the Qur'anic verses in question.

2) These reports are considered as background information for understanding the meaning of some verses.

3) The occasion of revelation (*sabab nuzūl*) is not the occasion of existence (*sabab wujûd*). The connection between condition (*sabab*) and revelation (*nuzūl*) is not a conditional relationship.

4) It is incorrect to argue that revelation (*musabbab*) is dependent on the existence of an occasion (*sabab*). In fact, due to the considerable theological connotation of this topic, some Muslim scholars use the expression *sabab al-iqtirān* in place of *sabab al-nuzūl* which means that although God sends the verses because of His divine wisdom, His revelation comes down in connection to a particular point in time.

5) It is a fact that many verses of the Qur'ān were revealed without there being a specific occasion. This clearly indicates that events (conditions) in seventh-century Arabia did not determine the incidence of revelation; but, on the contrary, the revelation determined or shaped events.

6) Those verses that came as a direct response to specific questions should not be considered as answers only to those specific queries. Muslim scholars state this issue in the famous technical formula: 'the specific nature of the *sabab* (occasion) does not hinder the generality of the rule.'

7) These reports are not the real reason for the revelation but are a means for understanding the verse.

6.1.10 Books on *Asbāb an-Nuzūl*

Since early times, Muslim scholars have written books addressing this topic, some of which are:

- Ali b. al-Madini, (d. 238 A.H. / 848 C.E.), *Asbāb al-nuzūl.*
- Abū al-Mutrif Abd al-Rahman b. Muhammad al-Qurtubī, (d. 402 A.H. / 1010 C.E.), *al-Qasas wa al-asalib allati nazala min ajliha al-Qur'ān.*

- Wāḫidī, (d. 468 A.H. / 1075 C.E.), *Asbāb al-nuzūl.*
- Muhammad b. As'ad b. Muhammad al-Iraqi, (d. 567 A.H. / 1171 C.E.), *Asbāb al-nuzūl.*
- Ibn Taymiyya, (d. 728 A.H. / 1327 C.E.), *al-Ilm bi-asbāb al-nuzūl.*
- Ibn Ḫajar al-Asqalani, (d. 852 A.H. / 1448 C.E.), *al-Ujab fi bayan al-asbāb.*
- Jalal al-Din al-Suyūtī, (d. 911 A.H. / 1505 C.E.), *Lubab al-nuqul fi asbāb al-nuzūl.*
- Lubbi Muhammad Efendi, (d. 1166 A.H. / 1752 C.E.), *Lubbu al-tafasir fi ma'rifat asbāb al-nuzūl wa al-tafsīr.*

6.2 The Notion of *Isra'iliyyat*

Muslims believe that the Qur'ān comes directly from God as an update, an extension, correction, or commentary on both Jewish and Christian scriptures: filling the gaps, expanding or explaining some ambiguities and suggesting some corrections. At the same time, the Qur'ān contains many narrative passages concerning the Prophets and sages, but these are usually in an allusive style and frequently mention an event only once or refer briefly to a person who does not appear again. These passages are not intended as biography, history or entertainment. Many details are mentioned only briefly in the Qur'ān in order to spend more time on more weighty issues.

In order to understand every detail of the narratives of the Qur'ān, Muslim scholars felt it necessary to reference pre-Islamic sources, thus Muslims have used, and from time to time are still using, biblical and other sources in their interpretations of the Qur'ān. However, it cannot be said that Islam took everything from Judaism and Christianity or any other tradition. Islam is not Judaism and Christianity and vice versa; between them there is shared information and nuances.

6.2.1 Definition of *Isra'iliyyat*

Isra'iliyyat is the plural of the word '*isra'iliy*'. It means the information which came from Jewish sources and is used in the interpretation of Qur'anic verses. According to the reports '*isra'il*' is the title for Jacob.[460] He is mentioned in the Qur'ān and he is the ancestor of twelve Jewish tribes.[461] The Qur'ān usually mentions Jewish as '*banī isra'il*' (the children of Israel). This word is Hebrew and con-

[460] Asim Efendi, *Kamus Terjemesi*, 4/1006.

[461] Qur'ān, 2: 136, 140; 3:84.

sists of two parts; first part '*isra*' means 'servant' and second part '*il*' means 'God'; as a compound it is 'the servant of God'.[462]

In a restricted sense, *Isra'iliyyat* applies to the traditions and reports that contain elements of the legendary and religious literature of the Jews, but more inclusively and more commonly it also refers to Christian, Zoroastrian and other Near Eastern traditions including folklore. In other words, every non-Muslims element used in Muslim exegesis is called *Isra'iliyyat.*

The specific usage of the term *Isra'iliyyat* to denote these different elements is, however, due to the Arabic rule of *taghlib*, which prescribes that the term is appropriate when material mainly obtained from Jewish sources predominates. *Isra'iliyyat* reports include the following information; stories of the Prophets, narratives from creation to the current date, narratives about a specific period from Moses' death to the Israelites arriving in Palestine.

Ibn Khaldun said:

> The early scholars had already made complete compilations on the subject. However, their works and the information they transmit contain side by side important and unimportant matters, accepted and rejected statements. The reason is that the Arabs had no books or scholarship. The desert attitude and illiteracy prevailed among them. When they wanted to know certain things that human beings are usually curious to know, such as the reasons for the existing things, the beginning of creation, and the secrets of existence, they consulted the earlier People of the Book about it and got their information from them. The People of the Book were the Jews who had the Torah, and the Christians who followed the religion of (the Jews). Now, the people of the Torah who lived among the Arabs at that time were themselves Bedouins. They knew only as much about these matters as is known to ordinary People of the Book (in contrast to learned rabbis). The majority of those Jews were Himyaritic who had adopted Judaism. When they became Muslims, they clung to the (information) they possessed, such as information about the beginning of creation and information of the type of forecasts and predictions. That information had no connection with the (Jewish or Christian) religious laws they were preserving as theirs. Such men were Ka'b al-Akhbār, Wahb b. Munabbih, 'Abd Allah b. Salam, and similar people. The Qur'ān commentaries were filled with material of such tendencies transmitted on their authority. It is information that entirely depends on them. It has no relation to (religious) laws, such that one might claim for it the soundness that would make it necessary to act (in accordance with it). The Qur'ān interpreters

[462] R. Na'na', *al-Israiliyyat*, 72.

were not very rigorous in this respect. They filled the Qur'ān commentaries with such material, which originated, as we have stated, with the people of the Torah who lived in the desert and were not capable of verifying the information they transmitted. However, they were famous and highly esteemed, because they were people of rank in (their) religion and religious group. Therefore, their interpretation has been accepted from that time onwards.[463]

Summary of the Definition of *Isra'iliyyat*:

1. It is the plural of the word *'israiliy'*.
2. It means the information which came from Jewish sources and is used in the interpretation of Qur'anic verses.
3. In a restricted sense, *Isra'iliyyat* applies to the traditions and reports that contain elements of the legendary and religious literature of the Jews.
4. More inclusively, and more commonly, it also refers to Christian, Zoroastrian and other Near Eastern traditions including folklore.
5. *Isra'iliyyat* reports include; stories of the Prophets, narratives from creation to the current date, narratives about a specific period from Moses' death to the Israelites arriving in Palestine.

6.2.2 The Approaches towards *Isra'iliyyat*

There are three approaches towards these types of reports:

1) Muslims are told to adopt a non-committal attitude to what they hear.

Abū Huraira reported:

> The People of the Scripture (Jews) used to recite the Torah in Hebrew and they used to explain it in Arabic to the Muslims. On that God's Apostle (pbuh) said: 'Do not believe the People of the Scripture or disbelieve them, but say: 'We believe in God and what is revealed to us' (2: 136).[464]

The Prophet (pbuh) commanded his Companions: 'Do not ask the People of the Book because they will not guide you having already led themselves astray'. He also counselled the Companions, saying: 'If the People of the Book tell you something do not either accept it as true or reject it as false for they may tell you something which is false but you may accept it is true'.[465]

---

[463] Ibn Khaldun, *al-Muqaddima*, Chapter 6, Section 10, Translated by Franz Rosenthal.

[464] Bukhari, *Saḫīḫ, Prophetic Commentary on the Quran*, 12.

[465] Dhahabi, *al-Isra'iliyyat fi al-Tafsir wa al-Hadith*, Cairo 1971, 70-71.

2) The avoidance of information from Jewish and Christian sources:

Jabir reported:

> 'Umar wrote some part of the Torah in Arabic and brought it to the Prophet (pbuh). When he started reading what he wrote, the face of the Prophet (pbuh) changed. Then one of the *Ansār* told 'Umar: 'Shame on you O 'Umar! Look at the face of the Messenger of God.' The Prophet (pbuh) said: 'Do not ask the People of the Book about anything, because they will not show you the right path, having already led them astray. Otherwise you accuse the truth of falsehood and confirm the wrong; I swear that even if Moses was alive among you nothing would be opened to him but to follow me.[466]

Ibn 'Abbās warned the community of Muhammad (pbuh):

> O community of Muslims! Why do you ask the People of the Book about anything while you have the final and undistorted Book, which is revealed to the Prophet of God?' He added: 'Did God not inform you in His Book that the People of the Book have altered their book with their hands?' He recited 2:79: 'Then woe to those who write the book with their own hands and then say this is from God so that they may take for it a small price.' He continued, 'Does God not forbid you the knowledge that comes to you from questioning the People of the Book about what He has sent to you? By God we never saw any of them asking you about what God revealed to you.[467]

Muslim scholars not only forbid transmission from the scriptures of the People of the Book but they also forbid the study of these scriptures. Kattani mentions that the scholars agreed that it is unlawful to read, investigate and deal with the books of the People of the Book.

3) Accepting information from Jewish and Christian sources:

Although Muslims are apparently forbidden to study and copy Jewish or Christian scripture or to learn their religious practices, there are reports which suggest the contrary. Muslims were allowed to narrate from the Jews and Christians. The Prophet (pbuh) gave comprehensive directives in the following words:

> Convey (my teachings) to the people even if it were a single sentence, and tell others the stories of the People of Israel (which have been taught to you), for it is not sinful to do so. And whoever tells a lie about me intentionally, will surely take his place in the (Hell) Fire.[468]

---

466 Ahmad Ibn Hanbal, *Musnad*, İstanbul: Çağrı Yayınları 1992, 3/338, 387.

467 Bukhari, *Sahīh*, 4/375.

468 Bukhari, *Sahīh, Virtues and Merits of the Prophet*, 667.

Ibn Hishām reports: 'al-Aws and al-Khazraj were more knowledgeable about the Prophet (pbuh) than the Meccans because they used to listen to Jewish rabbis'.[469] Hafiz Ibn Kathīr, in the preface of his *Muqaddimah* tells us that God has taught us how to react to the narrations of this kind; i.e. those which neither conform to nor contradict the Islamic sources. The Qur'ān says:

> Some will say they were three, the dog being the fourth among them; and some will say they were five, the dog being the sixth – all guessing at random at (something related to) the Unseen. Still others will say: "They were seven, the dog being the eighth." Say (O Messenger): "My Lord knows their number better; it is but few that know (the truth about) them." So do not argue about them, being content with what is obvious (to you through Revelation), nor ask any of them (who argue even among themselves) to give you an opinion about them.[470]

In this verse God explains how to deal with useless details. When looked at closely, the narrations which are well known to have come from the Judeo-Christian legend are characterised by their amount of unnecessary detail thus relegating the lessons contained within to the background.

SUMMARY OF THE APPROACHES TOWARDS *ISRA'ILIYYAT*:

1. There are three approaches towards these types of report: a) Muslims are told to adopt a non-committal attitude to what they hear, b) the avoidance of information from Jewish and Christian sources, c) accepting information from Jewish and Christian sources.

6.2.3 When the Narration of *Isra'iliyyat* Started

These reports suggest that there was a close relationship between the Arabs and the People of the Book at an early stage of Islam. However, there is no consensus among Muslim scholars about the engagement in *Isra'iliyyat* during the time of the Companions. Some hold the view that *Isra'iliyyat* began during the Companions' time; while others maintain that there were no *Isra'iliyyat* during that time.[471] The second view is, to some extent, due to theological commitment rather than factual analysis of the narrated reports. Non-Muslim scholars, however, generally hold the view that, throughout the first and the beginning of the

469 Ibn Hishām, *Sīrah*, 1/232.

470 Qur'ān, 18: 22.

471 Ismail Albayrak, *Re-evaluation The Notion of Isra'iliyyat*, D.E.Ü. İlahiyat Fakültesi Dergisi Sayı XIII-XIV, İzmir 2001, ss. 69-88.

second Islamic centuries, Muslims were encouraged to learn about the biblical and extra-biblical pre-Islamic Prophets.[472] One important reason for this, according to Western scholars, came about from Muslims' having difficulty in making sense of significant portions of the Qur'ān. The second reason lies in the activities of the new converts to Islam. When they accepted Islam they brought with them their old religious traditions and legends.[473]

6.2.4 Important Figures in *Isra'iliyyat* Report Transmission

Key personalities who frequently commented on the verses with biblical references were 'Abd Allah b. Salam, Ka'b al-Ahbar and Wahb b. Munabbih. They were highly regarded by early scholars; for instance, Ka'b was considered the most learned of the People of the Book. Moreover, it is said that Wahb had read ninety-two books revealed by God. They found confirmation of the Qur'anic stories in the Jewish and Christian sources. The majority of their explanations are primarily based on Midrash, rabbinic exegesis on the Pentateuch or the Apocrypha, and the hagiographic writings of eastern Christianity, rather than on the Bible.[474]

6.2.5 Categories of *Isra'iliyyat*

Ibn Kathīr placed some limitations on these reports; he clarifies the matter by stating that *Isra'iliyyat* is quoted for supplementary attestation, not for full support.[475] The three categories of *Isra'iliyyat* which Ibn Kathīr proposed are still in use:

1) Those which are known to be true because they are attested to in the Qur'anic revelation.

2) Those whose falsehood is certified from the Qur'ān.

3) Those which fall into neither of the other classes.

[472] Albayrak, *Re-evaluation The Notion of Isra'iliyyat*, 69-88.

[473] Albayrak, ibid.

[474] Albayrak, ibid

[475] Ibn Kathīr, *Tafsir al-Qur'ān al-Aẕīm*, 1/7-8.

Chapter Seven

Clear and Ambiguous Verses (*Muḫkam and Mutashābih*)

Clear and Ambiguous Verses (*Muẖkam and Mutashābih*)

7.1 The Clear and Unclear Verses (*Muẖkam Mutashābih*)

In exegesis, there are some definitions which are very important for the interpretation of the Qur'ān. Since the Qur'ān is revealed in Arabic, it is important to know its language and its style of expression. The Qur'ān uses various different styles of expression that are suited to the topic and addressees. The usage of the words, the styles, the method for expressing the purpose, how the text conveys the desired meaning, etc. are all important for the interpretation of the Qur'ān. One of the key concepts in the exegesis is the notion of *Muẖkam and Mutashābih* verses.

7.1.1 Definition of *Muẖkam*

Muẖkam means:

a) to judge, to pass a verdict
b) to prevent, to obstruct
c) the things that are free from corruption
d) to bring something to perfection
e) to decide between two things
f) the things which are sound and real

In exegesis, *muẖkam* means, 'unambiguous' and 'contains no confusion'; it indicates the meaning of the verse clearly, and the verses whose interpretation is known and their meanings are clear. In other words, *muẖkam* verses are easily understood and do not need any explanation. The word *Muẖkamāt* is derived from the root *uẖkima* which means 'to decide between two things'. It is a verbal noun in the plural meaning 'judgements' and 'decisions'. In technical language it refers to all clearly decided verses of the Qur'ān; mostly those concerning legal rulings, but also to other clear definitions such as that between truth and falsehood, etc.[476] The verses regarding lawful or unlawful things, the prescribed daily prayers, fasting, *zakat*, *Hajj*, etc. are examples of *muḫkam* verses in the Qur'ān.

7.1.2 Definition of *Mutashābih*

Mutashābih means:

a) Similar or resembling
b) To complement one another
c) To be doubtful or uncertain in meaning
d) Difficult to differentiate because of equality in similarities

In the Qur'anic sciences, *mutashābih* means the verses which are not very clear or completely agreed upon, or those that are open to more than one interpretation. In other words, verses that have many meanings, need explanations and the meanings cannot be discovered through using reason alone. The time of the Day of Judgement and the *huruf al-muqatta'* (conjecture letters) at the beginning of some *surah* are examples of this type of verse.

The Prophet (pbuh) said:

> The lawful is clear and that which is unlawful is clear and between the two of them are '*mushtabihat*' doubtful [or ambiguous] matters about which not many people are knowledgeable. Thus, he who avoids these doubtful matters certainly clears himself in regard to his religion and his honour. But he who falls into the doubtful matters falls into that which is unlawful like the shepherd who pastures around a sanctuary, all but grazing therein. Verily every king has a sanctuary and God's sanctuary is His prohibition. In the body there is a morsel of flesh which, if it be sound, all the body is sound and which, if it be diseased, all the body is diseased. This part of the body is the heart.[477]

7.1.3 The Usage of *Muḫkam* and *Mutashābih* in the Qur'ān

Muḫkam and *Mutashābih* are used in the Qur'ān with different meanings:

> *Alif Lam Ra* a Book whose Revelations in verses have been made firm (absolutely free of doubt, alteration, or annulment) and full of wisdom, and arranged in sequence and distinctly detailed. It is from One All-Wise, All-Aware.[478]

---

476 Von Denffer, *'Ulūm al-Qur'ān*, 79.
477 Bukhari *Saḫīḫ, Iman*, 39: Muslim, *Saḫīḫ, Musaqaat*, 107;Abu Dāwud, *Sunan, Buyu*, 3.
478 Qur'ān, 11: 1.

In this verse the word 'أُحْكِمَتْ' (being made firm and free of doubt, alteration, or annulment) is used and this word has the same root as *'muḫkam'*. According to this verse, the whole Qur'ān is *muḫkam*; it means the verses of the Qur'ān have been made firm, they are absolutely free of doubt, alteration, or annulment and protected from any distortion.

> God sends down in parts the best of the words as a Book fully consistent in itself, and whose statements corroborate, expound and refer to one another. The skins of those who stand in awe of their Lord tingle at (the hearing and understanding of) it. Then, their skins and their hearts come to rest in the Remembrance of God (the Qur'ān). This is God's guidance, by which He guides whomever He wills. And whoever God leads astray, there is no guide for him.[479]

In this verse, the expression, كِتَابًا مُتَشَابِهًا (*mutashābih* book), infers that the whole Qur'ān is *mutashābih*. But here the word *mutashābih* means, 'the book whose statements corroborate, expound and refer to one another'.

هُوَ الَّذِي أَنزَلَ عَلَيْكَ الْكِتَابَ مِنْهُ آيَاتٌ مُّحْكَمَاتٌ هُنَّ أُمُّ الْكِتَابِ وَأُخَرُ مُتَشَابِهَاتٌ ۖ فَأَمَّا الَّذِينَ فِي قُلُوبِهِمْ زَيْغٌ فَيَتَّبِعُونَ مَا تَشَابَهَ مِنْهُ ابْتِغَاءَ الْفِتْنَةِ وَابْتِغَاءَ تَأْوِيلِهِ ۗ وَمَا يَعْلَمُ تَأْوِيلَهُ إِلَّا اللَّهُ ۘ وَالرَّاسِخُونَ فِي الْعِلْمِ يَقُولُونَ آمَنَّا بِهِ كُلٌّ مِّنْ عِندِ رَبِّنَا ۗ وَمَا يَذَّكَّرُ إِلَّا أُولُو الْأَلْبَابِ

> It is He Who has sent down on you this (glorious) Book, wherein are verses absolutely explicit and firm: they are the core of the Book, others being allegorical. Those in whose hearts is swerving pursue what is allegorical in it, seeking (to cause) dissension, and seeking to make it open to arbitrary interpretation, although none knows its interpretation save God. And those firmly rooted in knowledge say: "We believe in it (in the entirety of its verses, both explicit and allegorical); all is from our Lord"; yet none derives admonition except the people of discernment.[480]

According to this verse, some parts of the Qur'ān are *muḫkam* and others are *mutashābih*. There are two important *asbāb al-nuzūl* reports for the interpretation of this verse.

---

[479] Qur'ān, 39: 23

[480] Qur'ān, 3: 7.

The delegation of Najran, which consisted of sixty riders, came to see the Messenger of Allah (pbuh). There were among them fourteen noblemen, three of whom were their leaders. The first one was the deputy chief of Najran who was the head of the delegation, their ultimate advisor and the one whose orders they followed. His name was 'Abd al-Masih. The second was the master who was in charge of the well-being of the delegation and who also looked after their belongings. His name was al-Ayham. The third was Abū Harithah ibn 'Alqamah, their bishop, doctor and the head of their church. The latter was highly esteemed by his people; he had learned the Scriptures and became well versed in their religion. The Byzantine kings also held him in high esteem, financed him and built for him churches because of his knowledge and dedication. They came to the Messenger of God (pbuh) and entered his mosque when he had just finished the mid-afternoon (*'Asr*) prayer. They were wearing square, black attires which consisted of cloaks and long outer garments with wide sleeves. They had come riding the camels of the men of the Banī Harith ibn 'Amr. One of the Companions of the Prophet (pbuh), who saw them said: 'we had never seen a delegation like them before: When it was time for their prayer, they stood up and prayed in the mosque of the Prophet (pbuh). The Messenger of God (pbuh) allowed them to pray, and they prayed toward the East. The deputy chief and the master addressed the Messenger of God (pbuh), who said to them: 'Surrender to God' they said: 'We have surrendered to God before you. He said: 'You lie! You were prevented from surrendering by claiming that God has a son, by your worship of the cross and by your consumption of pork'. They said: 'If Jesus is not the son of God, who is his father?' They argued with him about Jesus, upon that the Messenger of God (pbuh) said: 'Do you not agree that a son must resemble his father?' They said: 'yes, we do: He said: 'Do you not know that our Lord is ever living and never dies while Jesus is subject to death?' they said: 'We do know that'. He said: 'do you not know that God oversees everything, protects and provides for it?' they said: 'We do!' He said: 'Does Jesus share any of that?' They said: No. He said: 'God has shaped Jesus in the womb of his mother as He willed, but our Lord does not eat or drink nor has He any need to relieve Himself. They said: 'We agree that this is the case. He said: 'Do you not know that Jesus was in his mother's womb in the way any other woman carries her child in the womb, and she gave birth to him like any other woman gives birth to a child, and then he was fed like any other child, and then he ate and drank and relieved himself?' They said: 'We do!' He said: 'Then how could he be the son of God as you claim?' At this point they did not answer. Then, God, glorious and majestic is He, revealed about them the beginning of *surah* Ali 'Imran up to the first eighty something verses of the same *surah*.[481]

[481] Wāqidī, *Asbāb an-Nuzūl*, 44, Tabarī, *Tafsir*, 3/162-163.

A group of non-Muslims (Jews) came to the Prophet (pbuh) and told him about the life of his community in the light of their reckoning of *huruf al-muqatta'a* (detached/abbreviated letters) and God revealed this *surah*.[482]

There are many comments on this verse and the meaning of *muḫkam* and *mutashābih* verses in the Qur'ān. Abū Hayyan and Suyūtī mention more than twenty meanings for *muḫkam* and *mutashābih*.[483] On examination, these various opinions are not contradictory but are, in fact, all similar and close in meaning:[484]

1) *Muḫkam* is *nāsikh* (abrogating) whereas *mutashābih* is *mansūkh* (abrogated).

2) *Muḫkam* is understandable by the people whereas *mutashābih* is known only by God.

3) *Muḫkam* has only one interpretation or dimension (requires no further comment), whereas *mutashābih* has more than one.

4) Legal verses, *ḫalal* and *ḫaram*, are *muḫkam* whereas the verses about the attributes of God, the nature of resurrection and the afterlife are *mutashābih*.

5) *Mutashābihāt* are those verses whose wording is repeated either fully or slightly differently.

6) *Wujūh* (several words with one meaning) and *Nazāir* (one word with several meanings) are *mutashābih*.

7) *Muḫkam* and *mutashābih* are lexical opposites in the verse 3:7 because of the existence of the word *ta'wil* (interpretation) at the end.

8) The *mutashābihāt* should be perceived as intricate or unclear but without an absolute ambiguity being intended. As long as *mutashābih* verses are read in the light of *muḫkam* verses they are not unclear.

9) *Muḫkam* means 'that which has been made firm and perfect', while *mutashābih* derives from the root '*shibh*', which means 'resemblance'. All the verses in the Qur'ān are *muḫkam* in the sense that there is no doubt about their Divine authorship, yet they are *mutashābih* as well in the sense that they are interrelated with one another.

The Prophet (pbuh) once recited this verse and then said: 'So when you see those who follow the *mutashābih* of the Qur'ān, then these are the ones whom God has mentioned, so beware of them'.[485] This Hadith explains that it is not right to

---

[482] Tabarī, *Tafsir*, 3/162-163.
[483] Suyūtī, *Itqān*, 2/3-7.
[484] Zarqānī , *Burhān*, 2/295.
[485] Bukhari, *Saḫīḫ, Tafsir of the Prophet*, 70.

interpret the *mutashābihāt* without understanding them according to the *muḫkamāt*. Therefore, those people who interpret the *mutashābihāt* in light of the *muhkam* are not blameworthy.

10) The *muḫkam* (singular) as an individual verse is not considered the Essence (or 'mother') of the Book, because only the *muḫkamāt* (plural) in their entirety can constitute the basis of the belief in *tawḫīd* (the Oneness of God).

The meaning of *ta'wil* in the verse:

a) To understand a word in light of one of its connotations, despite the fact that this connotation is not the primary intent of the word. This is due to some external evidence from the word itself, such as the context in which it occurs.
b) To explain a word or phrase.
c) The actuality of an event. In other words, when and how something occurs.[486]

Discussion of the grammatical position of the letter '*waw*', whether it is a conjunctive particle (*waw al-atf*) or a letter which shows the beginning of a new sentence (*waw al-isti'naf*) is very important to the interpretation of this verse. If the '*waw*' is considered *isti'nafiyya* (the beginning of a new sentence) it means only God knows the general and specific meanings of the *mutashābihāt* in their every detail. However, if the '*waw*' is considered as *al-atf* (conjunction), it means that some people who are firmly rooted in Islamic knowledge can know the meaning of the *mutashābihāt*. The last part of verse 3:7 '...yet none remembers but men possessed of minds' supports this argument. Both of these readings originate from the Companions. The first way was the reading of ibn Mas'ud and the second reading was that of Ibn 'Abbās. If one stops at this point, the context implies that the meaning of *ta'wil* is the interpretation. Therefore, 'those well-grounded in knowledge' are aware of the interpretation of the *mutashābih*. Ibn 'Abbās stated, 'I am of those well-grounded in knowledge, who knows the meaning of the *mutashābih*'.[487]

Indeed the particle '*waw*' is one of the *mutashābih*, and so both interpretations are equally valid and complete each other. God knows the real meaning of *mutashābihāt* but He also allows some of His servants to know or feel their meaning.

486 Qadhi, *Introduction to the Sciences of the Qur'ān*, 210.
487 Suyūtī, *Itqān*, 2/4.

Summary of the Clear and Unclear Verses (*Muḫkam Mutashābih*):

1. In exegesis, *Muḫkam* means, 'unambiguous' and 'contains no confusion'. *Muḫkam* verses are easily understood and do not need any explanation.
2. The verses regarding lawful or unlawful things, the prescribed daily prayers, fasting, *zakat, Hajj*, etc. are examples of *muḫkam* verses in the Qur'ān.
3. In the Qur'anic sciences, *mutashābih* means the verses which are not very clear or completely agreed upon, or those that are open to more than one interpretation. The time of the Day of Judgement and the *huruf al-muqatta'* (conjecture letters) at the beginning of some *surah* are examples of this type of verse.
4. *Muḫkam* and *mutashābih* are used in the Qur'ān with different meanings.
5. Abū Hayyan and Suyūtī mention more than twenty meanings for *muḫkam* and *mutashābih*. These various opinions are not contradictory but are, in fact, all similar and close in meaning.

7.1.4 How Can We Know *Mutashābih* Verses

When a verse is *mutashābih* it doesn't mean that there is no way to understand it, rather it means that there are many possible meanings and, for this reason, it is difficult to choose the right meaning. There are various ways to understand the meaning of the *mutashābihāt*; one is that they should be referred to the *muḫkamāt* since these are the essence of the Book. Every religious book sent by God contains both *muhkam* and *mutashābih* parts and the latter is always referred to the former. The *mutashābihāt* of the Torah were referred to the *muḫkamāt* of the Gospel, the *mutashābihāt* of the Gospel were referred to the *muḫkamāt* of the Qur'ān, and finally, the Qur'ān's *mutashābihāt* were, and continue to be, referred to its *muḫkamāt*. If the *mutashābihāt* are referred to the *muḫkamāt* they automatically become *muḫkam* leaving no conflict between the verses which say that the whole Qur'ān is *muḫkam* or the whole Qur'ān is *mutashābih*. Being strong in faith and firmly rooted in knowledge is a primary condition for understanding the *mutashābih*. The relationship between *'amal* (action) and *ilm* (knowledge) is very important for the interpretation of the verses.

In conclusion, the *muḫkam* verses are those verses whose meaning is so clear that they are not open to any ambiguity or equivocation. Such verses are the core of the Qur'ān. They embody admonition and instruction, as well as the refutation of erroneous doctrines. They also contain the essentials of the true faith, teachings related to faith, worship, daily life and morality, and the mandatory duties and prohibitions. These are the verses which will guide the genuine seeker of the truth; those who turn to the Qur'ān in order to find out what they ought or ought not to do.

The *mutashābih* verses are those which, having more than one meaning, require other evidence in order to be understood. Multiple reasons occur because time progresses, conditions change, human information increases, and there are as many levels of understanding as there are people. The Qur'ān, being the Word of God, addresses all levels of understanding from the time of its revelation to the Day of Resurrection. It explains to people matters which cannot be easily understood by using metaphors, similes, personifications, and parables. This method of explanation does not harm the unchanging, essential truths of the religion, for God has made it clear what He demands of us relating to faith, worship, morality, and the mandatory duties and prohibitions. The *mutashābih* (allegorical) verses contain relative truths which can be understood by considering the relevant verses and referring to the *muḫkam* verses.

Because of the realities of human life in this world, the relative truths are more in number than the absolute, unchanging ones. In order to understand this point, let us take a crystal chandelier as an example. While the light remains the same, those sitting around it perceive different colours or light of varying strength as their positions change. Such differences arise from the different shapes of the crystals in the chandelier, and the different angles of the crystals. In the same way, God included in the Qur'ān several allegorical verses to provide unlimited meanings with limited words to all people, whatever their level of knowledge or understanding might be, in order to teach them until the Last Day; in this way, they are invited to reflect on the Book and to be guided to the truth. It should not be forgotten that an exact resemblance is not sought between that which is compared and that to which it is being compared. Since the allegorical verses have multiple meanings, the interpreters of the Qur'ān may be able to discover one or more of those meanings. Each of their discoveries can be regarded as being true, provided it is in conformity with the *muḫkam* verses and the essentials of Islam, the rules of Qur'anic Arabic, and the rules of the science of interpretation. But, whichever true meaning is arrived at by a scholar, the exact meaning of these verses is always referred to God; this is exegesis.[488]

[488] Ali Unal, The Qur'ān with Annotated Interpretation, see the footnote for 3:7.

Summary of How Can We Know *Mutashābih* Verses:

1. *Mutashābihāt* means that the verse has many possible meanings for this reason it is difficult to choose the right meaning.
2. *Mutashābihāt* verses should firstly be referred to the *muẖkamāt* since these are the essence of the Book.
3. If the *mutashābihāt* are referred to the *muẖkamāt* they automatically become *muhkam* leaving no conflict between the verses which say that the whole Qur'ān is *muhkam* or the whole Qur'ān is *mutashābih*.
4. A primary condition for understanding the *mutashābih* is being strong in faith and firmly rooted in knowledge.
5. The reasons for the multiple meanings of *mutashābih* verses are that time progresses, conditions change, human information increases, and there are as many levels of understanding as there are people.
6. The *mutashābih* (allegorical) verses contain relative truths which can be understood by considering the relevant verses and referring to the *muhkam* verses.
7. Since the allegorical verses have multiple meanings, the interpreters of the Qur'ān may be able to discover one or more of those meanings.

7.1.5 Status of *Muẖkamāt*

Every *muẖkam* verse is individual from the *muẖkamāt*, but its meaning(s) and the rules it contains can only be known by comparing it with other *muẖkamāt*. In other words, like the *mutashābihāt* being referred to the *muẖkam*, the *muẖkamāt* are also referred to each other in order to clearly identify their meaning.

There are nuances in the relationship which occur among the *muẖkamāt*, such as *mutlaq-muqayyad* (unconditional or unrestricted vs. restricted), *āam-khās* (general vs. particular), *taqrir* vs. *tafsīr* and so on.

7.1.6 Categories of *Muẖkam* and *Mutashābih*

There are different classifications for *muẖkam* and *mutashābih*, such as:

1) Absolute *muẖkam*

2) Absolute *mutashābih*

3) Sometimes *muẖkam* while at other times *mutashābih*.

In general there are two types of *mutashābih*: the first type can be understood when studied in the light of *muẖkam* verses; the meaning of the second type is only known by God.

The unclearness or ambiguity in *mutashābih* verses may come from the words used or from the meanings or from both.[489]

a) Example for the perspective of the words; *yad* (hands of God: 48:10), *ayn* (His Eyes: 11:37), *wajh* (His Face: 55:27), *al-arsh* (His throne: 20:5) and so on.

b) Examples for the perspective of meanings:

> All praise and thanks are for God, the Originator of the heavens and the earth (each with particular features and ordered principles), Who appoints the angels as Messengers (conveying His commands) having wings, two, or three, or four (or more). He increases in creation what He wills. Surely God has full power over everything[490]

It is impossible to know how many wings the angels have.

c) Example of the unclearness from the perspective of both words and meaning:

> It is not virtue that you enter dwellings from the backs of them, but virtue is (the state of) one who (truly believing in God) strives to attain righteousness and piety (by carrying out His commandments and refraining from His prohibitions). So come to dwellings (in the normal way) by their doors[491]

The wording and meaning is ambiguous and this verse requires some study to understand the meaning.

The other classification of *mutashābih* is:

1. Verses whose meanings are only known by God.
2. Verses which *rāsikhūn* (the profound scholars) can know.
3. Verses which ordinary people can also know; there are some words in the Qur'ān which are ambiguous at first but can be known by anyone after some research.

There are absolute *mutashābihāt* which are known only by God, there are many which are connected with the meaning of one of the *muḫkamāt*, and there are others where the *mutashābih* meets the *muhkam* on various levels and shares several of its signs and significations. Consequently, the concept of the *mutashābih* as existing within the *muḫkam* and the *muḫkam* as existing within the *mutashābih*

---

489 Zarkashī, *al-Burhān*, 2/68-69 ; Suyūtī, *al-Itqān*, 2/2-13.

490 Qur'ān, 35: 1.

491 Qur'ān, 2: 189.

along with the levels of meaning will be apprehended by the people when the appropriate time comes. That time is determined by the ever changing needs of the people and the events which will occur gradually. Ambiguity cannot be removed by means of the ambiguous, nor doubt by means of doubt, but the ambiguity can be removed by referring the *mutashābih* to the *muḫkam*.

SUMMARY OF *MUḪKAM* AND *MUTASHĀBIH*:

1. There are different classifications for *muḫkam* and *mutashābih*, such as: absolute *muḫkam,* absolute *mutashābih* and sometimes *muḫkam* while at other times *mutashābih*.
2. *Mutashābih* falls under two types: those whose meaning can be known when studied in the light of *muḫkam* verses and those whose meaning is only known by God.
3. The unclearness or ambiguity in *mutashābih* verses may come from the perspective of words, meanings or both.
4. The other classifications of *mutashābih* are: verses whose meanings are only known by God, verses which profound scholars can know and verses which ordinary people can know.
5. The concept of the *mutashābih* as existing within the *muḫkam* and the *muḫkam* as existing within the *mutashābih*, along with the levels of meaning, will be apprehended by people when the appropriate time comes.

7.1.7 Benefits of *Mutashābih* in the Qur'ān

The presence of all the *mutashābihāt* indicates that there are abundant realities in the Qur'ān, many of which are unknown to humankind. Therefore, whatever a person's position and experience, (whether they are scholar or layman), they will inevitably face *mutashābihāt.* In fact there is a fresh *mutashābih* waiting before and after the clarification of every *mutashābih*. Therefore, the understanding of *mutashābih* is not static.

1. The existence of *mutashābihāt* is the clear evidence of the universality of the Qur'ān, because it enables the human mind to constantly contemplate them.

2. *Mutashābihāt* indicate the gulf between God's all-encompassing knowledge and that possible for human beings.

3. The progress and the development of human knowledge depend on the *mutashābihāt* verses.

4. *Mutashābihāt* teach us that human knowledge always remains deficient however great human achievements may be.

5. The distortion of the earlier scriptures (according to Muslim scholars) lies in their preoccupation with the *mutashābihāt* or their preference of *mutashābihāt* over *muḫkamāt.*

6. Only human beings are bound to the *muḫkam* and the *mutashābih* while God knows everything in all its detail.

7. With the help of *mutashābih* verses, the Qur'ān expresses many deep realities in very few words; this affected the volume of the Qur'ān and, as a result, it became easy to memorise. Indeed, this situation caused the establishment of the many Islamic sciences.[492]

8. *Mutashābih* verses are part of the trial of human beings and a test which indicates belief and disbelief.

Summary of the Benefits of *Mutashābih* in the Qur'ān:

There are many benefits in the presence of *mutashābihāt* in the Qur'ān. They give evidence of the universality of the Qur'ān, remind us of the gulf between God's total and humankind's limited knowledge, give humans the means to progress and develop in all areas of life and give a grounding for true faith.

7.2 Abbreviated / Detached Letters (*Huruf al-Muqatta'a*)

The Qur'anic alphabet has 28 letters; the Qur'ān uses half of these at the beginning of 29 *surah*, either singly like '*qaf*' (as in *surah* Qaf) and '*sad*' (as in *surah* Sad), or in two, three, four or five letter combinations. These letters are called *huruf al-muqatta'at. Muqatta'a* means 'what is cut', 'what is abbreviated'. In technical language the word is used for certain letters found at the beginning of several *surah* of the Qur'ān, called 'the abbreviated letters'. The so-called 'abbreviated letters' are an important section of the *mutashābihāt.* 'Ali b. Abī Tālib said, 'Every book has an essence and mystery, these letters are the essence of the Qur'ān'. Only half of the Arabic alphabet, 14 letters, occurred in this way in the Qur'ān. These letters are not only half of the alphabet but also half of the type of letters in Arabic according to how their sound is made. In Arabic, certain letters' sounds come from different parts of the mouth or throat; these letters constitute half of these.

There are many possible interpretations for these letters:

---

[492] Ismail Cerrahoglu, *Tefsir Usulu*, 128-129.

1. They refer to the names of God: الر 'I am Allah, I see always'

2. They are an abbreviation of certain symbols or meanings:

طسم Tur-u Sina and Moses

كهيعص Karim, Hādi, Ḫākim , Ālim and Sādiq

3. These letters are used to attract attention. They are equal to (اما or الا) 'be careful, listen carefully'.

4. The *surah* that begin with these letters contain a high frequency of detached letters.

5. Some scholars believe that these letters have some kind of numerical equivalence. For instance الر غلبت الروم refers to the number 583 H. when Muslims conquered Bayt al-Maqdis in Jerusalem.

6. Some Jewish scholars think that these letters indicate the life of the Muslim *ummah*.

7. Spelling these letters means that people had just begun to learn how to read and write. So, their presence at the beginning of some *surah* shows that the Qur'ān was sent down to an illiterate people.

8. They imply that the Qur'ān is a book composed of words and letters, which it is impossible for an illiterate person, such as the Prophet Muhammad (pbuh), to have produced.

9. The characters of the Arabic alphabet are variant forms, extended and curved, of the first letter *alif*, which itself is described as the extended form of the *nuktah*, or 'point'. This is a symbol of the reality that, like the letters, words and sentences of the Qur'ān, all the creatures of the universe originate from a single source and are interrelated. From this we may understand that, in order to be able to produce even a single atom in the universe or a word in the Qur'ān in its proper place, one must have the knowledge and power to produce the whole universe and the whole Qur'ān.

10. These letters are like ciphers between God and his Messenger (pbuh), the exact and complete meaning of which is known to the Messenger (pbuh) only. However, this does not mean no one else can grasp some of their meanings. Exacting scholars well-versed in the science of the mysteries of the letters have drawn many mysterious conclusions from them and discovered in them such truths that, in their view, these letters form a most brilliant miracle. For example, Imam Rabbānī Ahmad Faruq al-Sirhindi (1564–1624 C.E.) discovered in them the signs of many future events.

SUMMARY OF DETACHED LETTERS (*HURUF AL-MUQATTA'A*):

1. The Qur'anic alphabet has 28 letters; the Qur'ān uses half of these at the beginning of 29 *surah*, either singly or in two, three, four or five letter combinations.
2. These letters are called *huruf al-muqatta'at.*
3. The 'abbreviated letters' are an important section of the *mutashābihāt.*
4. Half of the Arabic alphabet (14 letters), are used in this way.
5. There are many possible interpretations for these letters: they refer to the names of God; they are an abbreviation of certain symbols or meanings; they are used to attract attention.
6. The *surah* that begin with these letters contain a high frequency of detached letters.
7. Some scholars believe that these letters have some kind of numerical equivalence whereas some Jewish scholars think that these letters indicate the life of the Muslim *ummah.*
8. Their presence at the beginning of some *surah* shows that the Qur'ān was sent down to an illiterate people. They imply that the Qur'ān is a book composed of words and letters, which it is impossible for an illiterate person like the Prophet Muhammad (pbuh), to have produced.
9. They indicate the divine source of the Qur'ān being the creator of the universe.
10. They act like ciphers between God and his Messenger (pbuh), the exact and complete meaning of which is known to the Messenger (pbuh) only but some of which can be divined by some exceptional scholars.

7.3 General and Specific (*Āam and Khās*)

The word *āam* applies to all the members of a specific set, no matter how small or large that set is. Some verses of the Qur'ān are of a very wide, general application including all human beings, or all Muslims, etc. Other verses are restricted in their application to certain special circumstances only. The following verses illustrate each of these applications:

> Every soul is bound to taste death[493]

> It is made lawful for you to go in to your wives on the night of the Fast[494]

[493] Qur'ān, 3: 185.

[494] Qur'ān, 2: 187.

> God commands you in (the matter of the division of the inheritance among) your children[495]

Khās (specific), on the other hand, is a word that is used to denote a limited number of things. The difference between *āam* and *khās* is that *khās* applies to a single subject or a specified number of objects; in other words, the scope of its application is limited, unlike the *āam*.[496]

There are three categories of *āam*:

1. That which is totally unspecified, for example:

> Allah is aware of all things.[497]

2. *Āam* in wording, but *khās* in meaning, for example:

> Then press on in multitude from where all the people press on, and implore God's forgiveness (for your opposing Him in any way before now and for the mistakes you have made during the *Hajj*). Surely God is All-Forgiving, All-Compassionate[498]

Even though in the verse 'all people' is used, only the pilgrims are meant.

3. It was *āam* but has been specified. This is the most common type of *āam* in the Qur'ān, for example:

> Forbidden to you (O believing men) are your mothers (including stepmothers and grandmothers) and daughters (including granddaughters), your sisters (including full sisters and half-sisters), your aunts paternal and maternal, your brothers' daughters, your sisters' daughters, your mothers who have given suck to you, your milk-sisters (all those as closely related to you through milk as through descent), your wives' mothers, your stepdaughters – who are your foster-children, born of your wives with whom you have consummated marriage; but if you have not consummated marriage with them, there will be no blame on you (should you marry their daughters) – and the spouses of your sons who are of your loins, and to take two sisters together in marriage (including a niece and her aunt maternal or paternal) – except what has happened (of that sort) in the past. Surely God is All-Forgiving, All-Compassionate.[499]

---

495 Qur'ān, 4: 11.
496 Hashim Kamali, *Principles of Islamic Jurisprudence*, 105.
497 Qur'ān, 4: 176.
498 Qur'ān, 2: 199.
499 Qur'ān, 4: 23.

This verse specified the forbidden ones for the marriage, so the verse which speaks in general tone regarding the forbidden ones for the marriage became *khās* (specified) with this verse.

SUMMARY OF GENERAL AND SPECIFIC (*ĀAM AND KHĀS*):

1. *Āam* verses apply to all people that are mentioned in the verse, e.g. all humans, all Muslims, etc.
2. *Khās* verses are applied to a limited number in the set.
3. The three categories of *āam* are: that which is totally unspecified; that which is *āam* in wording, but *khās* in meaning and that which is *āam* but has been specified. This is the most common type of *āam* in the Qur'ān.

7.4 The Unconditional (*Mutlaq*) and the Conditional (*Muqayyad*)

Some of the verses related to the rulings (*aḫkām*) are absolute and free from any conditions or circumstances (*mutlaq*), while others are bound (*muqayyad*) to special conditions or situations, and apply only therein. This differs from the *āam* in that the *āam* applies to all people that are included in its meanings simultaneously without exception, whereas the *mutlaq* can only apply to one person. In other words, *āam* applies to all the people of a specific set, whereas *mutlaq* only applies to any one person in that set, for example:

> Those who declare their wives unlawful for them and thereafter wish to go back on the words they have uttered must free *a slave* before they (the spouses) touch each other. This is what you are urged to do. And God is fully aware of what you do.[500]

The condition or quality of the slave has not been specified, so the verse is *mutlaq*. If the verse was about freeing all the slaves, it would be *āam*, but it is about freeing one slave, therefore this verse is *mutlaq*, but not *āam*.

The *muqayyad* (conditional) expression in the verses related to the rulings occurs when a *mutlaq* expression is specified by any condition or adjective.

> Yet (be circumspect), it is not for a believer to kill another believer unless it be by mistake. He who has killed a believer by mistake must set free *a believing slave*...[501]

---

[500] Qur'ān, 58: 3.

[501] Qur'ān, 4: 92.

In this verse, God mentioned the condition of freeing a slave as compensation for the crime of killing a believer; the slave who will be freed must be believer, and therefore this verse is *muqayyad*. If the verse said 'free any slave', the verse would be *mutlaq*.

SUMMARY OF THE UNCONDITIONAL (*MUTLAQ*)
AND THE CONDITIONAL (*MUQAYYAD*):

1. *Mutlaq* verses are absolute and free from any conditions or circumstances.
2. *Muqayyad* verses are bound to special conditions or situations and apply only to them.
3. *Mutlaq* only applies to any one person in the set.
4. The *muqayyad* (conditional) expression in the verses related to the rulings occurs when a *mutlaq* expression is specified by any condition or adjective.

7.5 Literal Meaning (*Mantuq*)

Mantuq literally means 'what was uttered'. In the Qur'anic sciences it also implies the literal meanings of the verses. The words of the verses are sufficient to understand the literal meaning. *Mantuq* has three categories; *naṣṣ, ẕāhir and muawwal.*

Naṣṣ: is the primary and the essential meaning of the verse, for the words clearly indicate the essential meaning, for example: 'God has made trading lawful, and interest unlawful.'[502] The essential meaning of this verse is that trade is lawful and permissible but usury is forbidden. Verses of this type create absolute binding rules.

Ẕāhir: the essential or primary meaning of the verse is not understood from its wording. However, it conveys the secondary meaning because the words are clear and unambiguous. This is similar to *naṣṣ* in that the meaning is understood from the words without needing any other explanations, but, in this case, the meaning is not the essential or principal meaning in context.

> If you fear that you will not be able to observe their rights with exact fairness when you marry the orphan girls (in your custody), you can marry, from among other women (who are permitted to you in marriage and) who seem good to you, two, or three, or four.[503]

---

[502] Qur'ān, 2:275.

[503] Qur'ān, 4:3.

When looked at without applying to other sources, this verse means it is permissible to marry with other women. However, this is not the true context of the verse. When looked at with the previous verses, the essential meaning of the verse is about protecting the rights of orphan girls. Marrying other women is the secondary meaning of the verse. It is only when looked at together with the previous verses that the essential meaning becomes clear.

Muawwal: if the literal meaning of the verse is not clear in accordance with Islamic beliefs then it must be interpreted; for example: 'Wherever you are Allah is with you;[504] It is not correct to understand this verse to mean God's physical presence because He is beyond time and space; therefore, this verse needs to be interpreted. The interpretation is that 'His power, knowledge and observation are upon you wherever you might be'.

SUMMARY OF MEANING (*MANTUQ*):

1. *Mantuq* is the literal meaning of the verse.
2. *Mantuq* has three categories; *naṣṣ, ẕāhir and muawwal.*
3. ***Naṣṣ:*** is the essential meaning of the verse.
4. ***Ẕāhir:*** is the secondary meaning of the verse. It is only when looked at together with other sources that the essential meaning becomes clear.
5. ***Muawwal:*** if the literal meaning is not proper according to the essentials of Islam the verse is interpreted.

7.6 Meaning (*Mafhum*)

Mafhum literally means 'the understood meaning'. In Qur'anic sciences it is the meaning of the verse which is not understood directly from its words but from different indications and after applying to different sources. It is an implied meaning which is not indicated in the text but is arrived at by the help of other indications. The words of the verse are not enough to understand the meaning, so the meaning has to be sought through reasoning.

Mafhum has two kinds; *Mafhum-u Muwāfiq* and *Mafhum-u Mukhālif.*

Mafhum Muwāfiq (harmonious meaning). If the extracted meaning is in harmony with its pronounced meaning it is considered to be *Mafhum Muwāfiq*. It is the extension of a ruling from a mentioned case to an unmentioned one due to a commonality between them. In this type of verse the meaning and the rul-

[504] Qur'ān, 57:4.

ing are parallel to each other and the meaning is same as that which is implied in the verse.

> Your Lord has decreed that you worship none but Him alone, and treat parents with the best of kindness. Should one of them, or both, attain old age in your lifetime, do not say "Ugh!" to them (as an indication of complaint or impatience), nor push them away, and always address them in gracious words.[505]

In this verse, the phrase 'do not say "Ugh"' also includes that it is *ḫaram* to beat parents. If the minimum disrespect is prohibited in the verse it is understood that the maximum is also prohibited. But the maximum is not clearly mentioned in the verse, nevertheless it is understood from the context and it is of the same kind and in the same line.

Mafhum Mukhālif (divergent meaning). When the extracted meaning of the verse is not in harmony with its pronounced meaning it is considered *Mafhum Mukhālif*. In other words, applying the opposite ruling of a case mentioned in the text to one that is not mentioned, for example:

> O you who have believed, if there comes to you a disobedient one with information, investigate, lest you harm a people out of ignorance and become, over what you have done, regretful[506]

It is understood from this verse that if a disobedient (unbelieving person) brings news it must be investigated before any action is taken based on that information. We also understand from this verse that if a righteous, obedient and pious person brings information it can be accepted without investigation. This type of meaning is known as *Mafhum Mukhālif* and it is applied to obtain the indirect meanings of verses.

Summary of Meaning (*Mafhum*):

1. *Mafhum* is the meaning of the verse which is not understood directly from its words but from different indications and after applying to different sources.
2. *Mafhum* has two kinds; *Mafhum-u Muwāfiq* and *Mafhum-u Mukhālif*.

---

505 Qur'ān, 17:23.

506 Qur'ān, 49:6.

3. *Mafhum Muwāfiq* is if the extracted meaning is in harmony with its pronounced meaning. It is the extension of a ruling from a mentioned case to an unmentioned one due to a commonality between them.
4. *Mafhum Mukhālif.* When the extracted meaning from the verse is not in harmony with its pronounced meaning it is considered as *Mafhum Mukhālif.* In other words, applying the opposite ruling of a case mentioned in the text to one that is not mentioned.

7.7 Literal Meaning (*Haqiqah*) and Metaphoric Meaning (*Majāz*)

Haqiqah means that the original and primary intent of the words in the verses refers to their real and literal meanings whereas *majāz* is when the words of verses are used in a metaphorical sense. An example of *majāz*:

> Lower to them the wing of humility out of mercy, and say: 'My Lord, have mercy on them even as they cared for me in childhood'[507]

In this verse the expression 'lower to them the wing of humility' is a metaphorical expression and it is not used literally.

> Inquire in the township where we were, and the caravan with whom we travelled hither. We are certainly telling the truth[508]

This verse describes the obtaining of information metaphorically as one cannot extract information from a town, but only from the people who live in the town.

7.8 The Ambivalent and the Unequivocal (*Mujmal* and *Mufassar*)

Mujmal denotes a word or text which is inherently unclear and gives no indication as to its precise meaning. The cause of ambiguity in *mujmal* is inherent in the locution itself. A word may be a homonym with more than one meaning, and there is no indication as to which might be the correct one.[509] This type of verse is named *mujmal* in the sciences of the Qur'ān.

Mufassar (unequivocal) refers to the word whose meaning is absolutely clear so there is no need to explain it further. For when the Qur'ān or the Sunnah provides the necessary explanation, the *mujmal* is explained and turns into

---

507 Qur'ān, 17: 24.
508 Qur'ān, 12: 82.
509 Hashim Kamali, *Principles of Islamic Jurisprudence*, 99.

mufassar. The *mujmal* becomes *mufassar* only if the clarification provided by the Qur'ān or the Sunnah is complete. However, if it is incomplete or insufficient to remove the ambiguity, the *mujmal* becomes *mushkil* (confusing and problematic), which is then open to research and *ijtihad*.[510] For example:

> As to those who devour interest, they turn out like one whom Satan has bewitched and confounded by his touch, and they will rise up (from their graves in the same way before God). That is because they say interest is just like trading, whereas God has made trading lawful, and interest unlawful.[511]

In this verse, the Arabic word '*riba*' means increasing. Since not every increase or profit is unlawful, the verse remains unclear as to what type of increase is meant. This verse needs further explanation. The Prophet (pbuh) explained the types of usury to remove the ambiguity of this verse.

Summary of the Ambivalent and the Unequivocal (*Mujmal and Mufassar*):

1. *Mujmal* denotes a word or text which is inherently unclear and gives no indication as to its precise meaning.
2. *Mufassar* (unequivocal) refers to the word whose meaning is absolutely clear and there is no need to explain it further.
3. When the Qur'ān or Sunnah provides the necessary explanation, the *mujmal* is explained and turns into *mufassar*.
4. If the clarification provided by the Qur'ān or the Sunnah is insufficient to remove the ambiguity, the *mujmal* becomes *mushkil*.

510 Kamali, 99.

511 Qur'ān, 2: 275.

Chapter Eight

The Notion of Abrogation (*Naskh*)

The Notion of Abrogation (*Naskh*)

8.1 Abrogation (*Naskh*)

Naskh literally means: 'obliteration, to remove, to abolish, to abrogate, to replace, to supersede, to transcribe (*istinsakh*) or to copy'. In the Qur'anic sciences, *naskh* means the suspension or replacement of one Islamic ruling by another, provided that the latter is of subsequent origin, and that the two rulings are enacted separately from one another.[512] Some of the verses related to commanding (*amr*) or prohibition (*nahy*) were totally abrogated or superseded by other verses and there is much wisdom behind this. A verse whose ruling has been abrogated is called '*mansūkh*' and the abrogating verse which brings the new regulation is called '*nāsikh*'. Knowledge of *nāsikh-mansūkh* provides believers with vital information to practise Islam correctly.

Naskh is also used in familiar Arabic expressions such as '*tanasukh al-arwah*' (reincarnation), and '*tanasukh al-mawarith*', the transfer of inheritance from person to person. The majority of scholars, however, agree that 'obliteration' (*al-raf wa al-izalah*) is the primary meaning, and 'transcription/transfer' is the secondary, meaning of *naskh*.[513] The application of *naskh* to the Qur'ān and Sunnah is confined, in terms of time, to one period only; the lifetime of the Prophet Muhammad (pbuh).

The word '*naskh*' and its derivations are used in the Qur'ān with different meanings, for example:

> This is Our Book (the record of your deeds that We prepared), speaking the truth against you. Assuredly We have had transcribed what you used to do (in the world)[514]

In this verse, the Arabic word '*nastansikhu*' which is derived from same root as '*naskh*' is used to mean 'writing, transcribing and copying'.

---

[512] Sayyid Sharif Jurjani, *Tārifāt*, 163.
[513] Ghazali, *Muṣtaṣfā*, I/69; Āmidī, *Aḫkām*, 3/ 102.
[514] Qur'ān, 45: 29.

> Never did We send a Messenger or a Prophet before you but that when he recited (God's Revelations to the people) Satan would make insinuations. But God *abrogates* whatever insinuations Satan may make, and then He confirms and establishes His Revelations. God is All-Knowing, All-Wise"[515]

In this verse, the word '*fayansakhu*' is used to mean 'to remove' and 'to abrogate'.

> We do not abrogate any verse or omit it but We bring one better than it or the like of it. Do you not know that God has full power over everything?[516]

Through this verse, scholars understand that God abrogates the rulings of some verses with other verses, or that He supersedes the rulings with new ones without removing the original rulings from the Qur'ān. *Naskh* is the change, not in *ilm* (knowledge of God), but *ma'lum* (what is known to us); it is not a change in the Creator's knowledge but it is a change in the rulings for humankind.

The Qur'anic revelations touch on a variety of subjects such as beliefs, history, tales of the Prophets, the Day of Judgement, Paradise and Hell, and many others. Particularly important are the *aẖkām* (legal rulings), because they prescribe the manner of legal relationships between people, as God wishes them to be observed. While the basic message of Islam always remains the same, the legal rulings have varied throughout the ages, and many Prophets before Muhammad (pbuh) brought particular codes of law (Shari'ah) for their respective communities.[517]

Islam has three principal approaches with regard to legislation:

a) Commands that pre-dated Islam written in the previous scriptures or practised in the community in which Islam appeared, and which were not contradictory with its essential principles, were retained.

b) Customs or rulings that did not conform to the principles of Islam were corrected or amended.

c) Completely new legislation was introduced.

In establishing new legislation in the Qur'ān, both life's unchanging (essential) and changing (temporal) aspects were considered. In the second case, God laid down rules in the Qur'ān that could be revised when necessary, according to the time and conditions, and in conformity with Islam's essentials of faith, wor-

---

515 Qur'ān, 22: 52

516 Qur'ān, 2: 106.

517 Von Denffer, *'Ulūm al-Qur'ān*, 102.

ship, and morality; and established legal principles to maintain this process. The same procedure was also followed in the time of the Prophet (pbuh) himself, during which the Qur'ān was revealed. God abrogated some verses, either with the injunction contained in their wording or with both their wording and the command they contained. This process was called *naskh*; abrogated verses were called *mansūkh*; and the new ones substituting the previous ones were called *nāsikh*.[518]

Summary of Abrogation (*Naskh*):

1. In the Qur'anic sciences, *naskh* means the suspension or replacement of one Shari'ah ruling by another, provided that the latter is of a subsequent origin, and that the two rulings are enacted separately from one another.
2. A verse whose ruling has been abrogated is called '*mansūkh*' and the abrogating verse which brings the new regulation is called '*nāsikh*'.
3. The application of *naskh* to the Qur'ān and Sunnah is confined, in terms of time, to one period only; the lifetime of the Prophet Muhammad (pbuh).
4. The Qur'anic revelations include *aḫkām* (legal rulings) which prescribe the manner of legal relationships between people, as God wishes them to be observed.
5. Islam has three principal approaches in regard to legislation: a) pre-Islamic commands that were not contradictory with its essential principles were retained, b) customs or rulings that did not conform to the principles of Islam were corrected or amended, c) completely new legislation was introduced.

8.2 Some Important Points Regarding *Naskh*

The issue of *naskh* is one of the most controversial topics in the history of Islam amongst Muslim scholars. Most scholars accept the notion of *naskh*, but some do not. Some used the term '*naskh*' in its broadest meaning, including *āam-khās*, *mutlaq-muqayyad* and *bayān*. The term '*bayān*' refers to clarity after being ambiguous and coming into existence after non-existence and '*khās*' refers to the limitation of a general statement, therefore neither term is related to the notion of '*naskh*'.

When the message of Islam was presented to the Arabs as something new and different from their way of life, it was introduced in stages. The Qur'ān brought

[518] Ali Unal, The Qur'ān with Annotated Interpretation, footnote for 2:106.

important changes gradually to allow the people to adjust to the new prescriptions. For example, in the Qur'ān[519] there are three verses concerning the drinking of wine. Wine drinking was widespread in pre-Islamic times and, although a social evil, highly esteemed. The three verses which finally led to the prohibition of intoxicating substances were revealed in stages.[520]

Naskh indicates that the first ruling has been contradicted by the later rulings and should be completely abrogated. In order for *naskh* to occur, a previous Islamic ruling on exactly the same topic must exist which is then abrogated by a later ruling. There should be intervals (*fasila/tarakhi*) between the rulings of *mansūkh* and *nāsikh*.

During the formative period of Islam various words were used to refer to *naskh*. Imam Shafi was the first person to limit this word to abrogation. Some people consider *naskh* as *bayān* (explanation), *khitāb* (discourse), or *raf'* (omit). All of them are close to the meaning of *naskh* (to abrogate the previous *ḥukm* with the new one), but none of them is *naskh*. Therefore, statements from the scholars of the first three generations that claim that a particular verse was 'abrogated' (*nasakha*) by another verse cannot be immediately taken as an example of *naskh*. It is this exact reason which has been one of the greatest causes of confusion regarding the number of *nāsikh/ mansūkh* verses in the Qur'ān.[521]

For example, marriage to one's step-mother was allowed in pre-Islamic Arabian culture. The Qur'ān prohibited this type of marriage in the following verse:

> And do not marry the women whom your fathers married – except what has happened (of that sort) in the past. This was indeed a shameful deed and hateful thing, and how evil a way![522]

This is not *naskh* because the Qur'ān annulled a pre-Islamic practice rather than an existing Qur'anic rule.

Naskh is only applicable to laws, not to matters of faith (the essentials of Islamic faith). In other words, *naskh* cannot occur with regards to belief in God, His Names and Attributes, the Day of Judgement, and other matters related to the fundamentals of belief. The following verse is a good example of this:

> Of the Religion, He has laid down for you as way of life what He willed to Noah, and that which We reveal to you, and what We willed to Abraham,

519 Qur'ān, 4: 43, 2: 219; 5: 93-94.
520 Von Denffer, *'Ulūm al-Qur'ān*, 103.
521 Qadhi, *The Sciences of the Qur'ān*, 234.
522 Qur'ān, 4: 22.

and Moses, and Jesus, (commanding): 'Establish the Religion and do not divide into opposing groups concerning it'.[523]

Naskh cannot occur with respect to *ijma* (general consensus) and *qiyāṣ* (analogy) but only with respect to the Qur'ān and Sunnah. This is closely related to the notion that *naskh* can only occur during the time of the Prophet (pbuh) when there was no need for *ijma* and *qiyāṣ*. Also, the Qur'ān and Sunnah have the authority to abrogate the rulings of some verses whereas *ijtihād* (personal reasoning) or *qiyāṣ* (analogy) or any other Islamic law sources cannot abrogate a ruling from the Qur'ān or Sunnah. Therefore, it is important to note that *naskh* is a primarily Madinian phenomenon where Islamic law was finalised. The knowledge of *nāsikh* and *mansūkh* is important because it concerns the correct and exact application of the laws of God. It is specifically concerned with legal revelations[524]:

a) It is one of the important pre-conditions for exegesis of the Qur'ān.

b) It is one of the important pre-conditions for the understanding and application of Islamic law.

c) It sheds light on the historical development of the Islamic legal code. It helps to understand the immediate meaning of the verses concerned.

Exegesis or legal ruling is not acceptable from a person who does not have such knowledge. Due to the importance of this topic, there have been a great many books written on the topic of *naskh* by scholars such as Qatāda as-Sadusi (d. 117 A.H.), Ibn Shihab az-Zuhri (d. 125 A.H.), Ahmad ibn Hanbal (d. 241 A.H.), Abū Dāwud (d. 275 A.H.) and Tirmidhi (d. 280 A.H.).

Summary of Some Important Points Regarding *Naskh*:

1. The issue of *naskh* is one of the most controversial topics in the history of Islam amongst Muslim scholars.
2. When the message of Islam was presented to the Arabs as something new and different from their way of life, it was introduced in stages to allow the people to adjust to the new prescriptions.
3. In order for *naskh* to occur, a previous Islamic ruling on exactly the same topic must exist which is then abrogated by a later ruling. There should be intervals (*fasila/tarakhi*) between the rulings of *mansūkh* and *nāsikh*.

---

523 Qur'ān, 42: 13.

524 Von Denffer, *'Ulūm al-Qur'ān*, 103.

4. Statements from the scholars of the first three generations that claim that a particular verse was 'abrogated' (*nasakha*) by another verse cannot be immediately taken as an example of *naskh*.
5. *Naskh* is only applicable to laws, not to matters of faith.
6. *Naskh* cannot occur with respect to *ijma* (general consensus) and *qiyāṣ* (analogy) but only to the Qur'ān and Sunnah.
7. *Naskh* could only occur during the time of the Prophet (pbuh) when there was no need for *ijma* and *qiyāṣ*.
8. Also, the Qur'ān and Sunnah have the authority to abrogate the rulings of some verses whereas *ijtihād* (personal reasoning) or *qiyāṣ* (analogy) or any other Islamic law sources cannot abrogate a ruling from the Qur'ān or Sunnah.
9. *Naskh* is a primarily Madinian phenomenon where Islamic law is finalised.
10. The knowledge of *nāsikh* and *mansūkh* is an important pre-condition for exegesis of the Qur'ān, for the understanding and application of Islamic law and for understanding the immediate meaning of the verses concerned.

8.3 The Way to Know *Naskh*

As in the field of *asbāb an-nuzūl*, information about *naskh* cannot be accepted upon mere personal opinion, but must be based on reliable Hadith, and should go back to the Prophet (pbuh) and his Companions. The report must clearly state which part of the revelation is abrogating and which is abrogated.

There are three ways of knowing about *naskh*[525]:

1) Reports from the Prophet (pbuh) or Companions.

2) *Ijma'* (consensus of the *umma* upon *naskh*).

3) Knowledge of the history and order of the revelation of verses.

For example:

> Those of you who (are about to) die leaving behind wives should make testament in their favour of one year's provision without expulsion. If they themselves leave (of their own accord), there is no blame on you for what they may do of lawful deeds by themselves. Surely God is All-Glorious with irresistible might, All-Wise[526]

[525] Qattan, 199.

[526] Qur'ān, 2: 240.

According to this verse, a widow can stay in her husband's house for one year. According to the scholars this verse is abrogated by the following verse:

> Those among you who die, leaving behind their wives: they (the wives) shall keep themselves in waiting for four months and ten days. When they have reached the end of the waiting term, then there is no blame on you for what they may do by themselves within (the bounds of) decency. God is fully aware of all that you do[527]

It can be understood on reading these verses that there is no *naskh* between them. One verse does not replace the other as they can be applied at the same time. The second verse indicates the obligatory time for which the widow must wait in order to get married with someone else; the first verse is a recommendation (not a command) for a man about to die to make one year's provision for his wife in his testament. There is no conflict between these two verses; therefore there is no need to apply *naskh* (to remove the ruling of one verse).

Summary of the Way to Know *Naskh*:

1. Information about *naskh* must be based on reliable Hadith, and should go back to the Prophet (pbuh) and his Companions.
2. The report must clearly state which part of the revelation is abrogating and which is abrogated.
3. *Naskh* can be known by reports from the Prophet (pbuh) or Companions, by *ijma'* and by knowledge of the history and order of the revelation of verses.

8.4 Evidence for the Existence of *Naskh*

The vast majority of scholars accepted the existence of *naskh* in the Qur'ān and Sunnah. In order to prove this they utilized four sources; a) the Qur'ān, b) Hadith reports, c) reports about *asbāb an-nuzūl* (the occasions of the revelation) and, d) the intellect. Their evidence;

In the Qur'ān, God says in three verses:

> We do not abrogate any verse or omit it but We bring one better than it or the like of it. Do you not know that God has full power over everything?[528]

---

[527] Qur'ān, 2: 234.

[528] Qur'ān, 2: 106.

> When We put a Revelation in place of another Revelation –and God knows best what He sends down – they say: "You are but a forger!" No, rather, most of them do not know[529]

> O (most illustrious) Prophet! Rouse the believers to fighting. If there be twenty of you who are steadfast, they will vanquish two hundred; and if there be of you a hundred, they will vanquish a thousand of those who disbelieve, for they (the disbelievers) are a people who do not ponder and seek to penetrate the essence of matters in order to grasp the truth. For now (while you lack in necessary equipment and training), God has lightened your burden, for He knows that there is weakness in you. So if there be a hundred of you who are strong-willed and steadfast, they will vanquish two hundred; and if there be a thousand of you, they will vanquish two thousand by God's leave. God is with those who are steadfast.[530]

The statement of the Prophet (pbuh): 'I used to forbid you to visit graves, but now you may freely do so, for they remind you of death'[531] is evidence for *naskh*.

A'isha reported:

> The Qur'ān revealed that ten clear sucklings make a marriage unlawful, then this was abrogated (and substituted) by five sucklings; then God's Apostle (pbuh) died but this ruling was found before that time in the Qur'ān (and was recited by the Muslims).[532]

'Abd Allah b. 'Abbās reported:

> 'Umar b. Khattāb sat on the pulpit of God's Messenger (pbuh) and said: Verily God sent Muhammad (pbuh) with the truth and he sent down the book upon him, and the verse of stoning was included in what was sent down to him. We recited it, retained it in our memory and understood it. God's Messenger (pbuh) awarded the punishment of stoning to death (to the married adulterer and adulteress) and after him, we also awarded the punishment of stoning. I am afraid that with the lapse of time, the people (may forget it) and may say: We do not find the punishment of stoning in the book of God, and thus go astray by abandoning this duty prescribed by God. Stoning is a duty laid down in God's book for married men and women who commit adultery when proof is established, or if there is pregnancy or a confession".[533]

---

[529] Qur'ān, 16: 102.

[530] Qur'ān, 8: 65-66.

[531] Ibn Majah, *Mishkat* p.154

[532] Muslim, *Sahīh*, 2/3421.

[533] Muslim, *Sahīh*, 3/4194; Bukhari, *Sahīh*, 8/816.

SUMMARY OF EVIDENCE FOR THE EXISTENCE OF *NASKH*:

1. The vast majority of scholars accepted the existence of *naskh* in the Qur'ān and Sunnah.
2. They utilized four sources to prove this; a) the Qur'ān, b) Hadith reports, c) reports about *asbāb an-nuzūl* (the occasions of the revelation) and, d) the intellect.

8.5 The Conditions for *Naskh*

Scholars have established a set of conditions in order to validate any claim of *naskh*. One of the reasons for this is that *naskh* is the last-resort, since the very concept of *naskh* implies discarding a ruling for another one. As long as both rulings in the verses can be applied, the concept of *naskh* is not applied. These conditions are[534]:

1) The two rulings must directly contradict each other so that it is impossible to apply both at the same time. This is because *naskh* is only called as a last-resort, when there exists no other way to explain the two rulings. Therefore, if one of the rulings can apply to a specific case, and the other ruling to a different case, this cannot be considered an example of *naskh*.

2) It must be indisputable that the *nāsikh* (abrogating) ruling was revealed after the *mansūkh* (the abrogated) ruling for the abrogation to take place. For the claim of *naskh* to be validated, a later ruling must repeal an earlier one. This can be ascertained in two ways: either there is a direct reference in the *nāsikh* ruling concerning the previous ruling (e.g. 2:187 and 8:66), or, the time-frame of the revelation of the verses in question is known (by the narrations concerning *Makkī* and *Madanī* revelations, the narrations concerning *asbāb an-nuzūl*, and other narrations). In other words, it must be known for certain that the *nāsikh* ruling was revealed after the *mansūkh* ruling.

3) Both the *nāsikh* and *mansūkh* rulings must originate in the Qur'ān or Sunnah. This is because analogy (*qiyāṣ*) and other forms of *ijtihād* cannot abrogate a command from God or the Prophet (pbuh). As for consensus (*ijma'*), it is not possible to occur against an explicit command in the Qur'ān or Sunnah; therefore, this also cannot be the source of *naskh*.

4) Most scholars have also added the condition that the *nāsikh* ruling must originate from an equal or greater authority than the *mansūkh*. In other words,

[534] Qadhi, *the Sciences of the Qur'ān*, 237.

a single report (*khabar wāḩid*) cannot abrogate the Qur'ān or a *Mutawātir* Sunnah, since it is of lesser authority.

Summary of the Conditions for *Naskh*:

1. Scholars have established a set of conditions in order to validate any claim of *naskh*.
2. The two rulings must directly contradict each other so that it is impossible to apply both at the same time.
3. It must be indisputable that the *nāsikh* (abrogating) ruling was revealed after the *mansūkh* (the abrogated) ruling for the abrogation to take place.
4. Both the *nāsikh* and *mansūkh* rulings must originate in the Qur'ān or Sunnah.
5. Most scholars have also added the condition that the *nāsikh* ruling must originate from an equal or greater authority than the *mansūkh*.

8.6 Classification of *Naskh*

The rulings that have been affected by *naskh* are classified in different categories: with respect to the sources, with respect to their existence or non-existence in the Qur'ān, or with respect to the rulings of the *mansūkh* in comparison with the *nāsikh*.

1) The Qur'ān abrogates the Qur'ān. For example, the verses regarding the stages of the prohibition of alcohol.

2) The Qur'ān abrogates the Sunnah. For example, when the Prophet (pbuh) came to Medina, he performed the daily prescribed prayers towards Jerusalem for 17 months. This practice was abrogated in the following verse:

> Certainly We have seen you (O Messenger) often turning your face to heaven (in expectation of a Revelation. Do not worry, for) We will surely turn you towards a direction that will please and satisfy you. (Now the time has come, so) turn your face towards the Sacred Mosque. (And you, O believers) turn your faces towards it wherever you are. Surely those who were given the Book (before, no matter if the hypocrites or the foolish among them deny or object to it) do know (the coming of this Prophet and this change of *qibla*) to be true (commandments) from their Lord. God is not unaware or unmindful of whatever they do.[535]

---

[535] Qur'ān, 2: 144.

3) The *mutawātir* (the strongest and most authentic Hadith) Sunnah abrogates the Qur'ān. For example, the following verse is abrogated by a *mutawātir* Hadith:

> Prescribed for you, when any of you is visited by death, if he leaves behind wealth, is to make testament in favour of his parents and near relatives according to customary good and religiously approvable practice – a duty for the truly God-revering, pious[536]

The ruling of this verse is abrogated by the Prophetic tradition 'God has given every person who has rights his due, and there is no bequest to an heir.[537]

4) The Sunnah abrogates the Sunnah. This category has a few subdivisions such as *mutawātir* abrogates *mutawātir* Hadith, *Aḫād* Hadith and vice versa. For example; 'I used to forbid you to visit graves, but now you may freely do so, for they remind you of death'.[538]

Classification in accordance with the verse and ruling;

a) Abrogation of the recited verse together with the legal ruling. An example for this is: A'isha reported that the Qur'ān revealed that ten clear sucklings make a marriage unlawful, then it was abrogated (and substituted) by five sucklings; then God's Apostle (pbuh) died and this was found in the Qur'ān before that time (and recited by the Muslims).[539]

b) Abrogation of the legal ruling without the recited verse. For example:

> O (most illustrious) Prophet! We have made lawful for you your wives to whom you have already paid their bridal-due...[540]

The ruling of this verse is abrogated by the following verse but still the former stayed in the Qur'ān:

> Other women will not be lawful for you to take; nor, are you allowed to change them for other wives, even though their fineness should please you, except those whom your right hands possess. God is ever watchful over everything.[541]

c) Abrogation of the recited verse without the legal ruling. For example: 'If the son of Adam has two valleys of gold, he would wish for the third one, for noth-

---

536 Qur'ān, 2: 180.

537 Nasaī, *Sunan, Kitāb al-Wasaya*, 3671.

538 Ibn Majah, *Mishkat* p.154

539 Muslim, *Saḫīḫ*, 2/3421.

540 Qur'ān,33: 50.

541 Qur'ān, 33: 52.

ing will fill the belly of Adam's son except dust'.[542] Another example for this is the previously mentioned statement of 'Umar about the stoning verse for the punishment of adultery.

SUMMARY OF CLASSIFICATION OF *NASKH*:

1. The rulings that have been affected by *naskh* are classified in different categories:
   - The Qur'ān abrogates the Qur'ān.
   - The Qur'ān abrogates the Sunnah.
   - The *mutawātir* (the strongest and most authentic Hadith) Sunnah abrogates the Qur'ān.
   - The Sunnah abrogates the Sunnah.
2. Classification in accordance with the verse and ruling:
   - Abrogation of the recited verse together with the legal ruling.
   - Abrogation of the legal ruling without the recited verse.
   - Abrogation of the recited verse without the legal ruling.

8.7 Difference Between Abrogation (*Naskh*) and Specification (*khās-takhsis*)

It is essential that the concept of *naskh* and that of *takhsis* (specification) are not confused. *Takhsis* is defined as the specification of a general ruling (*āam*), in that what seems to be a general ruling only applies in certain cases.

Naskh differs from *takhsis* in the following ways[543]:

1) *Naskh* only occurs with regards to laws and rulings (*aḫkām*). *Takhsis*, on the other hand, may occur with respect to other matters, for example:

> By Time, Most certainly, human is in loss, *except* those who believe and do good, righteous deeds, and exhort one another to truth, and exhort one another to steadfast[544]

The second verse is general (*āam*), implying that all of mankind will be in loss. The last verse, however, is an example of *takhsis* since it qualifies those of mankind who are not in a loss.

---

[542] Muslim, *Saḫīḫ*, *Zakat*, 39.

[543] Qadhi, *The Sciences of the Qur'ān*, 249-250.

[544] Qur'ān, 103: 1-3.

2) *Naskh* implies a total abolishment of the previous ruling, no matter what the case. *Takhsis*, on the other hand, is defined as the implementation of a previous ruling in only some of the original cases. In other words, after a *takhsis* occurs, the ruling is not totally invalid, but rather valid in specific cases.

3) The *nāsikh* (the abrogating verse) must be revealed after the *mansūkh* (the abrogated verse), whereas there is no such time restriction on *takhsis*.

4) *Naskh* only occurs with respect to the Qur'ān or the Sunnah. *Takhsis*, on the other hand, may apply to the Qur'ān, Sunnah, *ijma'* (the general consensus), or *qiyāṣ* (analogy). Also, the abrogating ruling may only come from the Qur'ān or Sunnah, whereas *takhsis* may be based on common sense or *ijtihad*.

Summary of the Difference Between Abrogation (*Naskh*) and Specification (*Takhsis*):

1. *Takhsis* is defined as the specification of a general ruling (*āam*), in that what seems to be a general ruling only applies in certain cases.
2. *Naskh* differs from *takhsis* in the following ways:
3. *Naskh* only occurs with regards to laws and rulings (*aḫkām*). *Takhsis*, on the other hand, may occur with respect to other matters.
4. *Naskh* implies a total abandonment of the previous ruling, no matter what the case. *Takhsis*, on the other hand, is defined as the implementation of a previous ruling in only some of the original cases.
5. The *nāsikh* (the abrogating verse) must be revealed after the *mansūkh* (the abrogated verse), whereas there is no such time restriction on *takhsis*.
6. *Naskh* only occurs with respect to the Qur'ān or the Sunnah. *Takhsis*, on the other hand, may apply to the Qur'ān, Sunnah, *ijma'* (the general consensus), or *qiyāṣ* (analogy).
7. The abrogating ruling may only come from the Qur'ān or Sunnah, whereas *takhsis* may be based on common sense or *ijtihad*.

8.8 The Number of *Naskh* Verses in the Qur'ān

The actual number of abrogated verses in the Qur'ān is disputed by scholars. The following list is an example of how scholars differ on this issue: Abū Ja'far al-Nahhas, 20 verses; Makkī b. Abī Tālib, 200 verses; Ibn Ḫazm, 214 verses; Abū Bakr Ibn Al-Arabi, 105 verses; Ibn al Jawzī, 22 verses; Al-Suyūtī, 20 verses; Al-Shanqiti, 7 verses; Shah Wali Allah al-Dihlawi, 5 verses.

The reason for such differences is that many verses are considered examples of *naskh*, when in fact they are examples of *takhsis* or do not fall under *naskh* at all. For example, those scholars who have over a hundred examples of *naskh* all consider the 'verse of the sword' as having abrogated dozens of verses. This verse gave permission for the Muslims to fight the disbelievers wherever they were:

> Then, when the (four) sacred months are over, then (declare war on them and) kill them wherever you may come upon them, and seize them, and confine them, and lie in wait for them at every conceivable place. Yet if they repent and (mending their ways) establish the Prescribed Prayer and pay the Prescribed Purifying Alms, let them go their way. Surely God is All-Forgiving, All-Compassionate[545]

According to Zarqānī this verse does not abrogate any verse.[546] For the scholars who accept this verse as abrogating, the rulings of the following verses are abrogated:

> And (remember) when We took a promise from the Children of Israel: You shall worship none save God (as the only Deity, Lord and Sovereign), and do good to parents in the best way possible, and to the near (relatives), to the orphans, and to the destitute; and *speak kindly and well to the people*...[547]

> Say: "O my people! Do all that lies within your power, indeed I (too) am at work (doing my task). So in time you will come to know to whom the ultimate abode of happiness will belong. Indeed the wrongdoers do not prosper and attain their goals[548]

> So leave them plunging about in play and amusement until the Day which they have been promised[549]

> (Even so, O Messenger) adopt the way of forbearance and tolerance, and enjoin what is good and right, and withdraw from the ignorant ones (do not care what they say and do)[550]

When we look at these verses, it is impossible to say that the rulings of these verses were abrogated by the verse of the sword. These verses have universal

---

545 Qur'ān, 9:5.
546 Zarqānī , 2/275-282.
547 Qur'ān, 2: 82.
548 Qur'ān, 6: 135.
549 Qur'ān, 43: 83.
550 Qur'ān, 7: 199.

values and cannot be abrogated. The verse of the sword aimed to put an end to terror activities on the Islamic border; it brought strict regulations for terrorist groups, but made it clear that violence should not be committed against non-terrorists as Islam never allows violence to be committed against them. The history of Islam and the life of the Prophet (pbuh) is the genuine witness for this. In Islam, war is always a last-resort. Islam always aims for peace, tranquillity and social harmony. An explanation of the aim of the verse of the sword and the verses that are similar to it are discussed below.

When considered together with other relevant verses of the Qur'ān, the verses 1-6 in *surah* 9 present significant principles concerned with the Islamic view of war[551];

1) The purpose of war is not to kill people. On the contrary, Islam attaches great value to life and regards the killing of one innocent person as being the same as killing all of humankind, and the saving the life of one person as being the same as saving the lives of all humankind. It aims at the survival of humanity and at helping everyone to find truth through education.

2) Even in warfare, Islam is ready to make peace and a treaty with the opposing side.

3) A Muslim government must remain faithful to any treaty it has made until the end of its term.

4) If the opposing side betrays the treaty, the Muslim government must publicly and officially declare to the other side that the agreement is no longer valid. Even though it can declare war as soon as the agreement loses its validity, it should grant them respite so that a new evaluation of the situation can be made.

5) If the opposing side continues its hostilities and does not change its attitude, even after the end of the term granted, it means that a state of war has begun.

6) In order to force the enemy to cease hostilities or to defeat them in war, Muslims must be powerful and remain steadfast. However, Muslims must always observe the rules of war which are stated in the Qur'ān and the Sunnah; they cannot wrong anyone even in war.

7) The sword verse is aimed at people who employ violence and who, as can also be inferred from the conclusion of that verse, do not recognize any rule or law and do not understand any language other than war. Therefore, the expression in this verse is of a deterring nature. The second part of the verse, which mentions repentance and the fact that God is All-Forgiving and All-Compassion-

---

551 Ali Unal, The Qur'ān with Annotated Interpretation, see appendix 3.

ate, reveals the main purpose of the verse. In addition, this verse also aims at removing from Mecca and Medina the violent, polytheist outlaws so it is important with respect to the security of the centre of Islam.

8) It is never the goal of Islam to kill people or conquer lands through war. Therefore, when the opposing side is inclined toward peace and making a treaty, the Muslims should also be inclined in this way. They should also give asylum to those who seek it and, without harming in any way the wealth or people of the asylum seekers, convey them to a place of safety.

9) Islam, aiming at universal peace and accepting the reality of human history, realizes that ensuring peace sometimes requires fighting. As declared in the Qur'ān: 'disorder is worse than killing' (2: 191); and 'disorder is even more grave and more sinful than killing' (2: 217); the conditions that give rise to war and disorder are more grievous than killing itself and, therefore, war, although not inherently a good thing, is permissible if it will remove these conditions.

Summary of the Number of *Naskh* Verses in the Qur'ān:

1. The actual number of abrogated verses in the Qur'ān is disputed by scholars.
2. The reason for such differences is that many verses are considered examples of *naskh*, when in fact they are examples of *takhsis* or do not fall under *naskh* at all.
3. Some scholars consider the 'verse of the sword' as having abrogated dozens of verses but it is impossible to say that the rulings of these verses were abrogated by the verse of the sword as they contain universal values.
4. When considered together with other relevant verses of the Qur'ān, the verses 1-6 in *surah* 9 present significant principles concerned with the Islamic view of war.
5. The purpose of war is not to kill people; Islam is always ready to make peace and a treaty; a Muslim government must adhere to any treaty made; it should grant the opposing side respite even if they betray the treaty; only when faced with renewed hostility can war begin again; Muslims must always observe the rules of war which are stated in the Qur'ān and the Sunnah; the wording in the verse of the sword is of a deterring nature; it is never the goal of Islam to kill people or conquer lands through war; Islam, aiming at universal peace and accepting the reality of human history, realizes that ensuring peace sometimes requires fighting.

8.9 Benefits of *Naskh*

Naskh is one of the important pre-conditions for understanding and applying Islamic law. There is much wisdom behind the notion of *naskh*:

a) It sheds light on the historical development of the Islamic legal code.
b) It helps to understand which verse was revealed first and which one was last.
c) It helps to understand the immediate meaning of the verses concerned.
d) It serves for the gradual progress and education of the Muslim community.
e) When the message of Islam was presented to the Arabs as something new, and different from their way of life, it was introduced in stages. The Qur'ān brought important changes gradually, to allow the people to adjust to the new prescriptions.

8.10 One Unique Approach to the Notion of *Naskh*

As was explained previously, *naskh* is declaring the expiration of a ruling of a verse by the indication of evidence from the Qur'ān or the Sunnah. Indeed, the ruling of one verse is changed with regard to the religious practise of Muslims, but there is no change in the knowledge of God.

Renowned Turkish scholar, Fethullah Gülen, approaches the notion of *naskh* in a unique and outstanding way[552]:

> 'We see that, the Qur'ān sometimes takes into consideration temporarily the understanding of its first addressees and the conditions when it was revealed and prepares them to the universal values which will be revealed later on. Even so, there are no conflicts or contradictions between the beginning of the revelation and its end. It seems that, one verse is the preparing of other verse and its pioneering; in turn, the other verse is the compliance for the previous one. This is one of the miracle aspects of the Qur'ān; even in the verses of *nāsikh-mansūkh*, there is a miracle of the Qur'ān. Now I will explain this aspect of miracles in the Qur'ān with examples;
>
> "And there are the fruits of the date-palm, and grapes: you derive from them intoxicants and good, wholesome nourishment. Surely in this there is a sign for people who reason and understand"[553]

---

552 Fethullah Gülen, *Kur'ân'ın Altın İkliminde*, pp. 128-132.
553 Qur'ān, 16: 67.

There is an implication for the last ruling regarding prohibition of alcohol in this verse, because Allah said in this verse, 'you derive from them intoxicants and good'. In this expression Allah says, 'you gain good provision from date-palm and grapes, but also you derive from them the intoxicants which is not good provision'. They are separated from each other in this verse indicating that although no verse at that time prohibited the consumption of alcohol, such a ruling was to come. Later on another verse revealed;

"They ask you about intoxicating drinks and games of chance. Say: 'In both there is great evil, though some use for people, but their evil is greater than their usefulness'"[554]

This is second step in the way of for the prohibition of alcohol and another warning, this verse says, 'apparently some of you may think that there are some benefits in intoxicating drinks and games of chance, but in both the harm is greater than their benefits. After this second warning the following verse was revealed;

"O you who believe! Do not come forward to (stand in) the Prayer while you are in state of drunkenness until you know what you are saying".[555]

In these three steps, some questions occurred in the minds of Muslims about alcohol and they were prepared gradually for the final ruling and Allah revealed it;

"O you who believe! Intoxicants, games of chance, sacrifices to idols and divination by arrows are a loathsome evil of Satan's doing; so turn wholly away from it so that you may prosper".[556]

Now let us investigate the thematic unity and strong interrelations between these verses. They are considered as abrogating and abrogated verses; even though they were revealed in different time frames, but there are no contradictions or conflicts between them, rather they are gradual steps which are connected to each other in the way of prohibition of alcohol. An example of this; in the first verse; "the fruits of the date-palm, and grapes: you derive from them intoxicants and good, wholesome nourishment" Allah is explaining that dates and grapes can be either beneficial or harmful, the Qur'ān doesn't name alcohol or intoxicating drinks as good and wholesome provision. If it is not good provision, Allah wouldn't be content with its consumption. Even when we remove the ruling of

---

[554] Qur'ān, 2: 219.
[555] Qur'ān, 4: 43.
[556] Qur'ān, 5: 90.

this verse there is no contradiction between this verse and the last one. What the verse in fact does, is gives some time and takes into consideration the conditions of the people in the time of ignorance, preparing them for the final ruling. In other words, Allah indicated the best rule for them by implying it in the earlier verses. In the second verse, since it was not the right time and the people were not ready for the final rule, Allah didn't mention the prohibition of alcohol clearly; "They ask you about intoxicating drinks and games of chance. Say: 'In both there is great evil, though some use for people, but their evil is greater than their usefulness.'"[557] If, in this verse, we accept the particle *'la'* in the word *'linnas'* as *'ahd'* (information), its meaning is that there is some benefit in alcohol for those people who produce it and sell it, but for the majority of people its harm is greater than its benefit. The ruling regarding alcohol is still not final in this verse, but when we carefully study this verse we can see the warning and prohibition in the style of its expressions. Incidentally, there were some Muslims who were continuing to drink alcohol at that time because it had not been explicitly prohibited. After a short while the third verse was revealed; "O you who believe! Do not come forward to (stand in) the Prayer while you are in (any sort of) state of drunkenness until you know what you are saying".[558] This verse was understood as that Allah will not accept the drunks to His presence in the prayers, even though every Muslim must come to the presence of Allah very often during the day. Indeed, every Muslim needs to meet with his Lord five times in a day and put his forehead in the prostrations as many as he can and open his heart to his Lord to relieve and come to the rest. But Allah said, 'if you want to come My presence to charge spiritually, you had better come not drunk'. Discerning people understood that they must abandon drinking alcohol for the sake of their Lord. Many of the Muslims, who understood the spirit of this verse, abandoned the drinking of alcohol after this verse was revealed, but those who did not have a deep understanding of the Qur'ān, were still drinking alcohol. After all these preparations and the gradual education, Allah marked the final point and declared the final ruling about alcohol; "O you who believe! Intoxicants, games of chance, sacrifices to (anything serving the function of) idols (and at places consecrated for offerings to other than God), and (the pagan practice of) divination by arrows (and similar practices) are a loathsome evil of Satan's doing; so turn wholly away from it so that you may prosper (in both worlds)".[559] Drinking alcohol and gambling were some of the addictions of people in the time of ignorance (time before Islam) and

---

557 Qur'ān, 2: 219.

558 Qur'ān, 4: 43.

559 Qur'ān, 5: 90.

they are loathsome evil of Satan's doing. Satan causes conflicts, quarrels and disagreements among the Muslims by utilizing alcohol, so the Qur'ān brought the attentions to this reality. In conclusion, even though these verses abrogate each other with regard to their rulings (*aḫkām*), nevertheless, there are no conflicts or contradictions between them with regard to their essential meanings. Similarly, there is a thematic unity and strong interrelation between these verses; indeed, this is the case for all the verses of the Qur'ān. It is impossible to find such thematic unity and strong interrelations in any book other than the Qur'ān.'

Chapter Nine

Qur'anic Readings and the Seven Letters (*Qiraat* and *Ahruf al-Sab'ah*)

Qur'anic Readings and the Seven Letters (*Qiraat* and *Ahruf al-Sab'ah*)

9.1 The Various Readings of the Qur'ān (*Qiraat*)

9.1.1 Definition of the Readings (*Qiraat*)

The Arabic word '*qiraat*' is the infinite form and derived from the root '*qa-ra-a*', which means reading and reciting. In the Qur'anic sciences, it means, the changes which occur in the words of the Qur'ān with regard to the extension (*madd*), shortening (*qasr*), punctuation of the written text, the order of the words in the text and their reading accordingly (*I'rāb*).[560] There are some terminological words pertaining to the topic of *qiraat* that should be mentioned to enable a better understanding of this subject.

One of them is the word '*qurra*', the plural of '*qārī*', which means a reader and a reciter. In the Qur'anic sciences it means the imams which represent the seven modes of the Qur'ān (*ahruf sab'a*) and the various readings of the Qur'ān (*qiraat*). It is also used for a scholar who has memorised the whole Qur'ān and has a detailed knowledge of the various readings.[561] During the Prophet's (pbuh) time, the word '*qārī*' meant someone who had memorised any revealed part of the Qur'ān.[562] Over time, the meaning of the word broadened until it came to the meaning which we understand today (an expert in the variant readings of the Qur'ān).

Another important concept and terminological word in the science of *qiraat* is '*riwāyah*'. It means the narrative style of each *qiraat* imam and the differences between these narrations. Disputes occurred as a result of these differences. Even students who learned their reading mode from the same imam differed from

560 Zarqānī , *Manāhil,* 1/412.

561 Zarqānī , 1/412; Ismail Cerrahoglu, *Tefsir Usulu,* 66.

562 Ismail Cerrahoglu, *ibid.,* 66.

each other in their narration and these differences (in the same mode of reading) are referred to as '*tarīq*'.[563]

SUMMARY OF DEFINITION OF THE READINGS (*QIRAAT*):

1. *Qiraa*t means the changes which occur in the words of the Qur'ān with regard to the extension, shortening, punctuation of the written text, the order of the words in the text and their reading accordingly.
2. *Qārī* means a reader and a reciter and is also used for a scholar who has memorised the whole Qur'ān and has a detailed knowledge of the various readings
3. *Qurra* means, the imams who represent the seven modes of the Qur'ān (*ahruf sab'a*) and the various readings of the Qur'ān (*qiraat*).
4. *Riwāyah* means the narrative style of each *qiraat* imam and the differences between these narrations.
5. *Tarīq* is the differences in narration between students who learned their reading mode from the same imam but differed from each other in their narration.

9.2 The Acknowledgment of the Various Readings

The Companions learned the Qur'ān from the Prophet (pbuh) in different ways. Some of them learned just one mode of reading, while others learned two, three or more modes of reading. In turn, the readings of the successors (*tabi'in*) who learned from the Companions were different from each other. So, these different readings continued after them and the various readings of the Qur'ān were established as an independent science. The imams of these various readings went to different cities of Islam and their reading styles became well-known among Muslims in those cities; as a result they named each reading mode after its imam. The famous imams of *qiraat* in that time were 'Abd Allah ibn Kathīr (d. 737 C.E.), Nāfi' (d. 785 C.E.), Abū 'Amr (d. 770 C.E.), Ibn Āmir (d. 736 C.E.), Āsim (d. 744 C.E.), Hamza (d. 803 C.E.) and al-Kisaī (d. 804 C.E.).[564]

Specialist scholars in the field of *qiraat* undertook to collect all the various readings of the Qur'ān around the end of the second century of *Hijra*. They ascribed each reading style to its well-known imam and classified the readings as authentic (*saḥīḥ*), exceptional (*shazz*) or fake (*mawdu'*) based on certain criteria and meth-

563 Suyūtī, *al-Itqān*, 1/76.
564 Subhi Salih, *Mabāhith*, 281.

odology.[565] From this, we can understand that the early works regarding the science of *qiraat,* had already started during the second century of *Hijra*. The most well-known scholar in this field is Harun b. Musa (d. 786 C.E.). However, all the works relating to the science of *qiraat* from this time were transmitted orally. The first books in the field of *qiraat* were written in the third century of *Hijra*. The first authors in the science of *qiraat* were Abū Ubayda al-Qāsım Sallām (d. 828 C.E.), Abū Hatim as- Sijistāni (d. 868 C.E.) and Ibn Jarir at-Tabarī (d. 922 C.E.). Due to the late development of the science of *qiraat* there were sometimes more than one report for each mode of reading. For this reason, the scholars who wrote the first books in this field mentioned more than seven ways of reading; for example, al-Rafi'i reports that Abū Ubayda mentioned twenty-five readings of the Qur'ān.[566]

In the fourth century of *Hijra*, the scholar Abū Bakr Mujahid (d. 935 C.E.) wrote *'Kitab as-Sab'a'*. In this book he collected the readings of the above-mentioned, well-known imams. His classification method was then adopted and there was a general consensus (*ijma'*) about the authenticity of these seven reading modes. Later still, Ibn al-Jazari, the profound scholar in the field of *qiraat*, added three more readings making the number of authentic readings ten; these ten readings are known as *'qiraat al-'ash'ara'* in the sciences of the Qur'ān. Ibn al-Jazari ascribed these three readings to Khalaf b. Hishām (d. 844 C.E.), Abū Ja'far Yazid al-Qa'qa' (d. 748 C.E.) and Abū Muhammad Ya'qub b. Isẖāq (d. 820 C.E.).[567] The sources in the field of *qiraat* describe the seven readings, which Abū Bakr b. Mujahid collected, as *'mutawātir'* (the most authentic narration) and the other three readings which Ibn al-Jazari collected, as *'mashhūr'* (well-known but not as trusted as *mutawātir*).[568] In addition to these ten readings, there are four more which are ascribed to Hasan al-Basrī (d. 728 C.E.), Ibn Muhaysin (d. 740 C.E.), Yahya b. al-Mubarak al-Yazidi (d. 817 C.E.) and Abū al-Faraj Muhammad b. Ahmad as-Shanbuzî (d. 998 C.E.), but these readings are *shazz* (exceptional) and not accepted as authentic.[569]

Summary of the Acknowledgment of the Various Readings:

1. The Companions learned various modes of reading from the Prophet (pbuh).
2. The successors (*tabi'in*) learned from the Companions and were different from each other.

565 Ibn al-Jazari, *an-Nashr*, 1/53.
566 Ar-Rafi'i, *Ijaz al-Qur'ān*, 42-43.
567 Ibn al-Jazari, *an-Nashr*, 1/98.
568 Zarkashī , *al-Burhān*, 1/318.
569 Ismail Karacam, *Kur'an-i Kerimin Nuzulu*, 276

3. Later, the various readings of the Qur'ān were established as an independent science. The imams of these various readings went to different cities of Islam and their reading styles became well-known among Muslims in those cities.
4. Each reading mode was named after its imam.
5. In the second century of *Hijra* scholars collected and classified the readings as authentic (*sahih*), exceptional (*shazz*) or fake (*mawdu'*).
6. All the works relating to the science of *qiraat* from this time were transmitted orally. The first books in the field of *qiraat* were written during the third century of *Hijra*. There were many modes of reading recorded at this time.
7. In the fourth century of *Hijra*, there was a general consensus on the work of Abū Bakr Mujahid who collated the seven well-known reading modes.
8. Ibn al-Jazari later added three more readings making the number of authentic readings ten; '*qiraat al-'ash'ara*'.
9. The first seven readings are '*mutawātir*' (the most authentic narration) and the other three readings which Ibn al-Jazari collected, are '*mashhūr*' (well-known but not as trusted as *mutawātir*).
10. There are four more readings which are *shazz* (exceptional) and not accepted as authentic.

9.3 The Classification of the Various Readings

The readings (*qiraat*) can be classified into two groups from the aspect of their transmission; authentic (*saẖīẖ*) and exceptional (*shazz*). Authentic readings are sub-divided into two groups; *mutawātir* (most authentic) and *mashhūr* (well-known). *Shazz* readings are three groups; '*āẖād*' (transmitted by single source), '*mudraj*' (mixed with unauthentic narrations) and '*mawdu*' (forgery).[570]

9.3.1 The Authentic Readings

The authentic readings must meet the following conditions based on general consensus:

1) The reading must be correct according to Arabic grammar (*muwafaqat al-'Arabiyyah*).
2) The reading must agree with the text of the Caliph Uthman (*Muwafaqat al-Muṣẖāf*).

[570] Suyūtī, *al-Itqān*, 1/215.

3) The reading must be transmitted through sound channels; in other words, it must reliably trace back to the Prophet (pbuh).[571]

It is not permissible to reject any reading which has these conditions and Muslims are obliged to believe in and accept them.[572]

The Most Authentic Readings (*Mutawātir Qiraat*)

Mutawātir qiraat are readings with the following conditions: [573]

1) They are reported by such a large number of people that it is impossible to reason that they would agree on a lie, and there is no break in the narration chain, (this is the definition of *mutawātir*).
2) They are correct according to Arabic grammar (*muwafaqat al-'Arabiyyah*).
3) They agree with the text of the Caliph Uthman (*Muwafaqat al-Muṣḥ̱āf*).

According to the majority of the scholars, seven readings are *mutawātir*.[574]

Well-Known Readings (*Mashhūr*)

The transmission chain is known to be authentic as it is narrated by a *qārī* who is just (*adālah*) and has healthy memory (*dabt*). This reading is also authentic since it meets the necessary conditions. The narration cannot reach the level of *mutawātir* because it is transmitted by fewer people; however, it is well-known by the scholars of *qiraat* and has become famous among them.[575] The readings of Abū Ja'far, Khalaf and Ya'qub are *mashhūr* readings.[576]

9.3.2 The Exceptional (*Shazz*) or Unauthentic Readings

These readings do not meet all or any of the three conditions of authentic readings.[577] They can be categorized into three groups; *āḫ̱ād, mawdu'* and *mudraj*.

Single Source Readings (*Āḫ̱ād*)

The transmission of this reading is authentic but it doesn't meet the other two conditions; correctness according to Arabic grammar and agreement with the text of the Caliph Uthman. This type of reading is classified as *āḫ̱ād*.[578]

---

[571] Zarqānī, *Manāhil*, 1/418.
[572] Zarqānī, *ibid.*, I.418.
[573] Zarkashī, *al-Burhān*, 1/318.
[574] Zarkashī, ibid, 1/318.
[575] Zarqānī, *Manāhil*, 1/ 430.
[576] Zarqānī, ibid, 1/ 433.
[577] Zarkashī, *al-Burhān*, 1/331.
[578] Zarkashī, *al-Burhān*, 1/331.

Mixed With Unauthentic Readings (*Mudraj*)

In the science of *qiraat*, a *mudraj* reading is when the narrator has made some additions to the original text for the purpose of explanation (*tafsīr*). These additions were not part of the Qur'ān but were personal notes to explain some words in the verses. These additional words were found particularly in the personal *Muṣḥāf* of 'Abd Allah ibn Mas'ud and 'Ubay ibn Ka'b. There is no doubt that the Companions who authored these notes were able to distinguish between their own notes and the original text of the Qur'ān. Their notes were just to explain the meanings of some of the words or verses.[579] For this reason, they didn't hesitate to write those non-Qur'anic words next to the original text. However, when later generations studied these texts, they understood that these notes referred to the reading mode of those particular Companions and ascribed the words as part of the original Qur'anic text. There are many examples of this type of addition; for example Sa'd b. Abī Waqqas 4:12, Ubay ibn Ka'b and Ibn Mas'ud 5:89 added extra words into these verses and read them in that way.[580]

Forged Readings (*Mawdu'*)

This type of reading does not have a sound chain of transmission, is baseless and forged. For example; Muhammad b. Ja'far al-Khuzaa reads the word 'Allah' with 'u' sound in the verse; إِنَّمَا يَخْشَى اللهَ مِنْ عِبَادِهِ الْعُلَمَاءُ and by this, changes the original meaning of this verse: 'Of all His servants, only those possessed of true knowledge stand in awe of God' which becomes: 'Allah only stands in awe of His servants, those possessed of true knowledge'. This type of reading is against the essentials of Islamic belief and is rejected.

Summary of the Classification of the Various Readings:

1. Readings can be classified into two groups: authentic (*saḫīḫ*) and unauthentic (*shazz*).
2. Authentic readings (*saḫīḫ*): must be correct in Arabic grammar, agree with the text of Uthman and be transmitted through sound channels. Muslims are obliged to accept them.
3. *Mutawātir qiraat* are the most authentic readings and are reported by such a large number of people it is impossible they could be forged. There is no break in their narration chain. Seven readings fall into this category.

[579] Zarqānī , *Manāhil*, 1/431.
[580] Ismail Cerrahoglu, *Tefsir Usulu*, 226.

4. *Mashhūr qiraat* have an authentic transmission chain but are transmitted by less people.
5. *Shazz* readings do not meet all or any of the three conditions of authentic readings and categorized into three groups; *āḫād* (authentic transmission but doesn't meet the other two conditions), *mudraj* (has notes from the recited mixed in with the original text) and *mawdu'* (forgery with no sound chain of transmission).

9.4 The Issue of Seven Letters (*Ahruf al-Sab'a*)

The Arabic word *'ahruf'* is the plural form of *'harf'* and has different meanings. The literal meaning of this word is each letter of the alphabet, but it is also used with other meanings in the Qur'ān.

1. Meaning the border and edge of something;

> Among people are also many a one who worships God on the borderline (of faith) in expectation of only worldly gains[581]

Fethullah Gülen interprets this verse as follows:

> Actually, God often tests the believers, hypocrites, and unbelievers in order to reveal the differences among their inner worlds. He puts their conscience to the test with troubles and disasters and even with the things relating to good. Thus, God reminds them of their actual worth or makes them aware of themselves. Allah tests His servants' sincerity and loyalty through their behaviour and on the scales of the judgments of their conscience. Those mentioned in the verse who failed in their test and incurred loss in both this world and the Hereafter were generally the hypocrites. They did not achieve the unity of the heart and the tongue; thus, they could not attain true faith. With their faith on the tip of their tongues, they watched occurrences suspiciously and lived a life at the edge of the religion, without ever adopting it fully and sincerely in their lives. They always remained on the borderline between belief and unbelief, being alert not to lose the worldly advantages of being a believer in the community of believers, like a fly that intends to light on the honey. In their opinion, they were deliberate and cautious against religious obligations and certain heavy duties that they found disadvantageous. In such a position they adopted, the hypocrites made plans to benefit from any advantages that Muslims might enjoy. If they got what they expected, they adhered to it and showed off as if perfect and contented

581 Qur'ān, 22: 11.

believers. Yet, if an affliction or tribulation appeared on the horizon, they immediately turned back to their previous attitudes.[582]

2. To take the words out of context to distort and distract from the truth.

> Among those who have become Jews (Judaized) are some who alter the words from their context to distort their meanings[583]

The Arabic word *sab'a* means seven and the expression *'ahruf sab'a'* means seven letters. In the Qur'anic sciences, it can be defined as the variety of modes of the Qur'ān transmitted to us, also expressed in various written forms of the text. In other words, it is the various ways that the verses of the Qur'ān can be read and recited. There are many more opinions about *ahruf sab'a*, so this definition is not accepted by all scholars. Nevertheless, a lot of evidence proves that the Qur'ān was revealed in seven letters (*ahruf sab'a*). The scholar, Suyūtī, mentions 21 Companions who inform us about the seven letters. Some of these Hadith are as follows:

1) Ibn 'Abbās reported:

> God's Apostle (pbuh) said: Gabriel recited the Qur'ān to me in one way. Then I requested him (to read it in another way), and continued asking him to recite it in other ways, and he recited it in several ways till he ultimately recited it in seven different ways[584]

2) Ubay ibn Ka'b reported:

> The Prophet (pbuh) was near the tank of Banī Ghifar that Gabriel came to him and said: 'God has commanded you to recite to your people the Qur'an in one dialect.' Upon this he said: 'I ask from God pardon and forgiveness. My people are not capable of doing it.' He then came for the second time and said: 'God has commanded you that you should recite the Qur'an to your people in two dialects.' Upon this he again said: I seek pardon and forgiveness from God, my people would not be able to do so.' He (Gabriel) came for the third time and said: 'God has commanded you to recite the Qur'an to your people in three dialects.' Upon this he said: 'I ask pardon and forgiveness from God. My people would not be able to do it.' He then came to him for the fourth time and said: 'God has com-

---

582 Fethullah Gülen, *Reflections on the Qur'ān*, 1/208-209.

583 Qur'ān, 4: 46.

584 Bukhari, *Sahīh*, 4/513

manded you to recite the Qur'an to your people in seven dialects, and in whichever dialect they would recite, they would be right.'[585]

3) 'Umar reported:

I was sitting in the *masjid* when I heard Hishām ibn Ḫākim recite *surah* al-Furqān. I was almost about to jump on him in his prayer, but I waited until he finished, and then grabbed him by his garment and asked him, 'Who taught you to recite in such a manner?' He replied, 'the Prophet (pbuh) himself taught me'. I responded, 'you are mistaken, for indeed I learnt this *surah* from the Prophet (pbuh) and it is different than from your recitation!' Therefore, I dragged him to the Prophet (pbuh) and complained to him that Hishām had recited Surah al-Furqān in a manner different from what the Prophet (pbuh) had taught me. At this, the Prophet (pbuh) told me to let Hishām be free, and asked him to recite *surah* al-Furqān. Hishām recited the *surah* in the same way I had heard him before. When he finished, the Prophet (pbuh) said, 'It was revealed in this way'. He then asked me to recite the same *surah*, when I had finished, the Prophet (pbuh) said again, 'it was (also) revealed this way. Indeed, the Qur'ān has been revealed in seven different ways, so recite whichever way is easy for you'.[586]

4) 'Ubay ibn Ka'b reported:

'Ubay ibn Ka'b heard two people reciting the Qur'ān in a manner different than from what he had learnt. After some discussion, both parties went to the Prophet (pbuh) and recited the same verses to him. He approved of both recitations. At this point, Ubay says, 'there occurred in my mind a sort of denial and doubt that did not exist even in the time of ignorance (time before Islam). When the Messenger (pbuh) saw how I was affected, he struck my chest, whereupon I started sweating, and felt as if seeing God in fear. Then the Prophet (pbuh) said, 'O 'Ubay! A message was sent to me to recite the Qur'ān in one way, but I implored God to make things easy on my nation. A second message came that I should recite the Qur'ān in two ways, but I again implored God to make things easy on my nation. I was then ordered to recite the Qur'ān in seven letters.

5) Once the Prophet (pbuh) met Gabriel, and said, 'O Gabriel! I have been sent to an illiterate nation. Among them are old and young men and women, and

[585] Muslim, *Saḫīḫ*, 4/1789

[586] Bukhari, *Saḫīḫ*, 4/514

those who have never read any writing'. Gabriel answered him, 'O Muhammad, the Qur'ān has been revealed in seven letters'.[587]

9.4.1 The Meaning of Seven Letters

There are many different opinions about the seven letters (*ahruf sab'a*); some of them are as follows:

1) Seven letters refers to the seven dialects of the tribes (*lughat*): Quraysh, Hudhayl, Tamim, Hawāzin, Thaqīf, Kinana and Yemen. People of this opinion believe that verses would be pronounced according to the pronunciation of the tribes. Where words did not match in each dialect, the corresponding word of the dialect would be used.

2) Seven letters refers to the seven ways of recitation (*lahajat*) such that words are replaced by their synonyms. The Letters have the exact same meaning but different wording.

3) It refers to the usage of words from the different languages in the Qur'ān.

4) It refers to different aspects of the revelation, such as order, prohibitions, promises, narrations, etc.

5) It may refer to different ways of pronouncing the words.

6) It refers to seven different categories of texts. For example: constrained and unconstrained, general and specific, literal and metaphoric, *nāsikh* and *mansūkh*. Other categories include those given by grammarians and linguists, specifying different verb forms.

7) It refers to seven different branches of knowledge, such as unity of God (*tawḫīd*), the rulings (*aḫkām*), etc.

8) It refers to seven types of verses in the Qur'ān: apparent, commands, recommendations, specific, particular, general and parables.

9) It refers to seven different ways that the verse can be changed:

a) 9.1. The wording: 101:5 '*kal 'ihn al-manfush*' 'humans will be like *moths scattered*' is changed to '*al-suf al-manfush*' which has the same meaning.

b) 9.2. Differences conform to the vowels and writing of the script of Uthman; the word '*fa-tabayyanu*' (investigate) in 49:6 is changed to *fa-tathabbatu* .

[587] Muslim ibid.

c) 9.3. The word order in the verses may be changed; the word *'wa qaatalu wa qutilu'* in 2: 195 is changed to *'wa qutilu wa qaatalu'*. This does not change the meaning of the verse.
d) 9.4. A letter or a word in a verse maybe added or subtracted; for example the verse 57:24 *'fa inna Allaha huwa al-ghaniyy al-hamid'* is recited as *'fa-inna Allaha ghaniyy al-hamid'* without the word *'huwa'* which means 'He'. This omission does not change the meaning at all.
e) 9.5. The change may occur in the form of the word in a verse; the word in the verse 23:8 *'li amānātihim'* (this word is plural and means trustees) is changed into the singular form, 'li *amānātihim'*. This does not change the meaning very much.
f) 9.6. The differences may occur in the diacritical markings, in other words, the sound of some letters may be different in regard to the 'a-i-u' sounds; for example, the word in the verse 2: 215 *'wa-ttakhadhu'* is changed to *'wa-ttakhidhu'*.
g) 9.7. Differences may occur in pronunciation with regard to lessening the effect of *hamzah* or *imalah*. For example, the word *'mu'minun'* is changed to *'muminun'*.

9.4.2 Benefits of Seven Letters in the Qur'ān

Knowledge of correct *qiraat* (the science of proper recitation) comes from the Prophet (pbuh) himself and the Sunnah dictated the manner of reciting each verse. Aspects of this are intrinsically linked with the Qur'anic revelations: the text was revealed verbally, and by promulgating it verbally the Prophet (pbuh) simultaneously provided both text and pronunciation to his community. Neither can be divorced from the other.[588] The seven letters are the basis of several distinct ways of reciting the Qur'ān, reflecting the different usage at the time of revelation, comprising variations in pronunciation and even minor differences in wording.[589] The seven letters are, however, not identical with the well-known seven readings. These came about in a later age. Although much of what the seven readings contain is also found in the seven letters, there are some differences between them.[590]

The unity of dialect which the Prophet (pbuh) had been accustomed to in Mecca vanished with his arrival in Medina. Islam's expansion over the Arabian

588 M. M. al-Azami, *The History of the Qur'anic Text*, 190.
589 Von Denffer, *'Ulūm al-Qur'ān*, 114-115.
590 Von Denffer, ibid.

peninsula meant the incorporation of new tribes with new dialects.[591] The main objective was to facilitate the Qur'ān's recitation for those who were unaccustomed to the Quraysh dialect and such a concession was granted through the grace of God.[592] Muslim scholars have put forward a number of explanations and benefits for Muslim that are derived from the revelation of the Qur'ān in seven letters. Among these, the following are the most important[593]:

1) To make reading, pronunciation and memorising easier, as many people were illiterate in the Prophet's (pbuh) time.

2) To unite the new Muslim community on the basis of one common language, the Arabic of the Quraysh, with minor variations accepted, according to spoken language.

3) To show something of the unique nature of the Qur'ān, in the realm of language.

4) To show something of the unique nature of the Qur'ān, in the realm of meaning and legal rulings.

5) To explain a legal ruling in more detail. As the Qur'ān is the main source for Muslims jurists to extract Islamic rulings, the seven letters provided more information for the derivation of legal rules.[594]

6) To prove the miraculous nature of the Qur'ān, for despite all these differences, the meanings of the seven letters did not contradict one another, but rather were complementary.

7) To prove the truthfulness of Prophet Muhammad (pbuh), for despite the fact that he was illiterate, the revelation of the Qur'ān occurred in different tribal dialects and different words, all of which consisted of the most fluent and eloquent speech of his time.[595]

Summary of the Benefits of Seven Letters in the Qur'ān:

1. The Prophet (pbuh) conveyed the knowledge of correct recitation of the Qur'ān.
2. The text was revealed verbally so both the text and its recitation cannot be divorced from each other.

---

591 al-Azami, *The History of the Qur'anic Text*, 191.

592 al-Azami, 192.

593 Von Denffer, *'Ulūm al-Qur'ān*, 113.

594 Ad-Dānī, *at-Taysir Fi Qirat as-Sab'a*, 98.

595 The last two are taken from Qadhi, 182.

3. The seven letters are the basis of distinct ways of reciting the Qur'ān.
4. The seven readings came about in a later age. Their content overlaps but has differences.
5. The aim of the seven letters was to aid the memorisation of the Qur'ān across the new Muslim world.
6. Their benefits include uniting the Muslim community, showing the unique nature of the Qur'ān, explaining legal rulings, proving the miraculous nature of the Qur'ān, and proving the truthfulness of the Prophet (pbuh).

9.4.3 Important Points about Seven Letters

There are some important points regarding the seven letters which are essential to consider when studying this topic. They are derived from the Hadith about the seven letters; some of them are as follows:

1. The different letters are all directly from God, and not from the Companions. In all the narrations where the Companions differed from each other, it was clear that each one had been taught directly by the Prophet (pbuh), who was inspired by God.

2. The reason the Prophet (pbuh) requested the number of ways of recitation to be increased was to make the memorisation and recitation of the Qur'ān easier for his followers.

3. The Prophet (pbuh) used to teach the different ways of recitation to different Companions, depending on the condition and situation of that Companion. The main idea was to help them to memorise the Qur'ān easily based on their personalities.

4. The differences between these letters were not so great as to prevent recognition of what was being recited. They were not radically different from each other.

5. Each one of these letters is complete and accepted by God.

6. The revelation of the Qur'ān in seven letters started in Medina.[596]

7. The Companions were very careful about the preservation of the correct recitation of the Qur'ān.

8. Qur'anic recitation is a Sunnah. The later generations must take it from the earlier generations. One has to recite it only as he has been taught. This is a fundamental principle.

---

[596] First six are taken from Qadhi, The Sciences of the Qur'ān, 174-175.

9. Because of the various readings of the Prophet (pbuh) and specific features of the Arabic text of the Qur'ān, there are some minor differences in recitation. The science of recitation is also related to the punctuation of the written text of the Qur'ān.

10. The readings are particular methodologies of reciting the Qur'ān. These *qiraat* are named after the reciter (*qārī*) who recited the Qur'ān in that particular manner and were famous as being the leaders in this field. They present the readings of the Prophet (pbuh) and the Companions.

11. These reciters sometimes differed from each other in the reading of some words, pronunciation and rules of recitation. Readings are not exactly the same as the seven letters.

12. The existence of seven, 10 or 14 readings does not mean that each reciter reads the verse totally differently. The difference is about a word or mostly about pronunciation.

13. There are two main ways of recitation in the Qur'ān: a) *Usūl* and b) *Farsh*; *Usūl* differences are mainly differences in phonetics, they are nothing to do with the actual words but are related to the sounds of the word; *imala, ishmam, tafkhim, tarqiq* or *madd*. *Farsh* differences are in the form and structure of the word. Nevertheless, these differences are generally minor differences and do not change the meaning; they are differences such as singular or plural, masculine or feminine or a minor omission. Most of the Qur'anic readings are *usūl* differences rather than *farsh*.

14. The narration chains (*isnad*) of *qiraat* are different from those of Hadith. There are *qiraat* which are transmitted by only one imam or narrator (*rawi*) but this does not mean that they are *āḥād* because *qiraat* are transmitted both written and orally. In other words, there is one reciter who transmitted a *qiraat* but in the same city thousands of people read the Qur'ān in the same way.

In conclusion, every reading that is in accordance with Arabic (grammar) even if only in some way, and in accordance with one of the *Masāḥif* (the Qur'ān books) of Uthman, even if (only) probable, and with sound chain of transmission, is a correct reading which must not be rejected. It belongs to the seven modes (*ahruf sab'a*) according to which the Qur'ān was revealed, and the people are obliged to accept it, no matter whether it is from the seven imams or the ten or from other accepted imams. However, when one of these three conditions is not fulfilled, it must be rejected as weak (*daif*) or exceptional (*shazz*) or void (*bātil*).[597]

[597] Suyūtī, al-Itqān, 1/75.

SUMMARY OF IMPORTANT POINTS ABOUT SEVEN LETTERS:

1. They come directly from God and were requested by the Prophet (pbuh) to aid the memorisation of the Qur'ān for his followers.
2. The differences between the seven letters were minor, each is accepted by God and the Companions were careful about preserving them correctly.
3. The revelation in seven letters started in Medina.
4. Reciting the Qur'ān is Sunnah and it must be recited as it was taught, even if there are some minor differences in recitation.
5. The readings are particular methodologies of reciting the Qur'ān. These *qiraat* are named after the reciter (*qārī*) who recited the Qur'ān in that particular manner and were famous as being the leaders in this field.
6. These reciters sometimes differ from each other in the reading of some words, pronunciation and rules of recitation. Readings are not exactly the same as the seven letters.
7. The existence of seven, 10 or 14 readings does not mean that each reciter reads the verse totally differently. The difference is about a word or mostly about pronunciation.
8. There are two main ways of recitation in the Qur'ān: a) *Usūl* and b) *Farsh*; *Usūl* differences are mainly differences in phonetics; *farsh* differences are in the form and structure of the word.
9. The narration chains (*isnad*) of *qiraat* are different from those of Hadith. *Qiraat* are transmitted both written and orally.
10. Every reading that is in accordance with Arabic (grammar) even if only in some way, and in accordance with one of the *Masāḩif* (the Qur'ān books) of Uthman, even if (only) probable, and with sound chain of transmission, is a correct reading which must not be rejected.
11. When one of these three conditions is not fulfilled, it must be rejected as weak (*daif*) or exceptional (*shazz*) or void (*bātil*).

9.5 Famous Readings (*Qiraat*) and the Reciters (*Qurra*)

1. Medina:

1.1. Nāfi (d. 785 C.E.): his full name was Abū Abdirrahman Nāfi b. Abī Nuaym al-Laythi. He was from Isfahan. He learned the knowledge of *qiraat* from 70 scholars. He stayed in Medina and taught *qiraat* to many people, therefore he is accepted as the Imam of Medina in the field of *qiraat*. The most famous narrators who transmitted his reading to the next generations were Qalun and Warsh. Imam Malik followed Nafi's reading method.[598]

1.2. Abū Ja'far (d. 749 C.E.) is not among the seven *mutawātir* readings. He was *tabi'in*, and learned his reading mode from Abd Allah ibn Qays. His narrators are Ibn Wardan and Ibn Jammaz.[599]

2. Mecca

2.1. Ibn Kathīr (d. 737 C.E.), took his *qiraat* from Abd Allah b. Saib al-Mahzumi. His famous narrators are Badhdhi (mu'adhdhin of Masjid Ḫarām) and Qumbul, Ibn Kathīr was Ibn Mujahid's *qiraat* teacher. Imam Shafi followed Ibn Kathīr's *qiraat.*[600]

3. Basra

3.1. Abū Amr (d. 770 C.E.). His full name was Abū Amr b. A'la al-Ma'azini. He was the imam for the people of Basra in the field of *qiraat*. He learned his *qiraat* from many *tabi'in*. There are two narrators for his *qiraat*: Duri (a blind man) and Susi. Abū Amr was the teacher of the famous Imam an-Nasaī and grammarian Sibawayh.[601]

3.2. Ya'qub ibn Isḫāq (d. 820 C.E.), is not among the seven *mutawātir* readings. His narrators are Ruways and Rawh.[602]

4. Damascus (Sham)

4.1. Ibn Amir (d. 736 C.E.). His full name is Abd Allah b. Âmir al-Yahsûbî. He was known as the imam of the people of Damascus. He took his *qiraat* from Companions such as Mu'awiya, Abū ad-Dardā, Fudala b. Ubayd and Wasila b. al-Ashqa. His narrators are Hishām and Ibn Zakwan. Ibn Amir was the teacher of Tirmidhi and imam of the Umayyad Mosque.[603]

5. Kūfa (Iraq)

5.1 Āsim (d. 745 C.E.). His full name is Abū Bakr Asim b. Abū an-Najud. He was the imam for the people of Kūfa. He took his *qiraat* from Abū Abdurrahman as-Sulami, Zarr b. Hubayhs and Abū Amr. His narrators are Shu'ba and Hafs. Asim was Abū Hanifa's teacher.[604]

---

598 Ad-Dānī, *Taysir*, 4.

599 Ibn al-Jazari, *Tabaqat*, 1/315.

600 Ibn al-Jazari, *Tabaqat*, 1/443-445

601 Ad-Dani, *Taysir*, 5.

602 Ibn al-Jazari, *Tabaqat*, 1/285.

603 Zarkashī , *Burhān*, 1/328.

604 Zarkashī , *Burhān*, 1/328.

5.2. Hamza (d. 772 C.E.). His full name was Abū Ammâre Hamza b. Habib az-Zayyât. He became imam in Kūfa after Asim and A'mash. His narrators are Khalaf and Khallad.[605]

6. Baghdad

6.1. Kisaī (d. 805 C.E.). His full name was Abū al-Hasan Ali b. Hamza al-Kisâî. He learned the knowledge of *qiraat* from Abū Layla. Ahmed b. Hanbel and Yahya ibn Main took lessons from him. His narrators are Layth and Duri.[606]

6.2. Khalaf b. Hishām (d. 843 C.E.) is not among the seven *mutawātir* readings. He was also the first narrator of Hamza's reading. His narrators are Isḫāq and Idris.[607]

Rawis (narrators) learned from the imams and each preserved some of the variations. Though the variations between the narrators are minor, there are some variations, for example, between Hafs and Shu'ba there are nearly 40 small variants.

The Readings of Today's Muslims:

Asim (Rawi: Hafs): 95% Most of the Muslim world

Nafi (Rawi: Warsh): 3% Algeria, Morocco, parts of Tunisia, West Africa, Sudan

Nafi (Rawi: Qalun): 0.7% Libya, Tunisia and Parts of Qatar

Abū Amr (Rawi: Duri): 0.3% Parts of Sudan and West Africa

Ibn Amir: 1% Parts of Yemen.

9.6 The Relationship between the Seven Letters and Various Readings

This relationship depends on the definition of the seven letters and also whether they still exist today or not. On this issue, scholars are divided into three groups. Tabarī, Taḫawī, Ibn Hibban and those who follow them, argue that only one letter from seven exists today. Tabarī maintains that when Uthman officially compiled the Qur'ān, he ordered the scribes to write it based on the Quraysh dialect, therefore, only one letter was preserved. On the other hand, Zarqānī argues that all of the seven letters were preserved, but he defines the *ahruf sab'a* (seven letters) as seven ways that the verse can be changed.[608]

---

[605] Ad-Dānī, *Taysir*, 6.

[606] Ad-Dānī, *Taysir*, 7.

[607] Zarkashī , *Burhān*, 1/330.

[608] Zarqānī , *Manāhil*, 1/170-172.

Abū Bakr Baqillānī and those who follow him hold that all the seven letters were preserved and still exist today. Their main argument is that the Companions would never leave a recitation that they used to recite during the lifetime of the Prophet (pbuh).

Ibn Taymiyyah, Shātibī, Rāzī, Ibn Kathīr, Ibn al-Jazari believe that Uthman preserved the seven letters to the extent that the script of his *Muṣḫāf* allowed him to do so. Ibn al-Jazari said:

> The majority of the early scholars and the later generations are of the opinion that the Muṣḫāf of Uthman contains seven letters in the term that its script allows. Seven letters are the recitations that the Prophet recited to Gabriel during the last year of his life. The present Muṣḫāf contains all this reading, and not a single letter from it is missing.[609]

The Companions were very careful in preserving the knowledge that they received from the Prophet (pbuh). They understood their responsibility in transferring this vast knowledge to the Muslims. It is because of this concern that detailed information exists about every topic of Islam, so much so that the Muslims even know how many white hairs the Prophet's (pbuh) beard contained.[610] The *Muṣḫāf* of Uthman was written without vowels and dots, this writing enabled the preservation of the seven letters. The various readings of the Qur'ān were taught by the Prophet (pbuh) and transmitted to us with sound and authentic channels. These *qiraat* have some integral relationship with the seven letters, so if we have various *qiraat* available today, in turn, we have seven letters as well.

Summary of the Relationship Between the Seven Letters and Various Readings:

1. Scholars are divided into three opinions over whether the seven letters exist today.
2. Tabarī, Taḫawī, Ibn Hibban and those who follow them, argue that only one letter from seven exists today.
3. Abū Bakr Baqillānī and those who follow him hold that all the seven letters were preserved and still exist today.
4. Ibn Taymiyyah, Shātibī, Rāzī, Ibn Kathīr and Ibn al-Jazari believe that Uthman preserved the seven letters to the extent that the script of his *Muṣḫāf* allowed him to do so.

---

609 Ibn Al-Jazari, *an-Nashr*, 1/31.

610 Tirmidhi, *Sunan, Shamāil*, 31.

5. The Companions were very careful in preserving the knowledge that they received from the Prophet (pbuh). They understood their responsibility in transferring this vast knowledge to the Muslims.
6. The *Muṣḥāf* of Uthman was written without vowels and dots, this writing enabled the preservation of the seven letters.

Chapter Ten

Qur'anic Stories (*Qasas al-Qur'ān*) and Thematic Unity in the Qur'ān (*Tanāsub*)

Qur'anic Stories (*Qasas al-Qur'ān*) and Thematic Unity in the Qur'ān (*Tanāsub*)

10.1 Qur'anic Stories (*Qasas al-Qur'ān*)

10.1.1 Major Features of Qur'anic Stories

The word '*qissa, qass, qisas*' literally means to scout or to narrate. In the Qur'anic sciences it is the stories which are mentioned in the Qur'ān. There are some stories in the Qur'ān which pertain to events that occurred in past nations. The stories of historical events are intended to help humankind avoid committing the same mistakes as previous generations. The fact that God has given these stories proves His love for believers in that He wants to help them and guide them to the truth. They also illustrate that disbelief is not tolerated as well as denial, wrong doing, the persecution of believers and the obstruction of Prophets. The stories in the Qur'ān confirm to the believers that the final victory belongs to the Messengers and believers.

The narration of these stories serves to strengthen the faith of believers. They are relayed in a vivid and authentic manner allowing the receivers to learn what actually happened as if they witnessed the events themselves. This is one of the miracles of the Qur'ān. The stories convey information about God's oneness, moral values, history and the laws of the religion. As we know from the principles of pedagogy and education, the narration of stories is an effective method for transmitting information. These stories teach humankind their duties in this world.

The stories mentioned in the Qur'ān are not imaginary stories; they relate real historical events. God says in the Qur'ān:

> And who is more truthful than Allah in statement.[611]

[611] Qur'ān, 4:87.

> And each [story] We relate to you from the news of the Messengers is that by which We make firm your heart. And there has come to you, in this, the truth and an instruction and a reminder for the believers.[612]

These verses inform us that the stories of the Qur'ān are comprised of historical realities. They are the truth and also the best stories:

> We relate to you, [O Muhammad], the best of stories in what We have revealed to you of this Qur'ān although you were, before it, among the unaware.[613]

There are manifold benefits to be gained from studying the Qur'anic stories. The language used to convey them is highly eloquent and they are rich in meaning and wisdom.

> There was certainly in their stories a lesson for those of understanding[614]

The stories in the Qur'ān, when studied, correct wrong thoughts, remedy hearts, teach the best way of conduct, lead to the most proper ways of behaviour and show us the best deeds.

Qur'anic stories are categorized into three groups:

1) The first group contains stories about the Messengers, their followers, the deniers or unbelievers and events relating to all of them.

2) The second group contains stories of unusual events that happened to people, the lessons from their stories and some exemplary events. The story of Maryam, Luqman, the companions of the cave, Zulqarneyn, etc. For example:

> Have you thought that the companions of the cave and the inscription were, among Our signs, a wonder? Mention, when the youths retreated to the cave and said, "Our Lord, grant us from Yourself mercy and prepare for us from our affair right guidance." So We cast (a cover of sleep) over their ears within the cave for a number of years. Then We awakened them that We might show which of the two factions was most precise in calculating what extent they had remained in time. It is We who relate to you, (O Muhammad), their story in truth...[615]

---

[612] Qur'ān, 11:120.
[613] Qur'ān, 12:3.
[614] Qur'ān, 12:111.
[615] Qur'ān, 18:9-21.

3) The third group contains stories related to the events which happened during the time of Prophet Muhammad (pbuh); the battles of Badr, Uhud, the Trench, etc.

Summary of Major Features of Qur'anic Stories:

1. God uses stories of historical events in the Qur'ān to teach lessons to humankind to help them avoid making the same mistakes as their predecessors.
2. The stories prove God's love for the believers; helps them and guides them to the truth.
3. He does not tolerate disbelief, denial, wrong doings or the persecution of believers.
4. The stories in the Qur'ān strengthen the faith of the believers, teach them wisdom and empower them against disbelief.
5. The stories mentioned in Qur'ān are not imaginary stories; they are real and historical events.
6. Qur'anic stories are categorized into three groups: stories about Messengers, followers and unbelievers; stories of unusual events happening to people; stories related to the events which happened during the time of Prophet Muhammad (pbuh).

10.1.2 The Wisdoms behind the Stories of the Qur'ān

Each of the Qur'anic stories contains much wisdom. The events related are historical but the wisdom they contain is universal and they can be used to give lessons to humanity. For example:

1) God himself explained the wisdom in the story and brought our attention to it.

> The Hour has come near, and the moon has split [in two]. And if they see a miracle, they turn away and say, "Passing magic." And they denied and followed their inclinations. But for every matter is a [time of] settlement. And there has already come to them of information that in which there is deterrence. Extensive wisdom, but warning does not avail [them].[616]

2) God is just and through stories He gives some outstanding examples from human history both warning humanity and explaining why He punished wrong doers.

---

[616] Qur'ān, 54, 1-5.

> And We did not wrong them, but they wronged themselves. And they were not availed at all by their gods which they invoked other than Allah when there came the command of your Lord. And they did not increase them in other than ruin. And thus is the seizure of your Lord when He seizes the cities while they are committing wrong. Indeed, His seizure is painful and severe.[617]

3) In some stories God proclaims His mercy and demonstrates how He bestowed favours upon believers. He invites all humanity to believe in Him alone by mentioning these favours.

> Indeed, We sent upon them a storm of stones, except the family of Lot, We saved them before dawn, As favour from us. Thus do We reward he who is grateful.[618]

4) God mentioned the previous Messengers to console Prophet Muhammad (pbuh).

> And if they deny you, then already have those before them denied. Their Messengers came to them with clear proofs and written ordinances and with the enlightening Scripture. Then I seized the ones who disbelieved, and how was My reproach.[619]

5) God mentioned past nations and their believers to encourage the believers to be patient and firm in their faith. The believers learned from the stories of the Qur'ān that God saved the early believers, He commanded them to fight in His way and He helped them to achieve victory over their enemies.

> So We responded to him and saved him from the distress. And thus do We save the believers.[620]

6) God mentioned that He destroyed past nations because of their disbelief and there is a lesson in this for today's unbelievers.

> Have they not travelled through the land and seen how was the end of those before them? Allah destroyed [everything] over them, and for the disbelievers is something comparable.[621]

---

617 Qur'ān, 11: 101-102.
618 Qur'ān, 54: 34-35.
619 Qur'ān, 35: 25-26.
620 Qur'ān, 21: 88.
621 Qur'ān, 47: 10.

7) The stories prove the Messengership of Muhammad (pbuh), because the news regarding the past nations can only be known by a real Messenger. God informed Muhammad (pbuh) about them and he in turn informed human beings.

> That is from the news of the unseen which We reveal to you, [O Muhammad]. You knew it not, neither you nor your people, before this. So be patient; indeed, the [best] outcome is for the righteous.[622]

SUMMARY OF THE WISDOMS BEHIND THE STORIES OF THE QUR'ĀN:

1. The wisdom the stories contain is universal and they can be used to give lessons to humanity.
2. God Himself explained the wisdom in the story and brought attention to it.
3. God is just and through stories He gives some outstanding examples from human history both warning humanity and explaining why He punished wrong doers.
4. God proclaims His mercy and demonstrates how He bestowed favours upon believers.
5. God mentioned the previous Messengers to console Prophet Muhammad (pbuh).
6. God mentioned past nations and their believers to encourage the believers to be patient and firm in their faith.
7. God mentioned that He destroyed past nations because of their disbelief and this is a lesson for today's unbelievers.
8. The stories prove the Messengership of Muhammad (pbuh).

10.1.3 The Repetitions of Qur'anic Narratives

In the Qur'ān, some stories are only mentioned once, such as Luqman and the companions of the cave. Some of them are repeated based on wisdom and necessity; each repetition reveals new information about them and tells them from a different perspective. In this regard, the repetitions are not exactly the same from the perspective of their length, narration style, information and approach to events.

There is a lot of wisdom in the repetition of stories, some of which is:

1) To bring attention to the importance of the story; if it is repeated in the Qur'ān it must be an important story for the believers.

---

[622] Qur'ān, 11: 49.

2) To teach lessons and place them in the hearts firmly, God repeated them in different places.

3) The stories are explained in a style which is compatible with their first addressees. The stories which were revealed in Mecca are short, very elegant and the style is very strong. On the other hand, the stories which came in Medina are opposite to this.

4) God explains same stories in variant styles which are compatible to the events, the time and the addressees; this clearly indicates the eloquence of the Qur'ān.

5) If one story can be explained from many different angles or perspectives as if seeing it, this shows that the Qur'ān is the speech of God; it came from the One who sees and knows everything.

10.1.4 The Books about the Stories of Qur'ān

Scholars have written many books about the stories in Qur'ān. Some of them are:

1) Ibn Kathīr, *Qiṣaṣ al-Qur'an.*

2) Sayf ad-Din Ahmad Mawsili, *Nafais-ul Marjan Fi Jam-i Qisas-ul Qur'ān.*

3) Tha'labi, *al-Arais.*

4) Rasul Mahalli, *Qiṣaṣ al-Qur'ān.*

5) Ahmad Hibatullah, *al-Fann-ul Qisasiyyu Fi Qur'ān-il Karim.*

6) Jar Allah Salila, *Qisas al-Qur'ān.*

7) Abd al-Karim al-Khatib, *al-Qiṣaṣ al-Qur'āniyya.*

8) Sarvat Abaza, *as-Sardut Qasasiyya Fi'l Qur'ān-il Karim.*

9) Abd al-Mun'im Khafaji, *Qasas min al-Qur'ān.*

10.2 The Notion of Unclear (*Mubhamāt*) in the Qur'ān

Mubhamāt refers to the names or places that are not mentioned clearly in the Qur'ān but are addressed using pronouns.[623] Examples of this include references to men, women, angels, *jinn,* tribes or groups. When reading these, the use of the pronoun makes it unclear who, or what, is being referred to. These details can only be made clear through the narrations of the Prophet (pbuh), the Companions or the next generation after the Companions. If the reports are not authentic, the information is not accepted. Using different sources, (such as Jewish or Christian), to explain the '*mubhamāt*' in the Qur'ān makes this ambiguity worse.

[623] Suyūtī, *al-Itqān Fi 'Ulūm al-Qur'ān,* 2/1089.

The reasons for the existence of *mubhamāt* in the Qur'ān are explained as follows:

1) The Qur'ān explained the *mubhamāt* in different verses and this style enriches the meanings of the Qur'ān:

"The path of those upon whom You have bestowed favour"[624]: This verse does not make it clear who has received God's favour. However, in a different verse it is explained and their names are given: "And whoever obeys Allah and the Messenger, those will be with the ones upon whom Allah has bestowed favour of the Prophets, the steadfast affirmers of truth, the martyrs and the righteous. And excellent are those as companions".[625]

2) There are some instances where a name is not mentioned because it is already well-known, so there could be no confusion about it.

> And We said, "O Adam, dwell, you and your wife, in Paradise and eat therefrom in [ease and] Abundance from wherever you will. But do not approach this tree, lest you be among the wrongdoers.[626]

In this verse God didn't mention Eve, rather He just mentioned her as "your wife", because she is already well-known and there is no need to mention her name. It is one of the aspects of the eloquence of the Qur'ān.

3) It is more eloquent to refer to someone using a pronoun instead of mentioning the name.

> And of the people is he whose speech pleases you in worldly life, and he calls Allah to witness as to what is in his heart, yet he is the fiercest of opponents.[627]

The verse does not indicate who it is referring to, but we know from other sources that it was referring to Ahnas ibn Sharik. He was a fierce opponent of Islam but later converted to the religion. The reason the verse did not mention him by name was to give an example to others with the same attitude. If he had been directly mentioned, it could have humiliated him and prevented him from later becoming Muslim. Instead, he recognised his mistake and embraced Islam.

4) If there is no benefit in identifying the *mubhamāt*, God didn't mention them clearly.

---

624 Qur'ān, 1: 7.
625 Qur'ān, 4: 69.
626 Qur'ān, 2: 35.
627 Qur'ān, 2: 204.

> Consider such an example as the one who passed by a township which had fallen into ruin. He said, "How will Allah bring this to life after its death?" So Allah caused him to die for a hundred years; then He revived him. He said, "How long have you remained?" The man said, "I have remained a day or part of a day." He said, "Rather, you have remained one hundred years. Look at your food and your drink; it has not changed with time. And look at your donkey; and We will make you a sign for the people. And look at the bones (of this donkey) how We raise them and then We cover them with flesh." And when it became clear to him, he said, "I know that Allah is over all things competent.[628]

> And ask them about the town that was by the sea - when they transgressed in [the matter of] the sabbath when their fish came to them openly on their sabbath day, and the day they had no sabbath they did not come to them. Thus did We give them trial because they were defiantly disobedient[629]

In both of the stories mentioned, the names and places are not identified. This is because knowledge of these does not bring the reader any benefit. The emphasis is placed on the subject of the verses rather than those details.

5) The use of the singular pronoun in this example gives a general meaning to the verse.

> And whoever emigrates for the cause of Allah will find on the earth many locations and Abundance. And whoever leaves his home as an emigrant to Allah and His Messenger and then death overtakes him; his reward has already become incumbent upon Allah. And Allah is ever Forgiving and Merciful.[630]

The singular pronoun "he" is used but the meaning is general; anyone who abandons his home or country for God will be rewarded.

6) The use of a pronoun instead of a name is also used to convey insignificance. For example:

"Indeed, your enemy is the one cut off".[631] There are three reasons why the name is not mentioned in this case. Firstly, there is no benefit in mentioning the person's name; secondly, the character of the person is so bad he does not deserve to have his name mentioned in the Qur'ān; thirdly, the use of a pronoun keeps

---

628 Qur'ān, 2:259.

629 Qur'ān, 7: 163.

630 Qur'ān, 4: 100.

631 Qur'ān, 108: 3.

the meaning of the verse general and indicates that anyone similar in thought or deed will also be cut off (sooner or later) from posterity. The verse itself is referring to those who satirise God's Messenger (pbuh) and warns they will be cut off from posterity.

7) Sometimes God praises someone about his/her good character without mentioning his/her name.

> Let not those of virtue among you and wealth swear not to give [aid] to their relatives and the needy and the emigrants for the cause of Allah, and let them pardon and overlook. Would you not like that Allah should forgive you? And Allah is Forgiving and Merciful.[632]

> And the one who has brought the truth (The Prophet) and he believed in it, those are the righteous.[633]

> If you do not aid the Prophet, Allah has already aided him when those who disbelieved had driven him out (of Mecca) as one of two, when they were in the cave and he said to his companion, "Do not grieve; indeed Allah is with us." And Allah sent down his tranquillity upon him and supported him with angels you did not see and made the word of those who disbelieved the lowest, while the word of Allah that is the highest. Allah is Exalted in Might and Wise[634]

All these verses are actually referring to Abū Bakr. God didn't mention his name but praised him and his good qualities to give an example for all believers. There is no benefit in mentioning his name as it is his characteristics which are noteworthy and should be emulated.

These examples clearly demonstrate that there are some *mubhamāt* in the Qur'ān. The purpose of *mubhamāt* is to direct the attention of the reader to the most important information in the verse without distracting it with unnecessary details. The Qur'ān, whilst containing information about historical events, is not a history book; it uses this information to educate people and invite them to the truth.

Summary of the Notion of Unclear (*Mubhamāt*) in the Qur'ān:

1. *Mubhamāt* refers to the names or places that are not mentioned clearly in the Qur'ān but are addressed by pronouns.

632 Qur'ān, 24: 22.
633 Qur'ān, 39: 33.
634 Qur'ān, 9: 40.

2. The Qur'ān explained the *mubhamāt* in different verses and this style enriches the meanings of the Qur'ān.
3. There are some instances where a name is not mentioned because it is already well-known, so there could be no confusion about it.
4. It is more eloquent to refer to someone using a pronoun instead of mentioning the name.
5. If there is no great benefit in identifying the *mubhamāt* in the verse, God didn't mention the name.
6. To indicate that it is a general statement even though it is mentioned in singular form. If it was named, it couldn't be a general statement.
7. God sometimes does not mention the name in order to humiliate a person; He just introduces the person by describing his low character.
8. Sometimes God praises someone with his good character without mentioning his name. The purpose of this is to give lessons and bring the attention to the most important information in the verses rather than distracting the attention with details of names and places when it is not necessary.

10.2.1 The Types of *Mubhamāt*

There are two types of *mubhamāt* in the Qur'ān; each is explained below with examples.

1) The names which are mentioned as male, female, *jinn* or as group but their names are known by the Qur'ān or Sunnah.

a) References to Maryam (Mary) and Isa (Jesus) are understood from the expressions in the verses 'the son of Mary or His mother'.[635]
b) The references to Masjid-i Kuba are understood from the verse "A mosque founded on righteousness from the first day is more worthy for you to stand in".[636]
c) We know that the vicegerent who is mentioned in the verse is Adam; "Remember (when) your Lord said to the angels: "I am setting on the earth a vicegerent".[637]

2) The names are mentioned as a group but only some of them are known.

---

[635] Qur'ān, 23: 50.
[636] Qur'ān, 9: 108.
[637] Qur'ān, 2: 30.

a) Some Muslims asked the Prophet (pbuh) about the new moon; "They ask you, [O Muhammad], about the new moons".[638] It is narrated that those Muslims who asked this question were Mu'adh b. Jabal and Tha'laba b. Ghanam.[639]

b) It is narrated that the chapter '*Kafirun*' is revealed about four unbelievers among them, Walid ibn Mughira and As b. Wail, but other two are unknown.[640]

c) Some unbelievers and hypocrites criticized the Prophet (pbuh) and Muslims when God ordered him to change the direction of the *qibla* towards the Ka'ba, among them were Rifaa ibn Qays, Qa'b ibn al-Ashraf, Rafi ibn Harmala and Hijaj ibn Amr[641]; "The foolish among the people will say, "What has turned them away from their Qibla, which they used to face?"[642]

10.3 The Notion of Addressing (*Khitāb*) in the Qur'ān

There are three main categories of addressing (*khitāb*) in the Qur'ān:

1. *Khitāb* to Prophet Muhammad (pbuh).
2. *Khitāb* to other people.
3. *Khitāb* to both.

These main categories have many sub-categories and there are many examples for them in the Qur'ān. There are 33 sub-catagories and each will be mentioned with one example[643];

1. *Khitāb* is general and the meaning is general: "Indeed, Allah does not wrong the people at all, but it is the people who are wronging themselves".[644]

2. *Khitāb* is specific and the meaning is specific: "O Messenger, announce that which has been revealed to you from your Lord".[645]

3. *Khitāb* is specific but the meaning is general: "O Prophet, when you divorce women, divorce them for [the commencement of] their waiting period and keep count of the waiting period, and fear Allah, your Lord".[646]

---

638 Qur'ān, 2: 189.
639 Suyūtī, *al-Itqān Fi 'Ulūm al-Qur'ān*, 2/1103.
640 Suyūtī, *al-Itqān*, 2/1103.
641 Suyūtī, 1103.
642 Qur'ān, 2: 142.
643 Zarkashī, *al-Burhān*, 2/217-253, Suyūtī, *al-Itqān*, 2/33-35.
644 Qur'ān, 10: 44.
645 Qur'ān, 5: 67.
646 Qur'ān, 65: 1.

4. *Khitāb* is general but the meaning is specific: there is disagreement among scholars about whether this type of *khitāb* exists in the Qur'ān. Most of the scholars accept it and give examples, such as: "And when it is said to them, 'Believe as *the people* have believed"[647] in this verse the word 'the people' is understood as Abd Allah ibn Salam.[648]

5. *Khitāb* to the species: all the verses which start as 'O Human beings' are examples for this type of *khitāb*.

6. *Khitāb* to a specific group: "O Children of Israel"[649]; in this type of *khitāb*, the children of Jacob are meant.

7. *Khitāb* to a specific person: 'O Moses', 'O Jesus' are examples for this type. All the Prophets in the Qur'ān are mentioned by name apart from Prophet Muhammad (pbuh). His elevated status amongst the Prophets is conveyed by the way he is addressed. He is most frequently addressed as The Prophet (pbuh) and The Messenger (pbuh).

8. *Khitāb* for praising: 'O Believers' is mostly praising *khitāb* for the Companions of the Prophet (pbuh).

9. *Khitāb* for condemning: "O you who have disbelieved, make no excuses that Day. You will only be recompensed for what you used to do".[650] In this verse the unbelievers are blamed, because they denied the truth deliberately.

10. *Khitāb* to honour someone: "O Adam, dwell, you and your wife, in Paradise".[651]

11. *Khitāb* for humiliating: "Allah said, 'then get out of it, for indeed, you are expelled. And indeed, upon you is the curse until the Day of Recompense".[652] Satan was cast out of Paradise by God and cursed by Him for his arrogance.

12. *Khitāb* to mock someone: "Taste the fire, Indeed, you are the honoured, the noble". This verse addresses Abū Jahil who valued his wealth and position in society above anything else and stated: 'I am so noble and honoured'. He is ridiculed and punished in Hell by God, Who reminded him of his arrogance.

13. *Khitāb* to a group by mentioning one of them: "O man, what has deceived you concerning your Lord, the Generous".[653] In this verse the word "*insan*" (man) is singular but the message is for all humankind.

---

[647] Qur'ān, 2: 13.
[648] Suyūtī, 2/33-35.
[649] Qur'ān, 2: 40.
[650] Qur'ān, 66:7.
[651] Qur'ān, 7: 19.
[652] Qur'ān, 15: 34-35.
[653] Qur'ān, 82: 6.

14. *Khitāb* to a single person by mentioning a group: "O Messengers eat from the good foods and work righteousness. Indeed, I, of what you do, know".[654] In this verse Allah meant Prophet Muhammad (pbuh) even though He mentioned all the Prophets.

15. *Khitāb* to a single person by mentioning two people: "You two, throw into Hell every obstinate disbeliever".[655] In this verse the meaning of 'you two' is the Malik who is the guard of the fire.[656]

16. *Khitāb* to two people by mentioning just one of them: "(Pharaoh) said, 'So who is the Lord of you two, O Moses?"[657] In this verse Aaron and Moses is meant but just one of them is mentioned.

17. *Khitāb* to a group after addressing one person: "And, [O Muhammad], you are not [engaged] in any matter or recite any of the Qur'ān and you [people] do not do any deed except that We are witness over you when you are involved in it".[658] In the verse, the first verbs are in singular form and then plural form. The first addressee is the Prophet (pbuh) and then his followers.

18. *Khitāb* to a person but meaning others: "O Prophet, fear Allah and do not obey the disbelievers and the hypocrites. Indeed, Allah is ever Knowing and Wise".[659] God mentions the Prophet (pbuh) but He means the Prophet's (pbuh) followers in this verse, because the Prophet (pbuh) is already protected from these bad deeds.

19. *Khitāb* for preaching and giving lessons: "he turned away from them and said, '*O my people*, I had certainly conveyed to you the message of my Lord and advised you, but you do not like advisors".[660] The Prophet Salih talked to his people in this manner to warm their hearts toward the message of God, but they didn't listen to him. There is a lesson for us in terms of addressing people.

20. *Khitāb* to others by changing the addressees: "And if they do not respond to you, then know that the Qur'ān was revealed with the knowledge of Allah and that there is no deity except Him. Then, would you be Muslims?"[661]

---

654 Qur'ān, 23: 51.
655 Qur'ān, 50: 24.
656 Zarkashī, *al-Burhān*, 2/217-253.
657 Qur'ān, 20: 49.
658 Qur'ān, 10: 61.
659 Qur'ān, 33: 1.
660 Qur'ān, 7:79.
661 Qur'ān 5 : 49.

21. *Khitāb* in the first person after talking in the third person or vice versa; "whatever you give for interest to increase within the wealth of people will not increase with Allah. But what you give in *zakat*, desiring the countenance of Allah, those are the multipliers".[662] The verse starts by addressing in the first person but it ends by addressing in the third persons.

22. *Khitāb* to unanimated objects: "Then He directed Himself to the heaven while it was smoke and said to it and to the earth, 'Come, willingly or by compulsion.' They said, 'we have come willingly"[663] God talked to the heavens and the earth in this verse.

23. *Khitāb* for encouragement: "O you who have believed, fear Allah and give up what remains [due to you] of interest, if you should be believers".[664] God named those people as believers first and then He encouraged them to leave the interest by saying 'if you are believers'.

24. *Khitāb* for threatening: "when We said to the angels, 'Prostrate to Adam,' and they prostrated, except for Iblees (Satan). He was of the *jinn* and departed from the command of his Lord. Then *will you take him and his descendants as allies other than Me while they are enemies to you?* Wretched it is for the wrong-doers as an exchange".[665]

25. *Khitāb* for heroism: "Indeed, Allah loves those who fight in His cause in a row as though they are a (single) structure joined firmly".[666] God encourages the believers to fight together in His way without fearing the enemy.

26. *Khitāb* for hatred: "O you who have believed, avoid much [negative] assumption. Indeed, some assumption is sin. And do not spy or backbite each other. *Would one of you like to eat the flesh of his brother when dead?* You would detest it. And fear Allah; indeed, Allah is accepting of repentance and Merciful".[667] This verse indicates the seriousness of the sin of backbiting: it is like eating the flesh of one's brother.

27. *Khitāb* to show his mercy: "Say, 'O My servants who have transgressed against themselves [by sinning], do not despair of the mercy of Allah. Indeed, Allah forgives all sins. Indeed, it is He who is the Forgiving, the Merciful".[668]

---

[662] Qur'ān 30: 39.
[663] Qur'ān 41: 11.
[664] Qur'ān, 2: 278.
[665] Qur'ān, 18: 50.
[666] Qur'ān, 61: 4.
[667] Qur'ān, 49: 12.
[668] Qur'ān, 39: 53.

28. *Khitāb* to show love: "when he said to his father, '*O my father*, why do you worship that which does not hear and does not see and will not benefit you at all?"[669] The expression 'o my father' indicates the love of Ibrahim towards his father.

29. *Khitāb* for challenging: "And if you are in doubt about what We have sent down upon Our Servant [Muhammad], then produce a *surah* the like thereof and call upon your witnesses other than Allah, if you should be truthful".[670]

30. *Khitāb* for refutation: "All food was lawful to the Children of Israel except what Israel had made unlawful to himself before the Torah was revealed. Say, [O Muhammad], 'So bring the Torah and recite it, if you should be truthful".[671] The Jews denied the information which the Prophet (pbuh) gave them and God revealed this verse to refute their claim.

31. *Khitāb* for cursing: "when they are alone, they bite their fingertips at you in rage. Say, '*Die in your rage*. Indeed, Allah knows of that within the breasts".[672]

32. *Khitāb* to show one's dignity or honour: this type of *khitāb* starts as 'tell'. The final three chapters of the Qur'ān are examples for this type.

33. *Khitāb* for non-existence: "when your Lord took from the children of Adam from their loins their descendants and made them testify of themselves, (saying to them), 'Am I not your Lord?' They said, 'Yes, we have testified".[673] This verse refers to God communicating with humankind before they were born. Scholars interpreted this verse to mean that humankind was created with innate faith.

10.4 Questions and Answers in the Qur'ān

The Qur'ān contains many questions and answers which scholars have categorised into 13 groups:

1) The answer comes right after the question: "They ask you what they should spend. Say, 'The excess (beyond needs)".[674]

2) The answer and question are separated from each other; in other words, the answer does not come immediately after the question. This can happen in two ways:

---

669 Qur'ān, 19: 42.
670 Qur'ān, 2: 23.
671 Qur'ān, 3: 93.
672 Qur'ān, 3: 119.
673 Qur'ān, 7: 172.
674 Qur'ān, 2: 219.

a) The question and answer are separated but they are in the same *surah* (chapter):

> They say, 'What is this Messenger that eats food and walks in the markets? Why was there not sent down to him an angel so he would be with him a warner?[675]

The answer came in the same *surah*:

> We did not send before you, (O Muhammad), any of the Messengers except that they ate food and walked in the markets. And We have made some of you [people] as trial for others, will you have patience? And ever is your Lord, Seeing.[676]

b) The question and answer are separated; "They say, 'what is the Most Merciful (Rahman)?"[677] The answer for this question came in a different *surah*; "The Most Merciful (Rahman), taught the Qur'ān, created man, taught him eloquence".[678]

3) The answer for the question is hidden in the verse; "if there was any Qur'ān by which the mountains would be removed or the earth would be broken apart or the dead would be made to speak?"[679] The answer for this question is hidden in the verse; it is 'if it was such a thing that would be the Qur'ān as well'.

4) Giving the answer without mentioning the question: "never would Allah have caused you to lose your faith (your prayers)".[680] When God changed the *qibla* direction towards Mecca some Companions were worried about 'what happens to the prayers which have been prayed towards Jerusalem? Are they wasted? What about the prayers of the Muslims who died before praying facing towards the Ka'ba?' The answer to all these questions is given in the above verse.

5) Giving two answers to one question: "They said, 'Why was this Qur'ān not sent down upon a great man from one of the two cities?"[681] There are two answers for this question:

> Do they distribute the mercy of your Lord? It is We who have apportioned among them their livelihood in the life of this world and have raised some of them above others in degrees[682]

---

675 Qur'ān, 25: 7.
676 Qur'ān, 25: 20.
677 Qur'ān, 25: 60
678 Qur'ān, 55: 1-4.
679 Qur'ān, 13: 31
680 Qur'ān, 2: 143.
681 Qur'ān, 43: 31.
682 Qur'ān, 43: 32.

The second answer; "your Lord creates what He wills and chooses; not for them was the choice".[683]

6) Giving one answer for two questions: "if it had not been for the favour of Allah upon you and His mercy?" The answer for these two questions is given by the incident of slander;

> Indeed, those who came with falsehood are a group among you. Do not think it bad for you; rather it is good for you. For every person among them is what [punishment] he has earned from the sin, and he who took upon himself the greater portion thereof, for him is a great punishment. Why, when you heard it, did not the believing men and believing women think good of one another and say, 'This is an obvious falsehood'. Why did they (who slandered) not produce for it four witnesses? And when they do not produce the witnesses, then it is they, in the sight of Allah, who are the liars.[684]

7) The answer is understood from the question and it is not mentioned:

> So is he who is on clear evidence from his Lord like him to whom the evil of his work has been made attractive and they follow their own desires?[685]

The answer is omitted but it is understood from the context.

8) The question and answer are seemingly unrelated and refer to different things: "Abraham, when he said to his people, 'Worship Allah and fear Him. That is best for you, if you should know?'[686] The answer to this request was completely different: "the answer of Abraham's people was not but that they said, 'Kill him or burn him'.[687]

9) The context includes the answer by stating the question:

> Sad. By the Qur'ān containing reminder, but those who disbelieve are in pride and dissension. How many a generation have We destroyed before them, and they then called out; but it was not a time for escape. And they wonder that there has come to them a warner from among themselves. And the disbelievers say, 'This is a magician and a liar.[688]

[683] Qur'ān, 28: 68.
[684] Qur'ān, 24: 11-13.
[685] Qur'ān, 47: 14.
[686] Qur'ān, 29: 16.
[687] Qur'ān, 29: 24.
[688] Qur'ān, 38: 1-4.

The Meccan polytheists didn't believe Prophet Muhammad (pbuh) but God swears and confirms his Prophethood by refuting their claim and condemning their attitude towards him.

10) The answer comes at the end of the statement:

> They will say there were three, the fourth of them being their dog; and they will say there were five, the sixth of them being their dog - guessing at the unseen; and they will say there were seven, and the eighth of them was their dog. Say, (O Muhammad), '*My Lord is most knowing of their number.*[689]

11) Answering as part of the question - the answer and question are part of each other:

> They said while approaching them, 'What is it you are missing?' They said, 'We are missing the measure of the king. And for he who produces it is the reward of a camel's load, and I am responsible for it.[690]

12) The answer is connected to time: "Your Lord says, 'Call upon Me; I will respond to you".[691] The Companions asked the Prophet (pbuh) when they should pray to God; after their question God sent the following verse:

> When My servants ask you, concerning Me, indeed I am near. I respond to the invocation of the supplicant when he calls upon Me. So let them respond to Me and believe in Me that they may be guided.[692]

13) The answer for the prohibition:

> O wives of the Prophet, you are not like anyone among women. If you fear Allah, then do not be soft in speech (to men), lest he in whose heart is disease should covet, but speak with appropriate speech.[693]

10.5 The Relationship between Chapters and Verses/Thematic Unity (*Tanāsub*)

One of the Qur'anic sciences which examines the coherence, interrelation and harmony between the verses and *surah* is the science of *tanāsub al-suvar wa al-āy.*

---

689 Qur'ān, 18: 22.
690 Qur'ān, 12: 71,72.
691 Qur'ān, 40: 60.
692 Qur'ān, 2: 186.
693 Qur'ān, 33: 32.

This science is very important to be able to see the whole picture and interrelations among *surah* and the verses.

The Qur'ān was revealed over 23 years at different times and on different occasions, but the connection between the verses is so strong that their position within the *surah* cannot be changed. It is as if the Qur'ān was revealed once as a whole. This is one of the miracles of the Qur'ān. There is no contradiction among the verses even though there was a great time difference between their revelation. For example, the *surah* Baqara took almost 10 years to be completely revealed but this cannot be sensed when it is read. The Qur'ān comes from an eternal knowledge which is beyond the limits of time. The whole of time is as one which explains the perfection of the Qur'ān. This ability is beyond the power of humankind which is why no one has been able to respond to the challenge of the Qur'ān; to bring just one *surah* which is similar. The Qur'ān itself testifies to the impossibility of the challenge.

Renowned scholars who highlighted the importance of this science in order to understand the Qur'ān as a whole were Fakhr al-Din al-Rāzī, Abū Bakr Ibn al-'Arābī, Zamakhsharī and Sakkaki. This science requires great attention and utmost care not to ruin the compromising meanings between the verses and *surah*. Many *mufassir* showed this interrelation among the verses in their *tafsīr* books. The *surah* Fatiha is like an introduction to the whole Qur'ān and all the following *surah* have a relationship with it.

There is also a strong connection among the *surah* and the order of them; they are not placed randomly. Some of them are designed according to their lengths or shortness, but this not the only measure to accord them their place. Their position was determined by the Prophet (pbuh) and there is a strong relationship between them. Because of this order in the Qur'ān, it is read and re-read without losing its appeal and memorizing it is easy.

Summary of the Relationship Between Chapters and Verses/Thematic Unity (*Tanāsub*):

1. This science (*tanāsub*) studies the coherence, interrelation and harmony between the verses and *surah* and is very important to be able to see the whole picture or interrelations among *surah* and the verses.
2. The Qur'ān was revealed over 23 years at different times and on different occasions, but the connection between the verses is so strong their position within the *surah* cannot be changed.

3. Renowned scholars who highlighted the importance of this science in order to understand the Qur'ān as a whole were Fakhr al-Din al-Rāzī, Abū Bakr Ibn al-'Arābī, Zamakhsharī and Sakkaki.
4. The *surah* Fatiha is like an introduction to the whole Qur'ān and all the following *surah* have a relationship with it.
5. There is also a strong connection among the *surah* and the order of them; they are not placed randomly.

10.5.1 The Examples for the Interrelation among the Verses

1. "Exalted is He who took His Servant by night from al-Masjid al-Ḫarām to al-Masjid al- Aqsa, whose surroundings We have blessed, to show him of Our signs. Indeed, He is the Hearing, the Seeing".[694] The next verse is "We gave Moses the Scripture and made it [695] guidance for the Children of Israel that you not take other than Me as Disposer of affairs". Without looking in-depth, these verses seem unrelated. However, when studied closely, we can see there is a strong interrelation between them. The first verse informs us about one of the Prophet's (miracles) and the second mentions how God saved Moses from Pharaoh and gave him the Torah. The intention of the second verse immediately following the first is to strengthen it and convince those who don't believe the Prophet (pbuh). In the time of Moses there were many people who did not believe him and this was also true in Muhammad's (pbuh) time. God spoke with Moses on the mountain of Tur-u Sina and similarly He ascended His servant Muhammad (pbuh) to the heavens and spoke with him. The verses illustrate the similarities between the two Prophets and show that they are acting on God's Will.

2. "They ask you, (O Muhammad), about the new moons. Say, 'They are measurements of time for the people and for *Hajj*.' And it is not righteousness to enter houses from the back, but righteousness is one who fears Allah. And enter houses from their doors. And fear Allah that you may succeed".[696] The seemingly unrelated topics in this verse (the new moons and the method of entering houses) both refer to wrong behaviour. God is indicating that rather than asking about the moons which can be observed, they should be asking about what is beneficial for them. He indicates their wrong behaviour by comparing it to those who enter their houses from the back instead of the proper way.

---

[694] Qur'ān, 17: 1.

[695] Qur'ān, 17: 2.

[696] Qur'ān, 2: 189.

3. The verses about the prohibition of interest came in the Qur'ān in the *surah* Baqara after the verses about charity, although they were revealed at different times. However, there is a strong connection between these verses, because both verses aim to protect the poor people in society.

10.5.2 Examples for the Interrelation between the *Surah*

Surah Duha and *surah* Inshirah are similar in regard to their aims; in both *surah*, God consoles the Prophet (pbuh) and supports him. The verses are intended to comfort the Prophet (pbuh) and assure him of his future success. God reminds the Prophet (pbuh) his Messengership is just beginning and assures him that, in the future, people will accept Islam. Although he will face difficulties, easiness will follow. He tells him to trust God and convey the message.

There is a relationship between *surah* Kawthar and *surah* Maun. God mentioned four qualities of the hypocrite in *surah* Maun: stinginess, abandoning the prayers, showing off if they perform the prayers and preventing the help of poor people. On the other hand, God mentioned four good qualities in contrast to the hypocrites; Kawthar which has many blessings, goodness and rewards, performing the prayer continuously, performing the prayer just for God and sacrificing animals and distributing meat to the poor. The scholar Abū Bakr an-Nisabūrī established this as a new Qur'anic science and wrote a book on this subject.

10.6 Thematic Unity in the Qur'ān

The thematic unity prevalent in the whole Qur'ān is one piece of evidence that it is the speech of God. The Qur'ān is like a master piece from the hand of an artist whose colours are coherent and nothing is out of place. There is not a single defect in the whole of the Qur'ān, nothing which bothers the eyes or ruins the pleasure.

All of the main themes present in the whole Qur'ān can also be found in every part. We can find the whole Qur'ān in the *surah* Baqara; similarly we can find Baqara in Fatiha and Fatiha in 'Basmala'. For this reason, if one reads one *surah* and says; 'I found the whole Qur'ān in this *surah*' the statement is not an exaggeration. Indeed every *surah* of the Qur'ān is like a small Qur'ān by itself.

The Qur'ān and its verses were revealed at different times, on different occasions and in different places, but there are very strong interrelations among the verses as if they were all revealed in one place, on one occasion and at one time. The whole Qur'ān is in 'Basmala' as a seed, this seed sprouts into Fatiha, grows and has branches in Baqara and it gives fruits in the whole Qur'ān. The relationship between the seed and the fruit is in between the verses of the Qur'ān. It is impossible to show every single relationship between the verses here, since they are countless, nevertheless I will give one example to give an idea about the thematic unity in the Qur'ān.

There is strong interrelationship between 'Basmala' and *surah* Fatiha; it seems that 'Basmala' is like one of its verses. Many scholars accepted 'Basmala' as one of the verses of Fatiha.[697] 'Basmala' starts with the Name of God who is eternal. There was nothing with Him and then He created everything based on His knowledge. He planted the light of Muhammad (pbuh) as a seed in non-existence and the tree of creation was born of this seed. The fruit of this tree is humankind. The best fruit among all these fruits is Muhammad (pbuh), so he was created as a seed for the whole of the tree of creation and he came as the best of its fruit at the end.

Indeed the 'Basmala' has strong relationship with the beginning and the end. In the beginning God created the universe from His divine attribute 'Rahman' (Compassionate). Then He created humankind and gave them many abilities from His divine attribute 'Rahim' (Mercy) such as free will, reason, the five senses and many more. With these abilities they became able to understand the meaning of the universe and their existence within it.

The *surah* Fatiha can be read as a letter of thanks to the mercy in 'Basmala'; nothing is excluded from this mercy and it attracts everything to itself. That is why we start to read the Qur'ān by reciting 'Basmala'. In order to thank God for His mercy in 'Basmala', we start *surah* Fatiha by praising God in the highest terms. We say: 'O God, thank you very much, you bestowed on us so many favours, we cannot count them, You are so merciful, all the praise is Your right and our duty'. God first bestowed on us existence and then created us as humans. Humankind was given free-will and other abilities and was entrusted with the earth. At the same time, humankind remained in need of divine guidance and those who use their free-will to find Him are guided by God. He guided us to Islam and honoured us with being the followers of Muhammad (pbuh), 'the Mercy of the world'.

It is impossible to fully comprehend God, His mercy and His favours. God is closer to us than ourselves but we are far from Him; in this station we are like a third person in the conversation. It would take an infinite awareness to see the whole universe and comprehend the acts of God, His names and His attributes. Understanding God is only possible by understanding the whole universe, and is

---

[697] *al-Mawsuatul Fiqhiya*, 8/83-86.

impossible for human beings with our limited faculties. For this reason we act in the role of third person in the creation, but the separation from God is something that makes us uncomfortable. It creates a yearning inside us and we search for ways to become closer to Him and get to know Him more. In this way we increase our faith. By observing the universe as an exhibit of God, we increase our knowledge and awareness of Him. When struggling to know Him in this way, there comes a point when we feel His presence within us and hear the call 'You'. At this point, we submit to the call and testify 'only You do we worship'.

It is a well-established custom that when visiting a king or ruler, the visitor goes with gifts. Not to do so would be offensive and unpardonable. Similarly, when we approach God, we offer our servanthood, our love and our obedience as gifts. We cannot give anything else as everything already belongs to Him. With our free will, which He bestowed on us, we can offer these as our gifts and as an admission that everything belongs to Him. He has the decision-making authority and nothing happens except that which He wishes. When we become closer to God we say 'only from You do we ask for help'. Our duty of worship can only be carried out by God's permission and with His help. There is no intermediary between us and God, so the servant asks for help directly from God and the most important request of his life: 'O Lord, please guide me to the straight path'.

There are three main themes in the Qur'ān: belief, worship and life. Belief is all the things which are mandatory to believe in, worship is the deeds and practises performed for God alone and life is applying the rules set down in the Qur'ān regarding the individual, family, society and government. The whole Qur'ān is based on these three topics and each *surah* is also based on them.

Now *surah* Fatiha will be analysed from this perspective:

> All praise and gratitude (whoever gives them to whomever for whatever reason and in whatever way from the first day of creation until eternity) are for God, the Lord of the worlds, The All-Merciful, the All-Compassionate, The Master of the Day of Judgment[698]

In these verses belief is explained, God is introduced as the One who deserves all praise. The essential oneness of God is conveyed; He administers all events in the universe and nothing happens without his permission; He creates, sustains and controls everything. The expression 'The Master of the Day of Judgment' encapsulates the resurrection after death, the accounting on the Day of Judgment, the divine scale (*Mizan*), Paradise, Hell, rewards and punishments. God is the Owner

---

[698] Qur'ān, 1: 1-3.

and Master of this day. All of the principles of belief are explained by these three verses.

'Only You, we worship' explains the other essential principle which is 'worship' and encompasses all forms of worship, physical or financial; daily prayers, *zakat*, fasting, *Hajj* and struggling in the way of God.

'Only from You, we ask for help' emphasizes that the most important source for the servant is God and it takes the servant to the higher levels of worship. To worship God alone is our duty and His right so we worship God alone and never associate any partners with him in any kind of worship.

> Guide us to the Straight Path, The Path of those whom You have favoured, not of those who have incurred (Your) wrath (punishment and condemnation), nor of those who are astray.[699]

This verse is related to the 'life' principle. The orbit of *surah* Fatiha is the straight path and the whole *surah* is finely balanced and turns around this. This path contains no extremism, it is balanced, moderate and the best way for human beings. Both the desires and the spirit are well-balanced on this way. The reason and the heart are aligned. The summary of *surah* Fatiha based on the three essential principles is: 'O God, guide us to the straight path in belief, in worship and in our lives'. The Qur'ān is this guide which holds the key to all these principles and gives human beings everything that they need to attain God's pleasure in this life and the afterlife.

Summary of Thematic Unity in the Qur'ān

1. The thematic unity prevalent in the whole Qur'ān is one piece of evidence that it is the speech of God.
2. All of the main themes present in the whole Qur'ān can also be found in every part.
3. The Qur'ān and its verses were revealed at different times, on different occasions and in different places, but there are very strong interrelations among the verses as if they were all revealed in one place, on one occasion and at one time.
4. There is strong interrelationship between 'Basmala' and Fatiha, it seems that 'Basmala' is like one of its verses.

---

[699] Qur'ān, 1: 5-7.

5. The *surah* Fatiha can be read as a letter of thanks to the mercy in 'Basmala'; nothing is excluded from this mercy and it attracts everything to itself. That is why we start to read Qur'ān by reciting 'Basmala'.
6. There are three main themes in the Qur'ān: belief, worship and life. Belief is all the things which are mandatory to believe in, worship is the deeds and practises done for God alone and life is applying the rules set down in the Qur'ān regarding the individual, family, society and government. The whole Qur'ān is based on these three topics and each *surah* is also based on them.
7. The Qur'ān is the guide which holds the key to all these principles and gives human beings everything that they need to attain God's pleasure in this life and the afterlife.

Chapter Eleven

Mystical Interpretation of the Qur'ān (*Ish'ārī Tafsīr*)

Mystical Interpretation of the Qur'ān (*Ish'ārī Tafsīr*)

11.1 Sufi Exegeses and Its Development

Sufism is the path followed by Sufis (mystics) to reach the highest level of servanthood to God. Sufism has many different definitions: the annihilation of the individual's ego, will, and self-centeredness by God and the subsequent spiritual revival with the light of His Essence; the continuous striving to cleanse one's self of all that is bad or evil in order to acquire virtue.[700] Abū Muhammad Jarir describes Sufism as resisting the temptations of the carnal, (evil-commanding) self (*nafs al-ammara*) and evil qualities and acquiring laudable moral qualities.[701] Some scholars describe Sufism as seeing behind the "outer" or surface appearance of things and events, and interpreting whatever happens in the world in relation to God, therefore every act of God becomes a window through which to "see" Him. M Fethullah Gülen describes Sufism as the path followed by an individual who, having been able to free himself or herself from human vices and weaknesses in order to acquire angelic qualities and conduct pleasing to God, lives in accordance with the requirements of God's knowledge and love, and in the resulting spiritual delight that ensues.[702]

The core meaning of Sufism is to worship God as if seeing Him, even though one doesn't see Him, He sees everyone. The Companions of the Prophet (pbuh) strived to achieve this level of servanthood and deprived themselves of worldly pleasures and endured hardships in this way. For them, '*ihsan*' (worshipping God as if seeing Him) ranked above *iman* (faith) and Islam based on the Gabriel Hadith; 'Umar reported:

> One day, while we were sitting with the Prophet (pbuh), a man came up to us whose clothes were extremely white, whose hair was extremely

700 M. Fethullah Gülen, *Sufism*, (tr: Ali Unal) New Jersey 2006, v.1 Sufism and Its Origins (Introduction).
701 Gülen, ibid.
702 Gülen, ibid.

> black, and upon whom no traces of travelling could be seen. None of us knew him. He sat down close to the Prophet (pbuh), so their knees rested against each other and placed his two hands upon his thighs and said, 'Muhammad, tell me about Islam.' The Messenger of God (pbuh) said, 'Islam is witnessing that there is no deity but Allah and that Muhammad is His Messenger, and you establish the prayer, and you give *zakat*, and you fast Ramadan, and you perform the *Hajj* of the House if you are able to journey to it.' He said, 'You have told the truth,' and we were amazed at him asking him and then telling him that he told the truth. He said, 'Tell me about *iman* (faith). He said, 'That you affirm God, His angels, His books, His Messengers, and the Last Day, and that you affirm the Decree, the good of it and the bad of it.' He said, 'You have told the truth.' He said, 'Tell me about *ihsan*.' He said, 'That you worship God as if you see Him, for if you don't see Him then truly He sees you.'[703]

Some of the Companions abstained from some permissible things (*ḫalāl*) to achieve the level of *ihsan* but God warned them with the following verse: "O you who have believed, do not prohibit the good things which Allah has made lawful to you and do not transgress. Indeed, Allah does not like transgressors".[704]

The Prophet (pbuh) lived a highly spiritual life, abandoning worldly pleasures in his struggle to achieve the contentment of God, but he warned his Companions away from extremes of worship that would make practising Islam difficult for them, such as not getting married, forbidding lawful things to oneself and praying for the whole night without sleeping. The religion of Islam is easy to practice and if one makes it difficult, he cannot carry out his duties; other than that, living Islam on a spiritual level is never prohibited, indeed it was encouraged by the Prophet (pbuh) and his Companions.

In the early days of Islam, religious commandments were not written down; rather, the practice and oral circulation of commandments related to belief, worship, and daily life led the people to memorize them. Since religious commandments were vital issues in a Muslim's individual and collective life, scholars prioritised these and compiled them into books: legal scholars collected and codified books on Islamic law, its rules and principles pertaining to all fields of life; scholars established the Prophetic traditions (Hadith) and way of life (Sunnah), and theologians dealt with issues concerning Muslim belief.[705] At the same time, Sufi masters were mostly concentrating on the pure, spiritual dimension of the Islamic truth. They

---

703 Bukhari, *Saḫīḫ, Belief*, 47; Muslim, *Saḫīḫ, The Book of Faith*, 1.

704 Qur'ān, 5: 87.

705 Gülen, ibid.

sought to reveal the essence of humanity's being, the real nature of existence, and the inner dynamics of humanity and the cosmos by calling attention to the reality of that which lies beneath and beyond their outer dimension.[706]

With the expansion of the borders of the Islamic world, Muslims encountered many new customs, cultures and races resulting in the development of Islamic thought and discussion on different issues, and leading to the establishment of many Islamic disciplines. Following this period, scholars were named by the field they studied and, similarly, those Muslims who lived Islam on a spiritual level were named "Sufi". It would be wrong to refute Sufism as being part of Islam just because it is not mentioned in the Qur'ān or Sunnah. Despite winning many battles and achieving the spoils of war, the Prophet (pbuh) and his Companions lived a very simple and spiritual life. It is important to remember that Islam is not just set of rules or acts to perform, it is a religion which combines both the spirit and body; it meets all the needs of human beings and satisfies their inner and outer dimensions. The Prophet (pbuh) never completely abandoned this world but he focused on the afterlife while living in this world and, following his example, the Companions did the same.

Islamic spiritual life, based on asceticism, regular worship, abstention from all major and minor sins, sincerity, purity of intention, love, yearning and the individual's admission of his or her essential impotence and destitution, became the subject matter of Sufism, a new science possessing its own method, principles, rules, and terminology.[707] In short, the basic core of this science has always been the essence of the Islamic truth.

The ascetic life began to be systemised from its early days and was based on two essential characteristics; fear and love. The fruit of this movement was born in Baghdad, Iraq, as Hasan Basrī, (d. 110 A.H. / 728 C.E.), an example representing the fear of God. Rabia al-Adawiyah (d. 135 A.H. / 752 C.E.) was a good example representing the love of God. The "Sufi" label was first applied to Abū Hashim al-Kūfī who lived after them.

It has been asserted by some that Sufism evolved out of other cultures with the expansion of the Islamic borders, and that Islam and Sufism are mutually exclusive. This unfortunate view ignores the fact that Sufism has its roots in the very earliest days of Islam and is merely the spiritual side of the religion and not different from it. Sufism is made up of austerity, self-control and criticism, and

---

706 Gülen, ibid.

707 Gülen, ibid.

the continuous struggle to resist the temptations of Satan and the evil-commanding self in order to fulfil religious obligations. Although this discrimination arises partly from assertions that the commandments of the Islam are represented by legal scholars or muftis, and the other by Sufis, it should be viewed more as the result of the natural, human tendency of assigning priority to that way which is most suitable for the individual practitioner.[708]

Sufi scholars have written many Sufi exegeses, the first of which *'Tafsīr Qur'ān al-Az̲īm'* was written by Abū Muhammad Sahl b. Abdillah at-Tustari, (d. 283 A.H. / 986 C.E.). Other well-known Sufi exegeses are Abū Abdirrahman Muhammad b. Musa as-Sulami, (d. 412 A.H. / 1021 C.E.), *'Haqāiq al-Tafsīr'*; Muhammad al-Qushayrī, (d. 465 A.H. / 1072 C.E.), *'Latāif al-Ishārat bi Tafsīr al-Qur'ān'*; Abū Muhammad Ruzbahan, *'Arāisu Bayan fi Haqāiq al-Qur'ān'*; Najmuddin Dāya, *'Ta'vilāt an-Najmiyya'*; Ni'matullah Nahjivānī, *'al-Fawatihu'l Ilāhiyya wa'l-Mafatihu'l-Ghaybiyya'* and Ismail Haqqi Bursawī, *'Ruhu'l-Bayān'*.

Sufi exegeses fall under two categories; 1) Theorical Sufi *tafsīr* and 2) *Ish'ārī* Sufi *tafsīr*. The first type bases a reading of the Qur'ān on pre-existing ideas and theories and attempts to interpret the book according to those; the second is interpretation born of the personal inspiration of the *mufassir* and therefore cannot be corroborated by any evidence. There are difficulties with each of these types of exegeses which are discussed below.

First, it is important to note that in Islam all scholars are in the service of the Qur'ān, they do not use it for their personal aims. This type of interpretation is not acceptable because it destroys the foundations of Islam.

Theorical Sufi *mufassir* interpreted the Qur'ān in line with their philosophical and theological opinions. The main aim of the Qur'ān is to guide humanity to the straight path and sometimes these *mufassir* found it difficult to find an interpretation that fitted with their ideas. This led to interpretations that were not supported by evidence from the Qur'ān or Sunnah, resulting in changing the aim of the Qur'ān. For example; Muhyiddin ibn 'Arābī interpreted some verses in his books *'Futuḫāt Makkiyya'* and *'Fusūs al-Ḫikam'* in a way that cannot be accepted. He interpreted the following verse; "Whoever is an enemy to Allah and His angels and His Messengers and Gabriel and Michael, then indeed, Allah is an enemy to the disbelievers"[709] as follows; Gabriel is the active reason, Michael is the soul of the sixth firmament and *Israfil* is the soul of the fourth firmament. He sees the

---

[708] Gülen, ibid.

[709] Qur'ān, 2: 98.

angels, who are in the charge of the plants which are for human beings as the reason, the angels who are in the charge of animals as trusted reason.[710]

According to some scholars, the founder of theorical *tafsīr* is Muhyiddin b. 'Arābī.[711] The essential theory of this school of thought is '*wahdat-i wujud*' (similar to pantheism). In attempting to interpret the verses in parallel with their theorical understanding, scholars of this school utilised the Arabic language, literal meanings and grammatical rules. In doing so, they disregarded any compromise between their explanations and the Arabic rules and, in their interpretation, strayed from the fundamental purpose of the Qur'ān. As a result very deep philosophical interpretations occurred and the clear, comprehensible Qur'ān became ambiguous and difficult to understand.[712]

The interpretation of the whole Qur'ān or the whole verse in the theorical *tafsīr* is rare. Rather, the *mufassir* focused on the parts of verses that fit their own ideas: for example, Muhyiddin b. 'Arābī rarely interpreted a whole verse in his books *Futuḫāt-i Makkiyya* and *Fusūs al-Ḫikam*.[713] Sadr al-Din Konawī and Abd al-Razzaq al-Kāshānī adopted the style of Muhyiddin b. 'Arābī in their *tafsīr, Kitāb al-I'jāz –al-Qur'ān* and *Ta'wilāt*. A reader of Ibn 'Arābī's *tafsīr* would be likely to think that he was under the influence of pantheism, despite that not being the case; however, the layman cannot differentiate his understanding from pantheism. For example, the verse "Our Lord, You did not create this aimlessly; exalted are You"[714] is interpreted as: "O Lord, You didn't create anything but Yourself, whatever besides You is not real. You created everything as reflection of your names and attributes. We glorify and exalt You from the existence of anything else other than You".[715] For him, everything in existence is destined to perish, so it cannot be labelled as real, so nothing other than God is real.

Ish'ārī Tafsīr is the interpretation of the Qur'ān by Sufis aided by inspiration. Their approach to the Qur'ān is not to prove their ideas, but to give meanings to the Qur'ān with the help of their inspiration.[716] In *surah* Kahf, the Qur'ān mentions the story of Moses with a man (Khādir) who was endowed with special knowledge from God. Sufis aim to achieve that special knowledge by applying certain methods in Sufism. This special knowledge is mostly related to the inner dimen-

---

710 Dhahabī, *at-Tafsir wal-Mufassirun*, v.3 pp. 6-7.
711 Dhahabī, *at-Tafsir wal-Mufassirun*, v.11, p. 340.
712 Dhahabī, *at-Tafsir*, v.11 p. 343.
713 Dhahabī, *at-Tafsir*, v.11 p. 340.
714 Qur'ān, 3: 191.
715 Dhahabī, *at-Tafsir*, v.11 p. 340.
716 Dhahabī, *at-Tafsir wal-Mufassirun*, v.3 p. 18; Zarqānī, *Manāhil al-Irfān*, v.1 p. 546.

sion of things, events and beings. Moses couldn't understand this knowledge at the beginning but Khādir explained it later at the end of their story. Sufis conceal this knowledge of inner things by utilising symbols, signs and metaphoric expressions in their explanations. This type of *tafsīr* was named '*Ish'ārī*' because it can only be achieved through a deep meditation on the verses rather than through a literal reading of them.

To accomplish the *Ish'ārī tafsīr* the Sufi, through certain methodology, purifies his heart from worldly pollution and becomes ready to understand the inner meanings of the Qur'ān. Sufis do not deny the literal meanings of the verses but believe that each verse has many levels and that inner meanings are hidden in the words and letters.[717]

Ish'ārī tafsīr was not invented by Sufism but has actually existed since the early time of Islam. This is supported by evidence from the Qur'ān and Sunnah.[718] God said in the Qur'ān:

> Do you not see that Allah has made subject to you whatever is in the heavens and whatever is in the earth and amply bestowed upon you His favours, [both] *apparent and unapparent*? But of the people is he who disputes about Allah without knowledge or guidance or an enlightening Book [from Him].[719]

The expression '*ẕāhir-bātin*', ('apparent' and 'unapparent'), indicates there are inner and outer dimensions of the Qur'ān. The Qur'ān is one of the favours which God bestowed upon human beings but, whilst the polytheist people in Mecca could understand its outer dimension because they spoke Arabic, they didn't understand its inner meanings. The Qur'ān blamed them for this. The Prophet (pbuh) said:

> In every verse there are outer meanings (*ẕāhir*), inner meanings (*bātin*), the last border [rulings] (*hadd*) and it's beyond [warnings of the last day and the afterlife] (*muttala'*). Each of these categories has twigs and branches.[720]

Ẕāhir is the literal meaning of the verse, *bātin* is its inner dimensions, *hadd* is the rulings within the verse pertaining to *ḫalal* or *ḫaram* and *muttala'* are the warnings and good tidings contained in the Qur'ān.

Sufi *mufassir* focused on the inner dimensions of the verses rather than their literal meanings. Other scholars debated and sometimes disagreed about the lit-

---

717 Dhahabī, *at-Tafsir wal-Mufassirun*, v.3 p. 18.

718 You can check this evidence at Sulami, *Tafsir*, pp. 16-24.

719 Qur'ān, 31: 20.

720 Ibn Hibban, *Saḫīḫ* 1:146.

eral meaning of the verses. Sufi's did not join this debate; they concentrated on understanding the deeper meanings of the Qur'ān through its language and Arabic grammar.

Ish'ārī mufassir and *Batini* interpreters, whilst both concentrating on extracting the inner meanings of the Qur'ān, should not be considered similar. *Ish'ārī mufassir* never ignored *Shari'ah* and its rules and believed it was necessary to perform all Islamic duties to achieve God's pleasure and access the inner dimension of Islam. The *Batini* people considered the inner meanings of the Qur'ān to be its most important dimension and where their interpretation differed from the literal meanings, they favoured their own explanations. Their disregard for all Islamic duties was harmful to the religion and led to false interpretations. Muslims perform five daily prayers to purify their hearts, but the *Batini* held that an already purified heart precludes the necessity of praying. *Ish'ari mufassir* performed all Islamic duties and never interpreted the Qur'ān in a way to annul its rules. They accepted the literal interpretation of the verses and adhered to them and, in addition, they used their inspiration to try and understand their inner meanings.

Imam Shātibī (d. 1388 C.E.) a prominent grammarian and legal theorist, held that the outer meaning of the verses is just the literal reading of them and the inner meaning of the verses gives the real understanding. God says in the Qur'ān; "What is the matter with those people that they can hardly understand any statement?"[721] This verse refers to the people who read and understand the Qur'ān at its most basic level but fail to grasp its significance. Unbelievers read the book in this way and deny it, using it to mock Islam. They fail to comprehend its true nature as a guide for all humanity.[722] *Ish'ārī tafsīr* are accepted by all Muslim scholars except the Ẕahirī School which only accepts literal interpretations; Ibn Ḫazm (994 – 1064 C.E.), a leading proponent and codifier of the Ẕahirī School, said the Prophet (pbuh) explained everything in Qur'ān and nothing is hidden in the religion.[723] Ibn Taymiyya (1263 – 1328 C.E.) of the Hanbali School didn't completely reject *Ish'ārī tafsīr* but stipulated certain conditions that must be met for them to be accepted:

> There are two types of inner knowledge; the first compromises the literal meaning of the verses and the second does not. If the inner meaning does not compromise the literal meaning of the verse it is rejected. Whoever claims: "I know one inner meaning but it contradicts the literal

---

[721] Qur'ān, 4: 78.

[722] Shātibī, *al-Muwafaqaat*, v.3 pp. 382-383.

[723] Ibn Ḫazm, *al-Fasl*, v.2 pp. 91-92.

> meaning" is wrong, either he is ignorant or corrupt. On the other hand, if the inner meaning complements the literal meaning, it is like the literal meaning. This can be proved with the words of the Qur'ān and Sunnah, but it is not accepted as the only meaning of the verse. Those who say that it is the only meaning of the verse are wrong. If they do not claim this, it can be accepted as part of the interpretation.[724]

Ish'ārī tafsīr are accepted if they meet the following conditions:

1) It is not contrary to the literal meaning of the Qur'ān
2) There is evidence from the Qur'ān or Sunnah which supports the interpretation.
3) Islam and logic do not contradict it.
4) There is no claim that this is the only meaning of the verse.

According to these conditions, it is possible to accept or reject *Ish'ārī tafsīr* books. Inspiration was the main source for this type of *tafsīr* and this is not sufficient evidence by itself alone as it is personal and may not be experienced by everyone. The experience is subjective and is a secret between the *mufassir* and God; the knowledge can be applied individually but others should not be expected to follow it. Islamic Sufism is neither philosophy, nor just the theory; it is the experienced knowledge; without experiencing those intuitions, inspirations and spiritual ecstasy, it is hard to understand it. Sufis accepted the Qur'ān and Sunnah as an authority and if their inspirations and intuitions complemented the Qur'ān and Sunnah, they accepted them, if not, they corrected themselves. The great Sufi, Bayazid al-Bistami emphasized this point: "if you see a man who is flying in the air or walking on the water without sinking, do not accept him before checking him with the Qur'ān and Sunnah."[725]

11.2 Important Sufi and *Ish'ārī* Exegetical Works

11.2.1 Tustarī and His *Tafsīr*

One of the most important scholars of *Ish'ārī tafsīr* was Abū Muhammad Sahl b. Abdillah at-Tustarī, born in Tustar in 815 C.E. Tustarī feared God, had a very good character and treated people well during his whole life. It is reported that he performed '*karamaat*' (extraordinary acts) and marvels. He was *mujtahid* (the jurist who is able to extract rulings from the sources) and he practised special Sufi

[724] Ibn Taymiyya, *Risāla Fi Ilm al-Bātin*, pp. 231-236.

[725] Gülen, ibid.

methods to discipline his carnal desires (i. e eating less, speaking less, sleeping less, not eating animal products, etc.) for a long time. He lived for a long time in Basra and died in 896 C.E.

Tustarī began his education early and had memorised the whole Qur'ān by age six or seven. His Sufi life also started early and he distributed all his wealth amongst the poor. He went to *Hajj* and whilst in Mecca he met and conversed with great Sufi Dhun-Nun al-Misri. Ibn Sālim the student of Tustarī, transmitted Tustari's opinions after his death and his teachings survived through the *tariqa of Salimiyya* (the path of Salimiyya).

Tustari was not an extreme Sufi, he was considered a moderate Sufi leader. He defined *ma'rifa* (knowledge of God), *yaqin* (certainty in faith), soul and life based on the fundamentals of Islam. For him, the soil for the worship of God is *ma'rifa*, its seed is *yaqin* and its water is knowledge. Life is also knowledge, therefore if one is ignorant and does not have knowledge, he is considered as metaphorically dead. Ignorance is against Islamic morality, even being suspicious is better than being ignorant. For Tustarī, continual repentance was just as important as other tenets of worship such as performing the five daily prayers, giving *zakat* or fasting during Ramadan. For him, being a good servant of God was related with earning and consuming *ḫalal* provision; if one worships God, he has to make money from *ḫalal* ways and provide *ḫalal* provision for his family.[726]

Tustarī wrote many books but unfortunately many of them didn't reach us. Some of his books are *Daqāiq al-Muhibbīn, Mawāiz al-Ārifīn, Jawābāt-u Ahlil Yaqīn, Qiṣaṣ al-Anbiya, al-Qāya Li Ahli'n Nihāya, Risāla* and *Tafsīr al-Qur'ān al-Aẕīm.*[727]

His *Tafsīr*

Tustari's *tafsīr* was published in Egypt in 1908. Some scholars argue that the book we have today is not his original book but is collated by others and contains the opinion of other scholars.[728] This fact is understood from the book which was transmitted orally by his student Abū Yusuf Ahmad b. Muhammad as-Sijizi and from the book which was written by Abū Bakr Muhammad al-Baladi. In this book, he separates his own words from the words of Tustarī. Ibn Nadīm doesn't mention this book and for this reason some scholars suspect its authenticity. However, most scholars accept it as Tustari's work and consider it the first *Ish'ārī tafsīr*. For example, Qādi Iyaz trusted this *tafsīr* and frequently quoted from it.

726 Tustarī, *Tafsir*, 46, 116, 121.
727 L. Massignon, Encydopedie de l>Islam, (Sahl at-Tustarī), IV. 65.
728 L. Massignon, ibid.

The book begins with acknowledgements that Tustarī obtained his knowledge of Qur'anic *tafsīr* from Muhammad b. Sawwar and is prefaced with details of the characteristics of people who do not want to understand the Qur'ān. This *tafsīr* book does not interpret the whole of the Qur'ān, it concentrates on just some of its verses.

In his book Tustarī explains four levels of meanings: *ẕāhir,* reading the Qur'ān; *bātin,* understanding the Qur'ān; hadd, *ẖalal* and *ẖaram*; *muttala'*, enlightening the heart by understanding the purpose of the verse. *Ẕāhir* is the literal meaning of the verse which can be achieved through reading it, but *bātin* requires intentional struggling to understand the meaning in this level. For example; God said in the Qur'ān:

"What is the matter with those people that they can hardly understand any statement?"[729]

He says that they read the verses but they don't want to understand them.[730] Tustarī stated that if God wants one of his servants to be closer to Him he teaches him the *ẕāhir* and *bātin* meanings of the Qur'ān. When he was asked about the meaning of *bātin* he explained that it is to understand the inner meanings of the Qur'ān; God intended for the Qur'ān to be comprehended not just read literally.[731] It can be understood from his expressions that *ẕāhir* is the literal meaning of the words and *bātin* is the meaning truly intended by God. Tustarī mostly dealt with the inner meanings of the verses in his *tafsīr* only occasionally explaining literal meanings: for example, in his interpretation of '*basmala*' he gives the meaning of each letter and also explains the grades of Sufis.[732]

> The people of Moses made, after [his departure], from their ornaments a calf, an image having a lowing sound. Did they not see that it could neither speak to them nor guide them to a way? They took it [for worship], and they were wrongdoers.[733]

For Tustarī this verse symbolised anything that separates people from worshipping the one true God. The golden calf represents family, children, worldly things, idols. Human beings can only get close to God by ridding themselves of these

---

729 Qur'ān, 4: 78.
730 Tustarī, *Tafsir* 3.
731 Tustarī, *Tafsir*, 5.
732 Tustarī, *Tafsir*, 6-7.
733 Qur'ān, 7: 148.

obstacles or false loves. The Jews overcame their carnal desires (and destroyed the golden calf) saving themselves from idol worship and becoming closer to God.[734]

> Who created me, and He [it is who] guides me. And it is He who feeds me and gives me drink. And when I am ill, it is He who cures me. And who will cause me to die and then bring me to life. And who I aspire that He will forgive me my sin on the Day of Recompense.[735]

He interprets this verse as: God created me to worship Him alone and guided me to the straight path to have me closer to Him. He is the One who feeds me with the pleasures of faith and gives me the drink of contentment. He protected me when I inclined to worldly pleasures and He prevented me from following my carnal desires. He kills and revives me by His names. When mentioning them I experience death and I experience life. I am kept at a point between fear and hope. He judges me with His mercy and forgiveness.[736]

"We ransomed him with a great sacrifice".[737]

He interprets this verse as: Abraham's human nature meant he loved his son very much. God ordered Abraham to kill his son in return for His favours and protection. God did not intend Abraham to literally sacrifice his son, it was symbolic; he wanted him to sacrifice the love of anything except Himself. He tested Abraham through the thing he loved the most. Abraham understood God's meaning and renounced the love of all worldly things and committed himself to God; in return God spared his son from sacrifice and replaced him with a ram.[738]

> Your Lord has decreed upon Himself mercy: that any of you who does wrong out of ignorance and then repents after that and corrects himself, indeed, He is Forgiving and Merciful.[739]

Tustarī's interpretation of this verse was that God revealed to the Prophet David the following: 'O David, whoever knows Me, he desires Me. Whoever desires Me, he loves Me. Whoever loves Me, he searches for Me. Whoever searches for Me, he finds Me. Whoever finds Me, he struggles not to lose Me'. Thereupon David

---

734 Tustarī, *Tafsir*, 39-40.
735 Qur'ān, 26: 78-82.
736 Tustarī, 69-70.
737 Qur'ān, 37: 107.
738 Tustarī, 52.
739 Qur'ān, 6: 54.

said, 'O my Lord, where can I find You when I search You?' God replied: 'You can find Me in the broken hearts that fear Me a lot'.[740]

These examples illustrate that Tustari's interpretations were neither illogical nor against Islamic principles. His explanations are accepted because they do not contradict the literal meaning of the verses. Tustarī struggled to purify the hearts, discipline the desires and embellish the minds with good thoughts in his interpretations. He related the stories of pious people from early generations as examples to prove his interpretations. For him the Qur'ān is the speech of God and it is not created. There is no end to God and similarly there is no end to the Qur'ān; the meanings of the Qur'ān are endless and God's servants can only grasp from its meaning as much as God inspires in their hearts.[741] Practising Islam and its obligations is a precondition for understanding the inner meanings of the verses of the Qur'ān. If one listens to the Qur'ān whole heartedly and practices it in his life, God gives him a distinguished understanding ability and he can extract the inner meanings of the Qur'ān with this understanding.

11.2.2 Sulami and His *Tafsīr*

The fourth century A.H. was a time of great change in the Islamic empire with rebellions and uprisings by rulers against their governments. It is an important era in Islamic history in terms of the development of the intellectual and political movements. Muhammad b. al-Husayn b. Muhammad b. Musa al-Azdī as-Sulami, (936 – 1021 C.E.), was born at this time in the town of Nisabūr in central Asia. His parents hailed from the Arab tribes of Azd (father's side) and Sulaym (mother's side), therefore he had the names al-Azdī as Sulami. His father Husayn b. Muhammad was a pious Sufi who always struggled in the way of God. He was a poor but noble man who was well-versed in Islamic law. He died when Sulami was a young boy and Sulami was taken care of by his grandfather, Abū Amr Ismail b. Nujayd. Sulami was well looked after by his grandfather who kept him by his side and took him to his lectures and meetings.

Sulami began his education by memorising the Qur'ān then learned Arabic literature. He later studied Hadith and increased his knowledge of Sufism. He travelled to Ray, Hamadan, Marw and Hijaz and gained knowledge from the scholars in those cities. Among these scholars were Abū Qāsım an-Nasrabazi, Abū Nasr as-Sarraj and his grandfather Abū Amr Ismail b. Nujayd. After his grandfa-

[740] Tustarī, 35.
[741] Tustarī, 59-60.

ther's death, Sulami inherited a large fortune. He used it to build a rich library and lodge. He died in 1021 and was buried in the yard of his lodge. He had many students and Abd al-Karim al-Qushayrī was well-known amongst them.

Sulami was a productive scholar and wrote many books in the fields of *tafsīr*, Hadith, history and Sufism. Many scholars talked about these books; some criticized them and some praised them. Hadith scholars criticized him for using fake Hadith in his books without checking their authenticity. When using Hadith about rulings, (*aḫkām*), scholars were very careful to check their authenticity. However, they were not as careful when using Hadith covering moral or ethical subjects. Sufi *mufassir* used many Hadith in their books covering topics about good character and values but did not check their authenticity and received harsh criticism from other scholars.

Sulami was well-versed in Sufism and wrote famous books in this field. He wrote many original books which had not been written until his time and he taught Hadith to his students for 40 years. Sulami was praised in regard to his Sufism both by contemporary scholars and those who came after him. While Ismail al-Farisi, Abū Abdillah ibn al-Bayyi, Hujwuri, Ibn al-Athīr, Khatib Baghdadi and Qushayrī praised him, Subkī, Dhahabī, Ibn al-Jawzī, Ibn Taymiyya, Wāḫidī and ibn Salah criticised him saying that he wrote *tafsīr* only for Sufis and that he fabricated some Hadith.

The claim that Sulami was the first scholar to write Sufi *tafsīr* is incorrect as both Tustari and Abū Bakr al-Wasiti wrote Sufi *tafsīr* books before him. Sulami was first criticised for fabricating Hadith by his contemporary Muhammad b. Yusuf al-Qattan and later scholars accepted this criticism without investigating its truth. The Hadith Sulami used covered topics such as renouncing worldly pleasures, humility, modesty, discouraging jealousy, arrogance and other bad characteristics. Sulami did not intentionally use fake Hadith, he learned them from his teachers and, therefore, trusted them. Imam Ghazali also used many weak, even false Hadith in his books but he cannot be accused of fabricating them.[742]

His *Tafsīr*

Most of Sulami's books have not survived. His *tafsīr* was not published but handwritten copies are held in different libraries.[743] This *tafsīr* is voluminous and very important for Islamic Sufism.[744] In his *tafsīr* Sulami collected the thoughts, under-

---

[742] Dhahabī, *Tazkirat'ul Huffaz*, 3/1046-1047, Suyūtī, *Tabaqaat al-Mufassirin*, 31.
[743] Sulayman Ates, *Sulami ve Onun Tefsiri*, 70-75.
[744] Ates, 70.

standings and feelings of early the Sufi scholars as well as their *tafsīr* in the same way that Tabarī collected the *tafsīr* of the early Islamic scholars. Although Sulami didn't include much of his own opinion in the book, it is still a rich source of Sufi history for those studying the subject.

The book covers every *surah* of the Qur'ān from the Sufi perspective. Sulami didn't deal with the literal meaning of the verses; rather he focused on their inner meanings and collected all the Sufi opinions about them. In the preface he wrote: 'My intention is to collate the inner meanings of the verses for Sufis in the same way that other scholars have collated the literal meanings of the verses for non-Sufis.'[745]

In compiling his *tafsīr,* Sulami benefitted from the following people: the Prophet (pbuh), Ali b. Abī Tālib, Abd Allah b. 'Abbās, Ja'far as-Sadiq, Ata Allah Iskandarani, Junayd al-Baghdadi, Fudayl b. Iyaz and Tustarī.[746] The book contains other people's opinions more than Sulami's own and those who study the book must be aware that some of the narrations (especially those from Jafar as-Sadiq) are not authentic. In other words, the statements related from some Companions or from other people may not be their actual words. In spite of this, the book is a great source for understanding Sufi thinking at the time of Sulami.

Whilst he mostly concentrated on explaining the inner meaning of the verses, Sulami occasionally explained both the literal and the inner meanings. For example, the verse: "Your Lord would not have destroyed the cities unjustly while their people were reformers"[747] was explained literally; if the people of cities are tolerant to each other and they did not harm one another, God wouldn't destroy them.[748] Similarly, he interpreted *surah* Fatiha literally and explained the difference between *hamd* (praise) and *shukr* (giving thanks). He said, *hamd* is performed in both good and bad times, but *shukr* is performed only after receiving favours.[749]

"We will surely test you with something of fear and hunger and a loss of wealth and lives and fruits, but give good tidings to the patient".[750]

He interpreted this verse by relating the words from Imam Shafi:

---

745 Dhahabī, *at-Tafsir wal-Mufassirun*, 3/51-52.
746 Ates, 76-95.
747 Qur'ān, 11: 117.
748 Sulami, *Haqāiqu't Tafsir*, 124.
749 Sulami, *Haqāiqu't Tafsir*, 6.
750 Qur'ān, 2: 155.

> Fear is the fear of the enemy, hunger is the hunger during the month of Ramadan, loss of wealth is *zakat*, loss of lives is the sicknesses and loss of the fruits is the charity. Give good tidings to those who carry out these duties.[751]

Extreme interpretations are rarely seen in Sulami's book. He did not change the literal meanings of the verses in his interpretation. He utilized the Qur'ān, the Sunnah and also Arab poems to prove his interpretations.[752] He also related some *Isra'iliyyat* (information from Jewish and Christian sources) to interpret the verses about the creation of Adam, Paradise, the angels, etc. For example: "The thunder exalts Allah with praise of Him and the angels as well from fear of Him, and He sends thunderbolts and strikes there with whom He wills"[753] To interpret this verse he related from Zanjani: "the thunder is the scream of angels, the thunderbolt is the yelling of hearts and rain is their crying".[754]

Sulami generally avoided interpreting verses that contained legal rulings. This is a major difference between Sufi and *Batini mufassir.* Sufis view the rulings of Islam (*Shariah*) as essential to their practise. Without following these rules and having a thorough knowledge of the religion, one cannot access the inner dimension of Islam. On the other hand, *Batini* interpret verses containing rulings in a way that removes the ruling and changes the meaning of the verses.

Sulami utilised Arabic grammar in his interpretations; for example, he explained the word "*kitāb*" grammatically.[755] He had a deep love and respect for the Sufi elders but did not accept their word unconditionally. When relating from them he would say "if it is true" even sometimes he rejected their ideas. For example when he interpreted "*basmala*", he disclaimed that "if it is true that it was related from the Prophet (pbuh)".[756] Sulami held that the conjecture letters at the beginning of some *surah* are the secrets between God and His Messenger (pbuh). He interpreted these letters but was unable to support his opinion with evidence.

There are examples of anthropomorphism in Sulami's *tafsīr*; for example the verse: "Safa and Marwah are among the symbols of Allah. So whoever makes

---

751 Sulami, *Haqāiqu't Tafsir*, 17.

752 Sulami, *Haqāiqu't Tafsir*, 96-97.

753 Qur'ān, 13: 13.

754 Sulami, *Haqāiqu't Tafsir*, 4.

755 Sulami, *Haqāiqu't Tafsir*, 7, 217.

756 Sulami, *Haqāiqu't Tafsir*, 2.

Hajj to the House or performs *umrah*, there is no blame upon him for walking between them"[757] is interpreted as:

> Safa is the soul which is purified from disobedience, Marwa is the *nafs* which uses good values in the service of its master, Safa is to be purified from world's pleasures and carnal desires, *sa'y* (walking) is escaping to Allah.[758]

The verse: "Every people knew their watering place"[759] is interpreted by Sulami as:

> The watering place is the place to which the leader guides one. If one's leader is his *nafs* (carnal desires) his watering place is hell. If his leader is the soul, his watering place is paradise, if his leader is his Lord his watering place is the place where he will watch God.[760]

Sulami held the opinion that achieving the knowledge of *bātin* (inner or Sufi) depends on the knowledge of *ẕāhir* (the outer or literal meaning of the verses). To attain the inner meanings of Islam the *Shari'ah* must be followed. He rejected the interpretation of *Batini* people. For him, a servant must be mindful that guidance is from God, God is the real reason for one to achieve the knowledge of *bātin*, and his struggling in this way is a sign of God's guidance.[761] If one doesn't obey the rules of Islam, rather he only follows the Sufi way, he is considered an unbeliever, because Sufism is just the inner side of Islam and without Islam, the Sufi way is impossible.

11.3 Narratives of Moses and Khidir

Khidir is mentioned in Islamic sources as a companion of Prophet Moses. The literal meaning of 'Khidir' is green or the place which has abundant green. Khidir is not a private name; rather it is a nickname; he might be one of God's righteous servants or he may have been a Prophet. He represents the eternal enlivening or the gaining of eternity through elixir. It is understood from Moses' companionship with him that his mission relates to the spiritual domain of existence. He was blessed with knowledge of God and some sort of perpetual life, and can explain the wisdom behind life's events. The nickname was given because

[757] Qur'ān, 2: 158.
[758] Haqāiqu't Tafsir, 13.
[759] Qur'ān, 2: 60.
[760] Ates, *Sulami ve Onun Tefsiri*, 108-109.
[761] Ates, ibid, 142.

wherever he sits, even if it is on barren soil, that place becomes green.[762] He drank from the fountain of Paradise and wherever he steps, it immediately becomes green.

Some Orientalists claimed that the notion of Khidir was passed on to Islam from primitive cultures which had gods of vegetation and plants. Another claim is that the notion of Khidir is related with a man mentioned in the Torah, 'a man named sprout' (Zachariah).[763] In fact, the notion of Khidir in Islam is totally different from all the assumptions of the Orientalist scholars.

In some Islamic sources, he is mentioned as the son of Cain Hazrun, or the grandson of Noah Balya b. Malkan, or he is descended from the line of Aaron Khidir b. Amiyya, or he is Ilyas or Elyasa who are mentioned in the Qur'ān.[764] Ibn Kathīr says the Balya b. Malkan is the same as Ilya who is mentioned in Jewish sources but the name is changed into Arabic as Balya.[765] When we examine the Qur'ān and Sunnah, it seems that Ilya and Ilyas are the same person but Khidir and Ilyas are different; there is no information to suggest otherwise.

The story of Khidir is narrated in the Qur'ān without mentioning his name:

(Now relate to them, O Messenger, the experience of Moses): When Moses said to his (young) attendant: "I will not give up (journeying) until I reach the junction of the two seas, though I may march on for ages." When they reached the junction of the two (seas), they forgot their fish, and it took its way amazingly through the sea as in an underground channel. So when they had passed further on, Moses said to his attendant: "Bring us our morning meal; assuredly we have endured much fatigue in this journey of ours." He (the servant) said: "Would you believe it? When we betook ourselves to that rock for a rest, I forgot about (our cooked) fish – and none but Satan caused me to forget to mention it (to you) – and it took its way into the sea in an amazing way." He (Moses) said: "That is what we have been seeking!" So they retraced their footsteps. And they found (there) one of Our servants to whom We had granted a mercy as a grace from Us and taught a special knowledge from Our Presence. Moses said to him: "May I follow you so that you may teach me something of the knowledge of guidance which you have been taught?" He said: "You will never be able to have patience with being in my company. "How could you be patient about something that you have never encompassed in your knowledge?" He (Moses) said: "You will find me patient,

[762] Buhkari, *Saḥīḥ, Anbiya*, 29.
[763] Islam Ansiklopedisi, 7/461.
[764] Islam Ansiklopedisi, 7/461.
[765] Ibn Kathīr, *al-Bidāya*, 1/299.

if God so wills and allows me to, and I will not disobey you in anything." (Khidir) explained: "Well, if you go with me, do not ask me concerning anything (that I may do) until I myself make mention of it to you." So they set forth until, when they embarked on the boat, he (Khidir) made a hole in it. He (Moses) said: "Have you made a hole in it in order to drown its people (who would be using it)? You have certainly done an awful thing!" He said: "Did I not tell you that you would never be able to bear patiently with my company?" He (Moses) said: "Do not take me to task because I forgot, and do not overburden me in my affair (in what you ask of me)." So they went on until, when they met a young boy, he (Khidir) killed him. (Moses) said: "Have you killed an innocent soul (not in lawful retaliation but) without his having killed anyone? Assuredly you have done a horrible thing!" He said: "Did I not tell you that you would never be able to have patience with being in my company?" (Moses) said: "If I should ever question you about anything after this, keep me no more in your company. You have already received (full) excuse from me." So they went on until when they came upon the people of a township, they asked its people for food, but they refused them hospitality. They found there a wall which was on the verge of tumbling down, and he (al- Khidir) restored it. (Moses) said: "If you had wished, you could have taken payment for it." He (Khidir) said: "This is the parting of ways between me and you. I will tell you the meaning of what you were unable to bear patiently. "As for the boat, it belonged to some destitute people who worked on the sea – and I wished to damage it, for there was a king after them who was seizing every boat by force." And as for the young boy, his parents were believers, and we feared lest he should oppress them with rebellion and unbelief. "So we wished that their Lord would grant them in his place one better than him in purity and nearer in affection (to his parents)." And as for the wall, it belonged to two orphan boys in the city, and beneath it was a treasure belonging to them. Their father had been a righteous man. So your Lord willed that they should come of age and bring forth their treasure as a mercy from your Lord. I did not do this (any of the actions that you witnessed) of my own accord. This is the meaning of all (those events) with which you were unable to have patience.[766]

The topic of Khidir is mentioned in Hadith books such as Buhkari, Muslim, Ibn Majah and Ahmad b. Hanbal. They repeat the information which is given in the Qur'ān and sometimes add extra information about him. One of them is as follows, Said ibn Jubayr reports:

---

[766] Qur'ān, 18: 60-82.

"Moses got up to deliver a speech before the children of Israel and he was asked, who is the most learned person among the people?' Moses replied, 'I (am the most learned).' God admonished him for he did not ascribe knowledge to God alone. So God revealed to him, 'at the junction of the two seas there is a slave of Ours who is more learned than you.' Moses asked, 'O my Lord, how can I meet him?' God said, 'take a fish and put it in a basket (and set out), and where you lose the fish, you will find him.' So Moses set out, along with his boy-servant Yusha b. Nun, till they reached a rock (on which) they both lay their heads and slept. The fish moved vigorously in the basket and got out of it and fell into the sea and there it took its way through the sea (straight) as in a tunnel). God stopped the current of water on both sides of the way created by the fish, and so that way was like a tunnel. When Moses got up, his companion forgot to tell him about the fish, and so they carried on their journey during the rest of the day and the whole night. The next morning Moses asked his boy-servant 'bring us our early meal, no doubt, we have suffered much fatigue in this journey of ours.' Moses did not get tired till he had passed the place which God had ordered him to seek. His boy-servant then said to him, 'do you remember when we be-took ourselves to the rock I indeed forgot the fish, none but Satan made me forget it. It took its course into the sea in a marvellous way.' So they went back retracing their footsteps and found a man covered with a garment. Moses greeted him. Khidir said in astonishment, 'is there such a greeting in your land?' Moses said, 'I am Moses.' He said, 'are you the Moses of the children of Israel?' Moses said, 'I have come to you so that you may teach me of what you have been taught.' After that both of them proceeded along the sea coast, till a boat passed by and they requested the crew to let them go on board. The crew recognized Khidir and allowed them to get on board free of charge. When they got on board suddenly Moses saw that Khidir had pulled out one of the planks of the boat with an adze. Moses said to him, 'these people gave us a free lift, yet you have scuttled their boat so as to drown its people! Truly, you have done a dreadful thing. Khidir said, didn't I say that you can have no patience with me?

Then a sparrow came and sat on the edge of the boat and dipped its beak once in the sea. Khidir said to Moses, 'my knowledge and your knowledge, compared to God's knowledge are like what this sparrow has taken out of the sea.' Then they both got out of the boat, and while they were walking on the sea shore, Khidir saw a boy playing with other boys. Khidir got hold of the head of that boy and pulled it out with his hands and killed him. Moses said, have you killed an innocent soul who has killed nobody! Truly, you have done an illegal thing.' He said, didn't I tell you that you can have no patience with me? Then they both proceeded until they came

> to the inhabitants of a town. They asked them food but they refused to entertain them. (In that town) they found a wall on the point of falling down. Khidir set it straight with his own hands. Moses said, these are people to whom we came, but they neither fed us nor received us as guests. If you had wished, you could surely have exacted some recompense for it. Khidir said, this is the parting between me and you (he explained all the reasons). God's Apostle (pbuh) said, we wished that Moses could have been more patient so that God might have described to us more about their story".[767]

Ubay b. Ka'b reports in a weak Hadith:

> Khidir was a young man who lived in the time of Pharaohs, he learned the true religion from a man of religion, but he hid it. Unfortunately, when he divorced his wife, she informed other people about this secret. Thereupon he escaped to an island and refuged there.[768]

Later Hadith and Sufism books describe Khidir as someone immortal who is still alive today and will live until the end of time. In some sources it is narrated that the life of Khidir is extended to give him a chance to refute the claims of the antichrist.[769] It is said that he was alive in the time of the Prophet (pbuh) and met the Companion Anas who was the envoy of the Prophet (pbuh)[770], that he visited the relatives of the Prophet (pbuh) to console them when he died.[771] Some Sufis such as Ibrahim b. Atham, Bishr Hafī, Maruf Karkhī, Junayd Baghdadi and Muhyiddin ibn 'Arābī claimed that they saw Khidir, met with him and talked to him.

Khidir is described as living in the oceans whereas Ilyas lives on land and they meet often. Khidir also meets Gabriel, Mikhail and Israfil every year on the mountain of Arafat.[772] Islamic sources give two reasons for Khidir having such a long life; firstly that Adam made a will and prayed for him to have a long life and secondly, that he drank from the fountain of life.[773] Some scholars say that, he had long life but he died before the Prophet Muhammad's (pbuh) Messengership. Many Hadith scholars such as Buhkari, Ibrahim al-Harbi, Abū Hayyan Andulusi, Abū'l Faraj, Ibn Jawzī, al-Munawi, Ibn Taymiyya and Suyūtī, reject that Khidir is alive today. Ibn Qayyim al-Jawzī says that all the narrations which indicate Khidir is

---

767 Buhkari, *Sahīh, Knowledge*, 143.
768 Ibn Majah, *Sunan Fitan*, 23.
769 Ibn Ḫajar, *al-Isāba*, 1/431.
770 Bayḫaqī, *Sunan*, 7/423.
771 Ibn Kathīr, al-Bidāya, 1/141.
772 Ibn Ḫajar, *al-Isāba*, 1/432.
773 Tabarī, *Tārikh*, 1/220.

still alive are not authentic.[774] They bring evidence from Qur'ān, Hadith and logic to prove their claim. For example, in the Qur'ān God says, "Muhammad is not but a Messenger. [Other] Messengers have passed on before him,"[775] and "Every soul will taste death, and you will only be given your [full] compensation on the Day of Resurrection".[776] In the Hadith, the Prophet (pbuh) said; "in 100 years, all the human beings who live now, will be dead".[777]

Other scholars believe that Khidir is alive. They hold that the idea is not against the Qur'ān and Sunnah. Bediuzzaman Said Nursi evaluated this issue from different perspective and he accepted the life of Khidir in the present time. He explained the issue as follows:

> Is Khidir still alive? If so, why do some scholars reject this? He is still alive. Of the five degrees of life, Khidir has the second. This is why such scholars reject this. The first degree is as we live here and now, which is bound by certain conditions. The second degree is manifested in the lives of Khidir and Elijah. To a certain extent it is free, for those who have it can be in different places at the same time and are not bound by ordinary human life's necessities. For example, they do not have to eat and drink. The experiences that some godly persons who can discern hidden truths have had with Khidir suffice to illuminate and prove this degree of life. Further, one spiritual degree or station that saints reach in their spiritual journey is the Station of Khidir. One who attains this degree may meet Khidir and be instructed by him directly. Sometimes, one who holds this station is even mistaken for Khidir. The third degree is manifested in the lives of Prophets Jesus and Enoch, who live in heaven with their physical bodies. Their bodies are not bound by human life's necessities and have acquired a sort of refinement and luminosity to the degree of astral bodies and an angelic type of life.[778]

11.4 The Special Knowledge of God's Presence (*'Ilm Ladun*)

The special knowledge of God's Presence, or *ilm ladun*, is knowledge of the unseen or knowledge of mysteries, or knowledge which God imparts into one's heart and the truths occurring to it.[779] In *surah* Kahf, the Qur'ān mentions a distinguished servant of God favoured with special knowledge of God's Presence. The Prophet

---

[774] Ibn Qayyim al-Jawzī, *al-Manar al-Munif*, 67.
[775] Qur'ān, 3: 144.
[776] Qur'ān, 3: 185.
[777] Buhkari, *Sahīh, Times of the Prayers*, 575.
[778] Bedizzaman Said Nursi, *The Letters*, *The First Letter*, p. 3.
[779] M Fethullah Gülen, *Sufism*, v. 3 p. 32.

(pbuh) named him as Khidir. Sufi scholars hold that this special knowledge was the knowledge of His Presence. Despite being one of the five greatest Prophets, Moses desired to comprehend the general frame of the special knowledge of God's Presence by following Khidir to learn a particular aspect of it. Khidir said to Moses, 'O Moses! I have some sort of knowledge from God, which you do not know, and you have some other sort of knowledge which I do not know'.[780]

It is true that in order to be favoured with this knowledge, one should have the ability and merit to receive it and enjoy particular nearness to God; but it is primarily a special favour of God to His servants whom He has chosen.[781] For this reason, it cannot be acquired through study, research, or other similar ways. It should be pointed out that although such knowledge is extremely attractive, enchanting, and desirable, and although it is related to certain divine mysteries, the knowledge of the religion and divine truths with which the Prophets were favoured is much more elevated than this knowledge; the knowledge of the Prophets is objective, applicable to everybody, and secures the worldly and otherworldly happiness of people.[782]

11.4.1 Verse of Light

There are particular Qur'anic verses which Sufi scholars frequently refer to; one of them is the verse of light in *surah* Nur:

> God is the Light of the heavens and the earth. The example of His Light is like a niche wherein is a lamp; the lamp is in a crystal, and the crystal shining as if a pearl-like radiant star, lit from the oil of a blessed olive tree that is neither of the east nor of the west. The oil would almost give light of itself though no fire touches it: light upon light. God guides to His Light whom He wills. God strikes parables for people. God has full knowledge of all things.[783]

This verse is one of the ambiguous, allegorical verses of the Qur'ān. Many interpretations have been made to explain its deep and hidden meanings. It is important to remember that the true essence of God cannot be known as there is nothing comparable to Him. He is infinitely beyond our understanding and anything we can conceive of Him. To be able to gain some limited understanding of Him the Qur'ān presents us His acts, and creates allegories to give some knowl-

---

[780] Buhkari, *Saḥīḥ*, *Knowledge*, 143

[781] Gülen, ibid.

[782] Gülen, ibid.

[783] Qur'ān, 24: 35.

edge of Him with His Attributes, and Names. The Acts lead to the Names, and the Names lead to the Attributes.

M Fethullah Gülen interprets this verse as follows:

> It is God Who has brought and brings everything into the Light of existence from the darkness of non-existence and has made the universe an exhibition and a book to be mediated upon, nourishing our consciences with meanings that provide light for our eyes and exhilarate our hearts. It is possible only through the Creator of Light, Who illuminates the heavens and the earth with whatever is in them, to advance from knowledge to faith and from faith to true knowledge of God and from true knowledge of God to a deep consciousness of servanthood to Him at the junction of the outer and inner human worlds. Indeed, it is also through this same Light that the sun and numerous other suns illuminate the universe, the earth is bedecked with innumerable kinds of beauties, and hearts are enlightened with insight and perception. The eyes of human beings see the colours, the harmony among the colours and in everything else, and the eternal poetry in the general harmony of existence and transfer them to the heart as information. The insight takes these pieces of information and re-analyses and synthesizes them, transforming them into knowledge about or recognition of God. They sense both the pieces and the whole, both the physical entities and their truths, they also sense the Truth of truths, which the universe and whatever occurs in it refers to and indicates, and they come into contact with Him through one of the ranks of certainty, each according to his or her capacity.
>
> We should direct our insight to the Creator and Illuminator of Light so that the information we acquire from the universe can be transformed into knowledge of God and so that our feelings and sensations may not cause us confusion. Therefore, the existence must be studied through the Light of lights' Book which is more radiant than the sun, and in the light of the Prophethood of the Spirit of existence, namely Muhammad, upon him be peace and blessings. God is the Light of the heavens and the earth. Starting with the Light of Prophet Muhammad, upon him be peace and blessings, about which the Prophet himself says, "The first thing that God created is my Light,"[784] the first nucleus or seed which was brought into existence was the Light of Prophet Muhammad, everything is the manifestation of His Light at different wavelengths and its appearance in different forms in the external world.
>
> The source of Light is God, Who is beyond time and space. Therefore, His Light should be approached and reviewed from this viewpoint. Indeed,

[784] Al-Ajluni, *Kashfu'l-Khafa*, Vol. I, pp. 311–312.

> light and things of light can be present at millions of places at once and can transfer from one place to another in an instant. As a matter of fact, since the blessed body of the Prophet Muhammad, upon him be peace and blessings, had acquired such refinement as to be able to accompany his spirit (the law of energy and matter changing into each other may be explanatory for this incident), the Prophet completed his Ascension in a few minutes and returned. Such a journey requires a trillion times a trillion years under normal conditions. However, the authentic narrations inform us that the Prophet's bed was still warm when he returned from his Ascension. It is as if he transcended time during this journey.[785]

Ali Unal made the following explanations for this verse:

> The metaphor of the glass, lamp, and crystal indicates modern electricity and electrical lamps, therefore some modern interpreters of the Qur'ān, in particular, think that this verse suggests electricity. Energy is comprehended through its effects, and electrical energy is used for illumination through a bulb. The glass, lamp, crystal, or pearl-like radiant star when taken together brings to mind the image of an electric lamp. In the past, light was mostly obtained from lamps lit by oil, and the brightest lamp was that which was lit from the oil of an olive tree that grew in an open and elevated place, receiving the rays of the sun not only in the morning, but in the afternoon and throughout the day. So, the statement, neither of the east nor of the west, implies the intensity of the light obtained from a lamp lit from the oil of such olive trees, as it is not restricted in any direction. It also suggests that God's Light does not emit from matter or belong to the universe. It is meta-universal or meta-physical and, therefore, glows forth of itself without needing fire to kindle it. Likewise, the Qur'anic revelation as the source of knowledge and Islam, which it has formed, belong to none other than God. These are a pure light from God which illuminates the minds and hearts of humankind.[786]

Ghazali interprets this verse as follows:

> The meanings of niche, the lamp, a crystal, a pearl-like radiant star, blessed olive tree are five grades in the spiritual journey to Allah and five souls are corresponding to each level of these grades. The first grade is a sensitive soul which is represented by 'niche' in the verse. This soul exists in a baby who suckles his mother. The second grade is the imaginary soul which is represented by the lamp. This soul saves whatever the senses

[785] M Fethullah Gülen, Reflections on the Qur'ān, 210-213.

[786] Ali Unal, The Qur'ān with Annotated Interpretation, Surah Nur.

receive and informs the mind. This soul exists in small children who can memorize things and don't forget them and in some animals. The third level is the reasoning soul which is represented by the glass. This is the essence of human kind and this soul comprehends the things which are outside of feelings and the imagination. This does not exist in children and in animals. The fourth grade is the thinking soul which is represented by the tree. This soul learns rational things; it makes analyses and obtains new knowledge by this process. The fifth grade is the sacred soul which is represented by olive oil. This soul exists in the Prophets and in some saints.[787]

---

[787] Ghazali, *Mishkat*, 52-53.

Chapter Twelve

Textual Analysis and Translation of the Qur'ān

Textual Analysis and Translation of the Qur'ān

12.1 The Need for Philological Exegesis

The relationship between understanding the Qur'ān and knowledge of the Arabic language is obvious; it is impossible to truly understand and interpret the Qur'ān without a detailed knowledge of Arabic. In fact, the Qur'ān itself states the importance of the Arabic language as the language of the revelation: "We have sent down to you an Arabic Qur'ān so that you may understand".[788] The depth and richness of the Arabic language necessitate pondering over the Qur'anic verses to extract their meanings.

The interpretation of the Qur'ān must comply with the rules of the Arabic language in terms of vocabulary, grammar, rhetoric and principles of discourse. Imam Malik (d. 179 A.H.), said: "If any person is brought to me, having interpreted the Qur'ān while he is ignorant of the Arabic language, I will make an example of him (by punishing him)."[789] Mujahid (d. 103 A.H.), said: "It is not permissible for any person who believes in God and the Last Day to speak concerning the Book of God if he is not knowledgeable in the dialects of the Arabs."[790] Imam Shātibī (d. 790 A.H.), said: "Whoever desires to understand the Qur'ān, then it will be understood from the speech of the Arabs, and there is no way other than this."[791]

It is due to its miraculous eloquence that the Qur'ān has such depth and richness of meaning. One of the elements on which the Qur'ān's eloquence is based is its creative style, rich in the arts. It frequently speaks in parables and adopts a figurative, symbolic rhetoric using metaphors and similes.

The interpretation of the Qur'ān is always based first on the Qur'ān, Sunnah and the narrations of the Companions. The direct word of God, the words and

---

788 Qur'ān, 12:2.

789 Hasanuddin Ahmed, *Introducing the Qur'an*, p. 126

790 Ahmed, *Introducing the Qur'an*, p. 127.

791 Shātibī, *Muwafaqaat*, 1/ 84.

practises of the Prophet (pbuh) and the knowledge of his Companions are greater than the knowledge of any later linguist or grammarian. Interpretation based on the Arabic language comes after these three sources; it should neither contradict the former nor supersede them.

Over time, certain groups developed which adopted their own style of interpreting the Qur'ān. One was an extreme literalist sect called Ẕāhiriyah (literalists) which concentrated on the literal interpretation of the verses and ignored the symbolic and eloquent style of the Qur'ān. In contrast, another extreme sect called Batiniyah (esoterics), only concerned themselves with the inner meanings of the text and disregarded the literal interpretations. Both of these sects are extreme and harmful to the religion as their methodology leads to inaccurate interpretations of the word of God.[792]

Arabic, in the time of the Prophet (pbuh), was very rich and contained many different dialects. The Quraysh tribe made efforts to understand the other dialects and the other tribes in turn tried to understand the Quraysh dialect. The Qur'ān unified them. The Prophet (pbuh) was the most eloquent person in his time and sometimes used other tribes' dialects and even made contracts with them. He spoke with envoys from different tribes to convey his message. They admired his eloquence and asked him how it was possible? The Prophet (pbuh) said; 'my Lord taught me this eloquence and He taught well'.[793]

During the Prophet's (pbuh) life the Companions would always ask him to give explanations for verses that they were unsure of. This protected the language and the Arabic language remained pure until the end of the Companions' time. When the Muslim world expanded, many more people, cultures and languages influenced Arabic and scholars tried to protect it by establishing grammar rules. It is well-known that, for good reasons, the interpretations of the Companions did not cover the whole Qur'ān. Their interpretations were for the words that were vague, unclear, difficult, ambiguous, general or limited. However, without the living example of the Prophet (pbuh) and the first-hand knowledge of the Companions, following generations of Muslims had a greater need to understand the Qur'ān from its text. They began to interpret it according to the principles of Arabic, in addition to the interpretations of the Companions. The words in the Qur'ān are essential for understanding its meaning. Many scholars approached the Qur'ān from the perspective of the Qur'anic language and wrote books such as '*Qarīb al-Qur'ān*'.

---

792 Ali Unal, Foreword for his translation of Qur'ān.

793 Suyūtī, *Jami al-Saghīr*, 1, 12.

Arabic linguist scholars concentrated on interpreting difficult words, metaphoric expressions and ambiguous statements in the Qur'ān and used certain methodology for this; they would find the root of the word (and examine all its derivations), its place in the sentence and explain its usage in the language. To aid them in discovering the meanings of words they also looked to Arab poetry. They tried to define the nature of metaphorical expressions, their boundaries and how they should be interpreted within the context. In the Qur'ān there are words with multiple meanings and groups of words that all have the same meaning. Linguists examined those words, checked their existence in the Arabic language, how they were used and explained the meaning of those words in their contexts. For this purpose they wrote books such as: *I'rāb al-Qur'ān*, *Mushkil al-Qur'ān* and *Qarīb al-Qur'ān*. These books are not directly related to the interpretation of the Qur'ān, but helped in understanding the language of the Qur'ān.

It is imperative for any Qur'anic exegete to have a detailed knowledge of the Arabic language and grammar. The following scholars explained the Qur'ān by applying linguistic components: Zamakhsharī, Qādi Baydawī, Nasafī, Abū as-Suud, Jalalayn, Abū Hayyan. Some of these philological works are still referenced by scholars today such as: *'al-Mufradaat fi Qarīb al-Qur'ān* (Rāghib al-Isfahānī) and *Basairu Dhaw-it Tamyiz* (Firuzābādī). The main purpose of all these works is to aid the correct interpretation of the Qur'ān.

As mentioned before, without a detailed knowledge of the fundamental principles of the Arabic language, one cannot understand the Qur'ān. The Qur'ān is the speech of God and has a high eloquence and unique style; it is necessary for scholars of the Qur'ān to be familiar with these aspects. Sometimes the phrasing of a verse in the Qur'ān might be general, whereas its context shows that it is specific. In other cases, words or even phrases might seem to be missing, yet this is a characteristic of eloquent Arabic, since the missing words are understood by the context. In some verses, it might appear that the logical sequence of words has been reversed, but such a reversal adds subtle meanings that would otherwise not be present. Such characteristics, and others, are well known to the Arabs, and are an indication of the eloquence of the Qur'ān.

As non-Arabs had a greater need than Arabs to study and understand the Qur'anic language. it evolved that they comprised the majority of linguistic scholars. These scholars were essential to preserving the purity of Qur'anic Arabic against the influence of other cultures and languages that came about as a result of the expanding Islamic world. Arab scholars focused on making the Qur'ān easy to read and understand and even consulted Arab poetry in their efforts. On the other hand, to be able to read and understand the Qur'ān, non-Arabs needed Arabic grammar books to study and learn the language. Ibn Khaldun says:

> Influenced by other cultures and different natures, Arabs began to lose their natural ability to understand their language. The Arabic language they were familiar with was becoming unfamiliar. Afraid of reaching a point where they would be unable to understand the Qur'ān and Hadith, scholars decided to establish the essentials of Arabic, its rules, grammar and so on. This led to the first works on Arabic grammar.[794]

Philology of Arabic started to develop during the second century of Islam. Important scholars in this field were: Abū Amr al-A'la, Isa b. Amr as-Thaqafī, Sibawayh and al-Ahfash. They were the earliest scholars to write books on Arabic grammar. Khalil b. Ahmad wrote the first Arabic dictionary, '*Kitāb al-Ayn*'. Linguistic scholars wrote many books called *Gharīb al-Qur'ān* about understanding the Qur'ān from the perspective of its language. Unfortunately, these books did not survive until the present day but we know of them because they are referenced in other books. Some of the linguistic exegeses until the fourth Islamic century were:

1. Zayd b. Ali, (d. 121 A.H. / 738 C.E.), *Tafsīr Gharīb al-Qur'ān al-Majīd.*
2. Wāsil b. Atā, (d. 131 A.H. / 748 C.E.), *Ma'āni al-Qur'ān.*
3. Abān b. Taghlab b. Rabah al-Jarīrī, (d. 141 A.H. / 758 C.E.), *Gharīb al-Qur'ān.*
4. Muarrij b. Amr b. al-Harith b. Mani' as-Sadūsī, (d. 174 A.H. / 790 C.E.), *Gharīb al-Qur'ān.*
5. al-Ahfash, (d. 177 A.H. / 793 C.E.), *Kitāb Ma'āni al-Qur'ān.*
6. Yunus b. Habib, (d. 183 A.H. / 790 C.E.), *Ma'āni al-Qur'ān.*
7. Abū al-Hasan Ali b. Hamza al-Kisaī, (d. 189 A.H. / 804 C.E.), *Ma'āni al-Qur'ān.*
8. Abū Fayd Marsad ibn al-Harith b. Sadūs, (d.195 A.H. / 810 C.E.), *Gharīb al-Qur'ān* and *Ma'āni al-Qur'ān.*
9. Abū al-Hasan Nadr b. Shumayl an-Nahwī, (d. 203 A.H. / 813 C.E.), *Gharīb al-Qur'ān.*
10. Muhammad b. al-Mustanir, Abu Ali al-Qutrub, (d. 206 A.H. / 821 C.E.), *Ma'āni al-Qur'ān.*
11. Abū Zakariyya Yahya b. Ziyad al-Farrā, (d. 207 A.H. / 822 C.E.), *Ma'āni al-Qur'ān.*
12. Abū Ubayda Ma'mar b. al-Muthanna, (d. 210 A.H. / 825 C.E.), *Majāz al-Qur'ān.*

---

[794] Ibn Khaldun, *Muqaddima*, 3/184.

13. Abū al-Hasan Sa'id b. Mas'ada al-Ahfash al-Awsat, (d. 221 A.H. / 835 C.E.), *Gharīb al-Qur'ān* and *Ma'āni al-Qur'ān.*
14. Abū Ubayd al-Qāsım b. Sallam, (d. 223 A.H. / 837 C.E.), *Gharīb al-Qur'ān* and *Ma'āni al-Qur'ān.*
15. Muhammad b. Sallam b. Abdillah b. Sālim al-Jumahi, (d. 232 A.H. / 846 C.E.), *Gharīb al-Qur'ān.*
16. Abū Muhammad Abd Allah b. Muslim b. Qutayba, (d. 276 A.H. / 889 C.E.), *Ta'wil-u Mushkil al-Qur'ān* and *Gharīb al-Qur'ān.*
17. Ismail b. Isḫāq b. Ismail b. Ḫammad al-Azdī, (d. 282 A.H. / 895 C.E.), *Ma'āni al-Qur'ān.*
18. Muhammad b. Yazid b. Abdi'l-Akbar, Abū al-'Abbās al-Mubarrad, (d. 285 A.H. / 898 C.E.), *Ma'āni al-Qur'ān.*

12.1.1 Al-Farrā and *Ma'āni al-Qur'ān*

One of the most profound scholars in the field of Arabic grammar was Abū Zakariyya Ziyad b. Abd Allah b. Mansur al-Kūfī al-Farrā (144 - 207 A.H.). He was born in Kūfa (Iraq) and was accomplished in linguistics, literature and other sciences. He received his education from Qays b. al-Rabi, Mandal b. Ali, al-Kisaī and Sufyan b. Uyayna. His memory was excellent and he didn't take notes while studying. He was writing books without needing to check any reference books.

If he hadn't existed, Arabic wouldn't have survived, for he established its foundations and also summarized it. His most important book was *Ma'āni al-Qur'ān*. He interpreted the verses of the Qur'ān according to Arabic grammar. For example:

> Their example is that of one who kindled a fire, but when it illuminated what was around him, Allah took away their light and left them in darkness [so] they could not see[795]

This verse is interpreted by him as a metaphoric expression, so it explains the situation of hypocrites and the deed of hypocrisy, not the real man.[796]

> And believe in what I have sent down confirming that which is [already] with you, and be not the first to disbelieve in it. And do not exchange My signs for a small price, and fear [only] Me.[797]

---

795 Qur'ān, 2:17.
796 Farrā, *Ma'ān al-Qur'ān*, 1/15.
797 Qur'ān, 2:41.

The word *'kafir'* (unbeliever) is used in its singular form in this verse even though it refers to a group of people. Al-Farrā said that this was a part of Arabic literature and he proved it with evidence from old Arabic poetry.[798] In his book, he also explained the words of the Qur'ān by narrating the opinions of the Companions and the followers.

12.1.2 Abū Ubayda and *Majāz al-Qur'ān*

One of the famous linguists from Basra was Abū Ubayda Ma'mar b. al-Muthanna at-Taymi (110 – 210 A.H.). He wrote on *tafsīr, fiqh* and other fields. His sarcastic and satirical style made him so unpopular amongst his contemporaries, even his funeral went unattended.[799] Jāhiz said: "he was the most profound scholar among the scholars of his time".[800]

Abū Ubayda said that the Qur'ān is a special name and that other books cannot use this name. For him *I'rāb* (understanding the meaning of a word from its place in the sentence and its grammatical rules) of the Qur'ān consisted of metaphoric words, letters of words, summarizing, changing the way of conversation, and so on.[801] He used the following expressions in his book; '*majāzuhu* (its metaphorical meaning), *manaha* (its meaning), *tafsīruhu* (its explanation), *takdiruhu*' (its supposed meaning); they are all words which share the same meaning and are used to explain the meaning of verses. He did not interpret every verse of the Qur'ān but concentrated on strange words, metaphorical expressions, *I'rāb* and words with multiple meanings. For example, he interpreted *surah* Fatiha from the aspect of *I'rāb* and the meaning.[802] He proved the meanings of the words using Arabic poetry and sometimes he just gave the literal meanings of the verse. Sometimes he explained that one word could have different meanings depending on the context in which it was used. By indicating the root of the word it was possible to discover the intended meaning. His book contains valuable information about how Arabic grammar affects the meanings of words, how they are used in Arabic and how the context can affect their meaning.

---

798 Farrā, *Ma'āni al-Qur'ān*, 1/32-33.

799 Ibn Nadīm, *Al-Fihrist*, 79.

800 Jāhiz, *al-Bayan wat-Tabyin*, 1/347.

801 Abu Ubayda, *Majāz al-Qur'ān*, 1/8-16.

802 *Majāz al-Qur'ān*, 22-23.

12.1.3 Ibn Qutayba and Ta'wil-u Mushkil al-Qur'ān

The first representative of the Baghdad Linguist School was Abū Muhammad Abd Allah b. Muslim b. Qutayba at-Dinawari (213 - 276 A.H.). He tried to combine the Basra and Kūfa Schools. He learned *Tafsīr, Hadith, Fiqh, Nahw, Lugat, Kalam*, and History from the well-known scholars of his time.[803]

Ibn Qutayba explained the difficult expressions (*mushkil*) in the Qur'ān not only from the metaphorical perspective but also from other perspectives. Unlike Abū Ubayda, he limited the use of *majāz* (metaphoric usage and its explanations). He held that most *mufassir* were making mistakes in their explanations of the metaphorical expressions.[804] In his book he attempted to prove that the Qur'ān contains no contradictions by explaining those verses that seem to contradict each other. He gave many examples on this topic and his book is not only extremely valuable as a source book regarding the disputes against the Qur'ān in his time but clearly demonstrates his skill as a linguistic scholar and his in-depth knowledge of both the Arab and Persian cultures.

12.2 Foreign Words in the Qur'ān

There was much dispute between scholars over whether the Qur'ān contains foreign words. Scholars such as Abū Ubayda, Ma'mar b. al-Muthanna, Shafi and Tabarī reject this idea whereas others accepted the possibility because the Quraysh tribe met with other cultures and learned some of their words. The Qur'ān was revealed in their language and it is possible that some foreign words were included in the revelation. The majority of scholars believed that these foreign expressions were adopted into the Arabic language; however, there are some dogmatic implications in this issue, especially in relation to the Arabic nature of the Qur'anic text. The scholars who wrote '*Gharīb al-Qur'ān*' aimed to illustrate and explain the foreign words in the Qur'ān.

12.3 *I'rāb al-Qur'ān*

I'rāb al-Qur'an is the investigation and analysis of the words in the Qur'ān according to their place in a sentence from the perspective of Arabic grammar.[805] '*I'rāb*' is to state the type of the word, its ruling and its position in a sentence and give the meaning accordingly. This science indicates each word in a sentence wheth-

---

803 Ahmad Saqar, *Muqaddima for Ta'wil-u Mushkil al-Qur'ān.*
804 Ibn Qutayba, *Ta'wil-u Mushkil al-Qur'ān*, 76.
805 Ali Turgut, *Tefsir Usulu Kaynaklari*, 190.

er it is a verb (*fi'il*), the object (*fā'il*) or the subject (*maf'ul*). It plays a pivotal role in understanding the Qur'ān. The following examples elaborate this topic.

During the caliphate of Ali ibn Abī Tālib, a Bedouin man came from the desert and was praying behind the imam. The imam was reciting *surah* at-Tawba and he recited the following verse:

أَنَّ اللهَ بَرِيءٌ مِنَ الْمُشْرِكِينَ وَرَسُولُهُ

> And [it is] an announcement from Allah and His Messenger to the people on the day of the greater pilgrimage that Allah is disassociated from the disbelievers, and [so is] His Messenger.[806]

Instead of reading the last word '*rasulahu*', he recited it as '*rasulihi*'. This mistake changed the meaning of the verse to mean that God is disassociated from the pagans and from the Messenger of God (pbuh). The Bedouin immediately recognised this grave mistake and laughed in the prayer. He broke his prayer and severely criticised the mistake. Ali was informed of this incident and wanted to prevent this happening again. He ordered for Abū al-Aswad ad-Dualī, an expert on the Arabic language, to write down its essentials. Abū al-Aswad's reply to this request was; 'go forth in this direction'. In this statement he used the word '*naḫw*' (direction) which is how the science of *Naḫw* got its name.

As a science, *Naḫw* focuses on the Arabic words, their rules, their place and the vowels of the last syllable of each word in a sentence. The above-mentioned incident clearly demonstrates the importance of knowledge of *naḫw* as there are many other examples in the Qur'ān where simply changing the last vowel of one letter can change the whole meaning of the word or verse. Another example is:

إِنَّمَا يَخْشَى اللهَ مِنْ عِبَادِهِ الْعُلَمَاءُ إِنَّ اللهَ عَزِيزٌ غَفُورٌ

"Only those fear Allah, from among His servants, who have knowledge".[807]

In this verse if the word '*Allaha*' is read as '*Allahu*' the meaning of this verse changes to: 'God fears among his servants who have knowledge'. This is great mistake and nullifies the prayer; if one makes this mistake intentionally he loses his faith.

12.4 *Wujūh* and *Nazāir*

As with every other language, the Qur'ān contains some words which have multiple meanings. In some places the meaning of the word changes according

[806] Qur'ān, 9:3.
[807] Qur'ān, 35:28.

to the context in which it is used. The Qur'anic science '*Wujūh*' focuses on this area. Contrary to this, the Qur'anic science of '*an-Nazāir*' studies the words in the Qur'ān which share the same meaning. [808] Scholars usually studied both sciences and their books on the subject were titled '*Wujūh* and *an-Nazāir*'. One of the earliest Qur'anic exegetes, Muqātil, wrote a book on this topic, '*Wujūh Harf al-Qur'ān*'. In order to understand the Qur'ān better, knowledge of *Wujūh* and *an-Nazāir* is necessary.

Muqātil elaborated on this topic in his book, giving examples of words which have multiple meanings and those which have different meanings in different verses. He claimed that there are 180 words in the Qur'ān which have multiple meanings. He indicated their location in the verses and explained their meaning in each place. The following two examples illustrate this topic: in Arabic, illiterate (*ummī*) defines a person who is like a newborn, without knowledge and unable to read or write; it is the adjective form of *umm* (mother). In Arabic, *umm* also means the original form of something.[809] Apart from its lexical meanings, *umm* also has some metaphorical meanings. In the Qur'ān, *umm* is used as the origin, that is, the place to be returned to, and a woman who suckles. The Arab nation was also defined as "*ummī*"; for a long time, Arabs had been known as a nation that could not read, write or calculate. "*Ummi*" also means center as it is in the expression *Ummu'l-Qura* (Mother of the Cities).

The word '*waḥy*' in the Qur'ān is another example:

The meanings of *waḥy* are: guidance by a sign, such as Zachariah's inspiration of the people by his gesture to glorify God's praises;[810] evil whisperings from Satan, such as the devil's inspiration of the people to dispute with believers;[811] inspiration of inanimate things, such as God's command to the earth or heavens;[812] guidance from God to the Angels,[813] and the revelation:

> 'It is not fitting for a man that God should speak to him except by inspiration, or from behind a veil, or by sending of a Messenger to reveal with God's permission what God wills: for He is Most High, Most Wise'.[814]

---

808 Suyūtī, *al-Itqān Fi 'Ulūm al-Qur'ān*, 445.
809 Firuzābādī, *al-Qāmus al-Muhīt*, check the word "am-ma".
810 Qur'ān, 19:11.
811 Qur'ān, 6:121.
812 Qur'ān, 41:12.
813 Qur'ān, 8:12.
814 Qur'ān, 42:51.

12.4.1 Words with Multiple Meanings

The Qur'ān, as was previously mentioned, contains some words with multiple meanings, the subject of which caused disagreements between interpreters and even formed the basis for different rulings among Islamic sects; an example of this is the following verse:

> Divorced women shall keep themselves in waiting for three menstrual courses, and it is not lawful for them, if they believe in God and the Last Day, to conceal what God has created in their wombs.[815]

The word '*quru*' in this verse has two meanings; the first is purification from menses and the second is the beginning of menses. This difference in meaning led to different rulings in the Islamic Schools; some chose the first meaning and based their ruling on this understanding and others chose the second meaning and formed their ruling according to that.

Another example is the verse: "Then a visitation from your Lord encompassed it while they were sleeping. So by morning it had become bleak".[816] In this verse the word '*sariim*' translated as 'bleak' has multiple meanings, including but not limited to: it became as dark as night; it became like day; it became like ashes after a fire; it is spoiled by very cold or hot weather. All these meanings are given for the word '*sariim*' in the Arabic dictionary and Arabs use each meaning in different contexts. For this reason, the scholars interpreted this verse in multiple ways because the word has multiple meanings.

12.4.2 Disagreement among Linguists About the Meaning of Words

Sometimes one word may be understood differently, not because the word has multiple meanings but because of the context in which it is used, for example: "There will circulate among them young boys made eternal".[817] The word '*mukhalladun*' can be understood either as they won't get older forever, or as they will be the same age and their age won't be changed.

12.4.3 Disagreements about Absolute or Restricted Expressions

There are some verses in the Qur'ān which can be understood as absolute or restricted statements. For example:

---

815 Qur'ān, 2:228.

816 Qur'ān, 68:19-20.

817 Qur'ān, 56:17.

> Allah will not impose blame upon you for what is meaningless in your oaths, but He will impose blame upon you for [breaking] what you intended of oaths. So its expiation is the feeding of ten needy people from the average of that which you feed your [own] families or clothing them or the freeing of a slave. But whoever cannot find [or afford it] - then a fast of three days [is required]. That is the expiation for oaths when you have sworn. But guard your oaths. Thus does Allah make clear to you His verses that you may be grateful.[818]

In this verse, three days fasting can be understood as absolute and without any restriction or it may be understood as fasting three days consecutively. Abū Ḫanīfa, Thawrī and their followers understood this verse as restricted and ruled that the fast must be three consecutive days. These scholars relied on Ubay ibn Ka'b and Abd Allah ibn Mas'ud and read this verse with the addition of '*mutatabiat*' (consecutive) from their personal Muṣḫāfs (this topic is also related with *ilm al-qiraat*). This is binding evidence and they formed their ruling based on this evidence. As a result, if one has to fast three days as compensation for breaking his oath, he cannot separate these days according to Abū Ḫanīfa and Thawrī. Imam Shafi didn't accept this evidence, because it is not among the accepted recitations of the Qur'ān. He took the meaning of the verse in its absolute sense and ruled accordingly; that it is permissible to separate the days when fasting.

12.4.4 Disagreements about Real or Metaphoric Expressions

The Qur'ān contains some expressions which can be understood either literally or metaphorically. For example: "And that it is He who makes laugh and weep".[819] The literal meaning of the verse is that God created human beings with the ability to laugh or cry. The metaphorical meaning is that the earth laughs when the plants grow in it, the sky cries when it rains. The essential meaning of this verse is happiness or sadness; laughing indicates happiness and crying indicates sadness.

12.4.5 Disagreements about General or Specific (*Āam-Khās*) Expressions

Linguists sometimes disagreed as to whether some verses contained general or specific expressions, which could affect the meaning of the verse, for example:

---

[818] Qur'ān, 5:89.

[819] Qur'ān, 53:43.

> Or do they envy people for what Allah has given them of His bounty? But we had already given the family of Abraham the Scripture and wisdom and conferred upon them a great kingdom.[820]

The word '*nās*' translated as 'people' in this verse caused disagreements among the linguists. Some linguists understood the word '*nās*' as the Prophet Muhammad (pbuh), because God bestowed on him Prophethood, but the Jews envied him since he was non-Jewish. Other linguists understood this word as the Prophet (pbuh), his family and his Companions. The first understanding is specific and the second understanding is general.

12.4.6 Disagreements about Some Letters

In some verses there are letters that strengthen the meaning of the verse. Some linguists hold that the removal of these letters does not affect the meaning of the word whereas other scholars do not accept this. They hold that the letters are essential not additional and that their removal would change the essential meaning of the words. For example: "I swear by the Day of Resurrection"[821] The letter '*la*' at the beginning of the verse is accepted as an additional letter. This letter only strengthens the meaning. Other linguists don't accept this and say the letter '*la*' is not additional, it is essential and the meaning of this letter is prohibition, therefore the issue of *Qiyamah* (Judgment Day or the end of days) is obvious and doesn't need any support to explain it.

12.4.7 Disagreement about the Reference of the Pronoun

As in normal language, pronouns are very often used in the Qur'ān. A pronoun without a reference point results in ambiguity of meaning. In some verses of the Qur'ān the reference point of the pronoun is unclear and this caused disagreement amongst scholars, for example: "And he certainly saw him in another descent."[822] The verse does not make the reference point clear and so it is not certain whether the Prophet (pbuh) saw God or the angel Gabriel in his ascension to the heavens.

12.4.8 Poetry in the Explanation of the Qur'ān

There are some verses in the Qur'ān and some Hadith which seem to prohibit poetry.

---

820 Qur'ān, 4:54.
821 Qur'ān, 75:1.
822 Qur'ān, 53:13.

> And the poets the deviators follow them, do you not see that in every valley they roam, And that they say what they do not do. Except those [poets] who believe and do righteous deeds and remember Allah often and defend [the Muslims] after they were wronged. And those who have wronged are going to know to what [kind of] return they will be returned.[823]

The Prophet (pbuh) said: "It is better for a man's chest to be filled with pus than to be filled with poetry".[824]

Abū Bakr al-Anbari said:

> There are numerous narrations from the Companions and Successors about explaining the obscure and rare words in the Qur'ān with poetry. Yet, despite this, some who have no knowledge have criticized the grammarians, and said, 'When you do this, you make poetry a source (of understanding) rather than the Qur'ān'. He says, 'we have not made poetry a primary source over the Qur'ān, but rather we wish to clarify the meanings of the obscure and rare words in it'. [825] Ibn 'Abbās says, 'If you ask me about the rare words in the language, then seek it in poetry, for poetry is the record of the Arabs.[826]

Once 'Umar asked the Companions the meaning of the verse: "Or He will take them upon *takhawwuf*."[827] Thereupon an old man from the tribe of Hudhayl stood up and said: 'This is from our dialect. *Takhawwuf* means suffering loss little by little'. 'Umar asked him: 'Is this something that the Arabs know from their poetry?' He answered: 'Yes' and recited to them the line of poetry. After that 'Umar said: 'Stick to the recordings, you will not be misled'. When he was asked: 'What are the recordings?' he replied: 'The poetry of pre-Islamic times. Therein are the explanations of your Book, and the meanings of your words'.[828]

12.5. Orientalist Works about the Qur'ān

It is well-known that non-Muslim, western scholars have been studying Islamic disciplines such as Islamic Jurisprudence, Hadith, the History of Islam, the Theology of Islam, Islamic Philosophy, the Qur'ān and the Interpretation of the Qur'ān. They produced many works on these Islamic fields, particularly about the Qur'ān

---

823 Qur'ān, 42:224-227.

824 Muslim, *Saḫīḫ, The Book of Poetry*, 5609

825 Zarkashī, *al-Burhān Fi 'Ulūm al-Qur'ān*, 294.

826 Zarkashī, ibid.

827 Qur'ān, 16:47.

828 Qadi Yasir, *An introduction to 'Ulūm al-Qur'ān*, 314.

and the sciences of the Qur'ān. They wrote books about the history, the translations, the methodology and the interpretations of the Qur'ān. Most of the western scholars approached the Qur'ān with pre-conceived ideas and a pre-existing agenda. When they study a Qur'anic *surah* containing a story which they have already seen in other scriptures, they naturally assume that the Qur'ān derives from those other scriptures.[829]

They are usually very critical of Islam and its primary sources such as the Qur'ān and Hadith. Some of them go further and try to instil doubt in the minds of Muslims about the authenticity of the Qur'ān (its divine authorship) to reduce the value of the Qur'ān to the level of their sacred books. The following sections elaborate on some of these works.[830]

12.5.1 Nicetes of Byzantium, Refutation of the Qur'ān

The book's title indicates that this is not a scientific and objective study but is rather born of enmity towards Islam. Almost all of the early non-Muslim writers on Islam tried to prove the authenticity of Christianity (the Gospels), at the same time objecting to the Muslims' belief in the Qur'ān. There are obviously signs that some first-hand sources were used in their works, however they also relied on many secondary sources. The main purpose of their activities and efforts was to discredit the Prophet (pbuh) and the Qur'ān.[831]

12.5.2 Ignaz Goldziher

Goldziher started his book (De Richuntgen der Islamiçhen Koranauslegung) by focusing on the readings of the Qur'ān after which he studied the sects which appeared among Muslims in the history of Islam and evaluated them from different perspectives. In the last chapter he mentions modern interpreters of the Qur'ān such as the scholars in Egypt and India and he also talks about the school of Manar. His work is translated into Arabic by Abdulhalim an-Najjar along with a criticism of the book.

12.5.3 Theodor Noldeke - F. Schwlly, the History of the Qur'ān

This book discusses the collection of the Qur'ān, the first scribes and collectors (the Qur'ān committee), the knowledge of the Qur'ān during the time of the first

829 M. R. Waldman, '*New Approaches to Biblical Materials in the Qur'ān*', *The Muslim World* 65 (1985) 1
830 Tihami Nakra, *Manāhij al-Mustashriqin*, Riyadh, 1985, pp. 24-25.
831 Neal Robinson, '*Massignon, Vatican II and Islam as an Abrahamic Religion*', Islam & Christian and Muslim Relations, 2 (1991) 185.

four caliphates, the personal Qur'ans (individual *Muṣḫāf*), the collection of Zayd ibn Thabit, the methodology and the content of the first collection of the Qur'ān, the personal copies of the Qur'ān of 'Ubay ibn Ka'b and 'Abd Allah ibn Mas'ud and multiple copies of the Qur'ān in the time of Caliph Uthman, and also the conjecture letters (*huruf al-muqatta'at*').

Theodor Noldeke also wrote '*Gecschichte de Qorans*', a three-volume work about the history of the Qur'ān. Orientalist Rudi Paret admired this work and often referred to it with praise for the author. This work is among the classical works in the field of the Qur'ān sciences.[832]

[832] Rudi Paret, *the Articles on the Qur'ān*, (tr. Omer Ozsoy), Ankara 1995, s. 15.

Glossary

Ahl al-kitab People of the Book (Jews, Christians).

Ahl al-sunnah The Sunnis; orthodox Muslims.

Ahl al-Hadith Followers of Hadith.

Ahl al-Qur'ān Followers of the Qur'ān.

Ahruf Translated at different times as 'letters', 'ways' or 'dialects'.

Alim (pl. ulama) Scholar of Islam.

Allah The One God, the Everlasting. He has always been, has no progeny, and in His image nothing has been created.

al-Lawh al-Mafuz The Preserved Tablet

Asbāb al-Nuzūl Occasions of the revelation.

Ansar Lit. 'supporters', the Muslims of Medina who, pledging allegiance to the Prophet (pbuh), joined the Muslim immigrants from Mecca in establishing the first Islamic state.

A.H. Anno Hegirae (in the year of the Hijra). In reference to the Prophet's (pbuh) journey from Mecca to Medina in the month of Rabi' al-Awwal, which heralded the beginning of the first Muslim state and, hence, of the Muslim calendar.

Ayah A verse of the Qur'ān; can also be used more generally to mean any of God's signs in the created universe.

C.E. Common Era, a customary substitute for A.D. (Anno Domini, Year of the Lord). The modern Gregorian calendar was founded by Pope Gregory XIII in 1582; all dates prior to this are back projections.

Caliph The title taken by the Prophet's (pbuh) successors as both heads of government and of religious affairs.

Companion Any Muslim who was a contemporary of the Prophet Muhammad (pbuh), having seen or heard him at least once while professing the faith. The hypocrites of Medina, and any who subsequently rejected Islam and died as apostates, are excluded from this definition.

Canon A list of religious texts officially recognized by members of that religion as authoritative.

Consonantal Text One that is devoid of vowels.

Diacritical Dots/Marks Also known as *tashkil* or *nuqat al-'Arābīc*. A means of designating the inflection of letters within words, usually through the addition of supplementary symbols.

Dirayah Understanding; reason; opinion.

Exegesis Explanatory or interpretive effort usually focused on a religious text.

Fiqh Jurisprudence, the science of religious law in Islam; Islamic law.

Fuqaha Jurists in Islamic law.

Ghayb What is hidden, unseen and inaccessible.

Hadith An account of what the Prophet (pbuh) said or did or of his tacit approval of something said or done in his presence.

Hadith Qudsi What God, speaking in the first person, addressed to the Prophet (pbuh) outside the Qur'anic revelation.

Hajj Annual pilgrimage to Mecca.

Ḫalāl Permitted or permissible in Islamic law.

Ḫarām What is prohibited in Islamic law.

Hijrah Emigration of the Prophet (pbuh) from Mecca to Medina in 622 C.E.

Hikmah Wisdom; underlying reason.

Huffaz (Sing., Hafiz) Muslims who have memorized the entire Qur'ān by heart.

Ḫukm A rule or injunction that seeks to regulate the conduct of individuals who are capable of bearing legal obligations.

Hypocrites During the Prophet's (pbuh) residence in Medina, a small sector of its residents who opposed him semi-secretly and who endeavoured on repeated occasions to undermine or betray him.

Ibadah Various forms of worship and rituals in Islam.

Ijma' Consensus.

Ijtihad Exercise of individual judgement in order to arrive at a solution to a problem in Islamic law.

Islam The name of the religion expounded in the Qur'ān, it denotes submission to the One God.

'Ilm Knowledge; the opposite of *jahl* (ignorance).

'Ilm al-Qiraat The discipline of recitation of the Qur'ān.

Imam Leader of the prayer; leader of an Islamic community.

Iman Faith; belief. In Islam, faith has three components: the internal conviction in the heart, the verbal expression and the performance of what is believed in action.

Isnad Chain of authorities; an essential part of the transmission of Hadith.

Jahiliyyah Period of ignorance; pre-Islamic period.

Kaba Lit. 'Cube'. The Great Sanctuary built in Mecca by the Prophets Ibrahim and Ismail.

Kufr-Kafir A person who refuses to submit himself to God; a disbeliever.

Kahin Soothsayer.

Kalam Speech; scholastic theology.

Kalam Allah Speech of God.

Kalimah Spoken word; utterance.

Khalq al-Qur'ān Creation of the Qur'ān; the famous debate over whether the Qur'ān is created or not, which occurred during the 'Abbāsid period.

Kitab Book; scripture.

Kitab Allah Scripture of God.

Kufr Unbelief.

Kufic Script One of a number of angular scripts which rose to prominence and supplanted the Hejaz as the predominant script for the Holy Qur'ān. 'Kufic' has now become an umbrella term under which several angular scripts are catalogued.

Mansūkh An abrogated verse.

Maslalah Public interest.

Mathal Parable, proverb or popular saying.

Muarada The phrase used in Hadith for the annual recitations between the Prophet (pbuh) and the Archangel Gabriel, with one initially reciting while the other listened, then vice versa.

Mubayyan Explained.

Mufassal The segment from *surah* Qaf until the end of the Qur'ān.

Mufassir Interpreter of the Qur'ān.

Muhajir Lit. 'Immigrants'. The Meccan Muslims who migrated to Medina, having been the first to champion the Prophet's (pbuh) cause.

Muhkam Clear; unambiguous.

Muhkamat Clear, unambiguous verses.

Mujmal Aggregate.

Mujtahid A person engaged in *ijtihad*.

Mu'min Believer; Muslim.

Muṣḫāf The name given to a complete text of the Qur'ān considered as a physical object; codex.

Mushrik Polytheist.

Mutashābih (pl. mutashābihat) Obscure; not clearly intelligible to the human mind; allegorical.

Mutawātir Hadith That, at every stage of transmission, has many narrators.

Naskh Abrogation.

Qari (Pl., Qurra) A professional reciter of the Qur'ān.

Qiraat Recitation, Reading

Qisas al-Anbiya Stories of the Prophets.

Qiyas Reasoning by analogy, the fourth source of Muslim law.

People of the Book Those hailing from a monotheistic tradition who were given scriptures, the Jews and Christians.

Ra'y Opinion.

Riba Usury, interest or unlawful addition or gain.

Riwayah Narration; in modern Arabic usage has become an equivalent of story, novel or play.

Sab'a al-Ahruf The seven ways; seven dialects.

Sahaba The Companions of the Prophet (pbuh).

Sahih A rigorously authentic Hadith or a collection thereof.

Salafiyyah Neo-orthodox brand of Islamic reformism, originating in the late nineteenth century and centred on Egypt, aiming to regenerate Islam by a return to the tradition of the 'pious forefathers'.

Salah Five daily obligatory prayers; prayer.

Sawm Fasting.

Shari'ah Rules and regulations governing the lives of Muslims, derived in principle from the Qur'ān and Hadith.

Seven Dialects (Ahruf Sab'a) A divine sanctioning of the Qur'ān in more than one dialect. This served as both an aid to Arab tribes that were unaccustomed to the Quraysh vernacular, and a way of illuminating various shades of meaning within particular verses.

Successors The Muslim generation immediately follows the Companions. They in turn were followed by the Succeeding Successors.

Suhuf Lit. 'sheets'. It refers to the master volume of the Qur'ān that was prepared, on the basis of first-hand Qur'anic fragments, during the reign of Caliph Abū Bakr.

Sunnah Normative behaviour of the Prophet (pbuh). It is used sometimes to refer to Hadith.

Sunni A religio-political group in Islam (as opposed to Shi'ah); mainstream Muslims.

Surah Designation used for the 114 independent units of the Qur'ān often translated as 'chapter'.

Tabi'in Successors; generation followed by Companions.

Tafsīr An interpretation, generally of the Qur'ān. In most cases a work titled *tafsīr* will follow the text of the Qur'ān from beginning to end.

Tafsīr bi al-Ra'y Interpretation based on reason.

Tafsīr bi al-Riwayah Interpretation based on text/tradition. It implies that the interpretation of the Qur'ān should be guided by the Qur'ān itself, or the Prophet's (pbuh) instructions and his actual interpretations, or by his Companions and Successors.

Ta'wil Interpretation; often used for mystical interpretation of the Qur'ān and dealing basically with the hidden meanings of its terms and concepts.

Ulama Scholars of religion.

Ummah Community.

Usūl al-Fiqh Works of *Usūl al-Fiqh* are concerned with the sources of the law (*fiqh*) and the methodology for extrapolating rules from revelation.

Usūl al-Tafsīr Principles of exegesis.

Uthman Muṣḫāf Refers not only to the Qur'anic compilation authorized by the third caliph, but also to its spelling conventions. Any writing which deviates from the consonantal text of Uthman's Muṣḫāf cannot be regarded as the Qur'ān.

Various Readings The presence of more than one wording, clouded by uncertainty as to which is correct.

Waḫy Revelation.

Waḫy Ghayr Matluw Unrecited revelation.

Waḫy Matluw Recited revelation.

Zakat Obligatory payment by Muslims of a determinate portion of specified categories of their lawful property for the benefit of other enumerated classes.

Bibliography

Abū Hayyan. *Tafsīr Bahr al-Muhit.*8 vols. Riyadh, no date.

Abū Ubayda, Ibrahim ibn Muhammad. *Lughat al-Qur'ān*. Riyadh: Dar al-Watan, 1993.

Ahmed, Hasanuddin. *Introducing the Qur'ān.* New Delhi, India: Goodword Books, 2005.

al-A'zami, Muhammad Mustafa. *The History of The Qur'anic Text.* Selangor, Mayalsia: Islamic Book Trust, 2011.

______ *Studies in Hadith Methodology, and Literature.* Indianapolis: 1977.

Abū Dawud. *Sunan.* ed. M.M. 'Abdulhamid, 4 vols. 2nd imp. Cairo: 1950. English translation by Ahmad Hasan. *Sunan Abū Dawud*, 3 vols. Lahore: 1984.

Arberry, Arthur J. *The Koran, Interpreted.* London: Oxford University Press, 1983.

Armstrong Caren. *A Western Attempt to Understand Islam.* Victor Gollanz Ltd.

Asad, Muhammad. *The message of the Qur' an translated and explained.* Gibraltar: Dar-al-Andalus, 1980.

Ali Unal. *The Qur'ān with Annotated Interpretation in Modern English.* Feedbooks, 2007.

Baqillani. *Ijaz al Qur'ān (The sections of poetry) A tenth century document of 'Arabic literary theory and criticism, translated and annotated by Gustane e.Von Grunebaum.* The University of Chicago II, 1950.

Banna, Ahmad ibn Muhammad. *Itihaaf al-Fudhala al-Bashar fi al-Qiraat alArbatha Ashar.* Beirut: Alim al-Kutub, 1987.

Burton, J. *The Collection of the Qur'ān.* UK: Cambridge University Press, 1977.

Bayhaqi. *as-Sunan al-Kubra.* 10 vols. Hyderabad: 1344-1355.

Baladhuri, Ahmad b. Yahya. *Ansab al-Ashraf.* ed. M. Hamidullah, Cairo: 1959.

Baqillani. *al-Intishar al-Qur'ān.* Frankfurt: 1986 [facsimile edition]).

al-Bukhari, Muhammad b. Ismail. *Khalq Af'al al-Ibad.* Mecca: 1970.

______ *Kitab ad-Duafa al-Sagir.* Haleb: 1976.

______ *Sahih with the Commentary of Ibn Hajar.* ed. F. Abdul-Baqi, 13 vols. Cairo: al-Matba'ah as-Salafiyya, 1380. English translation by M. Muhsin Khan. *The Translation of the Meanings of Sahih al-Bukhari*, 8 vols. 2nd revised ed. Pakistan: 1973.

Cerrahoğlu, Ismail. *Tefsir Usûlu.* Ankara: Fecr Yayin Evi, 1991.

______ *Tefsir Tarihi*, Ankara: Fecr Yayin Evi, 1988.

Curcani, S. Sharif. *at-Ta'rifaat.* Beirut: 1988.

Dani, Abū 'Amr. *al-Ahruf al-Sab'a fi al-Qur'ān.* ed. Adby al-Muhaymin Thah, Jeddah: Dar al-Manarah, 1997.

_____ *al-Muhkam fi Naqt al-Masahih.* ed. 1. Hasan, Damascus: 1960.

_____ *al-Muqni.* ed. M.S. Qamhawi, Cairo: no date.

_____ *Kitab an-Naqt.* ed. M.S. Qamhawi, Cairo: no date.

Darimi. *Sunan.* ed. Dahman. 2 vols. Damascus: 1349.

Denffer, Ahmad Von. *'ulūm AI- Qur'ān, An Introduction to the Sciences of the Qur' an.* London: Islamic Foundation, 1985.

Dhahabi, al-imam Shams ad-Din Muhammad ibn Ahmad. *Ma'rifat al-Qurra al-Kibar 'ala at-Tabaqati wal Athat.* ed. Shu'ayb al-Arnawut, et. al. Beirut: Muassasah ar-Risalah, 1988.

_____ *Siyar A'lam an-Nubala.* ed. Shu'ayb ai-Arnawut, et. al. Beirut: Muassasah ar-Risalah, 1996.

Diraz, Muhammad 'Abdullah. *Madkhal ilal al-Qur'ān al-Karim.* Kuwait: Dar al-Qur'ān al-Karim, 1971.

Doi, A, Rahman I. *Introduction to the Qur'ān*. Lagos: Islamic Publications Bureau, 1976.

Flogel, Gustavus. *Corani texti 'Arabicus; Concordantiae Corani 'Arabicae.* Leipzig: Brett, 1834, 1898.

Fuad, Muhammad Abdul Baqi. *Al-Mu'ajam al Mufharras Li Alfazil Qur'ān al-Kareem*. Cairo: 1988.

Ghazali, Abū Hamid. *Ihya al-'ulūm ad-Din.* Beirut: Dar al-Ma'rifah, 1980-1993.

Gülen, M. Fethullah. *Kur'ân'ın Altın İkliminde.* Izmir: Nil Yayinlari, 2011.

_____ *Reflections on the Qur'ān*. tr; Ayşenur Kaplan & Harun Gültekin. New Jersey: Tughra Books, 2012.

Goldziher, Ignaz. *Die Richtungen der Islamischen Kormzauslegung*. Bril, Leiden: 1970.

Guillaume, A. *The Life of Muhammad: A Translation of Ibn Ishaq's Sirat Rasulullah*, 8th imp. Karachi: 1987.

Hamad, Ghanim Qaduri. *Rasm al-Masahif; dirasat lughawiya wa tarikhiya*. Masters diss., Cairo University: 1976.

Haythami, 'Ali b. Abū Bakr. *Majma' az-Zawiz'id.* 10 vols. Cairo: 1352.

Haji Khalifa, Mustafa b. 'Abdullah. *Kasha z-Zunun.* 3rd ed. Tehran: 1967.

Ḫākim, Muhammad b. 'Abdullah, *al-Mustadrak*. ed. M.A. 'Ata'. Beirut: 1990.

Ibn Abi Dawud. *Kitab al-Masahif.* ed. A. Jeffery. Cairo: 1936, in: id., *Materials for the History of the Text of the Qur'ān.* Leiden: The Old Codices, 1937.

_____ *Kitab al-Masahif of Ibn Abi Dawud.* ed. M. Wa'I. 2nd ed. Beirut: 2002.

Ibn Abi Shayba, 'Abd Allah b. Muhammad. *Musannaf.* ed. M.A. Shahin. 9 vols. Beirut: 1995.

Ibn Athir, Mubarak ibn Muhammad al-Jazari. *al-Nihayah fi Gharib al-Hadith.* Cairo: Maktabah al-Islamiyya, 1965.

Ibn Hajar al-'Asqalani, Ahmad b. 'Ali. *Fath al-Bari.* ed. F. 'Abdul-Baqi. 13 vols. Cairo: 1380-1390.

_____ *al Isaba fi Tamyiz as-Sahaba.* 4 vols. Beirut: no date [reprint of first ed. Cairo: 1328].

Ibn Hanbal, Ahmad. *Musnad.* 6 vols. Cairo: 1313. Reprinted by Ququba Press, Cairo: no date [c. 1988]) with Hadith serials in the margin.

Ibn Hazm, 'Ali b. Sa'id. *Jamhrat al-Ansab.* ed. E. Levi-Provencal. Cairo: 1948.

______ *al-Nāsikh wa al-Mansūkh fi al-Qur'ān al-Karim*, Dar al-Kutub al-Ilmiyyah, Beirut, 1986.

Ibn Hibban al-Busti, Muhammad. *al-Majhurin.* ed. M. Zayed. 3 vols. Halab: 1396.

Ibn Hisham. *Sirah.* ed. M. Saqqa et al. 4 vols. 2nd ed. Cairo: 1955.

Ibn Ishaq. *as-Siyar wa al-Maghazi.* the version of Ibn Bukair. ed. S. Zakkar. Damascus: 1978.

Ibn Khaldun. *The Muqaddima, An Introduction to History.* trans. Franz Rosenthal. 3 vols. New York: 1958. 2nd revised ed, Princeton, NJ: Princeton University Press, 1967.

Ibn Jawzī. *Tafsīr Ibn al-Jawzī (Zad al-Masir fi 'Ilm al-Tafsīr).* 9 vols. Beirut: Al-maktab al-Islami, 1964.

Ibn al-Jazari, Muhammad ibn Muhammad. *an-Nashr fi al-Qiraat al-'Ashru.* Beirut: Dar Kutub al-Ilmiyyah, no date.

Ibn Kathir, Ismail. *Fadail al-Qur'ān.* in vol. 7 of Tafsīr Ibn Kathir.

______ *Tafiir al-Qur'ān.* 7 vols. Beirut: 1966.

______ *al-Bidaya wa an-Nihaya.* Cairo: 1348.

Ibn Majah, Muhammad B. Yazid. *Sunan.* Riyadh: Maktab al-Tarbiyah al-'Arābī, 1988.

Ibn Manzur, Muhammad b. Mukarram. *Mukhtarar Tarikh Dimashq li Ibn 'Asakir.* ed. M. al-Sagharji. 29 vols. in 15 Beirut/Damascus: 1989.

Ibn Manzur. *Lisan al-Arab.* Beirut: Dar Sadir; Dar Beirut, 1955-1956.

Ibn Mujahid. *Kitab as-Sab'a.* ed. S. Daif. Cairo: 1972.

Ibn Qayyim al-Jawzīyyah, Muhammad b. Abi Bakr. *I'lam al-Muwaqqi'in an Rabb al-Alamin.* Beirut: Dar al-Kutub, 1996.

Ibn Qudama, 'Abd Allah b. Ahmed. *al-Burhan fi Bayan al-Qur'ān.* Pt. Said: Matabah al-Huda, 1989.

______ *Rawdat an-Nadir.* Mecca: Maktabah Dar al-Baz. 1994.

Ibn Qutaybah. *Ta'wil Mushkil al-Qur'ān.* ed. al-Sayyid Ahmad Saqr. Cairo: 1954; Cairo: 1973; Medina: 1981.

______ *al-Ma'arif.* ed. Th. Ukasha. Cairo: 1969.

Ibn Sa'd, Muhammad. *Kitab at-Tabaqat al-Kubra.* ed. E. Sachau et al. 9 vols. Leiden: 1905-1917.

Ibn Sayyid an-Nas. *'Uyun al-Athar.* Cairo: 1356.

Ibn Salama. *al-Nāsikh wa al Mansūkh*. Cairo: Halabi, 1967.

Ibn Taymiya. *Muqaddima fi usual al Tafsīr*. Kuwait: 1971.

______ *Iqtida Siratal-Mustaqim*. ed. Dr. Nasir al-'Aql.RiyadhL: Maktabah ar-Rushd, 1994.

Isfahani, Imam Raghib. *Mufarradat al Qur'ān.* Lahore: Able Hadith Academy, 1971.

Izutsu, Toshiheko. *The Structure of the Ethical terms in the Koran. A study in semantics.* Tokyo: 1950.

al-Jazari, Tahir. *at-Tibyan.* ed. A. Abū Ghuddah. 3rd ed. Beirut: 1992.

al-Jazari, Muhammad b. Muhammad. *Tabaqat al-Qurra.* 3 vols. Baghdad: 1932.

Jeffery, A. (ed.): *al-Mabani li Muqaddimatan fi "ulūm al-Qur'ān.* Cairo: 1954.

Kamali, Mohammad Hashim. *Principles of Islamic Jurisprudence.* Selangor: Pelanduk Publications, 1995.

Khalifa b. Khayyat. *Tarikh.* ed. S. Zakkar. 2 vols. Damascus: 1968.

Khalifa Rashad. *Qur' an: Visual Presentation of the Miracle.* Tucson, Arizona: 1982.

Malik b. Anas. *al-Muwatta.* ed. M.F. 'Abdul-Baqi. Cairo: 1951.

Mawdudi, Abū'l A'la. *The Meaning of the Qur'ān.* 9 vols. Lahore: Islamic Publications, 1967-1979.

Muslim b. Hajjaj al-Qushair. *Sahih.* ed. F. Abdul-Baqi. 5 vols. Cairo: 1374. English translation by Abdul-Hamid Siddiqi. *Sahih Muslim.* 4 vols. Lahore: 1972.

Nadim, Muhammad b. lshaq al-Warraq. *al-Fihrist.* ed. R. Tajdud. Tehran: no date.

Nasafi, 'Abd Allah b. Ahmad b. Mahmud al-. *Madarik al-tanzil wa-baqa'iq al-ta'wil.* ed. Zakariyya 'Umayrat. 2 vols. Beirut: 1995.

Peters, F.E. *A Reader on Classical Islam.* Princeton: Princeton University Press, 1994.

Saeed, Abd Allah. *Interpreting the Qur'ān.* New York: Routledge, 2006

Sabūni, Muhammad 'Ali. *At-Tibyan fi 'ulūm al-Qur'ān.* Beirut: Dar al-Irshad, 1970.

______ *The Recited Koran. A history of the first recorded version.* Princeton: The Darwin Press, 1975.

Salahi, 'Adil. *Recitation and Memorisation of the Our'an.* in: The Muslim 3/4. 1976, 84-7.

Salih, Subhi. *Mabahith fi 'ulūm al Qur'ān.* Beirut: Dar al-Ilrn li-l-Maliyin, 1964.

Sijistani, Abū Bakr. *Tafsīr Gharib al-Qur'ān.* Cairo: Maktaba 'Alam al-Fikr, 1980.

Suyūtī, Jalal al-Din. *History of the Caliphs.* tr. by H. S. Jarrett. Calcutta: Baptist Mission Press, 1881.

______ *al-Itqān fi "ulūm al-Qur'ān.* 2 vols. Beirut: Maktab al-Thaqafiyya, 1973.

Noldeke, T. "The Koran". *Encyclopaedia Britannica, vol. 16 (9th ed., 1891), pp. 597ff.* Reprinted in Ibn Warraq (ed.). *The Origins of the Koran: Classic Essays on Islam's Holy Book.* pp. 36-63. New York: 1998.

Qadduri Ghanim. *Rasm al-Muṣḥāf Dirasatun Lughawiyyatun Tarikhiyyatun.* Baghdad: 1982.

Qadhi, Abū Ammar Yasir. *An Introduction to The Sciences of The Qur'ān.* Birmingham, UK: al-Hidaayah Publishing and Distribution, 2003.

Qattan, Manna'. *Mabahis fi "ulūm al-Qur'ān.* Riyadh: Dar al-Sa'udiya li-al-Nashr, 1971.

Qurtubi, Muhammad b. Ahmad al-Ansari. *al-Jami' li aḥkām al-Qur'ān.* 10 vols. Beirut: Dar al-Kutub al-IImiyyah, 1993.

Qutb, Sayyid. *Fi Zilal al-Qur'ān.* Beirut: Dar al-Shuruq, 1992.

Razi, Fakhr ad-Din. *al-Tafsīr al-Kabir.* Beirut: Dar al-Ihya al-Turath al-'Arābī, no date.

Tabarī, Muhammad b. Jarir. *Jarmi al Bayan- Ta'wil ayat al Qur'ān.* 30 vols. 3rd ed. Cairo: 1968.

Tahawi, Abū Ja'far Ahmad. *Sharh Mushkil al-Athar.* ed. by Shu'ayb Arnawud. Beirut: Muassasah ar-Risalah, 1994.

Rodwell, A. *The Coran, translation with the Surahs arranged in chronological order.* London: 1876.

Tirmidhi. *Sunan.* ed. A. Shakir et al. Cairo: 1937.

Wahidi al Nais Abūri. *Asbāb al- Nuzūl.* Cairo: 1968.

Watt, W. Montgomery Bell. *Introduction to the Qur'ān.* Edinburgh: Edinburgh University Press, l977.

Zamakhsari, Muhammad b. 'Umar. *al-Kashsah.* 4 volumes. Cairo: 1972.

Zarkashī, Badruddin. *Al Burhan fi 'ulūm al-Qur'ān.* Cairo: 1958.

Zuhri. *Tanzil al-Qur'ān.* ed. al-Munajjid. Beirut: 1963.

al-Zurqani, Muhammad Abd al-Azim. *Manahil al-'Irfan fi "ulūm al-Qur'ān.* 3 vols. Beirut: Dar al-Kutub al-'Ilmiyyah, 1988.

Ubaydat, Mahmud Salim. *Dirasat fi "ulūm al-Qur'ān.* Jordan: Dar Ammar, 1990.